How It Wa

How It Was Done in Paris

Russian Émigré Literature and French Modernism

Leonid Livak

THE UNIVERSITY OF WISCONSIN PRESS

The University of Wisconsin Press
1930 Monroe Street
Madison, Wisconsin 53711

www.wisc.edu/wisconsinpress/

3 Henrietta Street
London WC2E 8LU, England

5   4   3   2   1

Printed in the United States of America

Library of Congress Cataloging-in-Publication Data
Livak, Leonid.
How it was done in Paris : Russian émigré literature and French modernism /
    Leonid Livak.
    p. cm.
    Includes bibliographical references and index.
    ISBN 0-299-18510-9 (cloth : alk. paper)
    ISBN 0-299-18514-1 (pbk. : alk. paper)
    1. Russian literature—France—History and criticism.   2. Exiles' writings, Russian—
France—History and criticism.   3. Literature, Comparative—Russian and French.
4. Literature, Comparative—French and Russian.   5. Russian literature—French influ-
ences.
I. Title.
PG3520.F7 L58   2003
891.709′944—dc21   2002153729

Publication of this book has been made possible in part by the generous support of the
Anonymous Fund of the University of Wisconsin–Madison

Есть люди, умеющие пить водку, и есть люди, не умеющие пить водку, но все же пьющие ее. И вот первые получают удовольствие от горя и от радости, а вторые страдают за всех тех, кто пьет водку, не умея пить ее.
—Исаак Бабель, "Как это делалось в Одессе"

[There are people who know how to drink vodka, and there are those who do not know how to drink vodka but who drink it all the same. And so the former take pleasure in misery and in joy, while the latter suffer for all those who drink vodka without knowing how to drink it.]
—Isaac Babel, "How It Was Done in Odessa"

Contents

Acknowledgments

This study would not have been possible without the assistance of many people and institutions whose generous support I am gratefully acknowledging.

I want to thank Alexander Dolinin (University of Wisconsin–Madison), whose vast knowledge and incisive critical advice, high expectations and great reserves of patience were instrumental in shaping the present study and in the scholarly tempering of its author. I am also indebted to David Bethea (University of Wisconsin–Madison), who provided more than his share of suggestions and criticism for developing my ideas and whose unwavering and enthusiastic support accompanied me throughout my work on this project. I am grateful to Steven Winspur (University of Wisconsin–Madison), who generously offered his expertise in French literature and kindly agreed to toil under the burden of Russian letters. During my research in France I profited from Marie-Paule Berranger's seminar on French surrealism (Université de Paris X–Nanterre) and learnt much from Charles Senninger (Université de Paris III–Sorbonne Nouvelle), who directed my work on L.-F. Céline's novels. I also wish to thank my French colleagues Catherine Gousseff, René Guerra, and Hélène Menegaldo, who kindly and patiently responded to my numerous inquiries about the cultural life of Russian émigrés in France. I am grateful to Elizabeth Beaujour (Hunter College and CUNY Graduate Center) and Greta Slobin (University of California–Santa Cruz) for reading the manuscript and offering painstaking commentary and criticism of all aspects of my work. I am indebted to Adam Mehring, Steve Salemson, and Barbara Wojhoski who saw my manuscript through all stages of the editorial process at the University of Wisconsin Press. Last but not least, I thank my colleagues from the Depart-

ment of Slavic Languages and Literatures at the University of Toronto
for their psychological support and practical advice at the final stages of
my work on this book.

A study like mine is simply unfeasible without the professional expertise and generous assistance of archivists and librarians around the
world. I wish therefore to express my profound thanks to the curators
and staff of the following institutions: Amherst Center for Russian Culture (Amherst College); Archives de la Police (Paris); Bakhmeteff Archive of Russian and East European History and Culture (Columbia
University, New York); Bibliothèque littéraire Jacques Doucet (Paris);
Bibliothèque Nationale de France (Paris); Bibliothèque russe Tour-
guénév (Paris); Bibliothèque de l'Institut d'études slaves (Paris); Bibliothèque de documentation internationale contemporaine (Nanterre);
Beinecke Rare Book and Manuscript Library (Yale University); Hoover
Institution Library and Archives (Stanford University); the University of
Toronto Libraries; and the University of Wisconsin Memorial Library.

I am fortunate to have been able to run my ideas by a broader scholarly audience by way of publishing excerpts from the earlier versions of
this study in article format. The feedback I received from reviewers, editors, and readers has proven invaluable in refining and modifying many
facets of my investigation. Although in its present form my study departs a great deal from these earlier publications, I still wish to express
my gratitude for the willingness of the following scholarly journals
to open their pages to my research on Iurii Fel'zen (*Modern Language
Review* 95 [2000]), Gaito Gazdanov (*Wiener Slawistischer Almanach* 44
[1999]), Georgii Ivanov (*Russian Literature* 49 [2001]), Vladimir Nabokov
(*Comparative Literature* 54 [2002] and *Studies in the Novel* 34 [2002]), Boris
Poplavskii (*SEEJ* 44 [2000], *The Russian Review* 60 [2001], and *Comparative
Literature Studies* 38 [2001]), Marcel Proust (*French Forum* 25 [2000]), and
the semiotics of Russian literary life in France (*Kritika* 2 [2001]).

The University of Wisconsin partially sponsored my research at its
early stages with a travel grant, the Steenbock Fellowship, and the university fellowship. I also greatly profited from a grant offered by the
Eurasia Program of the Social Science Research Council with funds provided by the State Department under the Program for Research and
Training on Eastern Europe and the Independent States of the former
Soviet Union (Title VIII). Finally, I am indebted to Grinnell College and
the University of Toronto for their generous sponsorship of my research
in its later phases.

I would be terribly remiss if I did not thank humbly my wife and muse,

who stoically put up with my scholarly obsessions and academic neu-
roses and faithfully served as my first reader and advisor, even though
I was at times too distraught to decide, "Быть ли мне вкрадчиво—
нежным? Быть ли мне пленительно—грубым?" as her favorite *poeta*
has it.

How It Was Done in Paris

Introduction

European civilization offers a typology of geographical, cultural, and spiritual exile rich in paradigmatic examples that inform the artistic construction of exilic experience. Besides the archetypes of a Paradise Lost and Lucifer's expulsion from heaven, there are the journey of the Argonauts, the peregrinations of Odysseus and Aeneas, the Jewish Diaspora, the banishment of Ovid and Dante, the emigration of Mme. de Staël, Chateaubriand, Mickiewicz, Herzen, and so forth. The artistic construction of exile has captivated many scholars who study the ways in which expatriates translate their experience into prose and poetry. Observing that "exile had been regarded as an occupational hazard for poets," Harry Levin insists that the writer's alienation from home may occur even without the benefit of travel, as in Flaubert's view of the artist as a man without a country.[1] Furthermore, twentieth-century thought has elevated the figure of exile to cosmic proportions by placing spiritual homelessness at the center of the modern human condition.[2] Fusing metaphorical and literal meanings of modern exilic experience, George Steiner wrote: "It seems proper that those who create art in a civilization of quasi-barbarism which has made so many homeless . . . should themselves be poets unhoused."[3]

The present study explores the mechanisms of cultural and artistic interpretation of exile based on the example of the Russian refugees who took up residence in France after the Bolshevik coup of 1917. The importance that Russian exiles attributed to literary expression as a means of cultural preservation and continuity makes their literature a case study in cultural modeling. I focus on the younger—alias "second" and "unnoticed"—generation of writers, who matured artistically outside Russia. The body of works produced by this generation in

3

the 1920s and 1930s has been largely ignored in literary studies. Beyond the memoirs of contemporaries and a few monographs devoted to individual authors, no systematic investigation of the "unnoticed generation" has been conducted either in Russia, where the notion of a culture in exile remained taboo until the late 1980s, or in the West. I analyze the specific position of the "unnoticed generation" in the context of French modernist literature, examining the ways in which French literary life influenced émigré artistic identities and oeuvre.

I use the notion of literary modernism only insofar as the authors in question base their own artistic identities on it. Consequently, the evolution of the émigré theory of artistic modernism lies outside the thematic scope of the present study. My interest rests with the auxiliary function of "modernism" as a symbolic tool informing artistic identities. As I will show, both French and émigré writers who came to literature after the First World War utilized this concept in their self-definition in contrast to their immediate but "ancient" predecessors.

This study pursues two goals. First, it is an attempt at the systematic investigation and theoretical conceptualization of Russian exilic experience in France as modeled and institutionalized in émigré literary and critical discourses. I hope that the theoretical concepts and analytical methods proposed here will contribute to the positing of Russian literature and culture in exile as a valid field for a coherent scholarly inquiry that would surpass national boundaries, reaching out to French and comparative literary and cultural studies. Second, I aim to reintroduce into literary circulation—for both readers and critics—an unduly ignored group of Russian writers by showing that the "unnoticed generation" represents, in fact, one of the most interesting, original, and rich pages in Russian literary history.

Readers familiar with interbellum French literature may at times find my emphasis on certain French writers, works, and esthetic features thereof one-sided or skewed. This is the consequence of trying to view the rich literary life of postwar France "through the Russian eyes," that is, from the vantage point of Russian exiles, who, for various reasons that are discussed in subsequent chapters, chose to elevate some artistic figures and trends to the status of notable literary events—as in the cases of the surrealist movement, Marcel Proust, André Gide, and Louis-Ferdinand Céline—while ignoring other important personalities and currents in contemporary French letters. Furthermore, because of its focus, my investigation gives precedence to the reception and interpretation of French literary works by Russian writers and by their

French colleagues, whose critical view often influenced that of the exiles. This attention to historical context sometimes comes at the expense of the immanent analysis of French works in question. Such bias is inevitable in a critical inquiry whose space limitations demand that one stay on course by assigning priority to certain aspects of a given work while overlooking others.

The conjunction of Russian émigré and French letters in a comparative study seems justified because émigré literary life, by virtue of its concentration in Paris, developed in close connection with French literature. The prestige of French culture among the Russian elites determined in more than one way their interpretation of revolutionary experience, filtered through the prism of 1789 and its repercussions— emigration, Jacobinic terror, political Thermidor, and so forth. Roman Gul' called this widespread application of French paradigms in the Russian context the "French thermometer."[4] Thus, the very appellation "émigré" (emigrant), which Russian exiles overwhelmingly preferred to "immigrant," harks back to the French sociopolitical emigration, which boasted a number of prominent intellectuals and produced such works as Germaine de Staël's *Letters from Germany,* Chateaubriand's *René* and *Mémoires d'outre-tombe,* and Senancour's *Obermann.* The Soviet regime also accepted the term "émigré" as valid in the post-1917 situation. In addition, émigré writers of the second generation matured as artists only abroad. Unlike most older émigrés, who were impervious to the literary life of the host culture, they made West European, and especially French, culture part of their own artistic identity.

My study distinguishes between "Russian literature in exile" and "Russian émigré literature." The former thrived in Berlin as early as 1920 and antedated émigré letters, which appeared circa 1925 in response to the consolidation of the Soviet rule. By 1925 it became clear that the new order in Russia was a long-term phenomenon, and each exile had to define his or her position vis-à-vis the Soviet regime, coming to terms with the possibility of indefinite expatriation. The need for self-definition grew sharper in the literary diaspora inasmuch as artistic expression in the USSR came under ideological pressure.[5] The steady abatement of Russian literary life in Berlin in 1923–24, the mass migration of "émigrés" to Paris, and the return of "Soviet" writers to the USSR marked the birth of émigré literature.

Since by "literature" I mean not only written works and individual writers but a sum total of dynamic and mutually defining relations between writers, readers, and critics in a given historical period, the chronological scope of this study, circa 1925–40, coincides with the birth and demise of Russian émigré literature in its uncontested capital. If the rise of émigré letters cannot be neatly assigned to one year, its death is clearly delineated. The entry of France into war and its defeat and occupation put an effective end to the independent Russian press and publishing houses, which were the main venues for the commerce of émigré artistic and cultural ideas in Paris. The subsequent decimation of the émigrés of Jewish descent and the exodus of many exiles—both creators and consumers of émigré writings—into the "Free Zone" and overseas finalized the demise of émigré literary life.[6]

My study rests on the methodological premise that émigré works cannot be comprehended by an immanent analysis that disregards their historical context. I treat émigré literature as a dynamic and evolving system, a concept elaborated by René Wellek and Austin Warren, where each element is defined in relation to the historical whole of which it is a part (*Theory of Literature*, 255). Claudio Guillén showed that because of the *functional* importance of the relations between its parts, a literary system is akin to Ferdinand de Saussure's idea of a linguistic system, which had been brought to bear on the problems of literary history—before Guillén, Wellek, and Warren—by Roman Jakobson and Iurii Tynianov (*Literature as System*, 378, 495–96). Applying the models of structural linguistics to literature, these scholars argued that "language and literature had a systemic character"; that "every system necessarily existed as an evolution"; that the notions of *langue* and *parole* applied to literary systems; and that one could study literary evolution "through an analysis of the correlation between the literary series and other historical series. This correlation (system of systems) has its own structural laws, which must be submitted to investigation."[7]

Drawing on this tradition, a group of scholars have described twentieth-century Russian literature as a system of systems with Soviet and émigré letters as interdependent subsystems.[8] But they did not account for the third factor present in the émigré cultural capital—French literary life. As Paris replaced Berlin in the quality of the Russian cultural center, every émigré literary event was informed by the triangular esthetic opposition of émigré, French, and Soviet letters. But if the Russian-French dynamics were present from the beginning of Russian literature in Paris, the émigré-Soviet dichotomy began to acquire importance in the literary life of Russian exiles only in the second half of the 1920s.

The view of culture as a mechanism for organizing information, formulated by Clifford Geertz, presupposes the existence of a system of rules by which human experience is translated into culture, or text. Iurii Lotman and Boris Uspenskii consider this system of rules as the language of culture, which helps describe experience through a process that singles out some facts over others and creates what Paul Ricoeur has called "ideal models" for social phenomena.[9] These models inform experience with meaning and evolve to reflect the changes in their creators' circumstances. A product of selective interpretation, the meaning bestowed upon social phenomena may not coincide with the logical intentions of the original actors. Similarly to their counterparts in literary studies, Geertz, Lotman, Ricoeur, and Uspenskii have shown that, as a paradigm for explanation, the structural approach is not limited to linguistic signs if we understand culture as a system of signs that organizes the world into a social structure.[10] It applies to all signs that are analogous to linguistic signs and all social phenomena possessing the relations of a semiological system—the relation between code and message, relations among the units of the code, the relation between signifier and signified, the relation within and among social messages, and the structure of communication as an exchange of messages.

Giving meaning to exile, émigrés created dynamic ideal models for Russian, French, and Soviet literary traditions and writers, as well as the ideal models of émigré literature and writer, in the triangular equilibrium of émigré, Soviet, and French literary lives. The evolving ideal model of émigré literature defined the thematic scope, esthetic peculiarities, and cultural mission of émigré writing. I view the relation of this model to the actual events of émigré literary life as analogous to the relationship between *langue* and *parole* (Saussure) or schema and usage (Hjelmslev). It is only logical that cultural modeling reached high intensity in the milieu of émigré writers. As translators of experience into texts, artists tried to comprehend the social and cultural changes in their society through a sharp rise in semiotic behavior. The evolution of the ideal model of literary activity in exile constitutes the backbone of the history of émigré literature.

The trajectory of émigré artistic self-definition was complex and often counterintuitive. It initially involved the conceptualization of French literature by older exiles as "un-Russian" (read "formalist"). The introduction of the "Soviet" component tipped the balance: by 1930, émigrés found "Russian" features in French writings in contrast to Soviet letters. Their rejection of Soviet "formalism" was dictated more by the logic of émigré self-conceptualization than by the realia of

literary life. The "form-oriented" avant-garde was not the only trend in
Soviet letters; besides, the writers who had revolutionized literary language, plot construction, and narrative techniques were silenced by the
regime's cultural policies after 1927, at the very time when émigrés created their model of Soviet art as "formalist." The émigré-French rap-
prochement received a boost from younger exiles who established a
fourth vantage point, drawing on French modernism in order to depart
from older émigré praxis, stripping their literary fathers of "Russianness," and implicitly lumping them with Soviet writers. Soviet "antiformalist" campaigns modified yet again the émigré-French-Soviet
dynamics. By the mid-1930s, the émigré critical discourse, now dominated by younger writers, valorized artistic innovation (a "formalist"
trait), as exemplified by the French, against the backdrop of older émigré and Soviet conservatism.

The first chapter of my book scrutinizes the ways in which émigrés
gave meaning to exilic experience, focusing on the relations between literary events—works or meaningful deeds—and their interpretation
from the vantage point of ideal models. Subsequently, I examine the
role of the émigré-Soviet-French dynamics and the function of ideal
models in the artistic trajectories of individual émigré writers.

My study is not confined to written works only. I examine the patterns of meaningfully oriented behavior in the milieu of exiled artists as
"texts of life" that are shaped by the émigré-French-Soviet triangulation
and appeal to certain ideal models for meaning, holding no less esthetic
value in the eyes of contemporary observers than prose or poetry. Deliberate esthetic organization of behavior among artists is an international phenomenon. Reflecting on the construction and reading of life
as a text, Ricoeur wrote:

> In the same way that interlocution is overcome in writing, inter-
> action is overcome in numerous situations in which we treat ac-
> tion as a fixed text. . . . Action itself, action as meaningful, may
> become an object of science through a kind of objectivation sim-
> ilar to the fixation which occurs in writing. . . . As the fixation
> by writing is made possible by a dialectic of intentional exteri-
> orization immanent to the speech-act itself, a similar dialectic
> within the process of transaction prepares the detachment of the
> *meaning* of the action from the *event* of the action. ("Model of the
> Text," 80–81; original in English)

Ricoeur's insight into the hermeneutics of meaningfully oriented
behavior found support in Lotman's studies of the poetics of everyday

behavior, which introduced the concept of a "code of conduct" (*pove-dencheskii kod*) to describe a set of rules that functioned as a backdrop for human behavior and endowed it with special cultural significance.[11] These theoretical findings have been tested in the studies of Russian literature and culture by Svetlana Boym, Gregory Freidin, and Irina Paperno, who showed that the fusion of life and literature, rooted in the nineteenth-century ideal model of the Russian writer as a spiritual apostle who put ideas into practice, figured prominently in the careers of many Russian artists.[12] Establishing the patterns of meaningfully oriented behavior among émigrés, one can clarify the relationship of their self-interpretation to the ideal model of the émigré writer, created largely on the basis of the older model of the Russian writer. Further-more, as I will show, émigrés grafted French artistic praxis on Russian esthetic concepts, adding new dimensions to the Russian experience of deliberate esthetic organization of behavior, which became a vehicle for defining one's artistic identity in a culturally alien atmosphere.

Émigré cultural modeling relied on numerous myths supporting the translation of experience into texts. Mythical thought is intimately linked to the modeling of social existence, since both attempt to cope with existential perplexities.[13] The preoccupation with tradition (Rus-sian cultural traditions in the case of émigré writers) necessarily raises the question of a "beginning" that provides the tradition's uncorrupted paradigm. The creation of émigré cultural mythology was thus un-avoidable, for the main function of myth is to relate a story of the "be-ginning," furnishing a model for meaningful activities.[14] Because of the paucity of studies in émigré culture, the creators of its mythology re-main the primary sources of information about the life of Russian ex-iles. Although at the time of creation it was vital for the émigrés' artis-tic self-identification, today this cultural mythology presents a serious impediment to the study of émigré literature, especially as regards its interaction with French cultural life. A study of émigré letters neces-sarily entails the reexamination of commonly accepted notions about the Russian emigration and its artistic expression.

For instance, the very definition of a "Russian émigré" is problem-atic. According to Mark Raeff, émigrés were the people who went into exile after repudiating Bolshevism (*Russia Abroad*, 16). But the political spectrum of the Russian diaspora testifies to greater complexity. Along-side those who opposed the regime, there were those who fled from deprivations, left to join their families, unwittingly found themselves in newly formed countries (the Baltic states, Poland, Finland) and annexed provinces (Moldavia, Western Ukraine), or were too young at the time of departure to make a conscious choice. Throughout the 1920s, there was no clear borderline between émigrés and Soviet fellow travelers residing abroad.[15] Many *political* exiles eventually returned, as did Viktor Shklovskii, Il'ia Erenburg, Aleksei Tolstoi, and Maxim Gor'kii. A number of exiles reevaluated their attitude, forming pro-Soviet movements (The Change of Landmarks, The Eurasians) or joining the Communists of their host countries, as did Dmitrii Mirskii and Vladimir Pozner. Some, like Iurii Annenkov, participated in the émigré cultural life, all the while retaining Soviet citizenship. Yet others, like Boris Poplavskii and Sergei Sharshun, nurtured pro-Soviet sympathies before unequivocally denouncing Soviet culture. This evolution from "exiled" to "émigré" is understated in memoir literature, whose view of émigré experience is influenced by its later period, the 1930s, when émigré and Soviet cultures became sharply polarized.

The concept of a self-imposed mission to preserve the "true" Russian cultural traditions despoilt in the USSR is part of émigré mythology, and one must separate its later interpretations from its role in the émigré literary life. Contrary to later claims, émigré cultural elites did not leave Russia "on a mission."[16] This evolving construct was engendered in exile in opposition to Soviet culture. The relationship between émigré and French letters also requires considerable demythologizing. According to memoirists, émigrés lived in isolation from French cultural life and were overcome by the "feeling of emptiness" in "indifferent Paris . . . so alien to everything Russian."[17] The logic of the émigré mission provided reasons for this alleged isolation—foreign influence could bring about "denationalization." Among other explanations one cites the political barriers separating émigrés from French intellectuals who practiced "parlor Bolshevism." Such claims permeate the accounts of Russian cultural life in exile.[18] They reflect the émigrés' self-imposed conceptualization of their situation in France but do not necessarily correspond to the real conditions of the cultural life of Russian exiles.

The myths discussed above possessed considerable esthetic value in relation to another myth of émigré literature—the view of younger writers as an unnoticed generation. The term itself, coined by Vladimir Varshavskii in his book *Nezamechennoe pokolenie* (1956), implies an array of features with which younger émigrés characterized themselves. They modeled their situation as a state of cultural crisis, alienation, solitude, and anxiety resulting from the social turmoil that marked their lives.[19] This interpretation of their cultural situation motivated their "modernist" refusal of "traditional" literature, contradicting the conservationist ethos of the émigré mission. The notion of the literary failure that made this generation "unnoticed" may be the most tenacious of émigré cultural myths.[20] Simon Karlinsky, for example, characterized the literary activity of younger émigrés as "an unbelievable and heroic phenomenon," because they accomplished so much in the face of such "staggering odds" as material difficulties, cultural isolation, and alienation from the émigré literary establishment ("In Search of Poplavsky," 6). Although one cannot deny their material difficulties and struggle for recognition within émigré literature, the sheer volume of their published writings speaks against the artistic failure of the younger exiles.

Furthermore, younger writers exaggerated these difficulties, cultivating them as valuable elements in their artistic identity. Their refusal of "traditional" art with its notion of success naturally led to the cult of literary failure. Incidentally, the self-description of the "unnoticed generation" is attuned to that of the European modernist writer in general, and younger émigrés readily assumed the prestigious name of "modernist."[21] The myth of the "unnoticed generation" is unoriginal in the context of contemporary French literature, which indulged in its own cultural crisis, anxiety, and solitude, even though the émigrés ensured their originality by finding specifically exilic roots of their worldview—the precarious financial situation of a refugee, cultural exclusion, the impossibility to make a living by writing in Russian, and the burden of memory that impeded assimilation.[22] These claims require an examination of the relationship between life in exile and its modeling.

In 1995 Mark Raeff decried the unsystematic nature of émigré studies in Russia and abroad ("V pomoshch' issledovaniiu zarubezhnoi Rossii," 349–50). Since then the situation has hardly changed. More biographical dictionaries and bibliographies have been published, but none is either definitive or comprehensive, not to speak of the glaring disparities between these reference sources, whose sole methodology is the whim of their compilers. *The Bibliography of Russian Émigré Literature* (1970) by Liudmila Foster, *L'Émigration russe: Revues et recueils* (1988) by Tatiana Gladkova and Tatiana Ossorguine, and Michel Beyssac's *La Vie culturelle de l'émigration russe en France* (1971) remain the most reliable reference instruments. In recent years, Beyssac's book has been brilliantly complemented by the thorough oeuvre *L'Émigration russe:*

Chronique de la vie scientifique, culturelle et sociale (1995–97), directed by
Lev Mnukhin. More conference proceedings and collections of articles
have appeared, but they have hardly advanced our understanding of
émigré literature as a cultural phenomenon and have mostly remained
superficially descriptive. With rare exceptions, recent studies of émigré
writings either elude in-depth analysis or fall short of placing individual writers in a larger historical context, which would permit the
systematization of knowledge about émigré literary life. Gleb Struve's
seminal study *Russkaia literatura v izgnanii* (1956) remains the most
comprehensive to date, while the article by Boldt, Segal, and Fleishman,
"Problemy izucheniia literatury russkoi emigratsii pervoi treti XX veka"
(1978), has been the only attempt to conceptualize the literary experience of Russian exiles.

The critical studies of younger émigré writers are easily accounted
for because they are few. This was demonstrated by the incident in
which I partook several years ago at a job interview. One of the inter-
viewers, a scholar of Russian literature and a long-time student of older
émigré writers, asked me the following question: "Why are you study-
ing these people? They are not Russian!" Literary and political parti
pris aside, this scholar was simply misinformed, basing his opinion on
that of the older émigrés, who guarded their place in the literary establishment by branding newcomers as "un-Russian." (Ironically, the
same brand was applied by the sons to the émigré fathers in the 1930s,
when young literature affirmed its Russian identity by denying the
very same qualities to older exiles.) To make matters worse, the writings of most younger émigrés are still hard to come by, for they are
only now beginning to be reprinted in Russia. While Gaito Gazdanov
has recently found a publisher and Boris Poplavskii's complete works
were scheduled to come out in 2002, Lidiia Chervinskaia, Iurii Fel'zen,
Vasilii Ianovskii, Sergei Sharshun, and Anatolii Shteiger, to name just
a few, still await their publishers.

Thus, of the younger émigrés forming the focus of my study—Boris
Poplavskii, Gaito Gazdanov, Iurii Fel'zen, Vasilii Ianovskii, and Vladimir Nabokov—only Nabokov has received adequate scholarly attention. Hélène Menegaldo studied Poplavskii's poetics in her dissertation titled "L'univers imaginaire de Boris Poplavsky" (1981). Two more
theses were devoted to Poplavskii in the early 1990s.[23] In *The Bitter Air
of Exile*, Simon Karlinsky and Anthony Olcott accompanied Poplavskii's
poetry with essays on his life and work. Karlinsky also wrote a short article comparing Poplavskii to Soviet poets Churilin and Zabolotskii.

Aleksey Gibson devoted a chapter of his book to the poetry of Poplavskii and Shteiger, but his analysis is superficial. Recently there have appeared several insightful articles devoted to Poplavskii's prose by John M. Kopper, D. Ricci, and L. Magarotto. This largely constitutes the body of writings on Poplavskii in the West. Gazdanov has not been more favored: the only monograph devoted to him in the West is *Russian Literature in Exile: The Life and Work of Gajto Gazdanov* (1982) by Laszlo Dienes. The interest in émigré literature in post-Soviet Russia may change the present situation, having already produced several articles on Poplavskii and Gazdanov, mostly, however, of a descriptive and introductory nature.[24] Fel'zen and Ianovskii have received even less critical attention.

I hope that my investigation will prove instrumental in reaching a fuller understanding of the cultural mechanisms involved in the effort by an expatriate community to carry on a creative existence despite dispersion and socioeconomic and political handicaps. An investigation of the literary life that a society in exile carries on in an alien cultural environment reveals major patterns of behavior applicable not only to the cases of literary activity in a foreign context but also to the study of any, direct or indirect, literary exchanges between cultures. Ultimately, I would like to think that the results of my research will not remain confined to exilic studies exclusively but contribute to the scholarly inquiry into the more general problems bearing on the processes of exchange, dissemination, and interaction that constitute key aspects in the formation of any culture.

Transliteration of Russian words in this volume follows the system of the Library of Congress except in instances where common English usage allows one to do otherwise (e.g., Dostoevsky, Tolstoy). All translations from the original French and Russian are my own unless otherwise specified.

1

Exilic Experience as a
Cultural Construct

"Russian" and "French"

From the beginning of émigré experience in France, exiles contrasted
Russian and French esthetics. Seeing Russian works as formally unso-
phisticated, they insisted that Russians could not match the style and
structural organization of French literature. Russian "amorphous emo-
tionality" clashed with "Latin clarity"; "French intellect" was a far cry
from the irrationality of "Russian depth" and "chaos," whose lack of order betrayed an anti-French mindset.[1] Unlike the French, Russian writers strove for spirituality and humanism at the expense of formalism. The
term "formalism" comprised syntax, semantic precision, and the or-
derliness and logical consistency of narrative. Russian writers were "formally inferior" to the French because the "Russian literary tradition had
an entirely different orientation."[2] This contrast of traditions brought
about value judgment, whereby "Russian" qualities were marked as
high and "French" as low. Opposing Russian literary discourse to the
French "emptiness and vanity of speech" (*pustota i prazdnost' rechi*),
Adamovich attributed this esthetic gap to a spiritual split between two
peoples.[3] The ease with which émigré critics reversed their judgment
points to a good deal of flexibility in the system of Russian-French oppositions. Adamovich saw Baudelaire as "too pretty and dressed up,
too full of effects and eloquence." Later he exonerated Baudelaire but
immediately proposed another scapegoat—Anatole France—to justify
a "Russian" view of "French" esthetics.[4]

Despite such contradictions, most émigré evaluations were supported by the stock contrast of the Russian and the French traditions based on the oppositions sincerity-artificiality; psychological depth-esthetic superficiality; humanism-literature; spirituality-formalism. Dostoevsky was used as a symbol of Russian esthetics. Kirill Zaitsev bashed André Gide's novel *Les Faux-Monnayeurs* (*The Counterfeiters*) for its superficiality, intellect, and eloquence, which concealed indifference to things spiritual. He opposed Gide's brilliance and rational coldness to Dostoevsky's moralistic stance.[5] This judgment is stunningly inappropriate, considering that in his oeuvre Gide paid tremendous attention to moral and ethical questions, turning to Dostoevsky for inspiration. In *Les Faux-Monnayeurs*, Gide continued his treatment of the moral aspects of crime. But since the Russian-French dichotomy dictated that moral preoccupations stood in opposition to French estheticism, Zaitsev heeded only the formal aspect of Gide's novel, namely, its experimentation with the nineteenth-century novelistic canon.

The criteria constituting a "Russian" text in the émigré critical discourse make it obvious that most exiles maintained the nineteenth-century tradition of dividing the literary work into form and content. Endowing the notion of content with different meaning, based on ideological and esthetic preferences, they played down the importance of artistic craft. Critics persistently used such topoi as "irrational chaos," "spiritual depth," "humanism," "sincerity," and the preoccupation with the "most important" (*samoe vazhnoe*) in human existence to characterize the Russian literary tradition by opposition to the "artificiality," "rational coldness," "skill," "brilliance," and "formalism" of French letters. The repertory of the approved ("Russian") content consisted of existential problems and social questions, whose presence in a work could redeem the author's lack of skill.[6] Artistic skill was "entertainment," tolerable inasmuch as it brought the reader closer to "the most important." This view on the Russian tradition united the émigré critic Mark Slonim with his political and esthetic rival, Georgii Adamovich. For Slonim, the true tradition of Russian art lay in

> The deep and courageous treatment of the vital problems of individual and social existence. In Russia, literature has never been a trifle, game or entertainment. It has led the reader from petty preoccupations to the most important. . . . Now we miss this literature and crave the continuation of its tradition abroad. We are used to writers who regard their occupation as an important and

responsible task. We know that the best among them made their
way through suffering and struggle.[7]

This definition of the literary tradition draws on the nineteenth-
century model of the Russian writer as a spiritual apostle, created under the influence of religious literature. During the secularization of
Russian society in the eighteenth century, secular literature, especially
poetry, took on the functions of religious literature. Creators of religious
texts had been regarded not as text inventors but as carriers of Truth,
whose personalities were inseparable from their writings. As the poet
became a prophet, filling the vacant place of spiritual authority, the authority of his text and his right to be a carrier of Truth depended on the
place of virtue in his life or personal mythology. The poet was even expected to undergo physical or moral suffering by which he resembled
saints and Christ himself. In the nineteenth century, this model was extended to all writers and amalgamated the civic tradition of the Russian
intelligentsia. The writer was modeled as a sociopolitical prophet who
took upon himself the suffering of his people; Russian literary authorship became a "charismatic institution."[8]

The émigré contrast of "sincerity" and "artificiality" springs from this
model of the writer as a carrier of Truth. The model also presupposes
the division of the literary work into "form" and "content," subjugating
artistic considerations to political, biographical, social, and metaphysical concerns. The opposition of "form" and "content" was accepted by
all generations of exiles, with rare exceptions (Vladislav Khodasevich,
Vladimir Nabokov). Younger writers of different esthetic leanings uniformly condemned "pure estheticism" and "art for art's sake." They saw
the Russian tradition in literature as a form of service that required the
sacrifice of art ("fiction") for the sake of Truth ("sincerity") and the
affirmation of the primacy of "ideas" over "estheticism." As "Russian"
writers, émigrés had to follow Dostoevsky's example, "carrying Russia's fate on their shoulders" and making an extra-artistic, ethical effort
because their place and mission were in life.[9]

The persistent French view of Russian letters as reflective of a "Russian soul" was a mirror image of the Russian-French dichotomy as construed by the émigrés and, in the final analysis, all but reinforced it. According to French critics, Russian works possessed the ungraspable
complexity and depth that seduced the French reader by its chaotic and
irrational nature. The French reviewers of émigré works emphasized
without fail their "Russian" character, whose "heavily psychological"

atmosphere evoked Tolstoy and Dostoevsky and showed the monopoly of the "Slavic genius" on certain nuances of suffering. Viewing émigré writings against the backdrop of nineteenth-century Russian literature, French critics encouraged the interpretation of the Russian tradition as "deep," "chaotic," "irrational," and "formless."[10] They found Russian roots even for those traits that were perceived by émigrés as French.[11] The concept of the "Russian soul" shocked émigrés by its crude applications in French popular novels, but it appealed to those who espoused the system of Russian-French oppositions.[12] Adamovich was convinced that the "Russian soul" existed. As a proof, he cited the differences between French and Russian literary traditions, closing the logical circle. Since the Russian-French dichotomy stipulated the existence of a spiritual gap between the two traditions, French critics' assertion that the "Russian soul" differed from their own seemed to find its confirmation in literature. Both sides, despite their alleged spiritual divergence, agreed on this point.[13]

The system of Russian-French oppositions served as a weapon in feuds among émigré writers. Nabokov's example is illustrative. Many critics placed his writings outside the Russian tradition. The perception of Nabokov's "un-Russianness" resided in his alleged unconcern for ethical, religious, philosophical, and social questions, and in his indifference to the ultimate problems of being, that is, in his reluctance to bring extraliterary preoccupations into literature. Favorably disposed critics refuted the accusations of Nabokov's un-Russianness by endowing his works with "high"/"Russian" qualities. For them, Nabokov "synthesized the Russian literary tradition (in its orientation toward the eternal, universal human content) and the West European artistic consciousness (with its primacy of form)."[14] Others aired reservations in regard to the "brilliant" style, puns, compositional games, elaborate plots, and fantasy of his novels, expressing anxiety for Nabokov's spirituality because his oeuvre contained too much "formal exercise."[15] Georgii Ivanov, settling personal scores, claimed that Nabokov wrote literature for literature's sake; that his "well worked and brilliantly polished" writings presented fake spiritual life; and were thus filled with smug vulgarity (*poshlost'*).[16] Using the topoi of the Russian-French dichotomy, Ivanov literally repeated Zaitsev's critique of *Les Faux-Monnayeurs*, whose "superficiality," "brilliance," and "refinement" also set an example of *poshlost'*.

It is not accidental that two critics with opposite artistic tastes pronounce identical judgments of rather different writers. They use the same system of esthetic coordinates that by 1926 had an established value hierarchy and vocabulary. Ivanov's use of the Russian-French dichotomy testifies to the flexibility of this weapon in critical debates. In the same review, he contrasts Nabokov to his peers Iurii Fel'zen and Gaito Gazdanov, whose novels were viewed as dependent on Proust's oeuvre. Ivanov cites Fel'zen and Gazdanov as positive examples of foreign influence: their link to Proust is "organic" because they are capable of translating "French" qualities into "Russian." Other émigré critics, however, called Gazdanov's and Fel'zen's writings "counterfeit" and a "corruption" of Proust.[17]

Even those émigrés who refused to divide a work of art into form and content made use of this procedure in esthetic feuds. Reviewing Ivanov's *Raspad atoma* (Disintegration of an atom, 1938), Khodasevich debunks the book by praising its technical skill and refusing it the status of a "human document." The "human document" that the critic opposed was a popular literary form among émigré writers in Paris. Its deliberate stylistic imperfection showed one's indifference to literary skill; its confessional "sincerity" evoked Dostoevsky's psychologism; finally, its pessimism and anxiety revealed the author's preoccupation with the "most important." Commenting on the way in which Ivanov's protagonist contemplated the abomination of the modern human condition, Khodasevich wrote that Ivanov "arranged his inelegant images so elegantly" that they "looked too smooth, too polished, and, finally, almost beautiful"; the book, according to the critic, "could pass for one of those 'human documents,' so fashionable nowadays, but this would be incorrect and unjust. . . . It is too artificial and skillful to be classified in this wretched type of literature" ("Raspad atoma," 9). The review's sharp pin was hidden in the praise of the author's skill, since "formal" achievement was marked as a suspicious or even negative quality in the émigré model of the Russian literary tradition. Khodasevich turned the tables on Ivanov, resorting to the critical idiom that Ivanov himself had used to debunk Nabokov.

Fitting into the system of Russian-French oppositions, the concept of the "Russian soul" was an equally flexible weapon in literary politics. It could be used to condemn a writer's denationalization or to praise his cultural universality, depending on the critic's attitude toward the author. Adamovich made use of this ambiguity. He defended young émigrés' orientation toward French literary models, arguing that a writer who gave up his external national features and lost his national identity committed an exploit, for he sacrificed his national self for the sake of cultural universality. But the same argument did not apply to his foe, Nabokov. Adamovich taunted the critical enthusiasm around Nabokov's novel *Zashchita Luzhina* (1929; translated as *The Defense*, 1964), saying that the work was original only in a Russian context and would go unnoticed in the *Nouvelle revue française*.[18]

The émigré reaction to the exiles who wrote exclusively in French shows that all accusations of "un-Russianness" on the basis of foreign influence were but literary politics. When, in 1938, Henri Troyat (Lev Tarasov) received the Goncourt prize, it was clear to everybody that he could not write in Russian by virtue of age and education.[19] Yet most émigré commentators regarded his career as a choice. Troyat's path revealed a "special spiritual disposition" that would have barred him from becoming a Russian writer anyway, because only by losing his "Russianness" could one "squeeze in the narrow door" of French literature.[20] Émigré critics stressed the selfless nature of Russian letters in exile and linked them to religious experience as an exploit and self-sacrifice.[21] To affirm this vision of the Russian writer as an ascetic apostle of Truth, Adamovich suggested that Troyat's choice was dictated by monetary considerations, while Khodasevich treated all Russian exiles writing exclusively in French as "renegades."[22] The perception of Troyat's career as lucrative defection does not correspond to the facts of French literary life. Émigrés knew that most French writers could not subsist on literary income alone.[23] But they forgot about this when dealing with the ideal model of Russian literary activity in emigration.

How "French" Became "Russian"

The distinction between the Russian and French traditions that the exiles made may appear unexpected considering the fascination with all things French nurtured by the Russian cultural elite at home. The émigrés indeed wondered about the discrepancy of their expectations and what they construed as the reality of French art, refusing to acknowledge their own dependence on old stereotypes, handy as long as French literature remained the only reference for their artistic self-identification.[24] The ignorance of contemporary French writing and the lack of cultural flexibility among older émigrés contributed to the clash of literary traditions.[25] With time, however, exiles began to modify their views. The structure of the Russian-French dichotomy remained intact, but French works were more and more often endowed with "Russian" traits. An opposite trend simultaneously developed vis-à-vis Soviet literature, which

the émigrés began to encode as "un-Russian." These modifications resulted from many factors: better familiarity with French literary life,
growing opposition to Soviet literature, and the activity of the Western-
oriented younger generation. But the crucial factor may have been the
gradual increase in émigré-French cultural contacts.

Although they concerned only cultural elites, these ties existed from
the beginning of exile.[26] Influential exiles appealed for interaction, justifying it by the émigré mission of cultural continuity: émigré-French
exchanges enriched Russian artists and educated the French about
things Russian.[27] The interest was reciprocal. The situation of exiles as
"troubled troublemakers" ("situation de gêneurs et de gênés") sparked
curiosity, stimulating attention to émigré culture.[28] A number of émigrés collaborated in French periodicals and collections.[29] Charles Du
Bos, André Gide, Édmond Jaloux, René Lalou, and Jacques Maritain lob-
bied for the publication of émigré works in French.[30] Critics stressed that
French interest for Russian letters produced a stream of translations
from contemporary writers, many of them émigré.[31] Translation was often initiated by publishers despite questionable financial prospects.[32]
Unlike younger exiles, older writers saw their works translated, all the
while complaining about the insufficient number of translations and
French inattention.[33] Thus, in his article "Les Russes de France," André
Beucler assumed that French readers were familiar with the art of older
émigrés and concentrated on the younger writers whose works remained untranslated (885).

Publishing was not the only venue for émigré-French commerce. Personal contacts were at least as important. Among the most significant
were the debates in Pontigny and the Studio franco-russe. The "Décades
de Pontigny," organized by Paul Desjardins in the former Cistercian
Abbey of Pontigny, united representatives of European cultural elites for
three ten-day sessions ("décades"), each dealing with a sociopolitical,
philosophical, or literary subject. Topics were provided in advance, and
a typical "décade" opened with an exposition, followed by debates,
both formal and informal, since guests lived in close quarters. Charged
with selecting participants, Charles Du Bos and André Gide invited a
number of émigrés. In Pontigny, Nikolai Berdiaev, Ivan Bunin, Lev
Shestov, Boris Shletser, and Boris Zaitsev met with major figures of
French literature, from Roger Martin du Gard and Paul Valéry to
François Mauriac and André Maurois. Personal ties born in Pontigny
continued in Paris.[34] Russian participants spread the news of the de-

bates in the exiled community; accounts of the "décades" appeared in the émigré press.[35]

Émigré-French contacts peaked between 1929 and 1934, when émigré literature was at its acme.[36] The trend toward intellectual exchange coincided with the growing importance of younger writers, who masterminded the Studio franco-russe and similar meetings under the tutelage of the review *Chisla* (Numbers).[37] Inspired by Pontigny, the young émigré writer Vsevolod Fokht, well connected in French intellectual circles as a journalist for the daily *L'Intransigeant,* created a venue for French-émigré meetings.[38] Fokht's stated goal was not to stimulate French interest for Russian writers living in Paris—the existence of this interest he could not deny—but to explain to the French the difference between Soviet and émigré letters ("Soirées de Paris," 60). He convinced a director of *L'Intransigeant,* J. Probus-Corréard, who ran the society "Humanités Contemporaines," to sponsor the Studio franco-russe. Marcel Péguy, the editor of the *Cahiers de la Quinzaine* and Fokht's friend, as well as Jean Maxence, the editor of the *Cahiers 1929,* which counted Fokht among contributors, joined the "Humanités Contemporaines" and its review, *France et monde,* in support of the project. From October 1929 until May 1931, the studio united émigré and French intellectuals in public debates on literary, cultural, and philosophical topics.[39] Full transcripts of these meetings appeared in the *Cahiers de la Quinzaine.*

Émigré critics remarked on the large number of prominent French figures in attendance at the studio.[40] French participants varied by political and esthetic convictions: the studio brought together the *académicien* Paul Valéry and the unrepentant avant-gardist Philippe Soupault; it pitched the "Catholics" Georges Bernanos and François Mauriac against the communist sympathizer André Malraux; and confronted the advocate of "Europeanism" Benjamin Crémieux with the promoter of fascism Robert Brasillac. Lists of participants, published at the end of each transcript, contradict the complaints of French indifference toward émigré cultural life.[41] The Studio closed because of Fokht's departure from France.[42] But the personal and professional links it initiated survived well beyond its lifetime.[43]

Russian-French contacts sped up the modification of the émigré view of French art. Expressing their opinions of French writing as cerebral and estheticized at the expense of spirituality, émigrés ran into French opposition.[44] Such direct confrontation forced many exiles to "rehabilitate" the French literary tradition in the late 1920s. Adamovich admitted that the émigré judgment was superficial and suggested the beneficial nature of French literary models for Russian letters. Veidle went even further. He characterized the Russian view as misinterpretation and endowed French letters with the "Russian" qualities of depth and humanism, bringing the proposed literary model into accordance with émigré esthetic expectations.[45] This shift is reflected in the contemporary evaluations of French writers.

In 1926, as we have seen, Kirill Zaitsev criticized *Les Faux-Monnayeurs* for esthetic refinement and lack of spirituality. In 1930 Adamovich endowed Gide's novel with "Russian" qualities, employing the same logic and terminology. The critics clashed at the Studio franco-russe. Both justified their views by postulating the presence or absence of "Russian" characteristics in Gide's oeuvre and never left the system of oppositions: sincerity-artificiality, psychological depth-esthetic superficiality, humanism-literature. Both appealed to Dostoevsky as the test of Gide's "quality."[46] The evaluations of Proust also changed. For Shmelev, Proust could not satiate exigent spirit as too smooth and refined. Fel'zen also preferred artistically uncouth books to the "brilliant and smooth average." But now it was Proust who possessed the Russian quality of formal imperfection.[47] In the unchanged contrast of the irrational element of Russian chaos and the French intellect, Fel'zen placed Proust on the Russian side of the divide despite earlier émigré views.[48] Since the dichotomy of formal skill and spiritual depth favorably applied to Fel'zen's own work, émigrés began to see this "Russian" attitude in his writings as inspired by Proust.[49]

By the early 1930s even older exiles revised their views. In 1925 Boris Zaitsev described French literature as entertainment deprived of mysticism and romanticism. In 1930 he spoke of the values shared by émigré and young French writers in contrast to Soviet art: psychologism and spirituality brought recent French writing closer to émigré literature and required that exiles heed French cultural life.[50] After witnessing debates at the Studio franco-russe, Zaitsev argued that the postwar generations in émigré and French literatures shared the experience of maturing in the time of social turmoil; he saw the behavior of younger French writers ("nervous, almost neurasthenic and frenzied") as "reminiscent of Russia" and remote from the conception of French rational coldness ("Dnevnik pisatelia," 3).

Having spent ten years in France, émigré literati could not fail to see that French literature was in an antiesthetic and soul-searching period. Young French writers rejected "artificiality" and "insincerity" in literature as part of the general reaction against the culture of positivism in which they saw the source of the war. Their "antiliterary" sentiment lent itself to Russifying interpretations, for it sported such concepts as sincerity, humanism, simplicity, and promoted "content" over "form."[51] The Russification of French literature was further encouraged by the émigré-Soviet split. Coming to the fore after 1925, it exacerbated the émigrés' need to find a counterbalance to state-sponsored Soviet art. The affinities (real or construed) of émigré and French letters allowed one to project the universal prestige of French literature on the émigré mission of cultural continuity.

In 1919 Valéry wrote that the war had brought about a spiritual crisis of cultural elites. The postwar intellectual was a "European Hamlet" contemplating the skull of his civilization; he suffered from existential anxiety (*inquiétude*), for the golden age was dead, his present was in disarray, and his future uncertain; he was doubtful and lonely, because the culture that had nurtured him was compromised. All thinking people were afflicted by this *malaise*, thought Valéry.[52] French writers commonly aired this opinion in the 1920s. According to them, the war produced an insurmountable gap between the fathers, who had written before 1914, and the sons, who matured in the years of turmoil. Claiming exclusive rights to "Hamletism," young writers criticized the philosophical, moral, and esthetic foundations of the ruined civilization, whose rebuilding entailed a revision of values in art and life.[53] In the first issue of *Littérature* (1919), Breton, Soupault, and Aragon questioned the validity of literary activity by asking French writers: "Why are you writing?" In 1920–23 the dadaist movement all but upheld the existence of a postwar "malady."

Spiritual ailment became an attribute of the postwar literary generation, whose new malady of the century harked back to the Romantic malady.[54] In 1924 the novelist Marcel Arland wrote a manifesto, "Sur un Nouveau mal du siècle," comparing contemporary intellectual atmosphere to that engendered by the French revolution. He thought that young writers were overcome by anxiety and solitude because the positivist culture that had "killed God" had been ruined by the war. Losing the last "existential protection," still available to their fathers, they refuted "pure estheticism" and used art to extra-artistic ends. They did not conceive of literature apart from moral issues; in search of "existential protection," they redefined the human being through self-study. Wrote Arland, "There is one subject that interests me above all literature: myself." "Sincerity" replaced "fiction" in a "human" and "documentary"

literature that answered the urgent questions of existence by reflecting
the psychological and intellectual vicissitudes of its creators.[55]

While older critics demythologized Arland's theses as *esthetically*
valuable,[56] many literary reviews in the 1920s published "examens de
conscience," in which writers aired their *inquiétude*. The symptoms of the
"new malady" became commonplaces.[57] Antiesthetic and extraliterary
considerations ranged from dadaist riots to the surrealist use of art as
a psychological tool to moralizing "Catholic" novels by Mauriac and
Bernanos. Postwar "sensibility" gave birth to a literary type—an anxious and disoriented young man. In 1920 one found him in Jacques de
Lacretelle's *La Vie inquiète de Jean Hermelin*, André Obey's *L'Enfant in-
quiet*, and Louis Chadourne's *L'Inquiète adolescence*. There followed Drieu
La Rochelle's *État civil* (1921) and in 1923 Soupault's *A la dérive* and *Le
Bon Apôtre* and Raymond Radiguet's *Le Diable au corps*. The hero suffered
from a personality crisis illustrative of the war rupture, which he evaded
through introspective analysis and international escapades, prompting
critics to unite these texts under the rubric of "literature of evasion."[58]
Disoriented young men soon invaded such different novels as Jean
Cocteau's *Enfants terribles* (1929) and L.-F. Céline's *Voyage au bout de la nuit*
(1932).

The novel was taken to task as the most "bourgeois" and "fake" of literary genres. Gide took apart the conventions of the nineteenth-century
novel in *Les Faux-Monnayeurs*, but his work was deemed too "literary."[59]
The first surrealist manifesto denounced the novel as a genre. Surrealist narratives, structured as records of a quest for truth, offered documentary proofs (photographs, posters, etc.) as an alibi against "fiction."
In an ostensible shift from literature to confession, novels about disoriented young men resembled autobiographies.[60] Young novelists strove
to express themselves in a confessional form whose discursive and uneventful nature and deliberate artistic imperfection violated literary
conventions.[61]

"New children of the century" shocked the reader by self-analysis
that violated social taboos. René Crevel filled his novels (*Mon corps et moi*
[1925], *La Mort difficile* [1926]) with intimate details, ranging from sex and
hygiene to suicidal desires. Soupault called the hero of *Le Bon Apôtre*
"Philippe Soupault" and did not shy away from scandalous confessions.
Escaping from "literature," L.-F. Céline, Eugène Dabit, and Raymond
Queneau used colloquial language and slang. And all, in unison,
claimed that they were "human beings" and "thinkers," but not "writers."[62] Ensuring an extraliterary alibi, many joined political and religious

causes. Surrealists flirted with communism. Gide and Malraux rallied for the "Russian experiment." Malraux wrote "leftist" novels (*La Condition humaine* [1933], *Le Temps du mépris* [1935]); Céline's pamphlets battled the Jewish conspiracy; Drieu La Rochelle joined the Action française and filled his novels (*Comédie de Charleroi* [1934], *Rêveuse bourgeoisie* [1937]) with the criticism of liberal democracy. *La Joie* by Bernanos (1929) and *Le Noeud de vipères* by Mauriac (1932) attested to the authors' involvement in Jacques Maritain's movement of "Catholic renewal."

Younger émigré writers related to the spiritual malaise of their French peers.[63] The "new malady" linked them with the French Romantics, who, for the most part, were also émigrés. Accepting French intellectual atmosphere as a model for artistic activity, émigrés used its elements to justify their own esthetic preferences, such as the taste for crisis, which they had brought from Russia. After arriving in France, Adamovich described the apparent health and energy of contemporary French letters as suspiciously "late Roman," although "Spengler's *Decline of the West* was still unknown in France" ("Literaturnye zametki," *Zveno* 68: 2). The critic was not alone in his desire to see things in Europe go bad: debates à la Spengler were the peculiarity of émigré table talk.[64] But having familiarized themselves with contemporary French writing, Russian exiles found it to be fruitful ground for their aspirations. They interpreted the "new malady" as part of the general European crisis heralded by Spengler. Wrote Adamovich: "Our monopoly on anxiety, on 'sacred distress' ['sviatoe bespokoistvo'] ceases to be a monopoly. . . . While there may not be much sanctity in contemporary French literature, its anxiety is not fake—hence the word *inquiétude* in every French article about literature."[65] The postwar "sensibility" of French literature opened possibilities for dialogue. (Thus, the first meeting of the Studio franco-russe dealt with anxiety in literature.) The symptoms of the "new malady" corresponded to the cultural uprootedness and disorientation of an exile. Émigrés Russified the fashionable malaise of the French writers, interpreting it by the logic of the Russian-French dichotomy. The "new malady" meant French literature's rejection of its former "estheticism" and brought French writers closer to the Russian tradition.[66]

In 1929 Adamovich wrote that those preoccupied with things spiritual should heed depth and humanity in French writing, which, "no matter how strange this may sound, was generally more attentive to the human being than Russian"; a few years later he claimed that émigrés *owed* their anxiety to French literature, which poisoned them with refined individualism that put to shame crude Soviet collectivism.[67] The view

of the decline of the West also changed. It began to appear healthier and
more human than Soviet "progress," and had more artistic potential.[68]

In the 1930s younger exiles often discussed the cultural catastrophe
that had dug a chasm between past and present, begetting the "émigré
young man" ("emigrantskii molodoi chelovek"), also known as "man
of the thirties" ("chelovek tridtsatykh godov") and "émigré Hamlet"
("emigrantskii Gamlet")—a cousin of Valéry's "European Hamlet."
These concepts described the esthetic and philosophical split between
émigré generations. The anxious young hero of French novels found a
cousin in the "hero of young émigré literature."[69] The ideal of "absolute
sincerity," as expressed by Arland, was echoed in Poplavskii's definition
of young émigré literature as "literature of truth."[70] The concept of the
"Paris note," ascribed to Poplavskii, was also distilled from the French
critical discourse. As a uniting mark of young émigré writing, it amalgamated the social, spiritual, philosophical, and artistic implications of
the "new malady." These were pessimism, frequent references to death
and boredom, solitude and anxiety, stylistic and compositional "simplicity," and confessional discourse at the expense of imagination.[71]

Solitude was the main ingredient of the "Paris note,"[72] often motivated by the absence of émigré-French interaction. As we have seen, this
allegation hardly corresponds to historical facts. To the contrary, it
seems that exposure to the French esthetics of the "new malady" imbued
émigrés with a taste for solitude. Complaining about isolation in his
memoirs, Adamovich wrote that "in order to penetrate into French
'circles,' even if one wanted to do so, one had to be persistent not without servility" (*Odinochestvo i svoboda*, 37). Thus, one had to *want* to reach
out to the French. The critic gives even more reasons to suspect the artificial nature of this alleged isolation when he writes that "'the bitter
sweetness of solitude'—an expression coined by Jean Moréas, a French
poet, whose works we relished still in St. Petersburg . . . a cult of this
sweetness we brought with us from Russia" (*Odinochestvo i svoboda*, 301).
Vladimir Veidle, familiar with Adamovich's involvement in émigré-
French exchanges, debunked the critic's claims to solitude as unrelated
to the émigrés' life in Paris: "He should be ashamed of speaking about
specifically émigré solitude, and of mixing inner and external solitude. . . . No other Russian émigré man of letters was more surrounded
by people than Adamovich. He could feel inner solitude even then, but
his life in emigration had nothing to do with this feeling" ("O tekh, kogo
uzhe net," 391).

But even as early as 1936, Adamovich was blamed for using the concept of solitude to esthetic ends.[73] His insistence on cultural isolation finds a better explanation not in the actual émigré experience but in its artistic construction. Adamovich wrote in his poem:

> За все, за все спасибо: за войну,
> За революцию и за изгнанье,
> За равнодушно-светлую страну,
> Где мы теперь 'влачим существованье'.
> Нет блага большего—все потерять,
> Нет радостней судьбы—скитальцем стать,
> И никогда ты не был к Богу ближе,
> Чем здесь, устав скучать, устав дышать,
> Без сил, без денег, без любви, в Париже.

❦

> [Thank you for everything: for the war,
> The revolution, and the exile,
> For the indifferent and bright country
> Where we are now "dragging our existence."
> No fortune is greater than to lose everything.
> No fate is more joyous than that of a wanderer,
> And you have never been closer to God
> Than here, tired of being bored, tired of breathing,
> Without forces, without money, without love, in Paris.]
> 　　　　　　　　　　　　　("Dva stikhotvoreniia," 3)

The expression "dragging our existence" hardly applies to the poet's life in Paris, where he found intellectual and artistic freedom. He means earthly existence, with respect to which elements of the "new malady" acquire esthetic and spiritual value. Deprived of cultural and social protection, he finds himself in isolation, which brings him closer to God, deepens his self-knowledge, and stimulates his art. According to Adamovich, such perfect exile liberates the writer's consciousness and opens it to "the most important."[74] The loss of material security is equally valuable, since the model of the Russian writer postulates the prevalence of the spiritual over the material. Adamovich's poem alludes to Lermontov's romantic posturing in the poem "Blagodarnost'" ("Za vse, za vse tebia blagodariu ia" ["I thank you for everything"]) and, by extension, to his *Hero of Our Time*, which grafted the original "malady of the century" onto Russian literature and proposed a Russian child of the century. Like Lermontov, Adamovich Russifies a French spiritual malaise.

The adoption of the "new malady" entailed the Russification of its French carriers, such as L.-F. Céline. The life of Bardamu, the hero of *Voy-*

age au bout de la nuit, is shaped by the shock of war. After failed international escapades, he settles in a squalid Parisian suburb and practices medicine amid social degeneration. This naturalistic narrative of joyless existence culminates in the death of Bardamu's friend. The narrative is steeped in slang to create the effect of antiliterariness. Crude descriptions show "true" life in contrast to the "estheticism" of fiction. At a meeting of the group Kochev'e, Céline's novel was said to possess a Russian consciousness, thanks to emphatic truthfulness, a mood "evocative of the Russian striving to speak about 'the most important,'" and "hopelessness, which Russians see as their monopoly."[75] More precisely, the novel appeared "Russian" to *younger* writers, who formed Kochev'e and shared the esthetics of the "new malady," expressed by Céline with great vigor.

Defending the positions of younger exiles, Adamovich rooted the literature of "émigré Hamlets" in the émigré mission. Attuned to the European intellectual atmosphere, these writers chose literary "documents" at the expense of "harmony, grace, unity and other beautiful things"; their reflection on the modern human condition was part of their mission.[76] Khodasevich disagreed that "documents" stemmed from the existential situation of émigrés: he viewed them as a literary fad, but did not detect their French roots.[77] Other critics saw more clearly the mythology of the new generation and its indebtedness to French literature.[78] Nevertheless, younger exiles persisted in claiming their own, special position in European culture, which impacted their writings. This was the situation of the "children of Russia's terrible years" ("deti strashnykh let Rossii") who "could not forget anything" ("zabyt' ne v silakh nichego"), as Alexander Blok had predicted.[79] A parallel émigré mythological construct was created, following the French model. Both justified the esthetics of new literary generations by their existential needs vis-à-vis the crisis of European civilization.

"Russian" and "French" versus "Soviet"

The émigré opinion of Soviet literature was a reaction to the Soviet writers' search for new literary forms for a new society, which translated into experiments in language, versification, plot construction, and narrative technique. Although most experimental forms and movements (formalist criticism, futurism, "ornamental" prose) had originated before the revolution, experimentation became especially pronounced in Russia in the 1920s, allowing émigrés to classify an array of literary features as "Soviet" esthetic phenomena.

The avant-garde saw its heyday despite the esthetic conservatism of the new regime. Futurists recapitulated their rejection of previous art in the name of the proletariat. In the name of materialism they denounced the prevalence of "content" over "form" in the Russian tradition and cited Marx's theses on Feuerbach to justify their concept of art as a reality-transforming force. The esthetic principle of Maiakovskii's Levyi Front Iskusstv (Left Front of the Arts, LEF) rested on the conviction that revolutionary art required new "forms." Art had to be "life edifying" and pragmatic. Hence proceeded the propagandistic poetry and the industrial esthetics of the Soviet avant-garde. Striving to revolutionize life by placing it under the sign of art, futurist esthetics slid into crude utilitarianism in the service of the regime.

Politically moderate writers were also obsessed with revolutionizing literature. The Serapion Brothers group adhered to the theories of Russian formalist critics, who tended to use the categories of "form" and "content" by reducing the literary work to a combination of devices with "content" as only a pretext for their manipulation.[80] The Serapions stressed their divorce from nineteenth-century literature, which they despised for its cult of "ideas." Along with other original writers— Zamiatin, Pil'niak, and Platonov—they turned their works into the testing ground for literary language (expressionist "ornamental" prose), plot construction (linear plot yielded to disconnected episodes with no central characters), and narrative technique. They used the formalist procedures of montage, estrangement, and laying bare the device. A break with nineteenth-century praxis could be observed even in the artistically conservative "proletarian" writers, who distanced themselves from tradition.[81]

Soviet experimentation followed the dichotomy of "form" and "content" all too familiar to the émigrés. This fact illustrates the structural affinity of the opposed literary subsystems. Under such conditions, an esthetic preference in one would be unacceptable in another. As autonomous subsystems with interdependent value hierarchies, Soviet and émigré literatures were, by 1930, locked in a mutually defining relationship based on the esthetics of opposition—they rejected each other's values as "noncultural."[82] Modeling exilic experience as "true" Russian culture, many émigrés marked Soviet experience as both noncultural and un-Russian. This was logical, since cultural models mark off their sphere against the backdrop of the noncultural; culture needs this opposition to nonculture as its privileged member.[83] Indeed, a rejection of tradition in the USSR was countered by the self-imposed mis-

sion of continuity in emigration.[84] An orientation toward "form" in Soviet letters met with its opposite in exile. The lack of psychological analysis, the superficial heroes of many Soviet writers—the result of a rebellion against the "psychological" novel—brought émigré accusations
of inhumanity and spiritual blindness.

In the context of the growing émigré-Soviet literary antagonism, esthetic choices acquired political connotations. A work marked by "Soviet" esthetics (futurist trans-sense language in poetry, expressionist
"ornamentalism" in prose, montage in plot construction, the formalist
procedures of estrangement and laying bare the device) could be considered ideologically pro-Soviet. Khodasevich denounced futurism
as literary formalism and classified it, along with formalist criticism,
as Bolshevik mentality: both "disrespected Russian literature and its
ideas"; such disrespect translated into the contempt for human personality characteristic of Bolshevism ("O formalizme i formalistakh,"
2–3). The implications were clear to all émigrés. Since "formalism" was
contempt for "content," which in Russian letters was incarnated by
"ideas," disrespect for "ideas" meant contempt for the Russian literary
tradition. One was not an "émigré" writer if one rejected this tradition.
The future of Russian literature lay with those émigrés who were not
"poisoned with political or literary Bolshevism."[85]

If discovered in a work by an émigré, traces of "Soviet" experimentation could bring about political suspicion, as in the response to B.
Temiriazev's *Povest' o pustiakakh* (Story about trifles, 1934). This novel
about revolution was perceived as Soviet, thanks to its narrative, full of
emphatic "devices" and based on the technique of montage, and to its
language evocative of Soviet-style "ornamentalism." Some saw in it a
provocation, suggesting that the novel had been authored by a Soviet
writer. Others argued that it was "Soviet" only in form and saw Temiriazev as a sheep disguised in a wolf's skin.[86] Later it turned out that "B.
Temiriazev" was the pen name of the émigré painter Iurii Annenkov. The
example of Boris Poplavskii is also illustrative. From 1921 on, Poplavskii
was active in Parisian avant-garde circles inspired by futurism and
Dada. Realizing the incompatibility of his esthetics with those of mainstream émigré reviews, Poplavskii did not publish until 1928. Entering
the émigré literary scene at the cost of withholding or editing his early
poems, he tailored his subsequent texts to émigré expectations. Described by memoirists as an "émigré" poet, Poplavskii himself considered his move a shameful compromise.[87]

Most of Poplavskii's peers abandoned "Soviet" esthetics when the émigré-Soviet split was just becoming a factor in their artistic self-definition. In late 1924 Soiuz Molodykh Poetov i Pisatelei (Union of Young Poets and Writers) was formed in Paris. Its program bore political implications. Reacting to Soviet "formalism," the union envisioned a "reexamination of values regarding the relationship of form and content" and postulated the need to counter "formalism" with "spiritually grounded art" in accordance with the true tradition of Russian literature.[88] An editorial in the union's review, *Novyi dom* (The new home), announced a commitment to cultural continuity, which had become impossible in Russia. It rallied for the rejection of estheticism and for the primacy of ideas (*ideinost'*) in art, affirming the group's orientation toward the nineteenth-century "engaged" Russian art.[89]

This statement illustrates new developments in émigré artistic self-modeling, as Soviet literary esthetics were superimposed on the system of Russian-French oppositions. Exiles ascribed "estheticism" to French literature. Yet *Novyi dom* argued that Soviet estheticism violated the Russian tradition. Two extremes, Russian avant-garde experiments and the stylistic "smoothness" of the average French work, became phenomena of the same series. Both shared "formal" orientation in contrast to the "spirituality" of the Russian tradition. But the identification of Soviet and French esthetics was short-lived. The shift toward French literature can be felt already in *Novyi dom*'s editorial, whose authors want to combine the Russian tradition with European spiritual values. They justify their interest in French models by the émigré-Soviet antagonism and imply their readiness to distinguish "true" French literature from the "estheticism" contained in it, just as they distinguish between "Russian" and "Soviet" paradigms. Thus presented, French influence appeared to exiles both justified and desirable.[90] Several years later, the *maître* of "émigré Hamlets," Adamovich, routinely divided French literature into "ours" (texts with "Russian" elements) and "theirs" (texts oriented toward the values of the Soviet subsystem).[91]

Using the nineteenth-century "engaged" art as a point of reference, young émigrés did not follow its example. Critics remarked that no "primacy of ideas" could be detected in the literary section of *Novyi dom*, but its poetry contrasted stylistically with futurist texts—it was "simpler" and "clearer."[92] Two of the review's editors, Knut and Terapiano, had belonged to avant-garde groups. Their condemnation of "Soviet" esthetics did not mean that they could give up their dadaist-futurist schooling and confine themselves to "civic" poetry à la Nekrasov. Instead, they followed the French "antiformalist" fashion, which presented itself as a

new word in literature. Against the backdrop of the émigré-Soviet polarization, the esthetics of the "new malady" motivated such perfectly
literary concerns as stylistic "simplification" and a new set of topics, allowing one to join mainstream émigré literature and still remain on the
forefront of European modernism.

To Knut and Terapiano, this reorientation brought increased awareness of the formal side of poetry. They joined the group Perekrestok,
whose mentor, Khodasevich, stressed technical skill on the basis of classical versification—"simple" in contrast to futurist "excesses." In this
"simple" form they spoke about the "most important." So did those who
preferred Adamovich's program demanding that the poet sacrifice skill
for "humanism" and "sincerity" as mandated by the "new malady."
These poets—the converted Poplavskii, Lidiia Chervinskaia, Anatolii
Shteiger—also saw their poetry as simple, although the task of making
it "imperfect" required considerable sophistication. (Characteristically, Soviet readers perceived the "ascetic" style of young émigrés as
extremely refined.)[93] Terapiano and Knut were quickly seduced by
Adamovich's view of literary simplicity. By 1930, Terapiano, in his own
words, overcame his interest for neoclassicism and discovered a new
metaphysical world-view, becoming an ardent proponent of "émigré
Hamletism."[94] Knut did as much: his quest for literary "truthfulness" resulted in programmatic linguistic and structural imperfection, too cal-
culated to appear either spontaneous or "sincere."[95]

In 1927 Soviet literary life began to evolve rapidly. In this year Stalin
consolidated his power, announcing the first five-year plan and the
cultural revolution, which entailed the "proletarianization" of professional groups and cultural institutions. Trotskii's political defeat brought
about the fall of critics who had protected fellow-traveler writers.[96] The
attacks of the Rossiiskaia Assotsiatsiia Proletarskikh Pisatelei (Russian
Association of Proletarian Writers, RAPP) on fellow travelers became
more dangerous, for the RAPP now appealed to the party's own cultural agenda. The new literary climate found its expression in the
RAPP's 1929 campaign against Pil'niak and Zamiatin—the heads of the
Moscow and Leningrad branches of Vserossiiskii Soiuz Pisatelei (All-
Russian Writers' Union), which included many fellow travelers. Victims
and observers perceived this campaign, which also targeted Bulgakov
and Platonov, as state sanctioned and aimed at the overall independence
of literary expression from the state.[97]

The campaign against fellow travelers coincided with a surge in col-
lectivization and in the purges of party, industrial, and cultural appara-

tuses. In a sign of antagonism toward the emigration, cultural watchdogs used as a pretext for their ideological warfare the foreign contacts of Soviet intellectuals.[98] To be sure, censorship of texts from abroad predated these events. In 1923, books by Russian exiles were barred from the country, although some materials were imported for scrutiny by loyal critics; in 1928 even this stream dried up.[99] In 1929 a director of the Pushkin House was arrested and charged with maintaining foreign relations. Zamiatin and Pil'niak were stigmatized as saboteurs "communicating with the White emigration" because they were published abroad. The editor of *Krasnaia nov'* (The red virgin soil), a liberal review that had patronized fellow travelers, now thought that a Soviet writer could not collaborate in the émigré press.[100] Vserossiiskii Soiuz Pisatelei condemned Zamiatin and Pil'niak. At the same time, many fellow travelers signed petitions demanding the death penalty in the political trials of 1930–31. These events reinforced the émigré conviction that Soviet writers had transgressed the ideal of the Russian writer—they had allied themselves with political authority and betrayed their calling as prophets of Truth.[101]

The growth of ideological pressure on Soviet literature intensified the émigré debate on the fate of Russian letters. By 1930 the Soviet-émigré opposition sharpened to the point that both sides denied each other's right to exist. As the demise of émigré art became a critical commonplace in the USSR, Dovid Knut aired the commonly shared opinion that the capital of Russian literature had moved to Paris.[102] The exiles' political leanings were often revealed by their take on this literary antagonism. "Leftists," like Mark Slonim, preached the imminent death of émigré literature because it had lost the traditional link of Russian literature to Russia's everyday life.[103] In extremis, public renunciations of émigré literature symbolized an exile's political conversion.[104] On the other end of the political spectrum, Khodasevich heralded the death of Soviet letters. For him, émigré literature could die not because it was divorced from Russian realia but because it was "not enough émigré" ("Literatura v izgnanii," in *Literaturnye stat'i i vospominaniia*, 258, 261, 267). But as Soviet art ossified under state control, exiles of all political hues had to agree that literary vitality sprang from freedom of expression available only in emigration.[105] Thus, Adamovich, who held a moderate opinion of Soviet art until the early 1930s, "buried" Soviet letters once fellow travelers were silenced by the dogma of socialist realism.

In April 1932 the party disbanded all literary associations and formed Soiuz Pisatelei SSSR (Union of Writers of the USSR), perfecting the state's control of literary expression. This event was followed by the introduction of socialist realism. Although the new esthetic dogma was elaborated in the course of several years, its implications were clear to the émigrés from the outset. It aborted all independent literary life that had survived ideological pressure after 1927.[106] The tightening of controls on Soviet writers stimulated the reevaluation of the émigré-French dichotomy. Adamovich argued that, since émigrés had to pass on to future readers the values of the "true" Russian literature, they had to give up their instinct of self-preservation, that is, the esthetic conservatism of older writers.[107] The new generation saw its mission in developing rather than in preserving the tradition. This program implied both a rebellion against émigré artistic conservatism and an orientation toward Western models.

As "Russian" and "French" esthetics drew closer, the exiles became increasingly ready to excuse the pro-Soviet mood of many French intellectuals.[108] "Misunderstanding" and "snobbery" were the terms in which they described French infatuation with communism.[109] Émigrés commonly distinguished Western communism from its Russian version: the "special and warm concept of communism" espoused by French intellectuals was a positive moral symptom because it sprang from a quest for social truth in the "abomination of capitalism and liberalism."[110] Whether snubbing or justifying French "parlor Bolshevism," émigrés did not see in it an isolating factor, as it has been presented in memoir literature.[111] It furnished, in fact, additional reasons for émigré-French interaction, because explaining the true nature of communism was part of the émigré mission.[112]

The polemics of Konstantin Bal'mont with Romain Rolland (1928), Andrei Levinson's obituary of Maiakovskii (1930), and the clash with French communists at the *Chisla* soirée "André Gide and the USSR" (1933) shared the desire for publicity in French intellectual circles. Bal'-mont's open letters, bashing Rolland's eulogy of the Soviet regime, were published in the émigré daily *Poslednie novosti* and the French daily *L'Avenir.* Levinson's denunciation of the myth of Maiakovskii the revolutionary poet appeared in the *Nouvelles littéraires.* "André Gide and the USSR" was conceived as a debate with French intellectuals. The high turnout of communists resulted in a violent clash of opinions, but instead of deploring French communist leanings, an émigré critic castigated Russian participants for lack of stamina in the debate, whereby they failed their mission.[113]

The Maiakovskii controversy shows the gap between the émigré-

French ideological dynamics and its presentation in memoir literature. Levinson's obituary said that the poet's émigré foes found this death too beautiful an end for a life like his ("ils trouvent une telle mort trop belle pour achever une pareille vie") ("La poésie chez les Soviets," 6). According to Berberova, French antiémigré sentiment found its "most glaring example" in "the physical beating by French surrealists of Andrey Levinson . . . after his obituary on Mayakovsky" (*Italics Are Mine*, 226–27). The émigré press told the story differently. Only one surrealist, Aragon, staged a scandal in Levinson's home; there was no beating; émigré commentators viewed the incident as an amusing anecdote; expressions of sympathy for Levinson were insincere, for the émigrés scoffed at Aragon as a professional scandalmonger.[114] A letter in defense of Maiakovskii by French and Russian artists was derided by émigrés as incompetent (on the French side) and ideologically biased (on the Russian).[115] A group of émigrés signed a letter in support of Levinson, targeting Maiakovskii's French admirers as "badly informed." It called the poet a composer of official verses in the service of the regime.[116] This document is a rare case of unanimity in the émigré opinion, one in which Adamovich's name flanks that of Nabokov. The entire debate took place in the *Nouvelles Littéraires,* a major weekly where the émigré opinion had wide resonance, contrary to the allegations of political exclusion.[117]

However, the attitude of the French cultural elites was far from uniformly pro-Soviet. Besides the uncompromising stance of Jacques Maritain and his associates, the Soviet regime was criticized by such former sympathizers as André Gide, Pierre Pascal, Victor Serge, Boris Souvarine, Drieu La Rochelle, and L.-F. Céline.[118] French interest in Soviet letters declined in the 1930s as a result of artistic ossification in the USSR; Gide publicly accused Soviet writers of cowardice and blamed the state for thwarting artistic expression.[119] This disillusionment was perceived by émigré commentators as a sign of evolution toward mutual understanding between French and exiled intellectuals.[120] The "Appeal of French Writers" in support of Soiuz Molodykh Poetov i Pisatelei, published in 1936 in several French dailies, only confirmed this view. The signatories—Marcel Aymé, Charles Du Bos, Gabriel Marcel, André Maurois, François Mauriac, Henri de Monthérlant, among others—called for financial assistance to émigré writers who chose the freedom of expression at the expense of material security.[121] Émigré commentators saw this group of signatories as composed of all leading representatives of French literature, a view that is at odds with the memoir descriptions of political isolation.[122]

An additional factor influenced the émigré-French ideological coexistence. The collaborators of the review *Chisla* rejected political preoccupations in art as a "Soviet" feature and attacked the émigré literary establishment for assimilating émigré art with anti-Bolshevik propaganda.[123] As it became clear that the Soviet regime could not be toppled by political means, cultural activity seemed to be the only fruitful form of resistance.[124] In the context of the émigré-Soviet opposition, the RAPP's ideological campaign of 1928–29, which lay stress on political vigilance in art, was a negative example. Beginning with this campaign, Soviet letters manifested some tendencies alarming in their functional similarity to the émigrés' own literary program: stress on psychological analysis, antiformalism, and, with the imposition of socialist realism, the acceptance of tradition. The emphasis of the points of divergence between the two literatures became ever more urgent.

The RAPP's campaign had major repercussions on Soviet letters. In 1929 formalist criticism was squashed, and its founders publicly repented; Maiakovskii left the LEF as too "formalist" and organized a Revoliutsionnyi Front Iskusstv (Revolutionary Front of the Arts, REF) to combat apolitical literature. Both groups disappeared in 1930, as Maiakovskii joined the RAPP.[125] Conducting an offensive on "nonproletarian" writers, the RAPP rallied for the imposition of a sole artistic method—proletarian realism with its "red Leo Tolstoy," a literary psychologist whose analysis would draw on dialectic materialism.[126] The "antiformalist" current intensified in the 1930s. Linguistic experimentation was debunked in favor of "correct" and "simple" language.[127] The RAPP promoted politically correct "content" over "form," arguing that excessive concentration on literary technique pushed Soviet writers toward the "disintegration of G. Ivanovs and G. Adamovichs." From the Soviet standpoint, "formalism" was an émigré literary feature.[128] In 1934, the party called for increased vigilance in view of the escalating struggle of classes, which spread to all spheres of life, including literature. Reaching its peak in 1936, the antiformalist campaign coincided with the trial of the Kamenev-Zinov'ev group, and Soviet critics began assimilating "formalism" in art to counterrevolution.[129]

Affinities between Soviet and émigré esthetics became obvious in the definition of socialist realism, presented as the heir to nineteenth-century literature ("tradition"). The dogma advocated "socialist humanism" by contrast to Western "bourgeois humanism," echoing the opposition of Russian spirituality and French estheticism. Both literatures now played down "form" and valorized extra-artistic considerations.[130] The definition of the Soviet writer as "an engineer of human souls" who led the way to the bright future was a crude adaptation of the ideal model of the Russian writer as a carrier of Truth—a major topos in émigré literature. This newly manifested similarity had to be countered. Soviet critics treated literature as a weapon in class struggle; individualist or apolitical art was anti-Soviet.[131] Now émigrés could exclude sociopolitical issues from the repertory of "the most important." The desire to oppose Soviet "collectivism" pushed younger émigrés toward the French "new malady" and its individualistic esthetics.[132] The Russian-French dichotomy was effectively undermined in view of the Russian-Soviet opposition.

The rejection of sociopolitical issues marked a major step in the evolution of the émigré literary subsystem. The collaborators of *Chisla* stopped paying lip service to the nineteenth-century tradition of "civic" art. The review had no place for politics as overshadowing "other equally important, if less urgent, issues."[133] The writings of its contributors reflected this program. Gazdanov's novel *Vecher u Kler* (1930; translated as *An Evening with Claire*, 1988) traced the life of an émigré, who joined the White Army not for ideological reasons but because he wanted to test himself. Spiritual experience overshadowed for him the issue of political choice. Bakunina expressed the same stance in a poem that refused to distinguish between the Reds and the Whites, portraying them as equally violent. The protagonist of Poplavskii's novel *Apollon Bezobrazov* (Apollo the ugly, 1930) wanted to comprehend the deeper meaning of exile, disregarding its political aspects as "metaphysically worthless." These political aspects had as little import for the hero of Fel'zen's novels: engrossed in self-analysis, he treated exile from a spiritual vantage point and criticized all warring sides for intolerance.[134]

Chisla's apolitical program stirred lively polemics in the émigré artistic circles. Turning away from the sociopolitical side of exile, younger writers stayed within the scope of "Russian" topics. Choosing from the approved literary subjects—"vital problems of individual and social existence" (Slonim, "Literatura v emigratsii," 1)—they opted for individual existence.[135] Furthermore, they reinterpreted the concept of the émigré mission to fit their own esthetic preferences. Viewing their opposition to the Soviet regime as primarily spiritual, younger émigrés presented their exclusive interest in the individual as a continuation of the Russian literary tradition.[136] Since the debate never left "Russian" esthetic coordinates, the politically and existentially preoccupied quickly found common ground. The fathers, who saw anti-Bolshevism as an essential quality of émigré literature, agreed with the sons in principle. Anti-Bolshevism meant that, instead of treating prescribed political topics (the way Soviet writers did), émigré artists would confront Soviet literature and culture "with creative activity based on the spiritual values suppressed by Bolshevism."[137]

As we have seen, by the end of the 1920s the émigré-French-Soviet triangle produced a set of criteria (stylistic, narrative, and semantic) applicable in the interpretation of artistic texts. These criteria allowed émigrés to identify any Russian literary work with the ideal model of émigré or Soviet literature and, subsequently, to classify it as "Russian" or "un-Russian." Later in my study I will refer to this set of interpretive criteria as *émigré poetics*.[138] From the outset of the Russian-French opposition, the signifiers "Russian" and "émigré" became synonymous, and the exiles saw the relation of their literature to French letters as "Russian" versus "un-Russian." But with the growth of émigré-Soviet antagonism, it became possible to mark French works as spiritually and esthetically "Russian." Furthermore, an additional, axiologically neutral category was introduced: now French texts could be described as "foreign" (marked neutrally), "Russian," and "un-Russian." By 1930 the exiles generally interpreted émigré literary production as esthetically and ethically "Russian," treating Soviet works as "un-Russian," that is, noncompliant with the émigré ideal model of the Russian literary tradition. A French text, however, could be identified with the body of "Russian" texts, if it appeared to share in the "high" values of émigré poetics; it could be treated as "foreign," in which case indifference was the dominant attitude toward it; and, if some "un-Russian" features were found in it, one tended to regard it as "pro-Soviet." Judgment varied by critic, but the oppositional system of evaluation remained the same.

"Russian Cultural Universality" or the Art of Being "Modern"

The projection of "Russian" qualities on French works and the opposition of French and Soviet esthetics were not the only ways to justify émigré interest in French models. One also interpreted the émigré mission as contingent on openness to foreign influences because cultural universality was traditionally Russian, as Dostoevsky pointed out in his speech on Pushkin. In the period dominated by the Russian-French dichotomy, émigrés rarely invoked this universality, but it came back with a vengeance in the 1930s. Now the "conservationist patriotism" of older writers betrayed "Russian universal spirit"; the question was no longer "What to preserve?" but "What can we take from the West?"[139] The rhetoric of the émigré mission (especially the claim of "turning to Europe for Russia's sake")[140] rationalized the fact that young exiles could not write like their older colleagues. Having little experience of adult Russian life, they could not describe the "good old days"; having matured as writers abroad, they were more exposed to the French than to the Russian tradition. The fact that émigré critics described foreign influences in works by younger writers as "normal" and "innocuous" testifies to the need to protect them from the conservatism of the fathers.[141] By the early 1930s there already existed a critical technique for justifying émigré interest in French literary models.

In this two-step procedure, one projected nineteenth-century Russian letters ("tradition") upon French writers to Russify them and undermined the "Russianness" of older émigrés, severing their ties to the tradition. Varshavskii argued that, since French writers paid more attention than older émigrés to "existence," to "noumenal things," and to "the fourth dimension," Gide was closer to Dostoevsky than were "émigré classics." The writer recoded the argumentative tools and vocabulary of the older generation. His reference to Dostoevsky recalls the same use of this signifier by the émigré opponents of "French estheticism," while the "fourth dimension" harks back to (and parodies) Shletser's view that French characters were "unidimensional" in contrast to the "three-dimensional" Russian heroes.[142] Poplavskii also thought that older émigrés lost touch with tradition, to which "new" writers gained access, thanks to contemporary French texts. Sticking to conventional oppositions of émigré poetics (form-content, rationalism-spirituality), the poet wrote:

> New émigré literature, the one that was born in exile, frankly admits that . . . Paris is its homeland. . . . "So, you are not Russian? . . . Write in French then." We will write neither about Russia nor in French, but the way we want, without asking permission but with Western sincerity. . . . The literati of the "generation of crime" (i.e., the loss of Russia) are losing ground, while the people of the generation of punishment . . . have survived, adapted to life and are now setting to work. . . . This is not a formalist movement but a new collective discovery in the metaphysics of the "dark Russian personality." ("Vokrug 'Chisel,'" 204–5)

Thus, young writers draw such "Russian" qualities as truth, sincerity, dark personality, antiformalism, and antipositivism from Western

(French) literature. An allusion to Dostoevsky's *Crime and Punishment* completes the recoding, stigmatizing older writers.

As examples of new literature Poplavskii cited novels, "human documents" by Sharshun, Bakunina, and Fel'zen. The narrative structure and thematics of Sharshun's *Dolgolikov* (Long face) drew on the French surrealist novel. Bakunina's *Telo*, a protofeminist story of corporeal emancipation, had emphatically simplified vocabulary and syntax, while its monotonous and uneventful narrative emulated the latest French achievements in "truthful" literature. Fel'zen's novel *Obman* (Deceit) was a neo-Proustian investigation carried out in long and syntactically complex periods. These different texts belonged, according to Poplavskii, to the same literary series. They shared sincerity, humanism, simplicity, and contempt for everything outside "the most important." Poplavskii implied that these "Russian" qualities were inspired by French literature.[143] The 1930s were marked by several such attempts to present younger writers as one movement based on common sensibility, which Varshavskii conveyed by the concepts of "émigré young man" and "hero of young émigré literature," Terapiano by that of the "émigré Hamlet," and which Poplavskii saw as the "mystical atmosphere of young émigré literature" and the "Paris note," Sharshun and Fel'zen as "magic realism."[144]

This heterogeneous group of writers, centered around Adamovich and *Chisla*, received the name of the Paris School and purported to represent "émigré modernism."[145] The desire to be "modern" and the "modernist" sense of breaking with the traditions of the recent past are felt in the attempts of these writers to define themselves. The new generation used nineteenth-century literature mostly to "Russify" (justify) its French models. Traditions of the émigré fathers died in the spiritual rupture of the war; older exiles became the writers who "emigrated but were not émigré" by contrast to the "émigré young men with Hamlet's soul."[146] This revolution in the ideal model of émigré literature was so effective that, as early as 1934, some critics began to use the term "émigré literature" almost exclusively in reference to those writers who had matured in exile.[147] In the "modern" tradition, where "Russian" and "French" esthetics merged in opposition to "Soviet," older exiles lost the main distinction between themselves and Soviet writers. Conspicuous influence of French modernist literature became an esthetic prerequisite among younger exiles in Paris.[148]

When used to rationalize émigré interest in French models, the concept of Russian cultural universality illustrates T. S. Eliot's argument about the advantages of "coming from a large, flat country which no one wants to visit" ("Henry James," in *Shock of Recognition*, 2: 857). The desire to exploit these advantages led to the creation of cultural myths that denied historical facts of émigré life in France. Émigrés found themselves exiled in the cultural center of the world and creative freedom; the circumstances of their exile stimulated artistic activity. Observing that the number of those who began to write abroad was disproportionately high vis-à-vis the size of the diaspora, Fel'zen suggested that "life in a foreign land, refreshing foreign influences stimulated creative activity, just as in the French emigration" ("My v Evrope," 158). Indeed, Russian exiles obtained de jure what European modernists cultivated artificially, namely, the notions of crossed borders, of breaking with the past, of cultural uprootedness, solitude, and crisis.[149] One found these notions in the cosmopolitan orientation of Dada and surrealism, whose rejection of tradition resulted in the solitude of a poet in advance of his culture. They marked the Proustian exile from childhood and the *inquiétude* of the "new malady."

But, as Veidle has noted, the border between literature and life in the artistic praxis of younger émigrés is very fluid. There exists intentional confusion between their literary expression and "Montparnasse lamentations" (*monparnasskaia skorb'*), as the critic called the cultural mythology of the "unnoticed generation" ("O tekh, kogo uzhe net," 387). Transforming their "everyday life into tragedy," to use Terapiano's phrase, young writers cited the absence of educational opportunities, the impossibility of making a living by writing, the hostility and indifference of older literati, and the necessity of physical labor as factors influencing their esthetics.[150] Most older émigrés were worse off financially and socially than younger writers because of the lack of linguistic skills and cultural flexibility, yet they did not motivate their art by such circumstances.[151] One finds a more likely explanation for "Montparnasse lamentations" in Virginia Woolf's description of "modern literature of confession and self-analysis" as a feat of prodigious difficulty accomplished in spite of adverse material conditions, universal indifference, and "every form of distraction and discouragement" (*Room of One's Own*, 51–52). The self-description of "émigré Hamlets" as writers despite everything fits Woolf's image of the modernist.

Émigré writers could move to several East European countries that financed Russian culture, but they preferred Paris, for it saved them from artistic provincialism.[152] As refugees were admitted to France because of the postwar labor shortage, their employment was encouraged and facilitated by the government.[153] But unlike many educated Russians, at first young artists found industrial jobs "offensive to poetic dignity."[154] They studied in France, spoke fluent French, and qualified for white-collar jobs.[155] And here begins a series of coincidences that look like a pattern of meaningful behavior. Terapiano left his position at the publishing house Hachette for the packaging unit of a pharmaceutical firm; Gazdanov also left Hachette to become a taxi driver; Knut was a chemical engineer before becoming a delivery boy. One could assume that they fell prey to discrimination. But thanks to the advocacy of the League of Nations, Russian refugees enjoyed an exceptional status among foreigners in France. In 1924–27, their naturalization was facilitated. Those who eschewed citizenship initially suffered in the economic crisis of the 1930s, but in 1933 the League of Nations adopted a convention on the legal status of Russian and Armenian refugees obliging member states to grant them equal rights with citizens.[156] Furthermore, Gazdanov, Knut, and Terapiano insisted that their professional reorientation was voluntary: it afforded them time to write and to lead a bohemian existence.[157]

Henri Troyat's French education dictated that a writer's freedom came from a second, stable and gainful, occupation. Not so for the "Russian" writer. The Sorbonne-educated Mandel'shtam turned down an academic job and hardly made ends meet with the daily *Vozrozhdenie*. Poplavskii, who also attended the Sorbonne, refused employment "on principle." Fel'zen, a law school graduate, preferred the stock exchange, often living at the expense of his sister. Those who did not give up their careers—Ianovskii as a physician, Smolenskii as an accountant, Ginger as an engineer—presented their jobs as a humiliating burden.[158] In his memoirs Ianovskii described the ideal of voluntary poverty cultivated by younger writers, who viewed financial security as shameful. Material stability contradicted the status of the "Russian" writer, as illustrated by Adamovich's alternative to the adoption of Soviet literary esthetics: "One would do better becoming a bank accountant."[159]

The Sorbonne-educated Gazdanov complained that young émigrés could not study and partake in French cultural life. According to his "coquettishly forgetful" self-descriptions (Bakhrakh's term), the writer's life consisted of literature and hard physical labor.[160] The same myth-generating manipulation marked Terapiano and Knut. The latter admitted that émigrés exploited the negative social and material implications of exile as "ideal conditions for lyrical poetry."[161] In this way they authenticated the motifs of suffering, solitude, and despair in their works, conflating and capitalizing on the model of the Russian writer as an ascetic prophet and on the French "modernist" rejection of literary recognition and success. Like Daniel-Rops, who claimed that French "new children of the century" wrote little and badly because they could not "live and express themselves at the same time," Varshavskii saw the "righteousness" of younger émigrés in the fact that they did not write "much and well."[162] The "new malady's" rejection of literary success as irrelevant for those who are "human beings and not writers" coincided with the cult of asceticism in the ideal model of the Russian writer. Together, they stimulated the presentation of émigré literary production as scarce or unpublished, linking artistic failure to the image of "Christ's poor knight."[163]

It was, therefore, only logical for "émigré Hamlets" to argue that they were not published, were not supported by the émigré literary establishment, and were ignored by readers.[164] Their claim to the indifference and hostility of the older generation reinforced the esthetically valuable notion of a gap between fathers and sons. In fact, publishing was possible with modest means, and many self-sponsored books by younger émigrés appeared after 1925.[165] The vogue of "young talents" dominated émigré literature in the late 1920s. Demand quickly surpassed the supply: critics promoted even those new writers who did not live up to high artistic standards.[166] In 1926 *Sovremennye zapiski* yielded to this pressure, while *Volia Rossii* and *Zveno* launched programs for the promotion of young writers.[167] There appeared two publishing houses, "New Writers" and "Parisian Union of Writers," for younger writers only.[168] The promotion of younger émigrés is evident in most literary reviews: *Blagonamerennyi* (1926), *Novyi dom* (1926), *Novyi korabl'* (1927–28), *Stikhotvorenie* (1927–28), *Chisla* (1930–34), *Novaia gazeta* (1931), *Krug* (1936–38), *Vstrechi* (1934), *Russkie Zapiski* (1937–40). By 1930 the second generation was firmly established in all émigré journals, including *Sovremennye zapiski.*[169]

Claims to artistic isolation are riddled with contradictions. Citing exceptions to the total indifference toward his peers, Varshavskii furnishes an exhaustive list of influential émigré literati. In the same breath he writes that *Chisla* was the only review open to younger contributors and that the majority of young exiles were regularly published in émigré periodicals. When they did not indulge in "Montparnasse lamentations," "émigré Hamlets" admitted that they were recognized, respected, and assisted by older writers, émigré periodicals, and publishers. At times even Adamovich and Khodasevich conceded that the Paris School resorted to foul play, motivating its esthetics by irrelevant social realia.[170] Many contemporaries of the "unnoticed generation" were technically correct when they described as preposterous its complaints of literary isolation, but they missed the underlying significance of the cultural mythology of "émigré Hamlets."[171]

The myth of the "unnoticed generation" owes its amplitude and longevity to the coincidence of cultural circumstances. This mythology motivated the Paris School's parti pris of anxiety and pessimism that went neck and neck with similar developments in French literature. It amalgamated the ideal model of the Russian writer with the ideal writer-figure of postwar French literature—a "sincere" producer of "documents," who despised literature as a compromised institution, rejected "estheticism" for the sake of "simplicity," and considered himself a "human being," not a "writer." The mythology of the "unnoticed generation" rationalized esthetically valuable notions shared by most French literary trends. The case of each younger émigré and his relation to French literary life must be studied individually, but such study is hardly possible outside the larger literary-historical context, whose main features I have outlined in this chapter.

2

The Surrealist Adventure of
Boris Poplavskii

Students of émigré letters have paid little attention to Russian literary activity in Paris before 1925, when the city finally emerged as the capital of Russia Abroad. The popularity of the pro-Soviet avant-garde among young Parisian exiles in the early 1920s helped to exclude this chapter from émigré literature proper.[1] But this "heroic period," to use Knut's expression, produced a number of émigré poets—Boris Bozhnev, Aleksandr Ginger, Dovid Knut, Viktor Mamchenko, and Sergei Sharshun, among others—whose artistic personae cannot be fully comprehended outside this initial phase of their careers.[2]

A case in point is Boris Iulianovich Poplavskii (1903–35), who matured at the crossroads of Soviet, émigré, and French letters. Schooled in the esthetics of futurism, Dada, and surrealism, the poet recoded his early artistic praxis by exploiting the topoi of émigré poetics in order to adapt in mainstream émigré literature. This recoding was so successful that most exiles overlooked the fact that the "prince of Russian Montparnasse" had begun his career in opposition to émigré art. Coming to terms with his status as émigré writer, Poplavskii relied upon the artistic authority of surrealism, which contrasted with the growing esthetic conservatism of Soviet letters and the traditionally conservative older émigré literature. To understand his place in émigré letters one must establish the ties of his artistic persona to French surrealism. The term "surrealism," as used by most students of Poplavskii's art, is problematic, for it implies any artistic exploration of dreams, shocking images, and the unconscious.[3] In my study, "surrealism" refers to the program of André Breton's group—the original and only meaning of the term familiar to Poplavskii.

Striving to create a "new man," surrealism saw itself as a group investigation of the unconscious and uncanny that could change the human condition.[4] Its program proposed a technique of semantic structuring ("automatic writing"); a set of symbols and topics; a philosophy; and a cultural mythology. Since the basic surrealist practice involved group praxis, Poplavskii, who was not a formal member of the group, cannot be considered a surrealist *stricto sensu*. He adapted the semantic and narrative devices of surrealism and drew on its symbolics, philosophy, and mythology, making them paramount to his own artistic self-definition. For instance, the association of systematic discovery with a loss of control during creation linked surrealism to Arthur Rimbaud's "illuminations" through rational derangement of the senses (*Une saison en enfer*) and to the antisocial ethos of the Count of Lautréamont (*Les Chants de Maldoror*).[5] Capitalizing on Rimbaud's and Lautréamont's rebellion against poetic language, creative consciousness, and daily life, the surrealists gave the dream and hallucination a function—the creation of a new man and esthetics.[6] They recovered psychic forces through "vertiginous internal descents" and "illumination of hidden places." Poplavskii used the same terminology to describe his creative activity.[7]

Rimbaud's and Lautréamont's role as literary precursors relied on their personal myths, which provided a paradigm for "life in poetry."[8] Seeing no value in art that was not supported by its creator's attitude to life, Breton treated both men as surrealists by virtue of lifestyle. Rimbaud and Lautréamont incarnated the ideal of evasion, whereby one escaped the vanity of art through silence, realized one's antisocial stance by leaving society, and fled reality conceived by the positivist theory in the unconscious, drugs, or death.[9] According to their myths, Rimbaud rejected art ("fell silent") and society (he left for Africa); Lautréamont was the author of a sole text who died young and left no biographical trace. These myths equated surrealism to an adventure that was lived out as much as written. The dadaist-surrealist split revealed tensions between Dada's ethically valuable posture of complete silence and surrealism's milder version of self-effacement permitting creative activity that produced psychological "documents." As "modest recording devices" of their unconscious, surrealists erased all distinction between the literary and nonliterary, rejecting the notions of talent and success. Written poetry lost its "poetic monopoly"; life itself became poetry.[10]

Combining the myths of Rimbaud and Lautréamont in one ideal model, Poplavskii described his own "disgust for literature" (*otvrashchenie ot literatury*). Wrote the poet: "All I want is to express and to express myself. To write one 'naked' mystical book, like Lautréamont's *Les Chants de Maldoror*, then *assomer* critics by leaving, becoming a soldier or a worker, doing away with the revolting dualism of real and described life. To concentrate on pain. To protect myself by contempt and silence."[11] It is, therefore, logical that Poplavskii's literary oeuvre has been overshadowed by his lifestyle of a "Russian Rimbaud" who "turned theory into practice."[12] His road to the French poet ran through surrealism—he admired Rimbaud as a visionary and a model for "life in poetry."[13] Consequently, my investigation of Poplavskii's surrealist connection does not limit itself to written texts. I explore Poplavskii's self-stylized mythology as a text of life that, along with his poetry and prose, tells the story of his surrealist adventure.

Boris Poplavskii in the Heroic Period of Young Émigré Poetry

Boris was introduced to avant-garde art by his sister, the Decadent poet Natal'ia Poplavskaia, even as the esthetic organization of behavior among Russian symbolists and Decadents reached its acme in the ideology of life creation (*zhiznetvorchestvo*), "deliberate construction of artistic images and esthetically organized plots in life."[14] His early poems conflate life and art in a way evocative of symbolist theories, where the Christian notion of incarnation provides a paradigm for the esthetic process: by making the spiritual material, incarnation unites the domains of the everyday and the "beyond." Symbolists and Decadents saw art as capable of creating life. Life was an object of artistic creation and a creative act. Since only life created by art, life as a product of the incarnation of spirit, was "real," the esthetic organization of life had far-reaching mystical implications.[15] Imitating symbolist models, Poplavskii treated his own drug sessions as life-creating events of mystical nature:

> Мы ходили с тобой кокаиниться в церкви,
> Улыбались икон расписные глаза,
> Перед нами огни то горели, то меркли,
> А бывало, видений пройдет полоса.

> ∼⊱

> [We used to sniff cocaine in church,
> The painted eyes of icons were smiling,
> Lights before us were coming and going,
> And at times a series of visions would pass.]
> ("Vot proshlo, navsegda ia uekhal na iug," in *Neizdannoe*, 355)

Youth afforded the poet a lot of esthetic flexibility. By the time he left Russia in late 1920, Poplavskii had embraced both the esthetics of symbolism and that of its archenemy, futurism. In 1919 he presented himself as "one of the hooligans from Maiakovskii's entourage" and wrote a poem, "Gerbertu Uellsu" ("To Herbert Wells"), published alongside Maiakovskii's drawings.[16] The choice of addressee is reminiscent of futurism: Velimir Khlebnikov appointed Wells a "chairman of the globe" ("Truba marsian," in *Tvoreniia*, 604). By its rhythmical pattern, industrial imagery, and iconoclastic ethos the text confirms Poplavskii's parti pris as Maiakovskii's epigone:

> А мы, на ступенях столетий столпившись,
> Рупором вставили трубы фабричные
> И выдули медные грохотов бивни
> В спину бегущей библейской опричнине:
> Мы будем швыряться веками картонными!
> Мы бога отыщем в рефлектор идей!
> По тучам проложим дороги понтонные
> И к Солнцу свезем на моторе людей!

❧

> [And we, having crowded the stairs of centuries,
> Raised the factory chimneys like a megaphone
> And blew out the copper tusks of dins
> In pursuit of the fleeing biblical *oprichnina:*
> We will be hurling around cardboard centuries!
> We will spot god with the reflector of ideas!
> We will pave the clouds with pontoon roads
> And bring people on a motor to the Sun.]
>
> (*Neizdannoe*, 363)

The poem fuses symbolist and futurist esthetics. The image of a celestial path recalls Vladimir Solov'ev's and Nikolai Fedorov's ideas, inherited by the symbolists. Both believed in the creation of a real bridge (*pontifex*) between heaven and earth and in the resurrection of human nature, modeled on that of Christ. After 1917 these theories were appropriated by a society steeped in revolutionary constructivist ethos. In Poplavskii's poem the *pontifex* is technologically materialized as a pontoon road that changes the human condition. Such fusion was possible because Russian symbolism and futurism shared in the utopian project of reorganizing the world and humankind. There was a continuity between the fin-de-siècle modernist esthetics and Soviet culture.[17] The futurist poet Il'ia Zdanevich proclaimed: "After the long isolation of the artist we have loudly summoned life and life has invaded art, it is time for art to invade life" ("Why Are We Painting Ourselves," in Bowlt, *Russian Art of the Avant-Garde*, 8). Futurism modified symbolist "life creation" into "life building" (*zhiznestroenie*), replacing mysticism with a technical (constructivist) approach to life, as reflected in Poplavskii's poem. Privy to symbolist and futurist esthetics, the young poet was ready to assimilate the praxis of artistically motivated behavior in Dada and surrealism. In Paris Zdanevich became his artistic mentor.[18]

Two features marked the literary life of young Parisian exiles in the early 1920s. First, the absence of anti-Soviet sentiment in their milieu coincided with the popularity of the Soviet avant-garde in poetry (futurism) and visual arts (constructivism). Young refugees joined the groups Gatarapak and Palata poetov run by Valentin Parnakh, Sergei Romov, and Sergei Sharshun, who partook in Dada's Parisian debut and invited dadaists to Russian literary events. Contacts with French dadaists constituted the second peculiarity of the period.[19] An aspiring poet and painter, Poplavskii was a regular at these meetings.[20] His mentor, Zdanevich, boycotted émigré circles, popularizing futurist poetry among Tristan Tzara's followers.[21] In December 1921 Palata poetov hosted Sharshun's soirée "Dada-lir-kan," attended by French dadaists. Poplavskii was present at this event, whose scandalous denouement was blamed on the conservatism of the émigré audience.[22] In May 1922 he went to Berlin in search of a Russian artistic "left," met Pasternak and Shklovskii, who encouraged his poetic ambition, and told his hosts that "besides Merezhkovskii, Bunin, and Gippius, Paris had its 'young' who opposed the 'fathers' in both art and politics."[23] Returning to Paris in late 1922, he joined the new group Cherez, which united Palata poetov and Gatarapak, forging close ties to Dada and Maiakovskii's LEF.[24] Before the blows dealt to Cherez by Dada's demise and by the conservatism of the Soviet regime, Poplavskii and other "leftists" ignored mainstream émigré literature.[25]

Thanks to Dada's affinities with futurism, Cherez backed Tzara in his war against Breton's faction until July 1923, when *Le Coeur à Barbe*, a show organized by Cherez, ended in a fight between dadaists and future surrealists. "This battle," wrote Zdanevich, "symbolized the demise of Dada and that of Cherez."[26] However, Cherez outlived Dada by revising its orientation: Zdanevich gave up trans-sense poetry, frequented the meetings of Breton's group, and befriended Paul Éluard and René Crevel.[27] Poplavskii's own "left" politics, his involvement in Dada and futurism, his personal ties to French avant-gardists, and his hands-on familiarity with their cultural mythology had prepared the poet to assimilate the theory and practice of surrealism.[28] The growing political and esthetic polarization of Russian artistic life left him with little choice but to keep aloof from émigré literary circles.

In November 1923 Paris offered young exiles an alternative milieu. Georgii Adamovich, Georgii Ivanov, and Nikolai Otsup—former acmeists hostile to the Soviet avant-garde—organized a "Tsekh Poetov" to fight for the souls of young poets.[29] As a result, several Cherez associates founded in 1924 Soiuz Molodykh Poetov i Pisatelei (Union of Young Poets and Writers), which opposed the "formalism" of the avant-garde with "spiritually grounded art" and "classical traditions." In the context of émigré literary life, this was an anti-Soviet declaration in art and politics.[30] Poplavskii did not contribute to the union's review, *Novyi dom*. After a meeting of May 1925, his name does not reappear among the group's participants until 1928. At this meeting the admirers of futurism clashed with "neo-classicists," having discovered the incompatibility of the union's orientation with "left" art.[31] Poplavskii's letters reveal the voluntary and politically motivated nature of this self-exclusion. He wrote:

> [Regarding] Stikhotvornyi (on zhe 'Smekhotvornyi') Vestnik [The poetic (alias risible) messenger] and its editors Bozhnev, Broslavskii and Mikh[ail] Struve. Struve's participation reveals the publication's political hue (that is why neither my poems nor Sveshnikov's nor Zdanevich in general will appear there). As for the members of Cherez—"God speed.". . . The review of the Poets' Club . . . invited Khodasevich as the editor. In general, it is a right-wing affair. . . . "Blagonamerennyi" [The well meaning] comes out on the fifth in Brussels, edited by Prince Shakhovskoi (the author of sonnets). Shura Ginger in a letter urged me to submit my works without specifying, as befits an idiot, "their" political orientation.[32]

This undated letter was written in the summer of 1925 (*Blagonamerennyi* appeared in 1926 only; Poplavskii says that he did not write all summer and is waiting for Zdanevich to arrive in September).[33] It testifies to the ongoing disintegration of Cherez. The dwindling ranks of the Russian avant-garde could not but propel Poplavskii toward the surrealists. Although at present there is almost no information about his life from 1923 to 1927, the poet's surrealist connection can be traced in his writings of this period.

The project to publish in 1926 Poplavskii's collection *Grammofon na Severnom poliuse* (The gramophone on the North Pole) failed, as did the attempt to publish *Dirizhabl' neizvestnogo napravleniia* (The dirigible of unknown destination) in 1927.[34] The recent discovery, in Zdanevich's archive, of the poems selected for *Grammofon* supplements the already known texts of 1923–27 from the 1965 edition of *Dirizhabl'*, compromised by editorial tampering.[35] *Grammofon* contains twenty-six poems attuned to the works of Breton and his peers. Some of them combine trans-sense language with the surrealist principles of semantic structuring, revealing Poplavskii's place at the intersection of the Russian and French avant-gardes. French surrealist texts representative of this period include *Les Champs magnétiques* by Breton and Soupault (1921), Breton's *Clair de terre* (1923) and *Poisson soluble* (1924), Éluard's *Répétitions* (1922), *Mourir de ne pas mourir* (1924), and *Nouveaux poèmes* (1925), Desnos's *Peine perdue* (1924) and *C'est les bottes de 7 lieues* (1926), and Aragon's *Le Paysan de Paris* (1926).

Subscribing to Tzara's postulate "Thought is made in the mouth," surrealists explored "the real functioning of thought." Since "no thought existed beyond words," its exploration implied the liberation of language from logical and social constraints. Automatic writing and dreams were designated as the means of producing "uncontrolled" thought. Automatic writing consisted of writing down everything that came to mind as fast as possible. The fast pace lifted the control of reason because "the speed of thought did not surpass the speed of words."[36] Arguing that the "emotive power" of the poetic image lay in the absurdity and arbitrariness produced by juxtaposing two semantically remote elements, Breton saw automatic writing as propitious for the creation of "surrealist" images ("Manifeste du surréalisme," in *Manifestes*, 49–50).

According to eyewitnesses, Poplavskii literally applied Breton's semi-jocular directions for the "magic surrealist art."[37] But while Poplavskii saw in automatic writing a literary method akin to Joyce's "stream of consciousness," Breton made the same comparison as a literary disclaimer, contrasting Joyce's artistic imitation to the psychological authenticity of automatic texts.[38] Yet, the product of Poplavskii's artistic imagination is akin to that of Breton's "liberated consciousness": the structural principle of the poetic image in *Grammofon* and *Dirizhabl'* follows the technique of semantic contrast presented by the poets of Breton's group as "surrealist." This contrast can be created by the juxtaposition of a noun and an adjective or a verb and an adverb, as in the poem "Stekliannaia deva" (*G*, 80): impossible tree (nevozmozhnoe drevo), unnatural enemy (neestestvennyi vrag), returnless friend (bezvozvratnyi tovarishch), flying gratuitously (bezvozmezdno letaet).[39] One finds similar usages in Breton's and Éluard's poems: "tous mes animaux sont obligatoires" (All my animals are obligatory, *Mourir*, 58), "un château sans signification" (a meaningless castle, *Poisson*, 27), "la Seine charriait de façon inexplicable un torse de femme" (the Seine carried a female torso in an inexplicable fashion, *Poisson*, 36).[40]

In more syntactically complex phrases the surrealist effect can be created by similes or metaphors composed of semantically unrelated elements: "the train was twisting like a sea worm" (sgibalsia poezd kak morskoi cherviak, *G*, 51), "a scream, like the tearing of new underpants" (i krik, tak rvutsia novye kal'sony, *D*, 30), "the moon has crouched like a soldier relieving himself" (luna prisela, kak soldat v nuzhde, *D*, 28; cf. "the sun [like a] lying down dog" [Le soleil chien couchant, *Clair*, 63], the phrase puns on two idioms: "chien couchant"—a setter; and "entre chien et loup"—at sunset); "the double-breasted coat of heavens blossomed / the violet tails silently languished" (tsvelo nebes dvupoloe pal'to / sirenevye faldy molcha mleli, *D*, 29; cf. "night came like a carp's jump on the surface of purple water" [la nuit est venue pareille à un saut de carpe à la surface d'une eau violette, *Poisson*, 38], the phrase puns on the idiom "un saut de carpe"—a brusque jump to one's feet from a horizontal position).

Violation of clichés is another way of creating the surrealist image. Thus, Breton titled his book of automatic poems *Clair de terre*. Besides its literal meaning of the light reflected from Earth into space, this expression reverses the poetic cliché "clair de lune" and shows Breton's rejection of the traditional poetic usage and of earlier literary esthetics. Aragon laid bare this device, replacing the idiom "blond comme les blés" (wheat blond) with a series of comparisons including blond as hysteria, blond as the sky, blond as fatigue, and blond as a kiss (blond comme le baiser). The latter created an additional semantic shock by distorting another cliché, "rouge comme le baiser" (*Paysan*, 51). Poplavskii also used linguistic clichés to this end. Transforming the idiom "to spin like a squirrel in a wheel" (kruzhit'sia kak belka v kolese) in "to spin like a squirrel in a clock" (kak belka v chasakh, *G*, 70), he plays on the phonetic affinity of "belka" (squirrel) and "strelka" (clock hand).[41] In the phrase "the heart is flying like a green rabbit" (letaet serdtse kak zelenyi zaiats, *G*, 59), he superimposes the stereotypical association of the noun "heart" with the verb "to jump" (serdtse prygaet) onto the idiom "the rabbit's heart" (zaiach'e serdtse), which denotes fear or agitation. Instead of comparing the "jumping heart" to a jumping rabbit, he makes the heart fly like a rabbit and paints his rabbit green.

Breaking mimetic and logical rules, surrealist texts strive to convince the reader that the author's activity is "unconscious." The question of authenticity is unessential: authentic or simulated, these texts *look* as if dictated by the unconscious. But the semantic anomalies that create the effect of uncontrolled discourse are not as arbitrary as presented. Michael Riffaterre has shown that surrealist writings relied on the principle of the "extended metaphor"—a series of metaphors connected both syntactically (as part of one phrase or narrative structure) and semantically (each expressing an aspect of the element represented by the first metaphor of the series) ("La Métaphore filée dans la poésie surréaliste," in *La Production du texte*, 217–34). The extended metaphor constitutes a special code since the images that compose it have meaning only in relation to the first metaphor of the series. Engaged in the active unraveling of an extended metaphor, the reader becomes the (re-)creator of a surrealist poem, following the logical path of its author.[42]

The development of an extended metaphor relies on automatic writing as a process of "formal verbal association" in which a word determines a verbal sequence by formal similarity (phonetic parallelism, puns) or stereotypical associations (phonetic groups, quotes, clichés).[43] Surrealist images appear obscure when taken in isolation but often can be explained in the context of preceding images. Automatic writing associates the signifiers of incompatible signifieds, violates the mimetic representation of reality, and replaces the referential function of language with its poetic function, that is, describes the form of the linguistic message. The poets of Breton's group were aware of this technical side of literary automatism. Éluard discussed a new function of the "image by analogy" (simile) and the "image by identification" (metaphor): both figures "got easily detached from the poem, becoming poems themselves" in the continuous development of constituent parts. But the poet provided this technical aspect of his art with extraliterary motivation—"involuntary" poetry was the result of his listening to the unconscious "flow of obscure news" without literary pretension, which would destroy the faithfulness of the record.[44]

Poplavskii artistically exploited the extended metaphor. For instance, the metaphor "the defenseless rain was still falling" (Eshche valilsia bezzashchitnyi dozhd', *G*, 41) encodes the rules of the ensuing derivation. The verb "valit'sia" (to fall) is not used to describe rain but can describe falling snow or a falling man. The semantically shocking application of the adjective "defenseless" reinforces association with a human body, which logically appears in the following line: "as a murdered man falls from a window" (kak padaet ubityi iz okna). The author uses another verb denoting the action of falling ("padat'"), which can be applied to both man and rain. The derivation results in the semantic incompatibility of compared elements—rain and a murdered man. In another poem he writes: "Years will be jumping like sparrows around excrement" ([budut] skakat' goda kak vorob'i nad kalom, *D*, 46). The metaphor "jumping years" violates the cliché "flying years" (gody letiat). And although the next image is also shocking (instead of pecking on crumbs, sparrows feast on excrement like flies), the derivation is justified by the stereotypical semantic association of "jumping" and "flying" with a sparrow.

Poplavskii's poem "Na belye perchatki melkikh dnei" (1926), dedicated to Zdanevich (*G*, 86–87), combines futurist and surrealist poetics. The first two stanzas read:

> На белые перчатки мелких дней
> Садится тень как контрабас в оркестр
> Она виясь танцует над столом
> Где четверо супов спокойно ждут
>
> Потом коровьим голосом закашляф
> Она стекает прямо на дорогу
> Как револьвер уроненный в тарелку
> Где огурцы и сладкие грибы

> [On the white gloves of petty days
> Shade sits down like a double bass into the orchestra
> Hovering it dances above the table
> Where four soups are calmly waiting
>
> Then having started coughing in a cow's voice
> It flows down straight onto the road
> Like a revolver dropped into a plate
> With cucumbers and sweet mushrooms]

The first two verses provide the code for the derivation. The verbs associated with "shade" are "to fall" (ten' padaet) and "to lie" (ten' lozhitsia), not "to sit down" (ten' saditsia). "To sit down" in relation to "gloves" can be perceived as referring to a fly ("mukha sela"). The fly casts shade in the light of short, "petty," days (the poem is written in January). Its noise is like the sound of a double bass (a fly in winter is "sleepy" [sonnaia mukha]). Hence the derivation: "Hovering, it dances above the table / where four soups are calmly waiting." "Soup" is evoked by association with the adjective "melkii" (petty or shallow), often used in combination with "plate" (melkaia tarelka). The agrammatical form of the noun "soup" suggests an animate subject, reinforcing the metaphor "soups are calmly waiting" and introducing an element of trans-sense language. This agrammaticality invades the next stanza: "to cough" is transcribed phonetically, evoking trans-sense poetry. The metaphor "coughing in a cow's voice" derives from the analogy between a cow's low-pitched moo and the sound of the double bass. "Flowing down" is evoked by the (spilt) soup. The revolver is suggested by the semantic associations of gun reports with the verb "to cough," whereas "to flow down" is used to speak about blood (krov' stekaet).

The use of trans-sense language increases toward the end of the poem, enhancing the impression of logical rupture. The literal reading proposed in the preceding discussion does not mean that the poem is "about" a fly in a soup. The prominent poetic function of its language draws one's attention to the form of this linguistic message—the combination of extended metaphors and trans-sense language—and to the author's futurist-surrealist artistic stance. The text polemicizes with the more conventional esthetics of the Parisian "Tsekh poetov" (the phonetic affinity between "soup" and "Otsup" may function as a satiric allusion). Thus, Poplavskii evokes the group's late founder, Nikolai Gumilev, as a burden to be replaced by his own esthetics: "Зане она замена гумилеху / обуза оседлавшая гувузу" (*G,* 87).

The extended metaphor draws its efficiency from the linear interdependence of elements: a modification in one image can change the entire sequence. Riffaterre views this structural feature as the basic stylistic device of "surrealist mimesis" ("La Métaphore filée," in *La Production du texte,* 233). In the poem "Voda vzdykhala" (*G,* 51), Poplavskii corrected the line "the blue sea where fish are diving" by replacing fish with birds in order to obtain the photographic negative of realist mimesis, a world upside down created as much by the logic of language as by the author's fantasy:

> А в синем море где ныряют птицы
> Где я плыву утопленник готов
> Купался долго вечер краснолицый
> Средь водорослей городских садов

> [And in the blue sea where birds dive
> Where I am floating already a drowned man
> The red-faced evening bathed for a long time
> Amid the seaweed of city gardens][45]

In March 1922 Breton's review *Littérature* began publishing dream accounts that soon became customary in surrealist journals. This issue of *Littérature* and Crevel's initiation into the technique of hypnotic dreams inaugurated the "Period of Dreams" (1922–24), in which Breton's dadaist associates formed the nucleus of the surrealist group with dreams and automatic writing as its rites of passage.[46] Hypnotic dreams provoked the "uncontrolled succession of images" (*Paysan*, 82) and permitted the immediate recording of "uncontrolled" discourse. Surrealists maintained the ambiguity of their experiments, insisting on the affinity of hypnotic dreams with drug-induced states and presenting surrealism as an "artificial paradise" and a "new vice."[47] Somnambulists spoke and wrote during hypnotic sessions, rejecting as unimportant the question of authenticity. Since thought drew upon the unconscious, one simply could not be "insincere."[48]

References to dreaming in the poetry of Breton's group far outnumber those to any other subject. There was hardly a poem in Éluard's *Mourir de ne pas mourir* that did not evoke dreaming; the same is true for Desnos's poems of this period. Breton opened *Clair de terre* with five dream accounts that are implicitly given the status of poetry. Poplavskii is no less obsessed with this subject. The poems of *Grammofon* can be divided into two groups: pure dream narratives (most of them with fantastic imagery) and more complex descriptions of his art based on automatic writing and dreams. Both types of poems refer to the role of the dream in creative activity through the image of speaking or writing in sleep. But the recognition of allusions to the artistic function of dreams and automatic writing requires familiarity with the system of symbols shared by the poets of Breton's group.

Surrealists constantly stress the unconscious nature of their discourse. Éluard's narrator "speaks without knowing it" (*Mourir*, 62), "tells the truth without telling it" (58), and "speaks with nothing to say" (56). Desnos's narrator is a "slave" who "comprises the dictionary of unknown language" and writes to its dictation despite his will (*Peine*, 33). Breton's narrator echoes this image of a linguistic slave: as a "prisoner of the world," he communicates with other prisoners by writing (*Clair*, 80). Emphasizing the unconscious nature of a text, these images also stress a new type of poetic language that no longer has one, literal meaning. Poplavskii's poems are full of similar images. His narrator speaks about "the mechanical piano of my soul" (*D*, 28, 35) and thus describes poetic activity:

> Мы в гробах одиночных и точных
> Где бесцельно воркует дыханье
> Мы в рубашках смирительных ночью
> Перестукиваемся стихами

⌦

> [We are in solitary and precise coffins
> Where breath is aimlessly cooing
> We in straitjackets at night
> Communicate by tapping our messages in verse]
>
> (G, 91)

"Solitary" coffins and message tapping refer to prison, slavery, and forced confinement. In the context of French surrealism, confinement alludes to a poet's dependent state as a "recording device," while the exchange of messages between prisoners suggests the surrealist artistic method. So does the adjective "precise," commonly used in surrealist poetry along with the nouns "clarity" and "light" to describe the result of "illumination." "Illuminated" reality becomes "clear" and "precise" in opposition to the world of the everyday.[49]

Surrealist illumination is symbolized by a set of conventionally accepted images. Automatic writing resembles the liberation of an underground source (*Poisson*, 82).[50] The signifiers with semantic connection to water may function as symbols of the unconscious. The most common among them are "water," "stream," "river," "sea," and, by extension, "fish" (cf. *Poisson soluble*), "shell," "ship," "submarine." Submersion into water, the observation of water, and water travel are common tropes for the exploration of the unconscious. Aragon's friends "dive into surrealism as into a sea and, like a treacherous sea, surrealism threatens to carry them away"; the narrator of Desnos's poem has an "ink-well periscope," and his pen returns into its shell; Éluard's narrator describes the river under his tongue that speaks when curtains are drawn.[51]

Water and related signifiers abound in Poplavskii's poems. They symbolize the process of "illuminating" the unconscious and refer to his artistic method. The opening poem in *Grammofon* starts with the line "Netonushchaia zhizn' au au" (hello, hello, unsinking life). It opposes the rationality of everyday ("unsinking") existence to another reality that culminates in a parade of infernal creatures as the everyday disintegrates. The title of *Grammofon* can be traced to automatic writing. The gramophone is a metaphor and a symbol of "automatism" and is associated with submergence: "Vot tonem my; vot my stoim na dne / nam mednyi grammofon poet privet" (Here we are sinking down; here we are standing on the bottom / a copper gramophone sings us a greeting, G, 52). In another poem, a speaking somnambulist has bell-shaped lips resembling a gramophone pipe (G, 91).

In "Zhizneopisanie pisaria," a scribe, who is not an artist but a "recorder," writes while dreaming and bathing in a stream:

> И тихо, тихо шевелит рукой—
> Клешнею розовою в синих пятнах,
> Пока под колесом, мостом, ногой
> Течет река беспечно и бесплатно

❧

> [And (he) quietly, quietly moves his hand—
> A pink claw with blue stains,
> While under the wheel, the bridge, the foot
> The river is flowing carelessly and gratuitously]
>
> (D, 42)

The comparison of the scribe's hand to the claw of a crustacean and the reference to a river derive from the poem's preceding images of bathing in a stream. The poem leaves open the possibility of interpreting dreaming as the description of its artistic method. Similar metadescription is prominent in another water trip, which ends in an effort to write it down:

> Плыву на дно: мне безразличны Вы.
> Тону: необходимы. Просыпаюсь.
> Рычат кареты за окном, как львы.
> Я за ружье чернильное хватаюсь.

❧

> [I am swimming to the bottom: I am indifferent to you.
> I am drowning: I need you. I am waking up.
> Carriages outside my window are growling like lions.
> I am grabbing for my ink rifle.]
>
> (G, 53)

The trip in "Petia Pan" ends similarly: the narrator wakes up, thanks to the shaking motion of his writing hand (G, 85). During another water trip, Poplavskii's narrator says:

> Тенебрум маре—море темноты.
> Пройдя, пролив чернила, мы в тебе.

❧

> [*Tenebrum mare*—the sea of darkness.
> Having crossed, having spilt ink, we are inside of you.]
>
> (G, 45)

The connection between ink and sea travel is enhanced by a pun: without a comma, the second verse can read "having crossed the strait of ink."

Following the rules of "surrealist mimesis," water is replaceable with air. If juxtaposed to the theme of air, the theme of water initiates new derivations of the extended metaphor type. Sea becomes sky, fish become birds, submarines become dirigibles. A river of stars carries away punctuation marks in Breton's poems (*Clair,* 63); Desnos evokes "liquid death on the shore of heavens" (*Peine,* 43); and Éluard's narrator describes a sea that is like the bright sky in which he falls asleep (*Mourir,* 55).[52] Poplavskii's dream narratives often shift from water to air, as in "Kladbishche pod Parizhem":

> Вертается умерший на бочек
> Мня: тесновато. Вдруг в уме скачок
> Удар о крышку головою сонной
> И крик (так рвутся новые кальсоны).
>
> Другой мертвец проснуться не желал
> И вдруг, извольте: заживо схоронен!
> Он бьет о доску нежною ладонью
> И затихает. Он смиреет. Тонет.
>
> И вот отравный дух—втекает сон,
> Ширеет гробик, уплывает камень.
> Его несет поток . . .
>
> И вот сиянье—то небесный град . . .

> [The deceased is turning on his side
> Thinking: kind of cramped. Suddenly in his mind a jump
> A knock on the lid with a sleepy head
> And a scream (like the tearing of new underpants).
>
> Another dead man did not want to wake up
> And suddenly, here you are: he is buried alive!
> He hits the wood with a tender palm
> And quiets down. He becomes calm. Sinks down.
>
> And lo, the poisonous spirit—sleep flows in,
> The coffin widens, the tombstone sails away.
> The stream is carrying him . . .
>
> Finally there is a shining—it is the heavenly city. . .]

(*D,* 30)

Confinement refers to a poet as a "recording device"; death symbolizes the dream; and the dream is a text-generating mechanism ("In soli-

tary and precise coffins. . . / [We] communicate by tapping our messages in verse," *G*, 90). The dead man with a "sleepy head" can be a
metaphor for the poet who seeks illumination in his "cramped" everyday reality. Illumination comes by way of his "head," that is, it is generated in his mind. The result is a semantically shocking utterance ("like
the tearing of new underpants") that may refer to the "uncontrolled" surrealist discourse. Another dead man falls asleep, "sinking down." The
image of sinking/drowning, derived from the semantic association of
sleep and water travel, engenders a series of water metaphors: sleep
"flows in"; the tombstone "sails away"; the coffin, carried by a stream,
turns into a boat. The comparison of sleep to a poisonous spirit evokes
the "poison" that propels Rimbaud's narrator in search of illumination.[53]
As water is replaced by air, the coffin becomes a flying boat and reaches
a heavenly city whose shining symbolizes the point of illumination.[54] A
reader familiar with surrealist poetics would proceed from the referential function of Poplavskii's text (a fantastic trip) to its poetic function—
reflection upon its artistic method.

The dream in "Voda vzdykhala" (*G*, 51) starts with the image of flying water, which initiates a series of metaphorical derivations: "shells of
a roof" (rakoviny kryshi), "jellyfish of clouds" (meduzy oblakov), "the
depth of the flying sea" (glubina letaiushchego moria), and "the weirdo-
dirigible roaming like a fish" (kak ryba ryskal dirizhabl'—chudak). The
image of a dirigible is especially important for Poplavskii (cf. *Dirizhabl'*).
His manuscripts contain several drawings of a bird standing on a fish
that looks like a dirigible. The image of the fish- and submarine-like dirigible haunts the writings of French surrealists. A dirigible resembled
both a cloud and a fish, while being a technological triumph; despite its
machinery, it was a prey to the breezes, going off in "unknown destinations"—the kind of spontaneity surrealists valued in art. In *Les Champs
magnétiques*, dirigibles float amid lakes in the sky, accompanied by the
winged carcass of a donkey (39). Éluard describes a dirigible as an air
icon that looks like a spinning giant fish (*Nouveaux poèmes*, 109–10). The
editorial of *La Révolution surréaliste* expressed the wish that human
bones be "inflated like dirigibles."[55]

A group of images derives from semantic association with water's
transparency and clarity and with the state of clarity and transparency
during "illumination." This group includes signifiers related to glass.
Poisson soluble describes a feast in a room filled with water. The revelers
have glass diving suits on and entertain a flock of women wearing glass
suits only (47). A similar image is found in Poplavskii's poem "Stek-

liannaia deva" (The glass maiden, *G*, 80): "A nude maiden comes in and drowns" (Obnazhennaia deva prikhodit i tonet). Here surrealist imagery polemicizes with the Russian poetic tradition by parodying one of its topoi—"rusalka" (water sprite). Alluding to the poem's parodic side, Poplavskii prefaced it with the epigraph "A poem in Zhukovskii's manner."

A common image in surrealist texts is a glass container in which the narrator finds himself or herself: a cube, a room, a house of glass haunted by fantastic visitors.[56] Several of Poplavskii's poems describe unconscious states as life in a glass house (*G*, 41, 68). In "Eshche valilsia bezzashchitnyi dozhd'" (*G*, 41), a trip to a glass house surrounded by water and filled with infernal creatures ends in catastrophe. The house is smashed by the "claw of terrible joy" (kleshnia uzhasnoi radosti) throwing about "blood of ink" (chernil'noi bryzzhet krov'iu). This house may be a glass inkwell that refers to the narrator's occupation as a "scribe"-somnambulist whose writing "claw" emerges in the poem "Zhizneopisanie pisaria" (*D*, 42). "Terrible joy" may refer to surrealist illumination.

Poplavskii's dream narratives are full of fantastic images steeped in graphic violence and mutilation. This aspect also hearkens to surrealist poetry, which is permeated with baroque images, showing how the surrealists oscillate between skepticism and belief in the supernatural.[57] In Breton's automatic texts, castles and flower beds are haunted by a ghost looking for his severed head (*Poisson*, 28, 30), while the narrator speaks to a wasp with a woman's waist (35–36). In other surrealist texts, glass skeletons dance in an earth of glass (*Clair*, 64) and accompany newly born children to the earth's surface (*Bottes*, 56); a bird drags a headless corpse on a mirrored surface (*Mourir*, 75); the Seine carries a "beautifully polished" female corpse with no head or limbs (*Poisson*, 36); and another female "boat of flesh" indicates that water travelers must hurry to their graves (*Bottes*, 59).

One critical opinion regarding Poplavskii's poetry should be contested. Gibson and Menegaldo argued that Poplavskii's poetry could not be justly considered surrealist because his versification was traditional—with meter, rhyme, and division into stanzas.[58] Basing their opinion on those early poems that Poplavskii deemed publishable in the émigré press, the scholars confused the dadaist and the surrealist artistic attitudes. Opposing the destructive anarchy of Dada, surrealism did not ground its antiliterary stance in antitraditionalism. Its designated ancestors ranged from Chateaubriand to Hugo. The style of Breton and Aragon was often called "classical"; Desnos and Éluard wrote regular verses with the attributes of traditional poetry, while experimenting with automatic writing.[59] So did Poplavskii, who wanted to publish his "automatic poems" without rhyme and meter as a separate collection. Most of these poems, too radical for mainstream émigré literature, saw the light of day only in 1999, largely because of Poplavskii's self-censorship.[60]

While mastering the surrealist discourse, Poplavskii enjoyed considerable freedom regarding surrealist theories. Not a member of the group, he did not risk expulsion for doubting the precepts of its charismatic leader. This critical distance differentiates his poems from the overly serious French surrealist texts. One of his parodies of surrealist poetry starts with the narrator's question as to whether readers have ever scrutinized the bottom of a city stream (*G*, 57). The evocation of objects from the bottom of a stream brings up associations with the refuse one habitually finds in a gutter. A water stream flowing along the curb is present in most Parisian streets as part of the city's cleaning effort. Dirt and refuse are swept into the curbside current that evacuates them into the gutter:

> Рассматривали вы когда друзья
> Те вещи что лежат на дне ручья
> Который через город протекает.
> Чего чего в ручье том не бывает! . . .
>
> В воде стоит литературный ад,
> Открытие и халтурный клад. . . .
>
> Там черепа воркуют над крылечком
> И красный дым ползет змеей из печки.
>
> Плыву туда как воробей в окно. . . .

⬦

> [Have you ever contemplated my friends
> The objects lying on the bottom of a stream
> That runs through the city.
> All kinds of things happen to be there! . . .
>
> A literary hell is reigning in the water,
> Discovery and false treasure. . . .
>
> Skulls are cooing there above a porch
> And red smoke is crawling from a chimney like a snake.
> I am swimming in like a sparrow into a window. . . .]

Stressing the poem's parodic nature, the narrator describes the contents of the stream as a "literary hell" in which discovery flanks "false treasure." Since the scrutiny of a stream is a metaphor for inquiry into the unconscious, those familiar with surrealist poetics would remark its grotesquely literal realization. The poem draws on the common imagery of surrealist "descents." Such habitués of surrealist dream accounts as skeletons and skulls "sit" in the stream; the narrator initiates action by "swimming in like a sparrow into a window"—a surrealist metaphor based on the semantic reversibility of water and air.

The ensuing infernal feast in a glass city (another surrealist cliché) travesties the baroque imagery in surrealist texts. The "beautifully polished" dismembered woman who charms the narrators of Breton and Desnos (*Poisson*, 36; *Bottes*, 59) is boiled and served under the "sauce of love." Poplavskii's narrator slices her "brilliant rear" with a knife. Intensifying the parody, the woman whose boiled "white breast" makes squeaky sounds under his fork is an allusion to Rimbaud's "white Ophelia," who floated down a river like a "large lily."[61] Poplavskii's Ophelia was abducted by a stream and floated, screaming "like a goose," until she reached the kitchen of the glass city. The narrator wonders if she is a false treasure or a discovery: "Ophelia, are you a fairy or a scam" (Ofeliia ty feia il' afera, *G*, 58). This feast on the body of Rimbaud's heroine alludes to the adaptation of Rimbaud's literary persona in surrealism and to his own adaptation of Shakespeare's character. Poplavskii's poem criticizes the surrealist literary model by stressing its clichés ("false treasures") rather than its discoveries. The poem shows that Poplavskii did not accept indiscriminately the poetics of the French avant-garde, even though it was the only "left" artistic outlet available to him in the growing polarization of Russian literary life.

As the Soviet state grew hostile to avant-garde art, the Russian artistic "left" in Paris found itself in a precarious situation. "Out of touch with reality ... we only imagined ourselves to be fellow travelers," said Zdanevich, dubbing this situation "an attempt with unfit means" (pokushenie s negodnymi sredstvami); in 1925 Poplavskii dedicated a sonnet under the same title to Zdanevich, who later read a paper titled "Pokushenie Poplavskogo s negodnymi sredstvami" (Poplavskii's attempt with unfit means, 1926).[62] The sonnet conveys the feeling of frustration vis-à-vis the changing artistic atmosphere of Russian Paris, whose orientation toward tradition left the poet "only five iambs" as a reminder of freedom. The last two stanzas read:

Так наша жизнь, на потешенье века,
Могуществом превыше человека,
Погружена в узилище судьбы.

Лишь пять шагов оставлено для бега,
Пять ямбов, слов мучительная нега
Не забывал свободу зверь дабы.

⤜⤛

[And thus our life, for the amusement of the age
Far mightier than the human being,
Is submerged into the prison of fate.

Only five steps are reserved for running,
Five iambs, the torturous languor of words
So that the beast would not forget freedom.]

(*F*, 11)

In the last line Poplavskii uses incorrect word order ("So that the beast not forget freedom would") to create a jarring contrast with the classical form of the sonnet (two quatrains, two tercets), its traditional . meter (iambic pentameter), and regular rhyme pattern. On the semantic level, this shock refers to the image of a caged beast as a symbol for the narrator's avant-garde poetics, which have been forced into the straitjacket of a regulated and traditional form. An allusion to an age that is "far mightier than the human being" explains this poetic confinement by external circumstances. One year later Poplavskii wrote another poem under the same title. It contained the lines "We are in solitary and precise coffins / Where breath is aimlessly cooing / We, in straitjackets at night / Communicate by tapping our messages in verse" (*G*, 91). Unlike the sonnet, this poem did not appear in print during the poet's life. The esthetic and political split in Russian Paris enriches these lines with additional meaning. Besides describing the poet's artistic method, they refer to the isolation in which Poplavskii and his associates found themselves by 1927.

Compromise: *Flagi*

Poplavskii remained aloof from émigré literary life until the last hope of publishing in the "left" circles was lost. Following Romov's failure to publish *Dirizhabl'*, Poplavskii suffered an artistic crisis. On February 4, 1928, he wrote to Zdanevich: "I am not writing poetry at all because of Romov (morally), but this is not important, well, actually, it is very important, but I would like to say that this is not important because otherwise I feel sick" (*Pokushenie,* 104). "From that point on," argued Zdanevich, "Poplavskii moved ever closer to the émigré press. This compromise won him a new sphere of action and coldness in relations with old friends" ("Boris Poplavskii," 168). In 1928 Poplavskii broke his seclusion, contributing several poems to émigré periodicals. But when he chose Nikolai Tatishchev as the executor of his archive, the poet demanded that his early writings see the light of day thirty years after his death.[63] He did not want to make public the texts whose esthetics contradicted his newly forged "émigré" image. Justifying his action to Zdanevich, Poplavskii wrote:

> You are accusing me of following the "great road of men," but do we dare, do we dare stay on the crystal path up there in the mountain? You will laugh: "Another one destroyed by Christianity." Yes, I am a Christian, even if I look to you like a scoundrel defecting ignominiously from the "courageous crowd." Yes, I have decided to "turn down the volume," to make myself comprehensible (and disgusting for myself). . . . But can you not see that the ways "beyond literature" have become shorter. . . . In a country so beautiful that "no one returns from within oneself," from "sacred nothingness," from "being a genius who dies unknown." But I do not want to die unknown, *I do not accept this Satanic pride* because I am a Christian. . . . *I curse your courage.*[64]

This letter shows that Poplavskii's reluctance to "follow the great road of men" was more than politically motivated. It sprang from the specifically surrealist view of art as self-cognition ("no one returns from within oneself") that rejects the literary establishment. The letter evokes Breton's statements: "It is unacceptable for the human being to leave a trace of passage on earth" ("sacred nothingness"), and "Today, many young writers are devoid of the smallest literary ambition" ("a genius who dies unknown," *Les Pas perdus,* 9, 73). The surrealists' artistic ambitions were also frustrated by self-imposed alienation from the literary establishment and public. In 1926 Artaud and Soupault were excluded from the group for publishing "too much" and contributing to nonsurrealist reviews.[65]

Poplavskii's letter illustrates the means by which the poet "enfranchised" himself. "Making oneself comprehensible" meant giving up the logical rupture of surrealist discourse, while "turning down the volume" implied his determination to play down surrealist imagery. The transcendental mysticism of surrealism was replaced by religious mysticism. The elitist aloofness of an avant-garde poet became "Satanic pride," while Christianity functioned as an anti-Soviet marker. In many respects the poet's about-face was a return to his old interests, dormant during his surrealist period—Christian mysticism, spiritualism, and Russian symbolism, especially the poetry of Alexander Blok.

With few exceptions most texts Poplavskii published in 1928–30 were written during that period. But the editing he performed on his early poems illustrates the technical side of his desire to write "comprehensibly" and to "turn down the volume." First of all, he introduced punctuation that is almost absent in the manuscripts of *Grammofon*. The absence of punctuation, common in surrealist texts, is a sign of "automatism" and often engenders semantic ambiguity and logical rupture. Poplavskii's orthographic "conversion" is apparent in *Flagi* (Flags, 1931)—his first published poetic collection. Zdanevich thought that the editor of *Flagi* introduced punctuation without consulting the poet ("Boris Poplavskii," 168). In fact, Poplavskii started observing traditional punctuation from his debut in the émigré press.

The poet also altered shocking phrases in his early writings. In the poem "À Élémir Bourge" (*G,* 74), published under the new title "Dolorosa" (*F,* 39), he modified two such phrases: "Na balkone korchilas' zaria" (dawn was twitching on the balcony) became "na balkone plakala zaria" (dawn was crying on the balcony). The phrase "On podnial ee devichii krup" (he lifted her maiden croup), where the female body is compared to that of a horse, was replaced with "podnialas' ona k nemu i vdrug" (she rose toward him and suddenly). As a result the shocking comparison of the falling night with a mysterious dying woman from Élémir Bourges's Decadent novels was softened and rendered compatible with the poem's new religious leitmotif. The dead woman was replaced by the mourning Mother of God. Compare the two versions (alterations are given in brackets/parentheses):

На балконе корчилась [плакала] заря
В ярко-красном платье маскарадном
И над нею наклонялся зря
Тонкий вечер в сюртуке парадном

А потом над кружевом решетки
Он поднял ее девичий круп
[Поднялась она к нему, и вдруг,]
И [Он] издав трамвайный стон короткий
Бросил вниз позеленевший труп . . .

Громко хлопнув музыкальной дверцей
Соскочила дама [осень] на ходу
И прижав соболью муфту к сердцу

[И прижав рукой больное сердце]
Закричала как кричат в аду . . .

И танцуя под фонарным шаром
Опадая в пустоте [тишине] бездонной
Смерть запела совершенно даром
Над лежащей на земле [М]адонной.

⟨≈⟩

[Dawn was twitching (crying) on the balcony
In a bright-red masquerade dress
While the slim evening in a formal suit
Was bending over her in vain

And then above the lace of the grate
He lifted her maiden croup
(She rose toward him, and suddenly,)
And (he) having uttered a short tramlike gasp
Threw down the green corpse . . .

Having loudly banged the music door
A woman (autumn) jumped off at full speed
And having clasped a sable muff to the heart
(And having pressed her hand against her sick heart)
Screamed like they scream in hell . . .

And dancing under the ball of the street lamp
Falling away in bottomless emptiness (silence)
Death began to sing completely gratuitously
Over (M)adonna lying on the ground.]

The poet goes from surrealism to Christian mysticism by eliminating some shocking images, replacing the word "woman" with the more ambiguous "autumn," and capitalizing "madonna" to transform a female stranger who suffers violent death into the mourning Mary. Finally, he introduces punctuation.

In "Sentimental'naia demonologiia," Poplavskii removed the ambiguity inherent in all poems that represent his surrealist experiments. In the original version one could interpret the narrator's adventures "underground" as a reference to the surrealist method. The new version permitted only a literal reading—a meeting with the devil. In the phrase "Vy pomnite kogda v kholodnyi den' / khodili vy pod gorodom na lyzhakh" (Do you remember the cold day / when you skied outside under the city") the preposition "za" replaces "pod" (*G*, 60; *F*, 15). Since "pod gorodom" can mean both "outside the city" and "under the city," "za" eliminates ambiguity. In the first version the narrator meets someone "dressed like / in a skeleton or even like a lady" (v skelet odetym ili dazhe damoi); in the new version the line reads "clothed in a dress-ing gown or even like a lady" (v khalat odetym). This alteration purges the comic ambiguity of the narrator's vision.

The poetic image was among the problems of Poplavskii's conver-sion. He had to justify fantastic or shocking imagery at a time when Parisian émigré poets—Adamovich, Chervinskaia, Ivanov, Shteiger—were heading in the direction of realistic and "simple" art.[66] In the con-text of surrealist poetics, fantastic imagery referred to surrealist experi-ence as a record of the unconscious. Outside this context it seemed too "literary." Poplavskii accompanied his edited poems with an article that reconciled surrealist and émigré poetics. He indicated that his art was traditionally Russian by citing Blok and Pushkin; he described the Rus-sian tradition as lacking in rational control: written "in a dream or an-other unconscious state," poetry was a "document" in which "every-thing could freely turn into anything" ("Zametki o poezii," 28–29). This argument encapsulated the program of surrealism and ran counter to the émigré opinion. If younger émigrés acknowledged the experimen-tal validity of surrealism, influential critics rejected it as naive because without the control of reason a text was a compilation of clichés; the flaw of Breton's program was in giving the irrational a rational task. As a result the predominant attitude toward surrealism was scornful dis-missal.[67] This attitude marked émigré reactions to Poplavskii's article and the poems it justified.[68]

The émigré requirement that the artist control his material was among the reasons for transformations in Poplavskii's poetry. Comprising al-most all of his poems published before 1931, *Flagi* presents a clear pic-ture of the poet's evolution. The poems in *Flagi* can be divided into four groups: those written before 1928 and marked by surrealist poetics; some poems of 1927 and all the poems of 1928, where the author no longer uses the extended metaphor technique and whose surrealist imagery is alien-ated from the context of surrealist poetics; the poems of 1929, in which fantastic imagery is motivated as children's dreams; and other poems of 1929–30 tending toward realistic motivation and imaginative restraint. Despite editing, the poems in the first group contrasted with mainstream émigré poetry, thanks to shocking images and fantastic plots ("Don Kikhot," "Otritsatel'nyi polius," "Angélique"), to logically incoherent narratives based on the extended metaphor technique ("Vesna v adu," "Lumière astrale"), and to metric patterns and neologisms reminiscent of futurism ("V bor'be so snegom," "Bor'ba so snom," "Arturu Rembo").

Poplavskii's effort to modify his poetics is explicit in the second group, where surrealist images and tropes are alienated from surrealist philosophy and symbolism. He abandoned the extended metaphor technique and reduced the amount of semantic shock. These poems teem with dream evocations, motifs of water and air travel, infernal descents, and fantastic imagery that are separated from the exploration of the unconscious as the goal and mode of creation. Estranged from surrealist philosophy, elements of surrealist poetics lose documentary motivation. Breton condemned as "literature" all imagination unjustified by extra-artistic concerns. The imagery of Poplavskii's post-1927 poems, which captivated readers and earned him renown as a surrealist, had little to do with surrealism proper.[69]

"Lunnyi dirizhabl'" exemplifies this evolution (*F*, 42–43). The poem describes a trip in a dirigible with conventional surrealist symbolics, interchangeable air and water imagery, and a descent into infernal spheres. But it lacks semantically and linguistically shocking images. The trip symbolizes neither a dream nor the process of poetic creation. The narrator is removed from the fantastic world, which he describes rather than explores. There is nothing incoherent in the succession of images. The dirigible's descent motivates logically the transfer from air to water imagery. The use of the word "dream" and its derivatives does not allow the surrealist ambiguity of dream and death. The narrator makes clear that he is describing not his own dream but a fantastic kingdom of sleep in which all characters are explicitly said to be sleeping. All metareference to the surrealist method is absent; the narrator insists on his status as a storyteller who invents and controls his narrative.

Poplavskii's use of surrealist signifiers devoid of their initial referents gives the impression of gratuitous fantasy. The poetry in *Flagi* has been called "visual" and "straight out of Giorgio de Chirico," although the same imagery (towers, banners) hardly had this effect in Poplavskii's early poetry.[70] Surrealism brought poetry and painting closer: visual automatism was developed simultaneously with automatic writing. Éluard described dadaist and surrealist painting in several poems.[71] The image of a tower in "Giorgio de Chirico" (*Mourir*, 62), for instance, does not produce the same "visual" effect as in *Flagi* because it is dependent on the derivation of an extended metaphor and has its referential function in the context of surrealist poetics. The poem's first stanza sets a derivational code:

Un mur dénonce un autre mur
Et l'ombre me défend de mon ombre peureuse.
O tour de mon amour autour de mon amour,
Tous les murs filaient blanc autour de mon silence . . .

⤙⤚

[A wall denounces/exposes/cuts short another wall
And the shadow protects/prohibits me from my fearful shadow.
Oh tower of my love around my love,
All the walls weaved/followed/ran white around my silence . . .]

The polysemy of "dénoncer"—to denounce, to expose, to end a relationship—initiates the parallel development of two motifs: confinement
("un mur . . . un autre mur") and a conflict of spatial relations (one wall
cuts short another). The relationship of shadows, evoked by the cliché
association of wall and shade, echoes that between walls, thanks to the
polysemy of "défendre"—to protect, prohibit. *Tour* (tower) is suggested
by a semantic link to *mur* (architectural affinity, ability to cast shade,
both protective and prohibitive function) and by their partial phonetic
coincidence. *Amour* derives from the phonetic superposition of *mur* and
tour. The second half of the third line is an exact phonetic rendition of its
first half. Phonetic affinity propels the semantic development of the initial metaphor, stressing the association of a tower with imprisonment
and establishing love in a polysemic function of both prisoner and war-
den. Self-imprisonment refers to the narrator's state as a "recording device" of the unconscious (evoked in the last stanza as the world he describes but is absent from). "Filaient blanc" evokes phonetically "filet
blanc" (the white part of a filet dish). *Blanc* can mean brief silence in a
conversation ("autour de mon silence") and a space between two lines
in writing, contributing to the poem's metadescription.

The image of dreaming flags, the most important trope of Poplavskii's
Flagi, was proposed by Breton as a metaphor for the lips of a surrealist
speaking in sleep (*Poisson*, 54). But by contrast to Breton's and Éluard's
writings, Poplavskii's towers and banners in the second and later groups
of poems neither derive from preceding images nor engender new ones,
having lost their surrealist referents. This is the case of the poem "Rim-
skoe utro," in which even the bilingual pun "siren'-matros" (*siren'* as
"lilac" versus a "siren" luring a sailor, *matros*) does not open surrealist
vistas. The first two stanzas read:

По вековой дороге бледно серой
Автомобиль сенатора скользит.

Блестит сирень, кричит матрос с галеры.
Христос на аэроплане вдаль летит.

Богиня всходит в сумерки на башню.
С огромной башни тихо вьется флаг.
Христос, постлав газеты лист вчерашний,
Спит в воздухе с звездою в волосах.

[Along the ageless pale gray road
A senator's automobile glides.
Lilac glistens, a sailor yells from a galley.
Christ flies into the distance on an airplane.

A goddess ascends a tower at dusk.
A flag quietly streams down from the enormous tower.
Christ, having spread the sheet of yesterday's newspaper,
Sleeps in the air with a star in his hair.]

(*F*, 49)

It seems that Poplavskii compensated for his divorce from surrealist poetics by an exaggerated use of surrealist tropes. Such amassment of repetitive images created a "visual" effect but was hardly an intentional borrowing from Chirico. One must contest the common view that in *Flagi* Poplavskii followed the surrealist technique of image construction.[72] In fact, he played down the basic precept of the surrealist image (semantic shock), employing the clichés of surrealist poetry instead. The decontextualization of his surrealist imagery produced the impression of "vitality amid a torrent of unwanted words."[73] The surviving instances of semantic shock in his writings drew accusations of linguistic incompetence.[74]

The poet's conversion entailed a change in versification. Futurist rhythmical patterns, common in his early poetry, gave way to a striving for "music"—an almost exclusive use of ternary meters. He presented "musical" meters as part of the Russian poetic tradition, incarnated by Blok, and assiduously implemented this shift, reviving his attachment to Russian symbolism.[75] The second group of poems in *Flagi* is steeped in the monotony of dactylic or anapestic verse. Such repetitiveness was artistically detrimental but seemed to prove his adherence to the Russian tradition. Émigré critics hailed Poplavskii's poetry for its musicality, reminiscent of Blok's "black music," which testified that he "turned away from Maiakovskii, looking in art for answers to doubt and anxiety."[76]

Entering émigré literature, Poplavskii joined his former foes, derided in "Na belye perchatki melkikh dnei." Adamovich introduced him into Gippius's literary salon and, along with Ivanov, promoted Poplavskii as a promising émigré poet. Pursuing their own agenda, both praised Poplavskii's poetry for its semantic imprecision, repetitiveness, and metrical monotony, interpreting the flaws of his art as a challenge to literary formalism.[77] Poplavskii was drawn into the polemics surrounding the nascent Paris School, which opposed technique and "estheticism," valuing imperfection as a proof of "truthfulness" and "simplicity." Adamovich's opponents saw Poplavskii's poetry as the exploitation of the latest literary fad, arguing that the repenting acmeists greeted Poplavskii's poetry for the very same qualities they had earlier denounced in Blok's poems.[78]

Poplavskii's poetry met with success. Less than a year after his first publication, he had been admitted to all major émigré reviews and became a "fashionable" poet. By the early 1930s his popularity among younger émigrés was unmatched.[79] Poplavskii's surrealist imagery, appealing by its novelty, "musical" meters, and deliberately "unskillful" semantic imprecision, was only partly responsible for his public success. The last two groups of poems in *Flagi* show that the poet was sensitive to émigré criticism. Critics wrote that if Poplavskii did not leave fantastic imagery and gain better control of his material, he would become trite.[80] The fact that he started doing away with the very features that contributed to his initial success illustrates Poplavskii's complex and contradictory position in émigré letters.

To acquit himself of all accusations of irrational creation, Poplavskii further modified his imagery. He abandoned fantastic journeys, ascribed all dreams to characters other than the narrator, and reduced the ambiguity of the relationship between dreams and death. In *Flagi* the dream became death's signifier, as in the poems about the dreams of children who die in sleep ("Smert' detei," "Detstvo Gamleta," "Devochka vozvratilas'," "Chernyi zaiats"). The new set of images in this cycle of poems replaced the infernal imagery of Poplavskii's former dreamer-narrator. Blok's second book of poems provided the source of this new imagery. Poplavskii's "little gnomes," "little priests," "little rabbits," and "little angels" harked back to Blok's sentimental imagery.[81]

Poplavskii's new imagery was accompanied by the introduction of an excessively sentimental "Christian theme." Poplavskii's Christ is a beautiful forest spirit in whose nimbus a "meek rabbit" is warming his paw (*F,* 79). The squashed paw of a rabbit is the symbol of "Christian pity" that Poplavskii derived, with Blok's help, from Dostoevsky's line that one tear of a tormented child was worth more than "supreme harmony." Citing Blok's poem about a "little priest" who lived in a swamp and prayed for the aching leg of a frog, Poplavskii wrote that one human tear could dissolve the crude beauty of the world, just as "one squashed rabbit paw was more important than the Louvre."[82] Beginning in 1929 "Christian pity" constituted an attribute of his poems, from "Zhalost' k Evrope" (*F*, 70) to the ultimate poem in *Flagi*, devoted to Adamovich.

The last group of texts in *Flagi* approaches the poems in Poplavskii's second collection *Snezhnyi chas* (The snowy hour, 1931–35) by linguistic and imaginative economy, the elimination of semantic imprecision, and the lack of dramatic action. The leitmotif of existential fatigue in these poems, conveyed in concrete and logically motivated images, supports his rejection of linguistic and artistic "vanity." Poplavskii was becoming "simpler." Following the Paris School precepts, he seemed ready to plunge into the fashionable existential anxiety of the "human document" and to speak about the "most important" questions of existence in light of his own favored theme of "Christian pity."

Surrealist Apology: *Apollon Bezobrazov*

According to Poplavskii's myth, the "unrecognized genius" ignored by émigré reviews published his "surrealist" collection *Flagi*, which was so badly received that he condemned its esthetics and "suffocated" among former acmeists.[83] Indeed, the poems in *Snezhnyi chas* seem to follow the program of Adamovich's circle, which rejected "poetry with decorations" and tended toward "dim colors, the lowering of tone, general alert and quiet restraint."[84] But, as we have seen, *Flagi* represents a movement away from surrealism. Recently discovered materials, however, testify to Poplavskii's persistent interest in surrealist discourse. In 1929, at Zdanevich's request, he wrote an invitation to a ball of Russian artists. Written in French, this text confirms Poplavskii's mastery of surrealist poetics and readiness to use them when circumstances permitted. He also continued to experiment with automatic writing, withholding its results from publication.[85]

Even in his published texts Poplavskii did not fully abandon avant-garde esthetics. Despite their differences, the Paris School had much in common with the French avant-garde. They shared the war-shock motivation, which validated a gap between "ancient" and "modern" practices; the focus on inner life as "true" reality; the antiesthetic penchant for "documentary" literature; and the valorization of failure and self-effacement over artistic success. Poplavskii exploited these affinities. In 1928 he revolted against the avant-garde ideal of a "genius who died unknown." But he unearthed this concept in the 1930s and integrated it into the antiartistic ethos of the Paris School, writing in his article that "love for art was *poshlost'*" and that "the most beautiful thing was 'To be a genius and to die unknown.'" The surrealist view of literature as a psychological record is visible in this article, which proclaims that art may survive only as a "document." Émigrés saw in this proclamation a reiteration of the Paris School "human document" doctrine, but the poet suggested that his idea of a "document" was closer to a psychological record than to a confession. In another article he stated that the "émigré young man" had "to learn from his 'brother' surrealists" the sharpness and articulation for affirming his mysticism.[86]

Exploiting the logic and topoi of émigré poetics, Poplavskii forged an original type of discourse that opened his texts to different readings contingent on one's proficiency in either émigré or surrealist literary esthetics. The adaptation of surrealist poetics to émigré expectations became the structural principle of his first novel, *Apollon Bezobrazov,* begun in late 1927. The poet destined *Apollon* to be an apology for his compromise. He informed Zdanevich in March 1928 that *Apollon* was "an attempt to justify our life," alluding to the life of the "courageous crowd" from which he "ignominiously defected" (*Pokushenie,* 106). John Kopper has argued that the surrealist element in *Apollon* is "defeated" by symbolist esthetics ("Surrealism under Fire," 245–64). Although Poplavskii's conversion indeed entailed a revival of his interest in symbolism, I contend that in *Apollon* he struck a balance between surrealism and symbolism, a balance visible through the prism of intimate knowledge of both Russian and French letters. Émigré readers saw that side of *Apollon* that harked back to the Russian tradition. Rooted in surrealist narrative, this novel was hailed as a "human document" and a confession despite its mythological characters and fantastic imagery. Zdanevich, to the contrary, saw *Apollon* as a proof of Poplavskii's avant-garde and anti-émigré artistic persona.[87]

Surrealists did not have a theory of the novel. Instead, they had an antipathy for certain novelistic attitudes codified by nineteenth-century realism. The aim of the surrealist novel was not to convince readers that it transcribed events from the world of the real or invented them according to its laws.[88] Realism was at fault for replicating the discontinuity of waking life and not accounting for the continuity of the unconscious and the conscious self. The surrealist novelist recorded unconscious reality in the continuity between conscious and unconscious existence. This task took the form of wandering in the streets of Paris in search of "objective chance" (le hasard objectif)—any manifestation of the occult in everyday reality revealing that daily life was caught in the net of supernatural forces. According to Breton, the recognition of the occult led to a better understanding of the power of the unconscious to transform the human condition.[89]

Surrealist narratives wander as aimlessly as their narrators in the streets of Paris. They shift effortlessly from abstract reflections to descriptions of the environment, to the evocations of memory and emotional states, to eruptions of chance coincidences. The search for mystery in the ever-changing city is an itinerary; city walks constitute the "action" of the hero of the surrealist novel. Aragon's *Le Paysan de Paris* (1926), Desnos's *La Liberté ou l'amour!* (1927), and Breton's *Nadja* (1928) embody the surrealist ideal in prose, for they succeeded in transforming the record of the writer's personal experiences of daily life into magical tales of poetic perception and expression.

The itinerary of the surrealist hero is "documented" by the meticulous notation of addresses; photographic reproductions of signs, posters, advertisements, and action sites; and the tone of a scientific report. This "documentary" motivation does not preclude fantastic descriptions, justified as the unconscious play of imagination, because one cannot rely on one's senses alone to find "superreality." In *Le Paysan de Paris* Aragon argued that the surrealist hero constructed a "modern mythology" and his itinerary engendered new myths in everyday life; the surrealist "science of life" was the freedom to mythologize reality through the marvelous and the uncanny one found or invented (15–16). To ensure the "documentary" nature of literary production, the author was identified with the narrator and the mythologization of everyday life was taken quite literally by the group's members.

Poplavskii also took this mythologization literally and considered *Le Paysan de Paris* as the model of the "new Western novel" ("Sredi somnenii i ochevidnostei," 96). *Apollon* is a Parisian itinerary narrated in the first-person singular. The streets, sites, signs, and advertisements that Poplavskii's narrator passes on his journey are cited in French to ensure the authenticity of his report. The narrator of Breton's *Nadja* accosts strange women during his walks until he finds the one who becomes the heroine of his narrative. Breton's novel is based on his chance meeting with a mentally ill prostitute who fascinated him by her "illuminations." According to witnesses, Poplavskii also conducted his search for "objective chance" in everyday life and shared this mythologizing obsession with passing women. He often abandoned his companions, pursued strange women who "inspired neither sympathy nor confidence," and explained his behavior by "some absolute nonsense of occult nature."[90]

Poplavskii's narrator meets his protagonists during wanderings. These are the demonic Apollon; the mystic Teresa; Zeus, a Siberian peasant and Orthodox sectarian; and Averoes, a former rabbi, theological student, and industrialist who cultivates flowers of unnatural colors. Poplavskii fancied the pseudonym "Apollon Bezobrazov" as early as 1921. At their first meeting, he gave Sharshun his business card, "Apollon Bezobrazov: Kloun" (Apollo the Ugly: Clown).[91] Apollon was an apt image for his "modern mythology." If Aragon's narrator sees Medusa in the window of a barber's shop (*Paysan*, 50–52), Poplavskii's meets an émigré Apollon endowed with supernatural qualities. The narrator Vasilii and Apollon are parts of one persona. Both are twenty-four, and this corresponds to the author's age in 1927, when he started working on his novel. They share the same clothes and eat from the same plate, and both have Poplavskii's boy-scout past. Vasilii knows in advance the intimate details of Apollon's childhood. They fall asleep simultaneously, see the same dreams, and converse in sleep, mixing "you" and "I," so that the reader cannot distinguish between interlocutors (*Apollon*, 40, 72).[92]

The oxymoronic name of "Apollo the Ugly" provides the key to the novel's semantic structure. The narrator's contradictory split personalities are the author's alter egos. Vasilii is a Christian mystic, weak in body and will, tearfully sentimental, and obsessed with "eternal questions." Apollon is an athlete, a boxer and a fan of the boxing champion Primo Carnero (*Apollon*, 54, 173). He cultivates intellectual and physical rigor, emotional restraint and reticence. He is a student of metaphysics, black magic, alchemy, astrology, and occultism, which give him an anti-Christian aura suggested by the title of the chapter in which the two alter egos meet—"Kak ia vpervye poznakomilsia s d'iavolom" (How I met the devil for the first time).[93] Both personalities correspond to Poplavskii's image. On one hand, he was a Christian mystic who advocated universal pity, mourned squashed rabbit paws, and appalled his acquaintances by lies, spinelessness, and monologues on "eternal questions." On the other hand, he was an athlete and a boxer who signed his articles on boxing and Primo Carnero "Apollon Bezobrazov" (*Chisla* 1 [1930] and 6 [1932]). He studied metaphysics, occultism, alchemy, and black magic in the Bibliothèque Sainte-Geneviève, where Apollon studied the same subjects (*Apollon*, 124).[94]

The motif of split personalities first appeared in Poplavskii's 1924 poem "Chernyi i belyi" ("Dvoetsarstvie," in *Flagi*), whose narrator describes how the "sword of death" slices in two his head and soul, his past and his future. His brain is pecked out by the "sparrows of dreams," and the two halves of his body are buried in heaven and hell (*D*, 39; *F*, 10). This opposition acquires a more concrete form in the coexistence of the saintly Vasilii and the devilish Apollon, whereby Apollon incarnates the surrealist attitude in life.

Émigré critics of *Apollon* did not discern or did not acknowledge the novel's surrealist undercurrent. However, the text is open to two readings. The first yields a "confession" about the author's émigré experience, in which the characters of Vasilii and Apollon do not merge. Vasilii is identified with Poplavskii himself, and his peregrinations are the "truthful" account of the writer's life. Apollon is a fictional character, the devil who tempts the good Christian Vasilii. Apollon's dreams justify the presence of fantastic elements and passages in rhythmical prose that accompany these dreams (*Apollon*, 39, 61, 74). In the second reading, done through the prism of French surrealist poetics, the two characters unite in one complex personality, offering an apology for Poplavskii's pre-1928 career, that very period he called "our time" and claimed to justify by this novel.[95]

In the first chapter Vasilii narrates his life "before Apollon." The epigraph from Éluard metaphorizes his existential situation: he is a bird trapped in flight.[96] Describing his Parisian "flights," Vasilii confesses to a feeling of confinement and a desire to break free from the people obsessed with the "metaphysically worthless" Russian Revolution. He prefers "civic death" (exclusion from the émigré community) to the mourning of lost material comfort—his interpretation of the White cause (24–25). His promenades are steeped in surrealist imagery. Constantly sleepy, he floats semiconsciously down the river of the Parisian summer (24); the Parisians move slowly, as if in water, while the trees give off a sweet, cadaverous smell (22). Poplavskii incorporated into this description lines from his early poems about fantastic water and air trips.[97] Vasilii craved some "presence" that would finalize his inner liberation through "civic death" and surrealist walks (25).

Finally he runs into Apollon, who sits in a boat surrounded by orange water and dreams with his eyes open (26). This meeting helps

Vasilii to find other "semiconscious wanderers" (25) and initiates the "legendary period" of his life (126). Apollon the dreamer, who never wakes from semiconscious meditation (30, 34), takes his companion underwater and underground. Vasilii's life becomes a succession of dreams. They are joined by other somnambulists, and their city walks end in water trips filled with surrealist imagery: submarines, dirigibles, glass houses, skeletons. Apollon's apartment looks like a submarine that easily becomes a dirigible (43, 46). Every time the tearful Christian would awaken in Vasilii, Apollon, the submarine's captain, said: "Let's sleep instead" (35, 43). As they "submerge," Paris submerges into the sea: giant fish swim through the Café du Dôme, waiters float upside down, a submarine crosses the boulevard d'Observatoire, and the beautiful floating corpses of Montparnasse prostitutes reflect the rising sun (122).

Those familiar with surrealist poetics could read these scenes as encoded messages. Poplavskii spoke about his poetry as a form of cryptic correspondence in "Pokushenie s negodnymi sredstvami" (*G*, 91). While the heroes of *Apollon* searched for soul mates "like the radio operators of a sinking steamboat," Poplavskii sent signals to the "courageous crowd" he had left behind (*Apollon*, 127).[98] His former associates from Zdanevich's circle could recognize his description of the "legendary" time when "they" opposed everybody else in Russian literary Paris by the lifestyle of dreamy existence and "automatic music" (131).

The somnambulists finally confront reality, their submarine resurfaces, and the "legendary" time ends (132). *Apollon* can be divided into the "legendary" time (chapters 1–13) and the time of awakening to reality (chapters 14–18). The clash of the Christian and the Satanic in the narrator's persona culminates in Apollon's departure. Echoing Poplavskii's "Christian" rejection of the avant-gardist "Satanic pride," this conflict is ambiguous. Vasilii's sympathy lies with the "paradise" he finds with Apollon (25). It is not Vasilii but Apollon who goes through crisis, condemning "his freedom and happiness" for the sake of Christian humility (167). Next to the passionate description of the surrealist "paradise," the demon's conversion is even more unconvincing than the condemnation of "Satanic pride" in Poplavskii's letter to Zdanevich. But it fits Poplavskii's new image. In his second novel, *Domoi s nebes* (Homeward from Heaven, 1932–35), Apollon is a student of theology at the Sorbonne. Incidentally, in a 1930 letter Poplavskii wrote that he, formerly an "ardent futurist," studied history of religion at the Sorbonne and had considered a career in religious philosophy ("Pis'ma Iu. P. Ivasku," 207–8). Left without a counterbalancing Apollon, the narrator of *Domoi s nebes* is a maudlin creature whose Paris is devoid of its former surrealist dimension.

Upon his conversion and departure, Apollon leaves a diary consisting of twenty-nine "automatic" poems that recall not only Poplavskii's texts in *Grammofon* and *Dirizhabl'* but also those in his collection *Avtomaticheskie stikhi* (Automatic poems), which includes several poems from Apollon's diary. But even after explaining these poems as the writings of his literary character, Poplavskii barred them from the published segments of *Apollon* as, no doubt, too radical for the émigré artistic tastes and unfitting for the émigré image the poet was actively forging for himself at this time.

In Poplavskii's poetry written after *Flagi*, Khodasevich saw signs of growing indifference to literary expression and a desire to express himself outside literature. Poplavskii's writings, argued Khodasevich, showed that the poet

> began to attribute incomparably less significance to the question "How to write?" in contrast to the question "How to live?". . . . He faced the danger of turning from the subject of literary activity, a poet, into its object—an interesting and complex personality that expressed itself in life and waited for someone else to express it in literature. . . . He may have even consciously provoked this danger. ("Dva poeta," 3)

Echoing Khodasevich's opinion, Adamovich considered Poplavskii "characteristic" of his time in that he strove to efface the boundary between art and a personal document, between literature and a diary ("Literaturnye zametki," *PN* 5516: 3). But this effacement was valued not only by the Paris School. Blurring the distinctions between literature and life, Poplavskii steeped his everyday existence—his text of life—in the "modern mythology" hailed by Aragon as the surrealist science of life (*Paysan*, 15–16). The cultural paradigms present in Poplavskii's literary esthetics influenced his lifestyle, especially since his artistic compromise hampered his literary expression. The poet's familiarity with Russian symbolism proved instrumental in his self-fashioning. The symbolist practice of esthetically organized behavior was all too familiar to surrealism. Thus, drawing on surrealist models of "life in poetry," Poplavskii could recode and present them in familiar "Russian" terms to his émigré audience.

The Making of a "Modern Myth": Poplavskii's Art of Life and Death

Christian mysticism was part of Poplavskii's émigré image. A manifestly anti-Soviet marker, Christianity was also the cornerstone of the ideal model of the Russian writer. Interested in Christian mysticism from the beginning of his career, Poplavskii turned it into a repository for surrealist mysticism. Seeing the goal of surrealism in reaching that point where the real and imaginary ceased to be contradictory, Breton drew on the esoteric and hermetic traditions.[99] His rejection of positivism and religion as oppressive dogmas made the opposition of esoteric and materialistic thought the dialectic tension of surrealism. Poplavskii translated surrealist mysticism and antipositivism into Christian mysticism, since his view of Christianity, shaped by symbolist attitudes, was far from conventional. Like the surrealists, he rejected positivism and institutionalized religion, adhered to the belief in the revelatory nature of dreams and hallucinatory states, and claimed that émigré artists should learn from surrealists the ways of affirming their mysticism.[100]

Poplavskii's surviving diaries testify to his preoccupation with religion and theosophy, but it is impossible to tell how many of the entries describe drug-induced states as religious experience. Menegaldo has pointed out several passages that obviously refer to drug use. In them "meditation," "prayer," and "joy" are accompanied by "visions," "dreams," and "voices"; the mystic confesses his addiction to a priest, but when he does not "pray" he suffers from physical discomfort.[101] Ignoring this ambiguity, commentators interpreted his diaries as proof of Poplavskii's deeply religious personality.[102] While the poet's mysticism is incontestable, his religious attitudes are highly problematic, because Poplavskii reconciled "insatiable hunger for mystical experience (any kind of mysticism) with drug experience (any kind of drugs)," as Simon Karlinsky put it. The same combination was familiar to French surrealists, who used drugs to reach "illumination."[103]

Dreams preserved for Poplavskii their surrealist function as a mysterious rite. In the diary of 1928–35 the words "prayer" and "dream" are interchangeable: "They think I am sleeping, I am praying"; "I am lying down to pray (to sleep)" (*Neizdannoe*, 115, 117). After Tatishchev, the executor of Poplavskii's archive, published parts of his diaries, Berdiaev wrote that, while the theme of these diaries was religious, the poet "did not have religious experience—he conducted religious experiments" ("Po povodu 'Dnevnikov' B. Poplavskogo," 443). A devout Christian,

Tatishchev supported the poet's self-interpretation as a Christian mystic without questioning Poplavskii's tampering with his diaries in view of posthumous publication. Upon reading the diaries, Adamovich suspected foul play on the editor's part, for Poplavskii he remembered was "much more eclectic"; Gazdanov blamed Tatishchev for not taking into account Poplavskii's "extraordinary freedom with poetic and 'metaphysical' material, including his 'affair with God' and his 'angelic accessories,' as he put it."[104]

The publication of Poplavskii's diary supported his image of a mystic and justified his imitation of Christ.[105] In the 1930s he was surrounded by young émigrés who saw him as a spiritual guide. Tatishchev followed Poplavskii like an apostle, recording the poet's random observations in a notebook that he later published.[106] But Poplavskii's image as a religious thinker had an effect (with the help of his disciples) only after his posthumous myth had taken root. (In 1935 the society Krug, which united émigré literati in religious discussions, rejected his candidacy as "suspect.")[107] Emmanuil Rais, another "apostle," provided a good summary of Poplavskii's personal mythology:

> Poplavskii did not resemble anyone and was incomparable. He turned out to be strong enough to reject from the outset the temptations of the home-grown academism of the "Paris note.". . . He even lived not like everybody else. Everyone worked, putting up with crude and poorly paid labor. . . . [Everyone] put up with the tyranny of conservative journal retrogrades who knew nothing about literature. . . . Poplavskii did not want to put up with anyone or anything. He was firm and pure; he lived in severe, unimaginable destitution, often went hungry but did not give up. He lived the way a genius must live. ("O Borise Poplavskom," in *Berega*, 298–99)

This description draws on the model of the Russian writer as a spiritual apostle who does not abide by social authority, who is uncompromising and pure, intransigent to artistic vanity and material temptations, and is thus saintly destitute, an unrecognized genius, and a persecuted martyr. It is in these terms that émigré observers testify to the impression of extreme poverty in Poplavskii's appearance.[108] But his conspicuous destitution did not spring from lack of means. Refusing gainful employment "on principle," he roomed and boarded at his parents' apartment and was an ardent book collector: after his death, his library contained more than two thousand volumes. Both his bibliophilia and fancy for drugs required money. The poet also owned a collection of Russian and French avant-garde paintings, sold after his death to sponsor the publication of his poetry.[109] Poplavskii's conspicuous penury seems to be a pose of poverty; he cultivated destitution as a virtue, writing in his diary that saints must be dirty and shabby. Imitating them, he came closer to the image of Christ, literally implementing the ideal model of the Russian writer.[110]

But the paradigm of the Russian writer was superimposed upon the French model of the avant-garde poet. The filter of "Christian sanctity" concealed the surrealist code of conduct. Poplavskii's "principled" refusal of employment is echoed in *Domoi s nebes*, whose hero, Oleg, boasts that he does not work because he values freedom. He supports his attitude with Rimbaud's (misquoted) words: "Je ne travaillerai jamais" (I will never work, 277, 329).[111] The evocation of the "ancestor" of surrealism is logical. The ethics of surrealism were formed in opposition to bourgeois values. "I am tired of hearing about the moral value of work. . . . The event we expect to reveal the meaning of life *cannot be attained at the price of work*," wrote Breton, instructing his friends to find rich wives.[112] Denouncing the value of work, Aragon described a friend-surrealist: "He is looking for a position but does not want to work: an advice to everyone." Consequently, Breton and Aragon quit their medical studies; Éluard and Rigaut worked but pretended to be idlers.[113]

Poplavskii tailored his appearance, seen by émigrés as that of an ascetic, through direct borrowing from the French avant-garde. He wore dark glasses in public. Some attributed this to an eye malady, others saw it as self-imposed penance. But the poet alluded to the answer in *Domoi s nebes*. After a meeting with Apollon, Oleg says: "It has been a long time. . . . With a monocle, in shabby pants. . . . My soul of 1925" (265). The line "With a monocle, in shabby pants" opened Poplavskii's unpublished poem "S monoklem, s bakhromoiu na shtanakh" and referred to a common attribute in the appearance of Parisian avant-gardists. Breton wore dark green glasses, which he alternated with a monocle; Joyce also wore dark glasses; Tzara, Éluard, and Péret wore monocles.[114] Wrote Breton: "We would like to be judged by our appearance alone. They are saying everywhere that I wear glasses. You will not believe me if I tell you why. I commemorate a grammar example: 'Noses are made to wear glasses; thus I have glasses'" (*Les Pas perdus*, 76). Poplavskii's glasses were motivated by a similar desire to surprise.

Another trait of Poplavskii's image was his passion for weightlifting and boxing, seen by émigrés as "humiliation of flesh akin to the chains worn by religious ascetics."[115] When Poplavskii did not claim indifference to literature, he modestly presented himself as a "poet and boxer."[116] Original in the Russian artistic milieu, this image was familiar in the French avant-garde because of the legendary persona of Arthur Cravan, a poet and Oscar Wilde's nephew, who was an amateur boxer. Cravan's fame came from his scandalous shows in prewar Paris. To convey his contempt for art, Cravan published on wrap paper from a butcher's store his poetic leaflet *Maintenant* and distributed it from a vegetable cart. The issue of March-April 1915 contained the text "Arthur Cravan: Poète et Boxeur."[117] Expressing contempt for traditional art, the combination of poetry and boxing symbolized dadaist and surrealist attitudes. Aragon's friend Jacques Baron, "a poet better known as a boxer," went by the nickname "Baron le boxeur" (*Paysan*, 24). Soupault created a semiparodic typical avant-gardist in his novel *En Joue!* (1925), emphasizing the same combination. His Julien writes poetry "without giving it more importance than it merits" because he has no literary ambition and prefers boxing and weightlifting to art.[118]

The paradigms present in Poplavskii's lifestyle may have brought about his demise, which many émigrés construed as suicide. His death harked back to the deaths of several French avant-gardists. Suicide was a leitmotif of surrealist thought.[119] The first issue of *La Révolution surréaliste* endowed dream and suicide with the same transcendental function: "It seems that killing oneself is like dreaming. It is not a moral question we are asking: is suicide a solution?"[120] Responses to the questionnaire confirmed the theoretical equivalency of dream and suicide. For René Crevel, who killed himself in 1935, those rejecting "reality" for the "sensation of truth" placed suicide higher than dreams. Antonin Artaud, who made several suicide attempts, insisted that his "appetite not to be" put him in a state of "suicide in progress," whose goal was a flight to the "other side of existence." Jacques Rigaut, who killed himself in 1929, viewed suicide as a "vocation" and the most efficient way of transcendence. Aragon saw suicides as "the only respectable dead," who chose "the better of all available *solutions*."[121] The first issue of *Le Disque vert* was also devoted to suicide. In it Crevel elaborated a theory of "provisional suicides," whereby the cult of self-destruction was as important as its actual realization ("Mais si la mort n'était qu'un mot," 29–31). The interpretation of Dada and surrealism as the products of the "new malady of the century" led observers to conclude that the suicidal tendencies of the avant-garde were akin to those in the Romantic "malady" and were as esthetically motivated as the suicides of Werther's admirers.[122]

While Rimbaud and Lautréamont embodied the ideal of artistic and existential evasion, their examples in the mythology of the French avant-garde were modernized by Jacques Vaché and Arthur Cravan. When he met Vaché in 1916, Breton was fascinated by his antisocial and antiartistic attitude. Vaché's virtue was "to have produced nothing," thanks to his contempt for art.[123] Cravan and Vaché were "ancestors" of surrealism not by virtue of lifestyle alone. In 1919 Vaché and his two friends were found dead, officially from an accidental opium overdose. But according to his myth, Vaché committed suicide and, in the last "joke," took his unwitting friends along. The interpretation of his death constituted a founding myth of Dada and surrealism—suicide as esthetic self-assertion and social and metaphysical transcendence. "His death was admirable in that it could pass for accidental," wrote Breton (*Les Pas perdus*, 24). In the same year Cravan disappeared on a boat promenade under mysterious circumstances. The ambiguity of Cravan's and Vaché's deaths perfected their myths, providing alibis against an artistic pose and laying ground for a model death style.

    In this model, suicide was closely associated with the concept of a "gratuitous act." Insisting, like Artaud and Crevel, that one's decision to die was more important than its realization, Rigaut supported his argument by a general contempt for life that was not worth the trouble of leaving it, just as literature was not worth the trouble of writing it. The ambiguous circumstances of Cravan's and Vaché's deaths recalled the "gratuitous act" as exemplified by the character of Lafcadio from André Gide's novel *Les Caves du Vatican* (1916). Lafcadio kills a man "for no reason," committing a gratuitous crime. Vaché had paid tribute to Gide's Lafcadio for his proto-dadaist spirit; Breton and Soupault, while debunking Gide's oeuvre in general, made an exception for *Les Caves du Vatican*; finally, according to Jean Cocteau, Cravan had served as Lafcadio's prototype.[124]

    The requirement of gratuity served as an alibi in an act of self-destruction: gratuity protected the artist from the charge of esthetic ambition. In Rigaut's program suicide was a good means of self-effacement, provided it was completely gratuitous. This meant that one could not kill oneself "for a reason." An act of self-destruction must be or must appear as spontaneous and unmotivated. According to his myth, Rigaut at all times disposed of a means of self-destruction in case of a spontaneous desire to kill himself. Rigaut developed both aspects of Vaché's death style—as an accident and as a joke in which the suicide finds himself company—and based his "modern mythology" on the reputation of a suicidal dandy.[125] He had organized dadaist events side by side with

Sharshun and participated in the meetings of Palata poetov and Cherez attended by Poplavskii. Rigaut's death in 1929 surprised everyone because it precluded all doubt vis-à-vis its nature. Wrote a critic: "His death recalls that of another initiator of Dada: Jacques Vaché. . . . I am surprised that Rigaut did not die exactly like Vaché, that is, making it unclear whether this was a suicide. . . . He must have understood that such accidents no longer fooled anyone."[126]

As early as 1923 Rigaut's suicidal "vocation" became a "literary fact." The protagonist of Jean Cocteau's novel *Le Grand écart* followed the recipe of "accidental suicide," trying to die by simulating a drug overdose. In the same year Drieu La Rochelle published his story "La Valise Vide," making fun of Rigaut's suicide on the installment plan. The story's protagonist, Gonzague, used suicide to cover up his artistic inadequacy. But Rigaut's death forced Drieu to change his mind. In 1931 he published the novel *Le Feu Follet*, which dealt with the life of an avant-gardist who preferred the sincerity of suicide to the lie of literature. Édmond Jaloux confirmed the cultural institutionalization of Rigaut's suicide as a model manifestation of the "new malady of the century" and a proof of artistic "sincerity." He commented on Rigaut's posthumously published manuscripts: "When writing the history of this period, future critics will have to account for them [Rigaut's texts] even if many of them appear negligible. The story of Jacques Rigaut is that of many young men of his time; his renunciation is a sign of purity."[127]

In 1933 Julien Torma disappeared during a mountain promenade. Like Rigaut, Torma was a former dadaist and shared the self-effacing attitude that marked the myths of Vaché and Cravan. His disappearance was construed as an "accidental suicide." In 1935 René Crevel killed himself shortly before Poplavskii's death. Notwithstanding the differences in circumstances, the deaths of Rigaut, Torma, and Crevel were interpreted similarly. Informed by the paradigm of the Vaché-Cravan suicidal model, these events were read as attempts to live up to the ideal of self-effacement in art and life and as ultimate proofs of artistic "sincerity."[128] Suicide provided a concrete mode of action for those who strove to implement literally the model of "complete silence" à la Rimbaud. "You are all poets," wrote Rigaut, "as for me, I am on death's side" (*Écrits posthumes*, 109). Although Rigaut continued writing, he stopped publishing after 1923, arguing that he had no literary ambition and was more interested in boxing.[129] Torma also insisted that literature was of no interest to him. After 1926 he "fell silent," led a nomadic life, and his trajectory was unknown except for one place where he took pains to be remarked—Charleville, the birthplace of Rimbaud.

Poplavskii wrote in a diary in March 1929: "Difference from the old decadence: we are joyful, golden. We are dying cheerfully, with a blessing, with a smile. Regarding death as the highest achievement. . . . The new slogan is—perishing. The émigrés will express themselves, their voice may resound in golden ages only if they perish, die, disappear, dissipate (*Neizdannoe*, 96)."

Outside the French avant-garde context, this entry was interpreted as a variation on the Russian fin-de-siècle decadent tradition.[130] But its reiteration in Poplavskii's article allows one to classify his "joyful" necrophilia as derivative of the dadaist-surrealist suicidal myth. Negating the necessity of art, Poplavskii argued that imaginative literature must be replaced by a "psychoanalytic record," whereas life must consist of dying; he specified that "death" meant the writer's self-effacement as a "genius who died unknown" ("O misticheskoi atmosfere molodoi literatury v emigratsii," 309, 311). Ironically, this statement came from one of the most popular poets in émigré literature. Poplavskii's artistic ideal, as articulated in his articles and diaries, evokes not only the surrealist view of art as psychological self-study but also Artaud's "continuous suicide," Rigaut's "vocation," and Crevel's "provisional suicide," equally ambiguous in their mythologizing necrophilia.

The Paris School placed physical and spiritual death among the most significant literary subjects.[131] Poplavskii's avant-gardistic necrophilia could be translated in these terms. Indeed, he presented his program of self-effacement as the immediate result of the existential solitude, isolation, and uprootedness of an exile. But the difference between his agenda and the esthetic toying with death among the Paris School writers became clear when the poet implemented the model death style of the French avant-garde.

His "accidental suicide" occurred on October 8, 1935. On the morning of October 9, Poplavskii was discovered dead in the company of Sergei Yarko, who died hours later. The medical expertise attributed their deaths to drug overdoses. The police investigation concluded that their deaths were accidental, as in the case of Jacques Vaché.[132] However, Poplavskii's text of life precluded the interpretation of the author's demise as natural. His death was construed as suicide by émigré observers who wanted to see the poet's end as an outcome of his esthetic and philosophical program.[133] The suicide version was further confirmed by the publication of Poplavskii's diary, where he wrote about his "physical thirst for death" (cf. Artaud's "appetite not to be"), which he anticipated with final preparations, "finishing and liquidating" old diaries and "cleaning up everything" (*Neizdannoe*, 114, 117).

Poplavskii's death bore uncanny resemblance to that of Vaché not only in its form of a group "accidental suicide" but also because of its announcement in advance. According to his legend, Vaché said shortly before his death: "I will die when I want to . . . but I will die with somebody. Dying alone is too boring. . . . I prefer one of my best friends."[134] Poplavskii also prepared the public opinion, informing his disciples of the imminent "ascension." Rais relates their dialogue several weeks before the event: the teacher hinted that he had made a serious decision but could not share it because Rais was "too weak" and had to wait until "everything was known." A similar premonitory conversation Poplavskii held with Tatishchev, repeating almost literally the presuicidal speech of the avant-garde dandy Julien from Soupault's *En Joue!*[135]

The nature of the rumors that circulated after Poplavskii's death is clear from the comments of his contemporaries. Khodasevich wrote: "Poplavskii died accidentally: from an overdose of poor quality narcotic substance. Had the dose been smaller, had the substance been of better quality—Poplavskii would have survived. Some friends of the deceased, well informed about his life and attitude, told me that this may not have been the case, that Poplavskii died willingly. It is also possible that someone else's despair found in him too deep a response and he let himself be taken from life" ("O smerti Poplavskogo," 3).

Thus, Poplavskii prepared his audience, which was already privy to esthetically motivated interpretations of suicide, for a double reading of his death—as an avant-gardistic "accidental suicide" or as the self-sacrifice of a Russian writer who died for someone else like the Christ he so obviously emulated.[136] In both cases his death served as a textual marker, as the sign of a tragic "fifth act" that logically concluded the development of the artist's text of life, informing each of its elements with cultural and esthetic significance.[137]

Interpretations of Poplavskii's death as a "Christian" suicide drew on two cultural models. On one hand, the deaths of Christ and saints had been described as suicides, thanks to the presence of intent in their striving for redemptive martyrdom.[138] Committing suicide for someone else, the poet died "like a saint." On the other hand, his suicide was informed by the model of the Russian writer in which the author's readiness to die guaranteed his righteousness and "truthfulness" in life and art.[139] The possibility of such reading had been confirmed in the wake of Maiakovskii's suicide. Poplavskii's death style, just like his lifestyle and art, combined Russian émigré, French, and Soviet cultural legacies.

Émigré commentators denigrated Maiakovskii for the incompatibility of his Soviet esthetics and behavior with those of a Russian writer. In his obituary Khodasevich argued that Maiakovskii was driven by opportunism and greed attesting to spiritual emptiness.[140] In response Jakobson offered his version of Maiakovskii as a martyr who shared the fate of other Russian poets (from Pushkin to Blok), dying "after long spiritual agony and unbearable physical torment." Including Maiakovskii in his list of martyrs, Jakobson traced their common fate to Christ's suffering and to the Russian tradition in which poets perished rather than died. Maiakovskii had walked the "poetic Golgotha" and died like an apostle, crowned with a "thorny wreath of revolution," in a "redemptive sacrifice for the future universal resurrection."[141] These mutually exclusive interpretations were supplemented by Breton, whose logic followed the surrealist suicide myth. Maiakovskii killed himself because he was an avant-gardist: like the surrealists, he had lived in a state of theoretical suicide in which his decision to die was more important than its realization.[142]

Poplavskii could have regarded the repercussions of Maiakovskii's death as a rehearsal of his own "fifth act." He prepared his audience for the reading of his liking, casting himself in the role of a Christ-like poet-martyr for the émigrés and of an avant-gardist for those familiar with the surrealist science of life and death. His fellow traveler, Sergei Yarko, was a Montparnasse Bohemian who had made previous suicide attempts and publicly announced his intention to kill himself. He was certainly familiar with French avant-garde mythology and used suicide announcements, like Vaché and Rigaut, as an artistic and existential "alibi." The rumor had it that Yarko was afraid to die alone.[143] Thus, in a self-sacrificial gesture, Poplavskii accompanied his friend. But there is yet another possibility. Following Vaché's example, the suicide's company had to die unwittingly. Both artists were versed enough in surrealist mythology to emulate Vaché's "accidental suicide." Indeed, Poplavskii invited to the drug session good friends of his—Lidiia Chervinskaia and Vasilii Ianovskii. Inviting Chervinskaia on the eve of the event, he said to her: "Our fates are tied forever." Both writers were spared by their decision not to come.[144]

Prefacing, some fifty years later, his "premonitory" novel *En Joue!* Philippe Soupault confessed that he recognized in its protagonist,

Julien, the ghosts of his friends Jacques Rigaut and René Crevel (13). In his semiparodic model of an avant-gardist "who bet his life on death," Soupault predicted down to details future suicides among dadaists and surrealists. Boris Poplavskii, whose literary oeuvre, life, and death were marked by the conflation of Russian émigré, Soviet, and French literary traditions, rightly belongs among the ghosts that haunted Soupault. The story of Poplavskii's artistic evolution and of his creative manipulation of émigré poetics to the end of adjustment in mainstream émigré letters is a striking example of an exile's artistic self-definition against the backdrop of the triangulated relationship of émigré, Soviet, and French literatures.

3

The Prodigal Children of Marcel Proust

The publication of *À la Recherche du temps perdu* (In search of lost time) was a major event in French postwar literature and in the self-definition of its new generation, which validated its sense of modernity by construing the war as a cultural and philosophical divide.[1] The brawl of ancients and moderns shaped the reception of *La Recherche:* looking for artistic authority, new writers drew on Proust to lay the foundation for their "modern" tradition. Although his career began in the 1890s, Proust identified with the new generation. Replying to Anatole France's rebuke of young authors for bad style, Proust rejected the idea of a stylistic canon because, for him, language expressed individual sensibility. He argued that new writers often seemed tiresome and opaque because they established unusual rapports between things. Using the pronoun "we," Proust indicated that he was also a "new writer."[2]

The construction of Proust as a cultural institution illustrates the gap between artistic theory and practice. Most French literati agreed that one could not write novels "after Proust" as they had been written before. But this hardly ensured Proust a place in the creative activity of the new generation. The critical reception of Proust's novel is a story of conscious misinterpretation to the ends of artistic self-definition. The gap between the theoretical eulogy of Proust's oeuvre by French "moderns" and their practical opposition to Proustian esthetics deserves special attention because it shaped in more than one way the émigré view of literary "Proustianism" and its artistic applications by Russian exiles.

The Creation of Marcel Proust and the "Influence of Anxiety"

The postwar esthetic evolution of French literature crystallized in the debates surrounding Proust. Proustian exegesis was a testing ground in the renewal of realist conventions, of the novelistic genre, and of literary language. After his death in 1922, Proust became a cult figure, acclaimed as the precursor of a new sensibility. In 1923 the *Nouvelle revue française* devoted an entire issue to Proust, laying the groundwork for his personal myth. A year later a young critic claimed that it would be extremely unjust and grossly erroneous "to relegate Proust among the old-timers" (parmi les vieilles barbes).[3] Interpreted as the epitome of modernism, Proust reached the peak of his fame in 1925.[4]

Immediately after the war, young writers viewed Proust differently. In 1922 Henri Rambaud and Pierre Varillon conducted the *Enquête sur les maîtres de la jeune littérature* (Questionnaire about the teachers of young literature), recording the view of Proust as a vain high-society novelist.[5] The *Enquête* asked young writers: "Who are your most important teachers?" and "What influences are crucial for the development of literature?" Among scores of respondents, only six named Proust, who was less popular than Anatole France.[6] Most opined that fathers had no serious influence—new writers needed a new and true teacher.[7] A year later Proust appeared as such a teacher.[8] By 1924 his appropriation was complete. "Old fogies ignore Proust," wrote Crémieux. "Only young writers—his anticipated progeny—realize that Proust is a great writer and innovator" (*XX-e siècle*, 10–11). Proust was credited with discovering new psychologism in art and with modernizing soul-searching through the concept of the unconscious.[9]

Lukewarm about Proust in the *Enquête,* Drieu La Rochelle wrote in 1923 that young writers had a secret link to Proust as the precursor who delivered them from the "miasma" of the fathers ("L'Exemple," in *HMP*, 320–21). In the period filled with interest for Freud, young writers saw Proust as the investigator of the unconscious. The fact that he had not read Freud attested to a new and universal sensibility.[10] Even dadaists went through an infatuation with Proust's work, finding in it antipositivist ethos, anxiety, and revolt against culture. A debate took place on the possibility of fusing Proustian analysis with surrealist imagination.[11] For those who rejected avant-gardistic extremes but espoused the notion of the unconscious as artistically fruitful, Proust's method appeared as a viable alternative to Dada and surrealism.

Many respondents to the *Enquête* emphasized that the "rebirth" of new writers followed a great rhythm governed by purifying inundations; this rhythm was an eternal movement of cultural cycles; the war was an inundation.[12] Such arguments reveal that the new generation based its identity on the myths of the eternal return and of the malady of the century. As part of a larger antipositivist reaction, the revolt against historical linearity had been elaborated by Nietzsche, who revived the myth of the eternal return. As for a malady of the century, it had already inaugurated a cultural cycle after 1789. French writers projected their situation upon the Romantic malaise, suggesting its cyclical recurrence.[13] The ethos of cultural renewal was important for Proust's appropriation by the "moderns." They were attracted to Proust's search for lost time as backward motion, a return to the pure sources of regeneration that were evocative of Freud's and Nietzsche's theories.[14]

Burying the West, the "new malady" stipulated its reconstruction from a tabula rasa by a culturally "naked" barbarian.[15] The anticipation of an undefined future and the cult of the new led to the exaltation of the present. Hence the abstract language in which postwar "moderns" spoke of the past, replacing historical memory by the ahistorical affinity of the present with archetypal extremes of history, such as the French Revolution. Reflecting on this "modernist" desire to erase the past in order to reach a point of origin that marks a new departure, Paul de Man described such falling away from literature and rejection of history as principles that give literature duration and historical existence.[16] In archaic civilizations cyclical time was a mode of existence that denied the value of historical events as deviations from an archetype; historical time was periodically abolished in collective ritual return to origins.[17] But the "modernist" revolt against history and longing for origins conflicted with the valorization of historical events, such as the Great War. Consequently, "European Hamlets" mythologized these historical events by projecting them upon cultural archetypes. Their inability to abolish historical time translated into the nostalgia for origins that replaced the myth of collective regeneration with that of an individual return to origins.

Freud offered a technique of individual return. His idea of recalling incidents of early childhood is pertinent to the myth of the eternal return. The goal of this time travel coincides with that of the ancient rites of cyclical regeneration: "burning" memories of events, one is freed from these events and renews one's existence. This ethos of deliverance underlay the "new malady" and distinguished it from its Romantic prototype, which saw ancestral past as the bedrock of new culture. "New children of the century" needed a cultural past in order to destroy it.[18] The unconscious became a new name for "that fatality which the ancients used to depict under the mask of divinity."[19] A new tragic opposition was added to the classical conflicts "man and destiny" and "man and passion." It was rooted in the conflict of one's contradictory selves, in the dissociation of personality by uncontrollable forces. The fact that the hero of *La Recherche* was irreligious (*Prisonnière*, 177) and more preoccupied with psychology than with metaphysics appealed to the "new children." But their assimilation of the novel to Freud's theories diverged from Proust's own project. There is an esthetic abyss between Proust's view of literature as the only true reality and the "European Hamlets'" requirement that art be "an exact painting" of life.[20]

Proust's protagonist does not "burn" his past. He seeks extratemporality in an identity of past and present that alleviates his fear of the future. Achieving extratemporal equilibrium, Marcel loses his fear of death (*Temps retrouvé*, 178–79). Proust and his self-proclaimed followers were linked by a common nostalgia for origins and by the means of seeking them through a "return to the depths" (*Temps retrouvé*, 203). But methodological affinities did not lead to shared conclusions. Return to the depths constitutes for Marcel the grandeur of art. He affirms his existence by rediscovering hidden life, and since he does this in a literary investigation, he concludes that literature is the only true life there is: "La vraie vie . . . c'est la littérature" (*Temps retrouvé*, 202). A "new child of the century," on the contrary, did not need to affirm his existence: he "knew that he was alive because he was not dead, having risked his life for five long years" (Crémieux in *Enquête*, 53). For this generation there could be no identity of past and present; true life was but material for regeneration. The formula "literature is life" drowned in the requirement that life should subordinate literature because "literature was not enough" (Crevel, "Après Dada," 5). But the rewritten formula was attributed to Proust. "Proust renews the eternal lesson of genius: art is not an enemy to life," stated Drieu La Rochelle ("L'Exemple," 322).

Seeing literature as exact painting of reality, "European Hamlets" succumbed to the referential illusion, a belief in the natural semantic relation of sign and referent based on the myth that language imitated ideas and signs were motivated.[21] Hence their reluctance to speak about realist illusion and imagination in art. The notions of illusion and imagination undermined the ethos of their activity—a renewal of mimetic conventions. Older critics saw Proust as a regenerator of mimetic conventions. *La Recherche* reinvigorated imagination: since everything a person made up was present in his or her unconscious, one could not be insincere in art.[22] Viewing literature as fiction, they credited Proust with reconciling contradictions in a writer's desire to be truthful. For the sons, reality had new meaning; Proust faithfully conveyed his search for hidden reality, and they followed him, replacing imagination with self-observation. "We cannot be insincere, but we can at least be more or less true," argued Dommartin.[23] New mimetic conventions encouraged the identification of author and hero. In this respect the generational split is evident. The fathers mock those who see *La Recherche* as autobiographical; the sons create a legend of Proust's life in art.[24]

The only link between Proust and his hero was the name Marcel, mentioned twice in the entire novel.[25] The novel's genesis shows that Proust tried to distance his narrator from himself. Had he had time to proofread the text, he would probably have eliminated these instances.[26] The publication of *Jean Santeuil* and *Contre Sainte-Beuve* confirmed Proust's research on the narrative technique for *La Recherche*. Having treated the subject matter of his novel in a third-person narrative and in an autobiographical essay, he chose the mode that best fit his purpose. Obfuscating his narrator, Proust reduced him to a set of mysteries that created the effect of multiplicity in the narrator's personality.[27] Both Proust and his hero criticized the conflation of author and text: since external reality was not true, one could not compare the author to his creation and art to the external world.[28]

If the ancients castigated Proust for incorrect usage, the moderns hailed his revolt against ossified literary language. Evocative of the complexity of his thought, Proust's usage was a small price to pay for coming closer to truth; this was a lesson in sincerity.[29] Proust's language was even interpreted as a return to the classical tradition, corrupted by the fathers.[30] Modern experience required new forms, unknown before the war. The postwar novel dropped several canonical qualities: it slowed down, thanks to psychological analysis, lost compositional rigor, and became a hybrid genre. Young writers demanded its interior reorganization, rejecting old linguistic and compositional requirements.[31] They saw Proust's linguistic revolt as part of his quest for a revolution in the novelistic genre.

Critics argued that Proust decomposed the canon by eliminating dramatic action, by flooding it with superfluous detail, by fleeing external description, by succumbing to the flow of psychological investigation, and by bringing in memoir and essay elements.[32] Young writers valorized *La Recherche* as the model for a "tradition of disorder."[33] Such interpretation contradicted Proust's own vision of his work. Reducing the description of external reality in favor of inner life, Proust used landscapes, social circles, and individuals as mirrors for the hero's self-study. The lack of external description is in itself a picture of inner states ("l'absence de toute description du milieu extérieure est déjà une description d'un état interne," *Guermantes II*, 535). Details appear insignificant only when contingent: in the novel's circular composition, the import of each detail is defined in relation to the narrator, for whom everything harks back to the first scene, the "bedtime drama" (*Temps retrouvé*, 351). *La Recherche* has a main story and secondary stories (Swann's love for Odette, Marcel's love for Gilberte, etc.). The main story is fully unveiled in the last volume, linking discrete details and events in one history of Marcel's literary vocation. That is why Proust denounced the view of his novel as chaotic and of details in it as superfluous.[34]

Reflection on the novel brought about the talk of its demise as a genre.[35] *La Recherche* embodied the decomposition of the novel to such an extent that its influence was proclaimed dangerous. In the postwar spiritual crisis, the decomposition of the novel mirrored the decomposition of human personality. Proust's method of depicting characters from multiple vantage points was interpreted as the fragmentation of the individual; Proust replaced spirituality with pure psychology, banished God from his work, and showed that the human being was an amalgam of contradictory forces with no unifying principle.[36] The voices in his defense, arguing that the decomposition of personality in *La Recherche* was suggested by "modern" decomposers, drowned in the "new children's" enthusiasm for erasing the old concept of personality. By advocating introversion, Proust opposed the generalizing psychology of the realist novel, which produced the static model of an individual shaped by social environment and held together by a unifying principle. New psychologism offered a more complex view of personality in transition. The danger that it could destroy human integrity was urgent only for the fathers.[37]

The sons saw Proust's characters as an exact and courageous painting of life.[38] Marcel indeed considers that "return to the depths" requires intellectual courage because it entails the demise of myths (*Temps retrouvé*, 203). Love is one of these myths, present in *La Recherche* as changes of heart ("intermittences du coeur"). Marcel does not negate the existence of love but denies its objective nature (*Swann*, 393). The source of changes of heart lies in the unconscious: coming closer to the source, one can predict these changes and use them as means for extracting emotions that furnish material for self-study (*Temps retrouvé*, 214–17). In tandem with other broken myths, Marcel's world-view, as seen by the "moderns," leads to solitude, pessimism, and despair—the central topoi of the "new malady."[39] For Proust, disintegration is only a prerequisite for the subsequent synthesis. His interpreters, however, flatly ignored the regeneration evident in *Le Temps retrouvé*.

Marcel's method rests on the axiom that he cannot go beyond appearances in an act of communication; another is perceived by senses and is an approximation (*Swann*, 84; *Prisonnière*, 372). He is made up of discrete momentary images. But after disintegrating scrutiny, all images must be considered together, in a temporal continuum that gives them unity and depth (*Temps retrouvé*, 230, 248). Since commerce beyond appearances is not feasible, solitude is a fact of life (*Guermantes II*, 308). But it is also a factor that stimulates creativity, eliminating the distraction of false communication (*Prisonnière*, 88–89; *Temps retrouvé*, 293). There exist only mental links between Marcel and another; they disappear with the erosion of memory, leaving an illusion of communication sustained by the myths of love, friendship, and respect (*Albertine disparue*, 34). The reconstruction of these links and the imaginary re-creation of another constitute the only reality there is and correspond to Marcel's literary vocation. Such positive conclusions from the affirmation of solitude are possible, thanks to his cult of art. In contrast, the "new children's" contempt for art as fiction placed them in the vicious circle of esthetically valuable despair and disintegration.

The construction of Proust as a cultural institution illustrates the gap between artistic theory and practice. Many writers and critics spoke about Proust without reading him; over 50 percent of those who read the first volume of *La Recherche* did not read the following ones.[40] Critics wrote about Proust's influence without providing examples. One could not find examples of his impact on the style or structure of French prose, limiting speculations about influence to affinity in subject matter, philosophy, and analysis.[41] An examination of the works cited as examples of Proust's influence makes the latter highly problematic.

In 1921 Drieu La Rochelle published his novel *État civil*. The novel starts with the protagonist's childhood; special attention is paid to his unconscious cognition of the world and himself through senses. Drieu describes his hero's reading list, schooling, and Parisian life in short sentences with affectedly simple syntax. The novel differs from the traditional bildungsroman by the presence of the fashionable "unconscious" in the hero's life and by his propensity for rebellion, since the war makes him a Hamlet. Despite the attempts to classify it as neo-Proustian, *État civil* is anti-Proustian in its style, its narrative structure (it has a linear plot), and its denial of the past.[42] Most important, Drieu's hero revisits the past to burn memories and deliver himself from the burden of his prewar life: "I am writing this to get rid of myself, or rather of the one I was, particularly during a certain war that coincided with my entrance into life. I dare hope that this effort of deracination also lays bare the foundations on which my youth did not erect its precarious structures. . . . I am tracing these pages in order to fixate on the outside all that from which I would like to separate myself" (*État civil*, 177–78).

Regeneration is the goal of this hero, who has "lost the secret of God" and sees no value in the past (179–80). This ethos of deliverance intensifies in Drieu's novel *Le jeune Européen* (1927), whose protagonist is a disoriented young man torn by anxiety, maladjustment, and cultural uprootedness that propel him into an intercontinental pilgrimage. The narrator of *État civil* dwells on the reading list of his childhood in order to flee the past by fixing his former self in writing. The hero of *Le jeune Européen* already curses this list because it gave him an uncontrollable desire to write. He can write only about himself, but when he does, the past gets hold of him. The only way to escape spiritual "marasmus" is to drown the desire to write in frantic travels (*Le jeune Européen suivi de Genève ou Moscou*, 44–45, 47). The conclusion is as transparent as it is anti-Proustian: active lifestyle in the present is the only available form of art; contemplation leads to ossification in the past.

The same conclusion is suggested in Soupault's *À la dérive* (1923), whose title is a mocking response to *La Recherche*. The life of Soupault's David, dubbed by a critic "little Hamlet at the cemetery of all European traditions," depends on the demolition of his past. Memory is a burden: it arrests action and causes senility.[43] Marcel's involuntary memory is disqualified as just a bar in the prison of life. David is a parodic anti-Marcel who mocks Marcel's "bedtime drama"—healthy and strong, he flees his mother and his bed (14, 17). Like the hero of *État civil*, he despises his family and runs away from his past. After he settles down, he is soon "paralyzed by memory" and dies. David's story is briefly summarized and drowned in discursive characterizations of his inner life.[44] Similar discursivity and lack of external description mark Drieu's novels, whose heroes are concerned not with the external world but with their feelings about it. This tempted critics to call both authors "Proustians," all the while admitting that the young writers were bad students of Proust.[45]

In *Le bon apôtre* (1923), Soupault summarized dramatic action in the introduction, devoting the rest of the novel to an excursion into the formative years of Philippe Soupault and Jean X. that determines what elements of the past are to be destroyed. That is why much attention is paid to their reading list. All main elements of the "literature of evasion" are present here: first-person narrative; confessional motivation; loss of God; anxiety; war shock; maladjustment; and intercontinental escapades. The story is related in the uneventful form of ruminating self-reflection. But instead of a secret connection to Proust, suggested by a reviewer, Soupault and Drieu shared a model of the novel of antieducation, mistaken by critics for a Proustian return to childhood.[46] Eager to reconcile the "new children's" hatred of the past with Proust's fusion of past and present, critics suggested that the issue of personality linking young writers to Proust received different treatment in their works under the influence of postwar anxiety.[47] By 1923 there emerged two novelistic models—adventure (alias the novel of energy) and introspective novels—which shared this "influence of anxiety" and "Proustian representation from within," that is, the projection of external life on the screen of inner life.[48] The claim that both models drew on Proustian discursivity was not entirely ungrounded. In *La Recherche* artistic vision implied submission to the reality of one's psyche; extratemporality was achieved outside action; artistic imagination was replaceable by the capacity to listen to the unconscious (*Temps retrouvé*, 178, 189, 208).

État civil, Le jeune Européen, A la dérive, Le bon apôtre, Arland's *Terres étrangères* (1923), Lacretelle's *La Vie inquiète de Jean Hermelin* (1920), Morand's *Tendres stocks* (1921), *Ouvert la nuit* (1922), and *Fermé la nuit* (1923), Cocteau's *Thomas l'imposteur* (1923) and *Le grand écart* (1923), Radiguet's *Le Diable au corps* (1923) belonged to the first type. While war and vagrancy dominated this model, it was far from a traditional adventure novel. This was a novel of antieducation. It described the formative years of an outcast, whose imagination and analytical mindset replaced external life and whose anxiety sprang from the war, whether or not he partook in it. Professing hatred of the past, "new children" gave Proust a sarcastic pinch. Like Soupault's David, Cocteau's Jacques considered the time spent with his mother "lost time."[49] Yet, representation from within was the model's binding principle; the reduction of dramatic action in favor of discursivity was viewed as a meritorious quest for simplicity and truth, taught by Proust.[50]

The introspective novel shared with its adventurous counterpart a contempt for dramatic action and external description. Here the protagonist's escape is fully internalized; discursivity becomes an ideal and is attributed to Proust.[51] Although the introspective novel was reproached for fragmenting personality through Proustian analysis, it was as far from Proust's search for extratemporality as the adventure novel was.[52] The past does not exist for the self-contemplating hero of this model: he is absorbed by his present. His striving for "sincerity" is conveyed through the form of an intimate diary, peculiar to most introspective novels, which are consequently laden with tension between the ideal of "sincerity" and the fact of literary fiction. Hence the metareflection on the relations of art and life underlying each intimate diary. In this model literary material is extracted from the hero's psyche by Marcel's method of romantic liaisons. Women are signs modeling Marcel's reality; he looks for situations in which they function as torturers by virtue of infidelity or "changes of heart."[53] The more misfortune one encounters, the more fruitful one's investigation becomes.

Betz's *L'Incertain* (1925), Drieu's *Journal d'un homme trompé* (1928), and Chardonne's *Eva ou le journal interrompu* (1930) exemplify this model. These diaries are narrated in the first-person singular and deal with tortuous romantic liaisons. Dramatic action is submerged in the discourse on the emotional vicissitudes and analysis of each relationship. The hero of *L'Incertain* scrutinizes his own wife, who never leaves their home (cf. Albertine in *La Prisonnière*). He suffers from anxiety, whose "profound" sources must be uncovered. His past is a muddle of fears that take hold of him through involuntary memory. Unlike Marcel, he longs for the "benefit of oblivion," which he attains through self-study (28–31). He needs his wife as a stimulus for "profound renewal." He is obsessed with possessing her, hence his acute jealousy reminiscent of Marcel's drive to possess another as a mirror asserting his own existence. This frustrated possession—one cannot penetrate beyond appearances— defines the nature of Marcel's affairs. His longing is inversely proportional to the degree of possession he can reach.[54] This is also true for the hero of *L'Incertain*. When his wife dies, his "solitude together" is ruined, and the novel ends on a note of desperation. The hero may keep finding female stimuli or commit suicide.

The same reworking of Marcel's method, the use of "female stimuli" to the end of deliverance from the past, marks *Journal d'un homme trompé*.[55] This diary, kept during the hero's flight to Spain from unhappy love, emphatically lacks external description. The hero's cult of solitude precludes attention to anything outside inner life and serves as the novel's documentary motivation (11, 46). Drieu builds his hero's monologue as a discursive mosaic from which the reader surmises that the hero loves a "grue" living at the expense of several men (cf. Swann and Odette, Saint-Loup and Rachel). His philosophy of love draws on the Proustian dialectics of possession; suspicion of infidelity triggers emotional calvary, which his diary describes and analyzes. Metadescription is the most interesting feature of this text.[56] Aware of the oxymoronic nature of literary documents, Drieu creates a semantic level where the protagonist's love and search of deliverance from the past metaphorize the novel's artistic method. The words about sincerity in love can be read as a commentary on sincerity in literature, since they are placed in the context of a generational split: "Our sincerity. Several years ago, at a bourgeois dinner where 'old couples' and 'young couples' mixed, I became the center of attention for justifying 'our generation' by its abhorrence of lies and its taste for sincerity" (20–21).

The novel leaves unresolved this double entendre in the hero's self-reflection as a parable for the author's artistic project. Sincerity may, after all, be possible because we learn at the end that the story of infidelity could have been a figment of the narrator's imagination.

The postwar French novelists, whose writings were seen as a continuation of Proust's project and who commonly appealed to Proust as a symbol of their sensibility, opposed Proust's view of the relationship between art and life and the ethos of his artistic investigation. They could not be farther from Proust in their striving for extraliterary "sincerity," which affirmed the primacy of life over art, and in their hatred of the past.

"Proustianism" and *Prustiantsy*

Many émigré writers treated *La Recherche* as the acme of French literature and echoed the French view that one could not write novels as they had been written "before Proust."[57] *Chisla* started its existence by soliciting opinions of Proust's place in art and of his possible influence on émigrés. The phrasing echoed French "modernist" opinions: *Chisla* inquired if exiles considered Proust as the epitome of their epoch.[58] Following French "moderns," "émigré Hamlets" posited Proust as emblematic of a generational split. *La Recherche* conveyed the sensibility of those who matured in social cataclysms and outside the traditions of the fathers; Proust was as radical an innovator as the surrealists.[59] Critics saw Proust's name in *Chisla* as a modernist pledge of allegiance.[60] But besides familiarizing themselves with Proust, émigré *prustiantsy* had to define their position in regard to the adventure and introspective novels and to French interpretations of Proust.

Émigrés were no strangers to the myth of eternal return. Russian symbolists, inspired by Nietzsche, had been keen on the idea of eternal return, by which they meant, variously, historical or cosmic cycles, reincarnation, and endlessness opposed to the enlightenment ideal of linear progress.[61] According to Adamovich, salvation from spiritual crisis was in writing "as if nothing existed before"; young émigrés had to start "from the beginning" (cf. the tabula rasa of French "new children"), forget that they were artists, and renounce imagination as insincerity.[62] "Émigré Hamlets" used Proustian exegesis as a battlefield for esthetic self-definition. Older exiles spoke about Proust's novel as a fairy tale whose power of verisimilitude broke stale mimetic conventions, creating new realist illusion. Younger writers regarded the novel as Proust's self-study and saw its stylistic program as a proof of antiartistic sincerity—Proust revolted against the smoothness and artifice of the average French work.[63] But in émigré literature the clash surrounding Proust's realism had more at stake than in French debates. The transformation of mimetic conventions followed the premises of émigré poetics, to which both generations appealed.

Shmelev and Vysheslavtsev saw Proust as a shallow high-society painter. But to Fel'zen and Tsvetaeva, Proust spoke "sincerely" about the "most important." This was a question of esthetic vision: where ancients saw superficiality, moderns saw suffering.[64] Adamovich challenged émigré writers to rise up to modern French letters and abandon external description, peculiar to Soviet art. External life, he argued, was secondary and subordinate to inner life. Bunin and Slonim also wanted literature to concentrate on inner life but thought that spiritual vicissitudes had to be illustrated from the outside so that the reader could see them. They condemned those who followed French examples that reduced the outside world to material for self-study with no figurative representation.[65]

Following in the French footsteps, émigrés pronounced Proust a decomposer of the novel and of human integrity; his art was esthetically and spiritually dangerous.[66] Since the novel was the backbone of the Russian tradition, émigrés poignantly felt its crisis as a crisis of human identity.[67] The banishment of the psychological novel in Soviet art in the 1920s additionally informed their view. The old psychological novel contradicted the utopian goal of the LEF—the creation of a new human being; Osip Mandel'shtam also thought that the psychological novel was obsolete; the Serapions clamored for the creation of a new novel based on Western examples.[68] Many writers, influenced by formalist theories, stressed such "Western" features as dramatic action and plot construction and scoffed at the Russian psychological novel in which literary craft was subordinate to social and metaphysical concerns. For the émigrés, "Western" markers were the opposite. "French psychological discursivity" contradicted "Soviet external descriptiveness"; Proustian solipsistic analysis emphasized the absence of spiritual intuition in the Soviet hero; Proust's language was the exact opposite of "Soviet" style.[69] The brand of dangerous influence encouraged Proust's appropriation by "émigré Hamlets." Proust was a product of the "brilliant and dangerous atmosphere of European modernism"; he was its "best and most poisonous flower."[70]

Soviet critics chastised Proust for individualism, "bourgeois mysticism," and indifference to the struggle of the classes, further encouraging the émigré adoption of "Proustianism."[71] Proustian "poison" was preferable to the crude integrity of the Soviet hero. That is why émigrés emphasized that Proust's influence was absent in Soviet art and saw "Proustianism" as the spiritual summit of French literature.[72] In the context of the émigré-Soviet antagonism, the fragmentation of personality in Proustian analysis did not seem too dangerous. New psychologism was as destructive as it was creative, for the crisis of European civilization, ostensibly absent in the USSR, revealed a potential for spiritual regeneration once the "all defining beginning" was found.[73] Affinity with Proust was also affinity with the West. This affinity implied a writer's opposition to Soviet literature and bestowed upon him the prestige of Western modernism.

Such was the cultural context in which Gaito Gazdanov and Iurii Fel'zen wrote their first novels. The complex web of artistic circumstances in which they found themselves could not fail to influence their view of Proust and "Proustianism." Forging their own artistic voices against the backdrop of *La Recherche*, French "neo-Proustian" novels, and Proustian exegesis, they arrived at very different results.

Flirting with Proust: Gaito Gazdanov's *Vecher u Kler*

Georgii Ivanovich Gazdanov (1903–71) started publishing as "Gaito Gazdanov" in 1926. *Vecher u Kler* (1930, translated as *An Evening with Claire*) was his first success. The novel begins in Paris, where Nikolai Sosedov finally possesses his first love, the French woman Claire, after

ten years of separation. As Claire falls asleep, he recalls his life from
childhood to the moment he left Russia. He was fourteen when he met
Claire in the resort town of Kislovodsk (cf. Marcel's meeting with Albertine in the resort town of Balbec). When Claire left for France, Nikolai joined the White Army, embarking on a journey with Claire as his
guiding star. Hence the novel's epigraph from *Eugene Onegin*: "My entire life has been the gage / Of a sure tryst with you." Steeped in the semantics of memory, the text was compared to *La Recherche*. Gazdanov
later admitted that he had not read Proust at the time, yet he accepted
the fashionable label of *prustianets* and discussed Proust publicly.[74] But
"reading" is an ambiguous term when it concerns a cultural institution.
La Recherche was so frequently discussed that the connection between
the two novels could not be only a coincidence in time, as Dienes has argued (*Russian Literature in Exile*, 70). One learnt about the style, subject
matter, analytical method, philosophy, and motifs of *La Recherche* from
the critical debates surrounding it. This contemporary discourse on *La
Recherche* accounts for the angle from which Gazdanov viewed "Proustianism" and for the initial classification of his own novel as neo-
Proustian.

Treating *Vecher u Kler* as a neo-Proustian text, émigré reviewers had
as their reference points not only *La Recherche* but also French postwar
novels interpreted as its offspring. Critics saw Proust's influence in Gazdanov's subject matter, a retrospective journey into childhood; in his language, full of long and syntactically complex periods; in the novel's discursivity and lack of dramatic action; in the amassment of apparently
superfluous details; in the narrative development by veiled associations
between contiguous elements; in the narrator's concentration on inner
life; and in the novel's confessional motivation, which suggested an
identification of the author with the hero.[75] Gazdanov encouraged autobiographical interpretations by mystifying his biography and arguing,
unlike Proust, for the direct dependence of art on its creator's life. He
cited Proust as an example of such literary "sincerity." According to Gazdanov, spiritual vision, absent in the positivist world-view, spanned the
gap between fiction and reality by recording the artist's psychological
vicissitudes.[76] This was the artistic method the French "moderns" ascribed to Proust.

Gazdanov's early stories were written in short periods with bright
metaphors and colloquial intonations modeled after Babel's writings.
The tide in his romance with Soviet letters turned in 1928. His stories
of this period ("Prevrashchenie," "Gavaiskie gitary") feature a more

somber style; an interest in Proustian topoi (time, memory, solipsistic analysis); a slower narrative pace; and the replacement of dialogues with indirect speech. *Vecher u Kler* finalized his "transition from Soviet to Western influences."[77] In the context of émigré poetics, his style functioned as an anti-Soviet marker; in contrast to Soviet prose, his language seemed simple.[78] But French and émigré views of stylistic simplicity differed. No French writer emulated Proust's style, too literary and archaic for expressing new sensibility. French "neo-Proustian" novels drifted toward shorter sentences with simpler syntax, eschewed literary times (*passé simple, imparfait du subjonctif*), which Proust overused, and introduced colloquial elements.[79] Gazdanov's motion in the opposite direction was hailed by émigré critics as a renewal of Russian stylistic traditions.

Gazdanov's view of a "Proustian" sentence derived from the discussions of *La Recherche* rather than from a familiarity with the text proper. *La Recherche* was presented as a web of very long periods, although, in fact, sentences longer than ten lines occupy less than a quarter of the novel.[80] Long periods with parentheses and subordinate clauses echo the construction of Proust's narrative in which episodes are grouped by parenthetic contiguity in clusters of associations and not by logical development in space (succession) or time (chronology). Spitzer calls Proust's longer sentences "sentence images," for their syntactic complexity illustrates a thinking mechanism centered on memory. Their reading requires memorizing and analytical work; linguistic behavior thus models psychological behavior as Proust sees it ("Le style de Marcel Proust," in *Études de style*, 410). For Proust linguistic articulation of intuitively found reality is an approximation: intelligence creates a gap between an object's "true impression" and the "nominal impression" of its description (*Temps retrouvé*, 176). This conflict of language and truth pushes Marcel toward indirect speech and makes him reiterate Proust's own view that "a writer's style is a question of vision rather than technique."[81]

What is for Proust a matter of artistic vision is for Gazdanov a marker of literary kinship with the *maître*. The language of his novel lacks the semantic aura of Proust's style; his "Proustian" sentence differs structurally from Proust's longer sentences. Adamovich saw Gazdanov's main stylistic device in the substitution of "poor, desperately outdated periods with commas and semicolons" ("'Sovremennye zapiski' kn. 50-ia," 3). This chaining of multiple clauses in one sentence is indeed a frequent device in the novel. Gazdanov's "chained" sentence evolves logically and requires no effort of memory. Unlike Proust's, most of his "Proustian" sentences can be broken up with no harm to semantic structure, like the links of the chains he describes:

> Я проходил мимо конюшен École Militaire; оттуда слышался звон цепей, на которых были привязаны лошади, и густой конский запах, столь неоычный для Парижа; потом я шагал по длинной и узкой улице Babylone, и в конце этой улицы в витрине фотографии, в неверном свете далеких фонарей на меня глядело лицо знаменитого писателя, все составленное из наклоненных плоскостей; всезнающие глаза под роговыми европейскими очками провожали меня полквартала—до тех пор, пока я не пересекал черную сверкающую полосу бульвара Raspail (*Kler,* 39).

> [I would walk past the École Militaire; from there one could hear the clanging of the chains to which the horses were tethered and smell the dense equine odor so unusual for Paris; I would then stroll down the long, narrow rue Babylone and at the end of this street, in the artificial light of distant street lamps, the face of an illustrious writer, composed of sloping planes, would stare at me halfway down the block until I finally crossed the black, glittering strip of the Boulevard Raspail] (*Claire,* 19).[82]

The structure of Proust's longer period is based on the deceleration of semantic progress by syntactic devices.[83] These include parenthetic clauses, correcting repetitions, ramifications, and disjunctions of syntactic patterns. Proust puts in parentheses secondary didactic elements: facts that do not directly concern inner life, reflections not in immediate rapport with the narrator's thought, passing impressions and commentaries. Striving for precision, he conveys sensations through approximations that delay semantic development. One often encounters such constructions as "this was not A but rather B" and "this was, if not A, then B," which resemble scientific discourse. Each distinction is made to eschew a possible error or to correct it a posteriori. By means of this autocorrection, Proust exposes an image through a series of anaphoric repetitions of syntactic patterns within one sentence. No such preoccupation with looking for the right word exists in Gazdanov's conspicuously polished language. His longer periods do not evolve by approximating parenthetic clauses. Instead, they represent a combination of syntactically autonomous sentences, in which one breaks the semantic structure of another, shocking the reader's expectations. He writes:

Он любил физические упражнения, был хорошим гимнастом, неутомимым наездником,—он все смеялся над "посадкой" его двух братьев, драгунских офицеров, которые, как он говорил, "даже кончив их эту самую лошадиную академию, не научились ездить верхом; впрочем, они и в детстве были не способны к верховой езде, а пошли в лошадиную академию потому, что там алгебры не надо учить,"—и прекрасным пловцом (*Kler,* 53).

⋙

[He liked physical exercise, was a good gymnast and an inde-fatigable equestrian—he always laughed at the "seat" of his two brothers, dragoon officers, who, he said, had not learned to ride "even by the time they'd finished that equine academy of theirs; and besides, even in childhood they had no talent for riding and went to the equine academy only because you didn't have to take algebra there"—and a good swimmer.][84]

Gazdanov's approach to building a longer period differs from Proust's inasmuch as the French writer links multiple parenthetical clauses in one sentence, both grammatically and syntactically. For instance, in the following excerpt from a long period, the semantic structure of the main clause preserves its continuity through several extensive parenthetic digressions, for its parts are linked by the conjunctions "but" and "because," conditional mode, and grammatical parallelism "this is not because . . . but because . . .":

Accessoirement comme moyen (car, si peu que notre vie doive durer, ce n'est que pendant que nous souffrons que nos pensées, en quelque sorte agitées de mouvements perpétuels et changeants, font monter comme dans une tempête, à un niveau d'où nous pouvons la voir, toute cette immensité réglée par des lois, sur laquelle, postés à une fenêtre mal placée, nous n'avons pas vue, car le calme du bonheur la laisse unie et à un niveau trop bas; . . .)—mais principalement parce que, si notre amour n'est pas seulement d'une Gilberte (ce qui nous fait tant souffrir), ce n'est pas parce qu'il est aussi l'amour d'une Albertine, mais parce qu'il . . . (*Temps retrouvé,* 203–4).

⋙

[This is first and least important (brief through our life may be, it is only while we are suffering that our thoughts, somehow agitated by perpetually changing movements, elevate, as if during a storm, to a level at which we can see the whole law-governed immensity, which normally, posted at a badly placed window, we could not see, because the calm weather of happiness leaves it smooth and beneath our line of vision; . . .)—but principally because, if our love is not only the love of a Gilberte (and this fact is what we find so painful), it is not because it is also the love of an Albertine but because it is . . .]

If one compares this period to Gazdanov's passage cited above, it becomes obvious that Gazdanov not only avoided grammatical and syntactic cohesion but understood linguistic "Proustianism" as the creation of a semantic shock through the combination of several autonomous sentences within an unusually large period. This explanation of Gazdanov's linguistic program seems especially plausible against the backdrop of the valorization of shocking usage in the contemporary critical discussions of Proust's style, whereby some commentators compared Proust to French surrealists.[85] Gazdanov excelled in this science of logical disruption, for some of his "Proustian" periods reach gargantuan proportions and shocking levels of syntactically created incoherence, as in the following example:

У этой девочки была любовь к необыкновенным приключениям: она то убегала на базар и вертелась там целый день среди торговок, карманщиков и воров покрупнее—людей в хороших костюмах, с широкими внизу штанами, точильщиков, букинистов, мясников и тех продавцов хлама, которые существуют, кажется, во всех городах земного шара, одинаково одеваются в черные лохмотья, плохо говорят на всех языках и торгуют обломками решительно никому не нужных вещей; и все-таки они живут, и в их семьях сменяются поколения, как бы самой судьбой предназначенные именно для такой торговли и никогда ничем другим не занимающиеся,—они олицетворяли в моих глазах великолепную неизменность; то снимала чулки и туфли, и ходила босиком по саду после дождя, и, вернувшись домой, хвасталась: Мама, посмотри, какие у меня ноги черные. (*Kler,* 74)

[This girl had a love for unusual adventures: she would dash off to the bazaar and wander around all day long among traders, pickpockets and thieves—people in good suits with wide-legged trousers, knife grinders, booksellers, butchers and those vendors of rubbish who exist, it seems, in all cities across the globe, who all dress in the same black rags, speak many languages badly, and trade the kind of debris that not a soul needs; and nonetheless they live and generations change in their families, as if fate itself had destined them for just that trade and they could never be anything else,—in my eyes they personified a magnificent immutability; or she'd take off her stockings and

shoes and go barefoot in the garden after it had rained, and returning home would boast: "Mama, look, I've got black feet."]
(*Claire*, 55)

Gazdanov's style corresponded to the émigré concept of "Proustian"
language: only one critic suggested that his language was just a pastiche
of Proust's style.[86] Furthermore, the novelist insisted upon the validity
of his style, the style of a "new writer." Following Proust's rejection of a
linguistic canon, he problematized the notion of correct usage in his
novel. Gazdanov's narrator is convinced that he speaks correct Russian.
Those with whom Nikolai clashes over usage—military school instruc-
tors and high school teachers—belong to the generation of "fathers"
(*Claire*, 49, 52; *Kler*, 69, 72). This linguistic gap symbolizes other gaps between the war-separated generations that *Vecher u Kler* portrays.

Structurally, Gazdanov's text is much closer to the discursive and uneventful postwar adventure novel than to *La Recherche*. Proust preserved
only two traditional novelistic figures, scene and temporal ellipsis, eliminating summarizing narrative and descriptive pause. He broke the
rhythm of the novelistic canon in which summarizing narrative provided generalizing resumes of nondramatic time, linking scenes with intense dramatic action. Some smaller scenes in *La Recherche* possess the
value of dramatic concentration (Swann's and Odette's cattleya evening;
the death of Marcel's grandmother), but in large clusters action yields to
psychological and social characterization. Proust replaced the scene as
dramatic locus with a temporal unit that grouped chronologically diverse information. Digressions concealed dramatic action; explanatory
discourse invaded the narrative to justify the novel's originality.[87] The adventure novel and Gazdanov's *Vecher u Kler* were less radical vis-à-vis
the traditional figures. Preserving the summarizing narrative and linear chronology, they reduced dramatic action in favor of psychological
characterization.

Nikolai scorns external events, focusing on his own feelings about
"insignificant" details (*Claire*, 102; *Kler*, 121). His vision is conveyed by
the disproportionate place of discourse in his uneventful adventures.
Dramatic action is emphatically reduced, nonclimactic episodes are singled out by the narrative focus, and historical and geographical context
is almost absent (even the location of his hometown is imprecise). Some
émigrés saw this "modern" narrative structure as too artificial. Others
praised it as a contribution to the Russian literary tradition, for it combined artistic innovation with observance of émigré poetics: the author
spoke about the "most important" (spiritual life) without resorting to

such "tricks" as eventfulness, complex plot, or linguistic expressionism, peculiar to Soviet literature.[88]

Unlike Gazdanov and his French peers, Proust rallied against the realist myth that truth could be expressed literally (*Guermantes I*, 59). In Marcel's view the writer striving for truth cannot manipulate his material, whose unintentional discovery in his own psyche constitutes the artistic process. It is this absence of intent that gives involuntary memory its authenticity (187). Consciously chosen reminiscences are a bad painting marred by the conventions of voluntary memory (*Guermantes I*, 6; *Contre Sainte-Beuve*, 44–46). To convey the absence of intent, Proust observes no strict chronology, grouping unrelated events into temporal units that serve as focal points for multiple narratives.[89] These temporal units—Mme. de Villeparisis's reception (*Guermantes I*), a dinner at the duchess of Guermantes's (*Guermantes II*), the princess of Guermantes's reception (*Sodome et Gomorrhe I–II*) and matinee (*Temps retrouvé*)—occupy the greater part of *La Recherche*. Nikolai, on the contrary, tells his story chronologically, while claiming involuntary memory as his method. Critics reproached Gazdanov this mixture of Proustian investigation with conventional memoiristic discourse.[90] But he hardly saw this as a deviation from "Proustianism," following the narrative model of the French "neo-Proustian" adventure novel.

Nikolai's spirit of adventure, interest in self-study, and hatred of the fathers harked back to the French adventure novel, whose protagonists he evoked even by the age at which he received his war shock, at sixteen.[91] Contemporaries saw Nikolai's anxiety and dismissal of voluntary memory as markers of Proustianism, but few recognized the intermediary link between Nikolai and Marcel—the myth of the eternal return as interpreted by French writers.[92] Gazdanov shared the French moderns' interest in circular time. In "Rasskazy o svobodnom vremeni" (Stories about free time, 1927), he "graphically represented time as a series of concentric circles" (*Sobranie sochinenii*, 3: 30). In 1929 he shocked the audience of the Studio franco-russe by calling the Russian revolution an event of local importance, one of many that recur in history.[93] As Gazdanov was finishing his novel, Mark Slonim decried the proliferation of memoirs in the literature of émigré fathers unable to adapt to contemporary non-Russian life ("Molodye pisateli za rubezhom," 116). Gazdanov hardly wanted to contribute to memoir literature. Just as the French adventure novel was an antibildungsroman, Nikolai's memoirs were antimemoiristic.

Symptomatically, the fathers were irritated by the way Gazdanov treated the cultural past. Speaking about Nikolai's eclectic reading list

(Avvakum, Cervantes, Dostoevsky, Hume, Andersen, and Verbitskaia), K. Zaitsev wondered if "he had actually read these things," for "there was no link—logical or psychological—between his narrative and these treatises!"[94] But a link there certainly was. Like the protagonists of Soupault and Drieu, Nikolai evokes his reading list not to venerate tradition but to burn it. There are two types of books in his past. The first, comprising *Don Quixote*, adventure novels, and fairy tales gives him his taste for adventure and shows the way of escape from the past. The second type, the books of the fathers, merits oblivion. Similar to French anxious heroes, Nikolai has too much imagination as a child and spends his formative years in solitude.[95] Like Marcel, he denounces friendship as "external noise" that impedes his listening to the "soft, incessant noise of spiritual life" (*Claire*, 42; *Kler*, 61; cf. *Guermantes II*, 382–83, 385). His imagination is fueled by books. As a result, he stops distinguishing between Russia and foreign lands, assimilates "home" and "abroad" in one imaginary space, and becomes a "Russian foreigner" alien to both Russians and foreigners (*Claire*, 31–32, 110; *Kler*, 52, 128).

During the war Nikolai met refugees who "bemoaned, as they said, the past" and, according to him, "did not possess the art of remembering" (*Claire*, 123; *Kler*, 142). But they recollected banal and idealized external events like church holidays or material comfort. Nikolai calls them "prostitutki s vospominaniiami"—"whores with recollections" or "whores with memoirs" (*Claire*, 143; *Kler*, 143). In the context of émigré literary life, this appellation targeted the fathers and their art. At a meeting of the Studio franco-russe attended by Gazdanov, Vysheslavtsev said that prewar Russians "had also tasted life in the manner of Proust. Charming lyrical recollections, analysis of emotions, resuscitated musical phrases . . . this 'lost time' was our ordinary occupation" ("Proust et la Tragédie objective," 24). Tsvetaeva showed as much impatience for this "whore with memoirs" as did Gazdanov. For her, Proust's feat was in rediscovering life by writing, while older Russians had lost theirs by bragging ("Les Débat," 50–51).

The fathers are not skilled in the art of memory because their concept of reality is outdated. Nikolai cannot distinguish between external reality and the products of his imagination. Such perception—he calls it a "malady" (*Claire*, 27; *Kler*, 47–48)—makes him indifferent to external life and gives his "true" reality a solipsistic bent: "My inner life began to exist in spite of immediate events. . . . Those times of complete withdrawal into myself . . . returned to me like attacks of a fading but incurable illness" (*Claire*, 32; *Kler*, 52). Preferring imagination to external re-

ality, he is engrossed in self-cognition. He scrutinizes his "second existence" (*Claire*, 46; *Kler*, 66) with the "memory of senses," different from
voluntary memory, which he considers his most imperfect capacity
(*Claire*, 28; *Kler*, 48). Nikolai's two existences are mutually exclusive. He
cannot react immediately to events of the external world and perceives
them, inasmuch as they find reflections in his inner life. The "memory
of senses" takes him on a downward journey into his unconscious,
which he describes as "a distant and illusory region to which my imagination descended only rarely, and where I would find, as it were, a ge-
ological stratification of my history [*moei istorii*]" (*Claire*, 56; *Kler*, 76).

The expression *"moia istoriia"* is intentionally ambiguous, for it can
also stand for "my story," in which case the passage takes on a metade-
scriptive function, referring to the mode of textual production—an investigation into the creator's unconscious. This ambiguity evokes the
story/history of Marcel's literary vocation: "La vocation invisible dont
cet ouvrage est *l'histoire*" (The invisible vocation whose story is what the
present work is about, *Guermantes II*, 385, emphasis added). But what
Nikolai finds deep down in his psyche makes all the difference between
the ethos of his search versus the ethos of Marcel's. Investigating his unconscious life, Marcel finds there an unadulterated record of his past. As
for Nikolai, he finds the "ruins" of his past because he can reach the profound sources of his imagination only after a "severe shock" from the
outside destroys his imaginary reality, forcing him to the "bottom of
consciousness" in search of sources for reconstruction (*Claire*, 56; *Kler*,
76). This shock can be generated by a critical situation, such as Nikolai's
presence at the scene of a suicide; strong emotional experiences, as his
love for Claire or his participation in the war; or a new book that im-
presses itself upon the mind.

This periodic regeneration is the only means at Nikolai's disposal to
fight his fear of death, because religion is banished from his universe
(*Claire*, 38, 49, 57, 72, 87; *Kler*, 58, 69, 77, 91, 106). Since every inner crisis
throws him into the depths of his psychological life, this downward
journey brings Nikolai near the realm where dream and death meet.
The comings and goings of these destructive but regenerating shocks follow the "unknown laws of internal movement" (*Claire*, 56; *Kler*, 76),
evocative of the myth of the eternal return. Although Nikolai has no control over these shocks, he can anticipate them; hence the permanent sensation of anxiety that haunts him from childhood (*Claire*, 25, 31, 76; *Kler*,
45, 51, 95) and which he describes as standing on the verge of a precipice
(*Claire*, 42; *Kler*, 62), a metaphor commonly used in reference to "Euro-

pean Hamlets." The anticipation of a shock and the cult of inner crises force Nikolai to hurry their advent by a lifestyle of adventure. His first adult action is to join the White Army in the hopes that war experience will regenerate him (*Claire*, 101; *Kler*, 119–20). He receives the "greatest shock of his life" (*Claire*, 76; *Kler*, 95), which sends him on a journey across Europe in the footsteps of the heroes of the French adventure novel.

Nikolai defines this taste for adventure as thirst for knowledge and possession (*Claire*, 78; *Kler*, 97), tracing this thirst to his reading list, which gave him the role model of a romantic hero—a mosaic of knights, hunters, and pioneers against whose nebulous background the figure of Don Quixote stands out (*Claire*, 28–29, 31, 70; *Kler*, 49, 51, 90). The mad knight embodies and subverts romantic ideals in the confrontation of imaginary and external reality, because Nikolai is too "modern" to act out the role of a romantic hero in all seriousness. He is aware of the gap between the two worlds but chooses to forget about the existence of external reality (*Claire*, 78; *Kler*, 97), denying it the status of true reality and erasing his negative experience of the external world through periodic inner regeneration.

Engaging the external world, Nikolai is faithful to inner reality. Hunting sparrows with a "Monté-Cristo" rifle, whose name recalls literary adventures, he reenacts his imaginary life, conceived with a book in hand. This is shown by means of a grammatical parallelism. Having learnt to read, he cried for two days over the story of an orphan, prompting his father to say: "Vot, nauchili tak rano chitat' mal'chika" (*Kler*, 50) ("See what happens! You taught the boy to read so early" [*Claire*, 30]). The structure of this phrase is echoed by Nikolai's aunt after the hero's misadventures in a fruit garden: "Vot, pustili mal'chika v sad" (*Kler*, 80) ("See what happens! You're the one who let the boy into the garden" [*Claire*, 60]). Nothing changes in Nikolai's perception once he goes to war. The seemingly insignificant events upon which he dwells are significant in relation to his concepts of history and memory. Treating the facts of war as unimportant, he rejects the linear concept of history with its stress on the original and the unprecedented. That is why every event he describes is a variation of another, similar event from his past.

A case in point is the story of Nikolai's grandfather. The only survivor of his horse-stealing trade, the old man radically changed his ways after the Russians conquered the Caucasus. For someone who "remembered much" (*Claire*, 60; *Kler*, 80), this operation involved the renunciation of the past and the reconstruction of the present from a tabula rasa. His peers perished because of their inability to part with their past. The episode with the grandfather recalls an earlier episode in which the narrator watches the battle of a tarantula with ants. Stronger than his enemies, the spider could flee but remains on the battlefield and is drawn into the anthill. This scene suggests to Nikolai the existence of a hidden knowledge in his consciousness (*Claire*, 58–59; *Kler*, 78–79), a knowledge that saves his grandfather and makes Nikolai denounce the irreversibility of time. The tarantula perishes because it never retreats (*Claire*, 58; *Kler*, 78). The same is true for the "whores with memoirs"— they believe in irreversible history and perish under the burden of the past, which prevents adaptation to new conditions. To shake off this burden, one must go back and burn the past. This is the ethos of Nikolai's art of memory, opposed to Marcel's quest but identical to that of the French moderns.

The image of fighting against the external world haunts Nikolai. The tarantula scene recalls the scene in which a wounded wolf runs from dogs, stumbling as if a "horrible terrestrial force was trying to rivet him to one place." The narrator applies this image to himself. The same force

like a huge magnet, rivets me in my mental wanderings and pins me to the bed; and once again I could hear Nanny's weak voice reach me as if it were coming from another bank of an invisible blue river:

Oh, I don't see my beloved
In the village or in Moscow,
I only see my beloved
In the dark night, in a sweet dream. (*Claire*, 70; *Kler*, 89)

This river could be either the Styx, beyond which dream and death meet, or the stream of oblivion, Lethe, or a conflation of both. Nanny's song symbolizes "home," that arresting terrestrial force that burdens Nikolai with memories. For Nikolai, who often imagines himself a sailor, it is also a siren's song. He has long stopped distinguishing between home and abroad, merging them in one space for mental wanderings. Giving into the magnetic force of home means ossification and death. He thus looks for deliverance from the burden of memory and finds it in a foreign siren—Claire.

As the war begins, Nikolai's anxiety intensifies in the anticipation of a flight from home. Claire's apparition signals the imminence of a liberating event; her image absorbs his past and alludes to future deliverance: "Claire's black stockings, her laughter and her eyes united in an inhuman and bizarre image in which the fantastic was mixed with the real, and the memory of my childhood was mixed with the vague premonition of catastrophe" (*Claire,* 69; *Kler,* 89). Claire's foreignness fits Nikolai's desire to leave home for unknown lands and intensifies Nikolai's "malady" of confusing reality and imagination (*Claire,* 69, 77; *Kler,* 89, 96). Stimulating his imagination, she supports his space of mental wanderings and prevents its fragmentation into "home" and "abroad," helping him to forget the call from "another bank." In Paris the song of the foreign siren scandalizes Nikolai by its lack of profundity:

> C'est une chemise rose
> Avec une petite femme dedans,
> Fraîche comme la fleur éclose,
> Simple comme la fleur des champs.
> (*Kler,* 43)

⁓

> It is a pink blouse
> With a small woman inside,
> Fresh as a newly blossomed flower,
> Simple as a wildflower.
> (*Claire,* 23)

Denouncing it as a case of "French superficiality," Nikolai uses the émigré critical lexicon: "It lacks the most important" (my translation; "В этом не хватает самого главного" [*Claire,* 24; *Kler,* 44]). But he is irritated with himself for applying an argument from the arsenal of the fathers to the present, symbolized by a French woman whose song alludes to her affinity with Proust's "jeunes filles en fleurs." Claire's laughter in response to his diatribe makes him feel the ridiculousness of his position; she is a mirror in which he is ashamed to recognize his past.

In his daydreams Nikolai juxtaposes Nanny's song with the watercolor "Leda and the Swan" in Claire's bedroom and a knight resembling Don Quixote on her floor rug. He is drawn into Claire's magnetic field, becoming a satellite in her orbit alongside Nanny, the swan, and the knight (*Claire,* 69–70; *Kler,* 89–90). The sexual nature of Claire's magnetism is clear from its projection onto the story of Leda's possession by Zeus. The swan is a three-tiered allusion. It refers to Proust's Swann, whose name, thanks to Odette's Anglophilia, was pronounced *à l'anglaise.* By extension it is a reference to Marcel's philosophy of love. Second, it is an allusion to Baudelaire's poem "Le Cygne," whose leitmotifs of memory and exile and dedication to the émigré Hugo foreshadow Nikolai's future in the combination of Parisian exile and unremitting desire. Baudelaire's narrator elaborates the image of a swan in the streets of Paris as a metaphor for an émigré in a foreign land:

> Aussi devant ce Louvre une image m'opprime:
> Je pense à mon grand cygne, avec ses gestes fous;
> Comme les exilés, ridicule et sublime,
> Et rongé d'un désir sans trêve!
> (*Les Fleurs du mal*, 60)

> [Thus, an image oppresses me in front of the Louvre:
> I am thinking of my big swan with his crazy movements;
> Similar to the exiles, ridiculous and sublime,
> And devoured by relentless desire.]

Finally, Nikolai draws on H. C. Andersen, whom he evokes as part of his reading list. In "The Wild Swans," Andersen tells the story of eleven princes exiled from home by their stepmother, who turns them into swans without voices. They are humans only by night and live beyond the sea. The brothers are delivered by their sister, who weaves coats of mail that give them "new skin" and make them permanently human. The youngest brother keeps a swan's wing in place of an arm, for one sleeve was wanting in his coat. The tale does not say whether the siblings return home: by their own admission, their new country is as beautiful as the one they left behind (*Andersen's Fairy Tales*, 199). The image of a swan without a voice describes the situation of an émigré writer; so does a bulky swan's wing in lieu of a better writing instrument—a hand. The dichotomy of two women, one delivering the swans from the spell of another, evokes Nikolai's home and foreign sirens. The fact that the men are delivered in exile suggests another parallel with Nikolai and Claire. The image of a prince with a wing conveys the tension between memory and happiness that an "émigré Hamlet," *Prince* Hamlet's progeny, found in Paris. Finally, the state of being human (oneself) by night recalls Nikolai's exile from daily reality into inner life ("night").

The image of Don Quixote is also a complex signifier. It symbolizes the conflict of imagination and the external world, in which the quest for a fair lady may lead to a pigsty. But it also recalls Turgenev's speech "Hamlet and Don Quixote"—part of the school curriculum in Russia. The association of these names was reinforced by the émigré critical discourse that used the concept of "émigré Hamlet," applicable to Nikolai. The coupling of Hamlet and Don Quixote projects Nikolai's love on Turgenev's model. For Turgenev, Don Quixote and Hamlet embodied two basic and opposed types of the human relation to an ideal. Don Quixote is the epitome of faith—he values life so long as it can be the means of attaining his ideal. Hamlet is a symbol of egocentric skepticism—his rationality precludes faith and puts his ideal in the service of self-contemplation ("Gamlet i Don Kikhot," in *Polnoe sobranie sochinenii i pisem*, 8: 173–75). Nikolai's love for Claire unites both trends. On one hand, Nikolai's life is devoted to a meeting with Claire. On the other hand, he uses Claire very rationally to the end of personal deliverance.

The quixotic conflict of imagination and reality is pivotal to Marcel's philosophy of love. He realizes that names refer to images rather than objects. That is why real Balbec and Florence do not correspond to their names (*Swann*, 380–81), and people "perish" if Marcel approaches them (*Guermantes I*, 4–5). To rescue the name and the image, he keeps aloof from "external reality" (*Guermantes II*, 550–51). For Marcel, carnal desire and traveling, women and places, are united by this split between the object and its image.[96] He perpetuates this discrepancy through a resolution to consider inner life, where imagination reigns, as true reality. Consequently, his, Swann's, and Saint-Loup's affairs are a chase after an imaginary construct; the lovers are aware of the gap between the imperfect object and its perfect image.[97] Swann loves Odette for her resemblance to Zephora in a Sistine Chapel fresco (*Swann*, 219, 221, 237, 242); Marcel values his objects of desire as stimuli for imagination, viewing their actual qualities as unimportant: "Let us leave pretty women to men without imagination" (*Albertine disparue*, 23). Distance between the woman and her image must be preserved in order not to upset the lover's imagination and ruin his interest in the desired object (*Guermantes I*, 5, 28; *Sodome et Gomorrhe II*, 138, 511).

Claire shares the flaws of Proustian women: she has bad taste in art; she is not as young and attractive as she used to be; she is deceptive and "easy," giving Nikolai reasons for jealousy. She also shares in the fragmented personality of Proust's heroines, appearing in multiple and contradictory personae (*Claire*, 25, 68–69; *Kler*, 45, 88). This fragmentation is literally realized in Nikolai's delirium, when Claire's body is brought to him in pieces (*Claire*, 70–71; *Kler*, 90). And yet he consciously constructs an idealized image of his beloved and spends ten years chasing it because his inner equilibrium requires an image functioning as a comprehensive amalgam of the past he needs to "burn." Gazdanov draws this addition to Marcel's philosophy of love—the use of women to the end of psychological deliverance—from the French introspective novel. To possess the object is to eliminate its distance from the image, killing love. For Proust's characters this creates tension between the desire for possession and the awareness that it will ruin the image: "One loves only those things in which he pursues something inaccessible, one loves only that which he does not possess" (*Prisonnière*, 369–70). Nikolai ignores this tension because the destruction of Claire's image is his goal.

Nikolai's object of desire has the advantage of being foreign. His quest for possession physically removes him from home. "I saw France," says Nikolai, "I had often imagined Claire and myself there, but the echoes and images of my former life did not reach there, as if they ran into an invisible wall of air" (*Claire*, 133; *Kler*, 152). The consummation of desire will kill the remains of the memories from "another bank," restoring equilibrium in his imaginary space for mental wanderings. Aboard a ship to Turkey, he realizes that his exile is, in fact, liberation: "'But Claire is French,' I suddenly remembered. 'And if this is so, then why was there this perpetual and anxious sorrow about the snow and the green planes and all those many lives which I had lived in a country which has disappeared behind a fiery curtain?' And I began to dream of how I would meet Claire in Paris" (*Claire*, 133; *Kler*, 152).

Their meeting in Paris is a second chance to consummate Nikolai's desire. In Kislovodsk, Claire tried to seduce him, but he resisted for fear of breaking Claire's image (*Claire*, 75–76; *Kler*, 94–95). During their second meeting he is ready to forget what remains of the song from "another bank." The operation involving the death of his guiding star and of the past she symbolizes fills Nikolai with nostalgia. He prolongs the moment preceding physical possession, as did Swann, who looked at Odette's face as if it were a landscape he was leaving forever.[98] Having consummated his ideal, Nikolai mourns "the end and approaching death of love" (*Claire*, 26; *Kler*, 46). He can no longer dream about Claire and proceeds to the final review of the memories amalgamated in her image. He feels the recession of memory in the impossibility of understanding and expressing the "endless succession of ideas, impressions and sensations" that led him to this moment in his life (*Claire*, 27; *Kler*, 47). The disintegration of Claire's image exposes to the light of day the film of memory, developed but not fixed, and the contents of its frames are disappearing forever in the hero's hands.

Nikolai's civil war experience culminated in his journey to the south with the retreating White Army. Recalling this journey, Nikolai observes that he never regretted leaving people and countries behind because he was doomed to carry along their images until the time of his "[l]ast deathly voyage, the slow fall into the black abyss . . . so long that while I am falling I will have time to forget about everything that I have seen

and remembered and felt and loved; and when I have forgotten everything that I have loved, then I will die" (*Claire*, 118; *Kler*, 137).

Yet he forgets the love of his life in the very beginning of the novel, as
if confirming the regenerating nature of this "death." The black abyss
may be the realm of the unconscious, where Nikolai descends in search
of regeneration. The key to the nature of his "death" may be hidden in
the last frame of the exposed film of memory.

Leaving the Russian coast, Nikolai hears a ship bell beat out time, a
sound that recalls the protracted and high-pitched resonance of a vi-
brating saw ("protiazhnyi i vibriruiushchii, kak zvuk zadrozhavshei
pily," "dolgii zvon drozhashchei pily," *Kler*, 153 [Claire, 134]). This sound
harks back to the time when, as a child, Nikolai was lured to an open
window by men sawing wood with "prolonged, metallic ringing that
was very delicate and clear" (*Claire*, 29; *Kler*, 49). He was narrowly saved
from falling down four stories. This first shock of his life remained his
only recollection of early childhood. The sound, recurring in the pivotal
moments of Nikolai's life, introduces a web of intertextual allusions explaining the meaning of his trip across the Black Sea at night—his literal fall into the black abyss.

The narrator of Alexander Blok's poem "Starost' mertvaia brodit
vokrug" (1905) is sawing a dormer at sunset, accompanying the arrival
of darkness with the yelping sounds of a saw (*Sobranie sochinenii v vos' mi
tomakh*, 2: 73). His physical elevation and desire to break free through a
window recall Nikolai's near-death experience. Blok metaphorizes the
setting of the sun as the departure of a ship that takes the narrator into
darkness. The poem contains all the elements of Nikolai's journey to the
south: departure into a sea at night (or the sea of night); the high-pitched
sound of a saw that symbolizes the severing of ties with the abandoned
land. The night sea may also be a metaphor for the unconscious state of
a dreamer or for death itself.

In the same year, Blok wrote another poem where departure was
marked by a high-pitched sound. In "Utikhaet svetlyi veter," the sound
of a "sleepy string" echoes a girl's farewell to her beloved, who leaves at
night for a "foreign and dark land." Central to her monologue is the
theme of memory: she asks him not to banish her image when he is
happy with another girl. The poem recalls the song of Nikolai's nanny
by its female narrative voice, motifs of parting and of night and dreams
as meeting places, meter (four-feet trochee), rhyming pattern (*aBaB*),
and the ultimate position of the word "dream":

В стороне чужой и темной
Как ты вспомнишь обо мне?
О моей любови скромной
Закручинишься ль во сне?
(Blok, *Sobranie sochinenii*, 2: 82)

Ах, не вижу я милова
Ни в деревне, ни в Москве,
Только вижу я милова
В темной ночке да в сладком сне.
(Gazdanov, *Kler*, 89)

[In a strange and dark land
How will you remember me?
For my modest love
Will you grieve in your dream?]

[Oh, I don't see my beloved
In the village or in Moscow,
I only see my beloved
In the dark night, in a sweet dream.]
(*Claire*, 70)

Blok's poem evokes the last journey into the night of a Serbian warrior, killed by a Turk, from Pushkin's poem "Pokhoronnaia pesnia Iakinfa Maglanovicha."[99] Incidentally, in his voyage Nikolai is headed for Turkey. Extended to Pushkin, the allusion embraces the novel's epigraph and links the novel's beginning and ending in a circle. Tatiana's letter to Onegin shares with Blok's poem and Nanny's song a female narrative voice and the motif of separation overcome only in dreams.[100] This subtext connects Onegin, a Russian Childe Harold afflicted by the Romantic "malady," to Nikolai—a "new child of the century."

In Blok's poem "Vzmor'e" (1904), the motif of departure once again brings about a long and high-pitched sound: a departing ship is accompanied by the voices of sirens, a burdensome sound (*tiagostnyi zvuk*) of death (*Sobranie sochinenii*, 2: 39). Thus, leaving for the land where he will be "happy with another girl," Nikolai hears his home siren's song. She is afraid that he will forget her, but oblivion is his goal in crossing the Lethe-Styx of the Black Sea.

The deadly ambiguity of his voyage is further informed by Blok's poems. In "Poslednii put'" (1907), ships that leave a snowy coast into the night are called back by a woman "chained in snow." But her call is dangerous: those who step on the "snowy path" never leave it, it is their last journey ("I na etot put' osnezhennyi / Esli vstanesh'—ne soidesh'" [And on that snowy path / Should you step—you will never leave [it], *Sobranie sochinenii*, 2: 214]). In "Poslednee naputstvie" (1914), the call of the home siren is countered by the call of a siren from another bank. One can read this poem as describing physical death, a voyage from suffering to peace, or as spiritual death and subsequent regeneration. As the traveler's ship passes the people and cities from his past, a female voice encircles him with a crystal sound that touches his heart like a tender violin. Once this "light terrestrial music" ("legkaia muzyka zemli") stops tormenting the traveler (cf. the "terrestrial force" arresting Nikolai's wanderings), his beloved leads him to the Elysian fields:

> А когда пройдет все мимо,
> Чем тревожила земля,
> Та, кого любил ты много,
> Поведет рукой любимой
> В Елисейские поля.
>   (*Sobranie sochinenii,* 3: 272–73)

❧

> [And when passes by all
> That troubled you on earth,
> She, whom you loved so much,
> Will lead you with a beloved hand
> To the Elysian fields.]

Choosing between two last journeys, Nikolai abandons the dangerous snowy path of Russia (cf. his "anxious sorrow about the snow . . . in a country which has disappeared behind a fiery curtain," *Claire* 133; *Kler,* 152), opting for the regenerating death at the hands of his foreign siren in Paris—the only city in the world that has the Elysian Fields. It is these fields that Claire mentions in her tune: "C'est une chemise rose / Avec une petite femme dedans, / Fraîche comme la fleur éclose, / Simple comme la fleur des *champs*" ("It is a pink blouse / With a small woman inside, / Fresh as a newly blossomed flower, / Simple as a wildflower," *Kler,* 43; *Claire,* 23, emphasis added).

Émigré critics disregarded the Russian literary subtexts in Gazdanov's novel, concentrating on its neo-Proustian nature. Slonim observed that Gazdanov's novel lacked detailed psychological analysis— the core of "Proustianism" ("Literaturnyi dnevnik," 456). Indeed, without engaging in analysis, Nikolai only says that he conducts it. By permeating his text with markers echoing contemporary debates on psychologism in literature ("bottom of consciousness," "psychological depth," "descent into oneself"), Gazdanov creates the impression of kinship with Proust. The same device is used for the novel's language: stylistic markers drawn from critical discussions associate it with the style of *La Recherche.* "Proustianism" does not appear essential to the novel's structure. After the initial response, critics began to qualify Gazdanov's "Proustianism" as a coquettish bow to fashion.[101] This criticism alone would not have convinced Gazdanov to abandon his "flirtation with Proust"—his provocative stance toward the émigré literary establishment dictated that he treat its opinions *à rebours*. One can explain his prompt departure from the "Proustian" style and thematics, obvious in 1931, as a result of the French anti-Proustian reaction of the early 1930s, which culminated in *Voyage au bout de la nuit*. Gazdanov figured among Céline's first émigré admirers.[102]

On Artistic Faithfulness: Iurii Fel'zen's "Roman s Pisatelem"

In the year of Gazdanov's "Proustian" fame another writer received the title of *prustianets*. This was Nikolai Berngardovich Freudenstein (1894–1943), alias "Iurii Fel'zen," who also debuted in émigré letters in 1926. Fel'zen wrote three novels united by one narrator, set of characters, and style. *Obman* (Deceit) appeared in 1930, *Schast'e* (Happiness) in 1932, and *Pis'ma o Lermontove* (Letters about Lermontov) in 1935. A number of Fel'zen's stories share the common traits of his novels.[103] Along with the novels, they are part of a text modeled after *La Recherche*. Fel'zen wanted to unite his works in a larger "Novel" titled as "effectively" as *À la Recherche du temps perdu* (Ianovskii, *Polia Eliseiskie*, 36). He may have found such a title in 1938, naming a story, acclaimed as his best piece to date, "Povtorenie proidennogo."[104] This phrase means both the "revision of the walked path" (including life itself) and the "revision of the covered material," in reference to the "Novel's" segments, which one must revisit in order to close the narrative circle, as does Marcel in *Le Temps retrouvé*. Deported to Auschwitz, Fel'zen left his novelistic project unfinished.

Gazdanov once argued that young émigré letters had only two gifted writers, Nabokov and Fel'zen. Nabokov was frequently compared to Gazdanov and Fel'zen in connection with Proust's influence on Russian exiles. In his attack on Nabokov, Ivanov cited them as good users of French models. Varshavskii criticized Nabokov's "smooth style" and "brilliant success" for concealing a spiritual void, evident by opposition to the "obscure tongue-tie" (*temnoe kosnoiazychie*) of his peers—a reference, among others, to *prustiantsy*. Nabokov did not live up to the formula Varshavskii attributed to Proust: "One is fond of those writers in whom he can recognize himself."[105] Nabokov answered his critics with a literary parody in which *prustiantsy* recognized themselves.

The protagonist of Nabokov's novel *Kamera obskura* (1932–33; translated as *Laughter in the Dark*, 1938), the art critic Bruno Krechmar, gets involved with Magda Peters, leaves his family, and, in the company of a business associate Robert Gorn, takes Magda to France. He is ignorant of Magda's affair with Gorn. In France, as Magda and Gorn board a train, Krechmar sees his acquaintance, the writer Zegel'krants—a German expatriate and a Proustian. Krechmar runs late and has to ride in a different car. The writer takes a seat next to Magda, without knowing who she is, and records his observations of Magda's and Gorn's conspicuous liaison as material for a new project. When Krechmar meets Zegel'krants again, the writer reads an excerpt from his new novel, opening Krechmar's eyes to Magda's affair.

Zegel'krants cultivates solitude, observation, and oversensitivity, writing "strange, complicated, and ductile" prose (*Kamera obskura*, 354, 360). His new book is a three-hundred-page novel about a visit to a dentist. "Proustian" uneventful discursivity is thus likened to pulling teeth. Zegel'krants's long and complex sentences contrast with the economical style of *Kamera obskura*. J. B. Foster interpreted this episode as a "pastiche of Proust's style, which perhaps betrays an anxiety of influence or at least some initial hostility toward Proust on Nabokov's part" (*Nabokov's Art of Memory and European Modernism*, 76). The critic, however, does not explain why Nabokov eliminated all allusions to Proust in the English version of his novel and changed Zegel'krants's name to Udo Conrad. What the English-speaking audience would have perceived as a spoof on Proust, the Russian émigré reader immediately saw as a mockery of expatriate *prustiantsy* (Osorgin, "V. Sirin," 459).

Zegel'krants's style evokes not *La Recherche* but Gazdanov's "Proustian" periods, which often combine two autonomous sentences with one shattering the semantic structure of another.[106] Zegel'krants's German name alludes to Fel'zen, who signed his articles and was mentioned in reviews by his real surname of Germanic origin, spelled and pronounced in Russian "Freidenshtein."[107] "Zegel'" evokes "Fel'zen" thanks to three shared phonemes: /e/, /z/, and palatalized /l/. "Krants" evokes the name of Hamlet's friend "Rosenkrantz," which Magda uses in lieu of "Zegel'krants," while Shakespeare is mentioned in the same episode (*Kamera obskura*, 362, 364). Usually pronounced together, the names of "Rosenkrantz and Gildenstern" evoke "Zegel' krants and Freidenshtein," especially since in Russian /stern/ becomes /shtern/. The inevitable reminiscence of Prince Hamlet recalls the Paris School description of its adepts as "émigré Hamlets." Despite a stylistic echo from Gazdanov, Fel'zen appears as the main target of Nabokov's parody.

Zegel'krants's narrative lacks compositional rigor. It is this want of a distinct plot for which Nabokov reproaches Fel'zen. His critique is clear in the contrast of Zegel'krants's novel with the larger structure of *Kamera obskura*. But while all dramatis personae of the episode are related to art (Krechmar as a critic, Magda as a cinema employee, Gorn as a cartoonist), Zegel'krants is the only true artist and decent person among them. Nabokov pays tribute to his attention to details: unlike Krechmar, Zegel'krants is not "blind." But compositional shapelessness undermines his method: for Nabokov, the meaning of details is fully conveyed in a rigorously organized narrative. Surprised by Krechmar's reaction to his novel, Zegel'krants realizes that his method lacks insight because he is not in full control of his material; he "mimicks life slavishly . . . without the distance and distortion that Nabokov deemed essential to art" (Weiner, *By Authors Possessed*, 212). Thus, when Krechmar goes blind in a car accident, Zegel'krants takes blame for this tragedy and suffers an artistic crisis.[108]

Nabokov's criticism of Fel'zen was not hostile, probably because both writers subscribed to Proust's denunciation of referential illusion. Evolution away from referential illusion constitutes the story/history of the literary vocation of Fel'zen's hero. Unlike Gazdanov, Fel'zen shared Proust's view of language as an imperfect tool, whose lack of precision required steadfast approximation (*Schast'e*, 152). Seen as striving for truth, Fel'zen's "Proustian" style provoked contradictory responses. Some found it too complex; others found it simple in contrast to Soviet "literary pretension." But the syntactic complexity and agrammaticality of Fel'zen's language were seen favorably: this was not imitation but spiritual affinity, which attested to the disciple's independence from his teacher.[109] Despite his familiarity with the text of *La Recherche*, Fel'zen bowed to the common view of Proust's style, as if fearing that otherwise readers would not recognize his "Proustianism." Long and complex periods dominate his works conceived as parts of the larger "Novel."

Engrossed in approximating elaboration, Fel'zen's narrator uses bulky hyphenated adjectives and adverbs.[110] Their frequent recurrence creates the impression that he slights the esthetic side of writing. In search of precision, Fel'zen's narrator invents new words.[111] Like Marcel, he uses approximating parenthetical digressions that blow up his sentences to shocking proportions. The syntax of Fel'zen's periods is giddily tangled, but, unlike Gazdanov's, they cannot be broken up into autonomous sentences without semantic loss. What may appear as a lack of stylistic mastery is, in fact, careful calculation:

Выбрал темно-красные розы, мокрые, свежие, еще свернутые на неестественно-прямых, поддержанных проволокой стеблях, и это было первое, что перенесло Лелю из воображаемой жизни в живую, первое, чем мое отношение к ней меня самого тронуло, какое-то обещание доброты, сразу обязавшее к доказательствам новым и непрерывным: точно также и всякие наши трогательно-прочные к людям отношения—длительная верность, бескорыстная саможертвенная заботливость, просто милое внимание—нередко начинаются с какого-нибудь случайно-капризного поступка, и потом уже нами руководят различные полусознательные соображения (умиленность перед собой, привычка к чужой благодарности, боязнь разочаровать, иногда несносная и скучная обязанность), поддерживающие нашу доброту, но еле связанные с первоначальной причиной—вероятно, многие из нас не помнят, почему оставляют в кафэ одному лакею вдвое больше, чем всем другим, и считают себя вынужденными своего предпочтения не менять.

[I chose dark-red roses, wet, fresh, still unopened, on unnaturally straight stems supported by wire, and this, for the first time, transported Lëlia from imaginary life into the real one, the first thing through which my own relation to her moved me, some promise of kindness, which immediately obliged me to produce new and incessant proofs: in the same way that our touchingly-committed relations to other people—long faithfulness, altruistic self-sacrificial concern, or merely charming attention—rather often begin with some randomly capricious acts, and only later we follow various half-conscious considerations (self-adoration, habit for expressions of gratitude, fear to disappoint, and, at times, intolerable and tedious obligation) that support our kindness but are barely linked to the original reason—many of us probably do not recall why they give to one café waiter twice as much tip as to all others and feel obliged not to change this preference of theirs.] (*Obman*, 29)

Fel'zen's violation of syntactic and lexical usage in search of precision, his invention of "odd" words and phrases are emphasized in the text of the "Novel" as conscious and intentional. His narrator insists on this point. Addressing his beloved in a diary, he claims his right to break the existing language, frustrating in its imprecision, for "by cowardly surrendering to language we sin both against human dignity and purpose in life. All this requires slow and passionate work on each word: let our word combinations be uncouth and gauche—at least we will express what we indeed want to say" (*Schast'e*, 69).

Émigré critics observed that Fel'zen's style was intentionally dull, lacking Proustian expressiveness.[112] Indeed, Fel'zen refused the metaphorization of discourse, which was an important part of Marcel's method (*Temps retrouvé,* 198). He fled bright metaphors that, from his vantage point, characterized Soviet literature and were "insincere."[113] Filtered through the lens of émigré poetics, the French interpretation of Proust's style as a reaction to the dead literary language of the fathers became in the eyes of "émigré Hamlets" a rebellion against the traditional "smoothness" of French writing. The same function was extended to Fel'zen's language. It contrasted with the "polished" style of the average French work and the "linguistic pretension" of Soviet art; decrying Fel'zen's "abuses," critics admitted that they constituted a style inherent to his artistic vision and philosophy.[114]

The émigré ancients saw Fel'zen's oeuvre as tedious and tortured, while the moderns cited it as exemplary of the "new sensibility" and émigré modernism, which rejected formal success for the sake of profundity and strove for imperfect but responsible literature.[115] While Gazdanov's case is interesting in that he had no firsthand knowledge of Proust, Fel'zen's link to Proust, based on thorough familiarity with *La Recherche,* is a striking example of an émigré's artistic self-fashioning after a French model. Fel'zen called this self-fashioning "roman s pisatelem," referring to the main preoccupation of his oeuvre and its source of inspiration (*Pis'ma,* 22–24). Since in Russian *roman* means both a novel and a love affair, the expression can be read as "a novel with/ about a writer" and as "an affair/liaison with a writer." The former alludes to the central position allotted in Fel'zen's "Novel" to the figure of its creator, making it a story of literary vocation. This trait links Fel'zen's oeuvre to *La Recherche* and distinguishes it from Gazdanov's "Proustianism."

Proust's novel is a story about writing whose hero describes the maturation of his vocation and resolves to write a novel about his own artistic coming of age. Deciding to devote his life to art that will recapture lost time, Marcel postulates this art as difficult and laborious because of constant transformations in the objects of observation (*Temps retrouvé,* 177, 206, 337); this art requires the great effort of tracing the reflections of images by means of memory and tends toward scientific precision (*Jeunes filles,* 478–79). Informed by scientific ethos, the notion of artistic gift acquires new meaning in Proust's novel. Since the narrator of *La Recherche* extracts artistic material from his own psyche, he thinks that the writer's imaginative capacity is replaceable by psychological intu-

ition (*Temps retrouvé*, 207). Hence Proust's conclusion that scientific vocation in a novelist is equivalent to artistic gift (*Sainte-Beuve*, 307). In this
context Fel'zen's self-description—"I do not have a gift. But I have a calling"—indicates the source of his artistic position and explains his ideal
of imaginative minimalism, as demonstrated by the repetitive plots of
his novels.[116]

Fel'zen's plots draw on Proust's philosophy of love: a writer's pro-
ductivity is directly proportional to the pain inflicted by a love interest.
In *Obman* an émigré, Volodia, falls in love with an émigrée, Elena Gerd
or Lëlia. She leaves him for a lover in Berlin and later gets involved with
Volodia's friend Bobka, whose departure restores the relationship. The
truce is crowned by a session of mutual analysis. In *Schast'e* the schema
repeats: Volodia's bliss alternates with jealousy, as Lëlia is involved with
his friend Shura. The suicide of her admirer, Mark Osipovich, brings her
back to Volodia. Peace is inaugurated by a session of analysis. In *Pis'ma
o Lermontove*, an epistolary novel chronologically anticipating developments in *Schast'e*, Volodia writes to Lëlia in Cannes, sparking her jealousy—she sees that he loves art more than her.[117] The ensuing mutual
analysis brings peace to the relationship. Stories related to the "Novel"
are mostly episodes in Volodia's jealousy.

Fel'zen insisted that plot and dramatic action were only pretexts for
Volodia's self-study, in which scenes with "insignificant conflicts"
(*Schast'e*, 59) were literary tricks for which Volodia apologized ("I pur-
posely use short 'effective' segments" [*Schast'e*, 66]). It comes as no surprise that the émigré moderns and Fel'zen himself justified such a narrative approach by the uneventful psychologism in French literature,
which upheld Fel'zen's contempt for the elaborate plot and dramatic action.[118] His own "Novel" drew on such features of the French introspective novel as uneventfulness; diary form; metareflection; and the use of
love as a metaphor for one's artistic method.

Initially, Fel'zen was enamored with the ideal of "truthful" literature
and convinced that art must be "serious, candid, and free of invention."[119] But under Proust's influence, he began to doubt the possibility
of "truthful" writing. These doubts are manifest in the shifts of narrative mode, as he attempts to achieve literary "sincerity." *Obman* is a diary whose narrator relates his inner life in indirect speech, modeled on
that of Marcel down to the vacillation from the subjective "I" to the generalizing "we."[120] Here Volodia writes for himself and resists the temptation of finding a reader (73, 175). *Schast'e* is also a diary but the narrator has an addressee, Lëlia, and thinks that she or another might read

his notes some day (8). He thus establishes an audience that will choose
to treat his text as a diary or a novel. *Pis'ma* is a throwback to documentary motivation, as if Fel'zen feared to have come too close to literary fiction in *Schast'e:* Volodia writes confessional letters to Lëlia. This tension
between the desire to write a document and what Fel'zen describes as
a "persistently-passionate need for creative activity" runs through the
"Novel" ("Probuzhdenie," 154).

The writer makes his protagonist a transparent adaptation of himself
(by age, social status, occupation) but gives him a fictional name. Volodia stresses that his method relies on the documentary recording of life,
while Fel'zen admits that Lëlia is "pure chemistry." Denouncing imagination as insincerity, Fel'zen debunks Sharshun for replacing art with
life in a novel that looks like a real diary rather than a "responsible literary form."[121] Critics added to this tension, seeing Fel'zen's writings as
an attempt to rejuvenate literary conventions; some treated his novels
as literary experiments in "truthfulness," as a self-imposed task doomed
to artistic failure.[122] But no notion was more prestigious in the Paris
School than the artistic failure of a writer in search of "truthfulness" and
"sincerity."

Contradictions between the ideal of sincerity and the fact of fiction
are finally resolved in the concept of true reality passed down from
Proust. Volodia lives in inner reality and loves Lëlia's image rather than
its referent. His Lëlia is an artificial construct (*Obman*, 73). He falls in love
with her image long before meeting Lëlia in person (*Obman*, 59–60). The
incompatibility of the prototype and its image constitutes the "deceit"
of Volodia's love. The source of contradiction between sincerity and fiction resides in the fact that Volodia cannot decide which reality is truer.
The definition of true reality is for him, as for Marcel, the most important ingredient in the maturation of his literary vocation. Volodia's hesitation regarding two versions of reality and, consequently, the relationship between art and life is reflected in his lucid view of his own
artistic method.

Volodia knows that the task of "sincerity" strips his writings of esthetic value. He curses his method as boring, dead, uninspired, and
naively serious (*Obman*, 20, 58, 182; *Schast'e*, 71; *Pis'ma*, 42), echoing Marcel's view of art as self-sacrificial labor. Seeing creative activity as intense labor and struggle with oneself (*Schast'e*, 84), he describes his own
writing as "creativity through refusal" ("tvorchestvo cherez otkaz," *Obman*, 190), which rejects artistic conventions, devices, imagination, inspiration, and success. But he dreams that one day he will go from di-

ary work to more imaginative writing. Like Marcel, he cherishes the idea
of a novel, an "imaginary novel" ("voobrazhaemyi roman," *Obman*, 19)
he would write had he not been committed to "sincerity" in order to stay
"faithful (even in failure) to some human calling" (*Obman*, 220). This
calling is the backbone of his vocation, but it contains a contradiction:
requiring "truthfulness," it runs counter to Volodia's vocation to write
an "imaginary novel" with fictional characters and events. Reconcilia-
tion comes when Volodia reaches that level of artistic maturity where the
tension between inner and external lives is resolved in favor of inner reality as unquestionably truer.

Volodia arrives at this decision in one of the last published parts of
Fel'zen's "Novel," the story "Kompozitsiia" (Composition). Like Gazdanov's Nikolai, he reminisces about his first love at a Russian summer
resort. But thematic kinship ends at the lovers' meeting abroad. For
Nikolai, this rendezvous shatters Claire's image; but when Volodia
meets Tonia in Berlin, nothing happens: only a "compositional miracle
of life" ("chudo zhiteiskoi kompozitsii") could resurrect his lost passion
("Kompozitsiia," 108). He is aware that their meeting smacks of a trite
plot from a psychological novel (109)—an allusion not only to *Vecher u
Kler* but also to Nabokov's *Mashen'ka* (1926; translated as *Mary*, 1970).
Leaving Berlin, Volodia receives flowers; he knows that they were sent
by another woman, but he could convince himself that they came from
Tonia, rounding up the tale "impressively and elegantly," like a "ready-
made story with stock vocabulary" (112). His artistic truthfulness does
not permit such effects in life. Volodia sees that his reminiscences were
shaped by literary clichés: on second thought, Tonia was not his first
love. He realizes that he "composed" his life, following the very literary
commonplaces he eschewed in writing. He concludes that inner life is
the only true reality, while its notation in writing could be liberated from
the falsehood of conventions: "It seems to me that only in art (where we
are stronger and more courageous than in life, at least spiritually and
creatively) we can overcome ourselves, get rid of necessary conventions,
and become fully free, the way we would be in life, if we did not want
to control and slightly compose it" (113).

Hence follows Volodia's decision that "art is life," linking his artistic
method to Marcel's esthetics. Like that of Marcel, Volodia's "imaginary
novel" has already been written. In his letters and diaries his own image is much closer to the ideal he wanted to express in the novel than to
his external self, whose conduct followed automatized conventions.

The story of Volodia's literary vocation is inseparable from his and

Fel'zen's own romance with Proust's "victorious martyrdom" (*Pis'ma*, 28–29). Volodia's choice of models is dictated by his place as an émigré who opposes dehumanizing collectivism and ideological pressure in Soviet literature. He cites Proust and the French introspective novel as his models—both human and modern in contrast to Soviet, machine-dominated but provincial, culture (*Schast'e*, 56; "Vozvrashchenie," 178). Volodia reiterates Fel'zen's own position, which earned him renown as the most un-Soviet émigré writer (Kel'berin, "Iurii Fel'zen," 184). Fel'zen described his own creative activity as "the cult of the individual and love in contrast to the Bolshevik crudeness and dissolution in the collective" ("Avtobiografiia," 121). French models taught the Russians "the genuine sincerity of tone, lack of special effects and embellishments, and seriousness of world-view"—the qualities marked in the émigré poetics as meritorious and hushed in Soviet literature "by Maiakovskii's drumbeat and Gor'kii's official optimism" ("My v Evrope," 155).

Volodia's artistic maturation is steeped in the vicissitudes of the "new malady." He fashions himself as an "émigré Hamlet"—a disoriented, introverted, and isolated being, and a failure in art and life (*Obman*, 83, 150; *Pis'ma*, 17–20, 76). In *Pis'ma* Volodia projects his own image as an aspiring writer upon those of Lermontov and Proust, creating the ideal writer-hero of his "imaginary novel." This combination comes from Fel'zen's belief that younger émigrés cannot rely on the Russian literary tradition alone to describe "their time." Considering Proust as the father of the modern psychological novel and Lermontov as that of the Russian psychological novel, Fel'zen alludes to his affinity with Lermontov by describing his own writings as "neoromantic."[123] The author of *Hero of Our Time*, whose protagonist, Pechorin, exemplifies a Russian "child of the century," links "new children" to their Romantic prototypes. Critics indeed saw references to Lermontov as confirming Volodia's and Fel'zen's own status as "new children of the century."[124]

Lermontov helps Volodia formulate the Russian element of his artistic method. He grounds Lermontov's image in the mythology of the "new malady" and "composes" it in accordance with his own ideal of a writer (*Pis'ma*, 47, 113). His Lermontov is a social failure and an unfortunate lover; an imperfect but sincere writer; an anxious child of his century; and an isolated self-analyst who is more attuned to "new sensibility" than Pushkin. One recognizes in Volodia's Lermontov the ideal model of a writer promoted by the Paris School, which decried Pushkin's "brilliant," "harmonious," and "optimistic" art and world-view as reflective of outdated sensibility, opposing them to Lermontov's art and persona—inherently pessimistic, full of contradictions, and filled with a sense of crisis.[125] Identifying Proust with Marcel and Lermontov with Pechorin, Volodia endows Lermontov's and Proust's images with the same qualities. He uses Proust to shed the "confining 'skin of unina-tionality'" (*Pis'ma*, 30) and to modernize Lermontov's image. Proust is closer to Volodia's own sensibility because he is the "discoverer and pre-cursor" of Volodia's generation (*Pis'ma*, 48), and as such he epitomizes its characteristics.[126] Conflating Lermontov and Proust, he produces the ideal model of an émigré modernist.

Similarly to other "new children," Volodia tries to forget his past, avoiding describing his life in Russia as the source and symbol of all that is negative in his present (*Pis'ma*, 20, 74). He goes back in time only twice, in the stories "Probuzhdenie" and "Kompozitsiia," motivating his return by the need to find the origins of his anxiety: "I have an ur-gent (if unrealizable) need to storm into the past and to fixate those vague years neither for the sake of the 'poetry of bygone days' nor for the sake of the poetry of reminiscences proper, but in order to trace meticulously, in the dark confusion of the predawn chaos of childhood, the birth of my independence, oriented toward some goal and immedi-ately marked by that terrible time that had prepared our desperate pres-ent" ("Probuzhdenie," 146–47).

Volodia sees these origins in the corpus of ideas he absorbed in school, in the Decadent atmosphere of his adolescence, and in the reli-gious and political intolerance—*sviataia nenavist'*—taught to his gener-ation by the fathers ("Probuzhdenie," 160, 168, 173; *Pis'ma*, 20–21). Volo-dia knows that he must destroy the memories of this past but refuses to do so, just as he refuses to "compose" the story of his first love.

He does not believe in the circularity of time and in the possibility of a regenerating destruction of memory. He espouses linear time and pro-gress, although both concepts "sound embarrassing today" (*Pis'ma*, 8). His view of progress as a last resort in the postwar crisis is at odds with the antipositivist ethos of the "new malady." In the linear concept of time, the past is irrevocable. Volodia likens the procedure of "burning" one's past to the publication of memoirs, highlighting the literary and conventional nature of the eternal return (*Pis'ma*, 32, 109, 136). He also refuses to flirt with the fashionable notion of the unconscious. By pos-tulating that spiritual depth is impermeable to conscious investigation, he implies the contrived nature of psychoanalysis and surrealism (*Ob-man*, 48; *Schast'e*, 152; *Pis'ma*, 11). Volodia echoes Fel'zen's own view of psychoanalysis and surrealism as negative elements in contemporary literature; Fel'zen strove to separate Freud and Proust, whose names were almost synonymous in contemporary critical debates ("Razroznennye mysli," 130).

It is by means of involuntary memory that one can discern the traces of unconscious life, revisit the past, and eschew "composition" (*Obman*, 130, 135, 144; *Pis'ma*, 11). But involuntary memory is too rare to be of use in systematic exploration. Polemicizing with the theory of the "new malady," Volodia locates the source of his own anxiety beyond the shock of war, a historical event that should be insignificant in the ahistoricity of circular time. His anxiety is rooted in the fear of death, discovered during his trip to childhood ("Probuzhdenie," 155; *Pis'ma*, 8–9). The most important issue is not the reconstruction of a ruined culture, since much of its destruction was invented, but the affirmation of the individual in the face of death, since traditional existential protection has been lost. Volodia escapes his own fear of death in love, more precisely, in Proust's philosophy of love.

Fear of death makes Marcel loathe the future until he finds atemporality in retrospective art (*Temps retrouvé*, 178–79, 343). Volodia considers Marcel's method synthetic, for it restores his own spiritual integrity, lost with the beliefs of the fathers, and allows him to defy death (*Schast'e*, 118; "Probuzhdenie," 173; *Pis'ma*, 77). His "belief in love" (*Obman*, 12) is neither romantic nor Christian, for he espouses Marcel's view of amorous liaisons as stimuli for self-study. This belief replaces belief in God, since he is incapable of irrational faith, and he views the hours of shared love as believers view the hours of prayer (*Obman*, 100). His affair with Lëlia, imaginary and tormenting as it may be, fills his life with meaning and supports his human calling and artistic vocation: "Only love equals and opposes death. . . . If all our activity, longing, and duty derive from love, then how can we not start with this essential element, how arrogant it is immediately to judge its derivatives instead. . . . My calling—similarly to that of other people with whom I feel an affinity—is to recreate these seemingly unnecessary details of love and unhurriedly to draw from them generalizing conclusions, hypothetical but not invented" (*Schast'e*, 193).

It is of great importance for Volodia's human calling and artistic vocation that Soviet culture professes intolerance akin to the one he discovered in his childhood and designated as the origin of everything negative in his present. His own artistic method is condemned in Soviet literature as bourgeois individualism. Commenting on Proust at the first congress of Soviet writers, Erenburg scornfully observed that the hero of the "degenerating bourgeois novel" did only one thing—he loved, a detail that paled vis-à-vis the question of the hero's socioeconomic condition ("Zasedanie sed'moe," 183). Volodia takes on the Soviet challenge: "Love, voluntary, not divine, not prescribed by anyone, is especially gratifying and necessary, thanks to the hatred surrounding us, which is, for the first time, 'class-conscious' and 'Bolshevik'" (*Pis'ma*, 18–19).

Volodia's dismissal of cyclical time, contempt for religious or political agenda in art, opposition to the artistic exploitation of memory and the unconscious, and view of Proust's method as synthetic acquire special significance in the context of the anti-Proustian reaction in the early 1930s. This was a reaction against the clichés of the literature of evasion.[127] Since Proust had been a model for the "new sensibility," attacks against his oeuvre were also directed at "European Hamlets." This reaction was religious, ethical, philosophical, and ideological. Proust's "dehumanizing" fragmentation of the individual had to yield to a new humanism that would reconstruct the human being by breaking his solipsistic seclusion and taking him back to society.[128] Proust's art was unappealing both to those who envisioned metaphysics as the stuff of literature and to the utilitarians, who demanded that writers become political and social thinkers.[129] The growing involvement of French writers in ideological battles jarred with Proust's view of sociopolitical preoccupations in art as a rationalization of artistic inadequacy (*Temps retrouvé*, 186).

Since most younger émigrés regarded political engagement in art as a Soviet trait (see chapter 1), many of them opted for a religious alternative. A number of exiles were close to Jacques Maritain's circle. The émigré critical opinion with regard to Proust and the French novels of the 1920s was close to that of Maritain's group—the postwar spiritual crisis could be helped only through a religious renaissance.[130] In this context Volodia's rejection of religious and political faiths is consistent with his faithfulness to Proust's method. He is aware of the disintegrating effect of Proustian analysis, but he also believes that it leads to an eventual synthesis (*Pis'ma*, 36, 78). Volodia's human calling clashes with the "new humanism" of the anti-Proustian reaction, echoing Fel'zen's own position vis-à-vis the critics of his stubborn Proustianism.[131] For Fel'zen, religious and ideological parti pris in art is a betrayal of the émigré mission to fight for the individual: "The writer's spiritual tension does not correspond to the enthusiasm of barricade fighters. . . . Direct participation in a debate makes him a banal 'propaganda agent'; this is what the Bolsheviks required from writers, thus killing their literature" ("O sud'be emigrantskoi literatury," 18).

Fel'zen publicly denounced the religious solution of the postwar crisis as ideologically biased and asserted his own belief in spiritual progress, in terms of which Proustian analysis was a constructive force that contributed to human self-cognition.[132]

Proust's fall from grace coincided with a drop in interest in Freud. Both were blamed for destroying the individual. The banalization of the concept of the unconscious brought the accusation that their analyses were fictional, compromising the perception of inner life as true reality and favoring the reorientation of writers toward sociopolitical issues.[133] Hence sprang Fel'zen's desire to separate Freud and Proust. The shift away from the view of Proust's writings as "truthful" fed Fel'zen's apprehension of the referential illusion, for this shift was now expressed in personal animosity toward Proust. As during the creation of Proust the precursor, critics now identified the writer's persona with that of Marcel, only this time the referential illusion worked against Proust— critics sought discrepancies between his work and biography to show the writer's insincerity and hypocrisy.[134]

In 1929 there appeared a *Manifeste du roman populiste* that called for the end of literature about idle and anxious self-diggers. The *Manifeste* advocated the externalization of the novelistic object; the treatment of social issues; and the "truthful" description of "simple folk" and their "crude but real" life based on the example of the naturalist novel (Lemonnier, *Manifeste du roman populiste*, 18, 35, 59–60). The *Revue mondiale* launched a similar attack on the "idlers who contemplated themselves according to Proustian or Freudian gospels" (Picard, "Faut-il revenir aux Écoles littéraires?" 233). The success of Dabit's *Hôtel du Nord* (1929) seemed to confirm that the tide was turning from Proust to Zola. But Céline's *Voyage au bout de la nuit* proved the tenacity of the literature of evasion. If the French introspective novel gradually came to naught, the adventure novel survived Proust's fall from grace. Paying tribute to Céline's "anxious voice," Fel'zen remained faithful to his "affair with Proust" and Proust's model of salvation—the affirmation of personality through art. "Those unable to adhere to religious or party beliefs," wrote the novelist, "gladly accept Proust's apology of artistic activity which creates life in the potentially possible combination of love, inspiration, and memory."[135]

Volodia's "belief in love" is also a belief in art, whose existence is threatened by the musings about the end of art from spiritual crisis and by new ideological pressures on art. Following the example of the French introspective novel, Volodia treats love as the means and metaphor of writing. Writing becomes "love's substitute," and it is often unclear whether Volodia is speaking about his love for Lëlia or about his vocation as a writer—the two share in the analytical method and in the ethos of his human calling.[136] Volodia's belief in love affirms the value of human personality; his writing is equally affirmative of the individual against the ideology of collectivism. Together they constitute the meaning of Fel'zen's artistic endeavor: "Stubborn creative activity 'despite everything'—the only dignified response that a resisting individual can offer to robots and slaves" ("Lichnost' i obshchestvo: Anketa," 133).

The influence of Proust's oeuvre on Iurii Fel'zen's art is both more direct than in Gazdanov's case and more fruitful.[137] Fel'zen went beyond such deceptive affinities as the semantics of memory and the stylistic imitation of the Proustian period, creatively reworking Proust's analytical method and philosophy according to his own artistic and existential needs. He overcame the inertia of literary fashions and critical filters that mediated between Proust's oeuvre and its readers. Remaining in the camp of "émigré Hamlets," Fel'zen found himself in opposition to the developments in both French and émigré literatures and went against the grain of the newly fashionable literary esthetics of the 1930s. This may have been a factor in Nabokov's favorable opinion of his art, since Nabokov also opposed the direction in which the Paris School evolved. Fel'zen's project, forgotten after the writer's untimely death, merits a critical reevaluation, for his "Novel" is among the most interesting and original Russian literary works created in exile.

4

The Esthetics of Disintegration

Dr. Céline and Mme Granier

Declaring the failure of their civilization, French writers gradually transformed desperate pessimism ("tragic lucidity") into a viable artistic credo.[1] The rise of what Lev Gomolitskii described as the "esthetics of disintegration" was heralded by the success of Eugène Dabit's novel *Hôtel du Nord* (1929), which dealt with the life of Parisian lower classes in a manner evocative of Zola. By 1930 existential anxiety and reflection on the human condition became the pivotal points of French literature. "We have left the era of esthetics to enter into the tragic age," wrote J.-R. Bloch.[2] Death was prominent among the issues tormenting "European Hamlets."[3] It haunted the suicidal heroes of Cocteau's *Les Enfants terribles* (1929) and the clergy of Bernanos's *Journal d'un curé de campagne* (1936); mesmerized the dandies of Soupault (*En Joue!* [1925]) and Drieu (*Le Feu follet* [1931]) to the same extent as the political fighters of Malraux (*Les Conquérants* [1928]; *La Condition humaine* [1933]). The rediscovered taste for dramatization found fruitful ground in the concept of the "human document," first developed by the French naturalists.[4]

In 1932 Dr. Louis Destouches, also known as Louis-Ferdinand Céline, published his *Voyage au bout de la nuit*, which has been acclaimed as an artistic epitome of Europe in crisis.[5] *Voyage* was the summit of the "literature of evasion." Its very title evoked a metaphor commonly used by "European Hamlets" to describe their perception of life.[6] Céline's Ferdinand Bardamu was a disoriented young man who embarked in the direction of anxiety ("parti dans une direction d'inquiétude" [*V*, 229–30]) in the footsteps of Soupault's, Morand's, and Drieu's anxious heroes.[7] The "new children of the century" admired the expression of "new sen-

sibility" in *Voyage:* its antiliterary language; erosion of the frontier between author and text; primary treatment of the essential questions of
existence with death as a leitmotif; and a disoriented young hero driven
by the shock of war.[8] *Voyage* discarded all previous existential protection
from death. It compromised religion, ridiculed science, mocked philosophy, lowered love to a physiological function, and presented work
as infernal delirium. Bardamu's flight from the sensation of death was
compared to a "monastic meditation in front of a skull" that recalled
Hamlet and "European Hamletism."[9]

   Voyage overshadowed many recent works without which Destouches
would not have become Céline.[10] But it also turned over a new leaf in the
"literature of evasion," deposing Proust in favor of a populist novel à la
Zola.[11] Proust had criticized Zola, branding as unrealistic his propensity
for the filth of life (*Guermantes II,* 483). The anti-Proustian reaction of the
1930s reevaluated Zola. Céline was an anti-Proust who "liberated his
generation" from Proustian introspection.[12] Describing a whorehouse,
he attacked Proust's view of love in order to postulate his own method
as truer to life (*V,* 73). Instead of a philosophy of love, Céline's characters have two basic drives, to kill and to have sex (*V,* 72).[13] Indifferent to
self-reflection, Bardamu is Marcel's antipode. His existence is externalized in the war, colonialism, and new forms of labor. Bardamu, the "new
child of the century," slaughters Marcel's paradise lost. Marcel's idyllic
life in Combray, the country property of his grandparents, is echoed in
Ferdinand's visit to his grandmother's property, which culminates in the
manual cleaning of a latrine (*M,* 583). Marcel's initiation to sex, as he
oversees lesbian foreplay, is described elliptically (*Swann,* 161). Ferdinand's sexual initiation is conveyed in full, graphically, and with obscene
vocabulary (*M,* 545).

   Céline's naturalistic descriptions blackened reality and supported
the antiliterary effect of his style. In *Voyage* the leitmotif of universal disintegration echoed the revolt against classical literary language. Céline
departed from previous stylistic praxis by elevating colloquial stylization to the status of the author's own language.[14] Older critics saw this
as a summit of preciosity—as doctors, neither Bardamu nor his creator
could speak such lowly idiom.[15] The expectation of "truthfulness"
forced Céline to claim that he wrote the way he spoke.[16] Other detrac-
tors described his novels as psychopathological documents and the exact opposite of art.[17] The latter statement was a supreme approbation in
the parlance of "new children," who exalted Céline's style as an escape
from literature into truth.[18] To crown his success, the Académie

Goncourt denied Céline its prize because "the entire French civilization" suffered from his "rude and intolerable expressions"(Godard, *Voyage*, 176).

Louis Destouches took pains convincing his readers that Louis-
Ferdinand Céline, Ferdinand Bardamu, and himself were one and the
same man. The potential for an autobiographical interpretation had
been programmed into *Voyage*, but the merger of author and text was
imposed by the readers. Céline at first presented *Voyage* as a "recollection of things witnessed" but only "as a pretext for recording dreams"
(*Cahiers Céline 1*, 88). Even this timid attempt to describe his text as "literature" was too much for the documentary taste of the day. "We do not
want to know whether Céline's painting is atrocious, we want to know
if it is true," wrote Bernanos in 1933. The "new children" went out of their
way to convince Céline that Bardamu was his self-portrait, and that his
work was not art but a "document."[19]

Céline began to furnish biographical data that identified him with
Bardamu. According to his legend, Céline was a literary beginner of
thirty-eight. Destouches's artistic career began in the mid-1920s (Vitoux,
La Vie de Céline, 113). Destouches started *Voyage* in 1929, but Céline told
a critic that the novel took ten years to write and, consequently, it was
not a bow to fashion.[20] This was an alibi: in 1922 the esthetics of the "new
malady" was still in gestation; in 1929 it was an artistic fad. Céline's and
Destouches's views of the war diverged. Céline's Bardamu rebelled
against patriotic rhetoric, Destouches was obedient and valiant; Bardamu dreamt of deserting, Destouches volunteered and was decorated.[21] Bardamu was a product of postwar experience, when the intellectual fashion explained to Destouches how to see the war and
suggested its artistic potential. Destouches had described Bardamu's
life in Africa, New York, and Paris in his play *L'Église* before Céline wrote
his *Voyage*. The play was a flop, and the turning point in the author's career came with the decision to tell the same story in the first person
("confession"), using the war shock as the hero's main motivation.[22]

Mort à crédit continued to close the gap between author and hero. Its
narrator's name is Ferdinand, and the name of Bardamu is absent. Making Ferdinand a doctor, a writer, and the author of *Voyage* (*M*, 531–32),
Destouches conflated Bardamu and Céline. But the narrator teases the
reader by the ambiguity of literary truth. He alludes to the text's imaginative nature, as if Destouches ridiculed the artistic naiveté of Céline and
his readers: "Mireille! I say to her . . . I know you are good at lying . . .
truth does not concern you . . . It's your imagination that interests me in

you. . . . I am a voyeur! You'll tell me some bullshit. . . . I'll make you part of a beautiful legend. . . . If you wish we'll sign it together" (*M*, 533).

Céline's narrator admitted that his depiction of life was obsessively partial (*M*, 515). He cultivates misery, solitude, and despair because "this is probably what one seeks in life, only this, the biggest possible sadness in order to become oneself before dying" (*V*, 236). While older critics saw Céline's penchant for dramatization as a device, the "new children" praised his indulgence in the esthetics of disintegration as attuned to his tragic age. Arland, an advocate of literature as exact painting of life, insisted on Céline's right to be partial in search for truth. Less dark, his book would have neither the same thrust nor the same value, argued the critic. It was not until the grotesque amount of filth in *Mort à crédit* surpassed the tolerance level of most "new children" that Arland admitted the thoroughly literary nature of Céline's earthly hell.[23]

Advocates of political commitment in art were puzzled by *Voyage* (Godard, *Voyage*, 26–27). Bardamu's anarchism and disbelief in the good nature of men nipped in the bud attempts to associate the novel with a political program. For communist critics *Voyage* neither showed the proletariat as the most progressive class nor preached revolution.[24] But it had a different reception in the circles of "Catholic renewal." A Christian renaissance was bound to scandalize bourgeois sensibilities, and Bardamu exemplified a scandalous search for God, whose "mercy was at the end of the night"; *Voyage* proved that the world could be saved through Christian love, which would flare up at the sight of extreme suffering; showing the modern human condition, Céline stirred compassion for humankind.[25] Bardamu's calvary recalled the physically repellent yet expiating nature of Christ's suffering. Wrote a critic: "Jesus on the cross was dirty, smeared in blood, excrement, pus, and those who passed by turned away to vomit out of disgust. But those who held his viscous corpse in their hands remain purified for centuries. Céline, you have not defeated death. . . . But you made death recoil a little, and this is already an achievement."[26]

This unexpected interpretation, a far cry from Céline's antireligious stance, appealed to all those who sought the remedy for Europe's spiritual crisis in inner regeneration. Along with the critical discourse of the French "new children," the view of "Catholic" intellectuals was among those filters through which émigré readers perceived Céline's oeuvre.

The émigrés elaborated their own concept of a "human document" in prose and poetry that targeted the effect of truthfulness through a set of linguistic, compositional, and narrative procedures. Following

Adamovich's postulate that "invented poetry was always bad," the Paris School denounced imagination: the "human document" was a "responsible literary form" that spoke only about the things the author had experienced; it "photographed rather than created."[27] Deliberate imperfection showed one's indifference to literary skill and desire to be simple; the tone of anxiety and despair indicated preoccupation with the "most important." Céline achieved the impossible—he turned a "human document" into an artistically sound form.[28] "Émigré Hamlets" were seduced by the correspondence of Céline's novel to the spirit of his time. If *Voyage* was successful, it was a success by recognition (*uspekh uznavaniia*).[29] The novel's "atmosphere of a dump yard" was so "truly real" that a transition "from Céline's joyless pictures to the 'most important' happened naturally."[30] Adamovich incorporated the expression "end of the night" into his critical vocabulary to denote death as the driving force of art ("Nesostoiavshaiasia progulka," 293).

Émigrés saw Céline's novels as artistic events of an amplitude equal to that of *La Recherche* but treated them as anti-Proustian endeavors.[31] The split between Proust and Céline sprang from their respective interests in the past and the present. In a characteristic logical twist, Terapiano deplored the interest of his peers in the past at the expense of the present and simultaneously translated Céline with the dictionary of the Russian cultural past. He projected Bardamu on Lermontov's Pechorin ("a hero of our time") and Demon: "A modern Russian book would not be very different from that of Céline if it had been written. This Russian book does not yet exist; it does not exist, probably, because the consciousness of new Russian writers is not completely established in the present. But all the ingredients of the sensibility, which makes Céline's hero Bardamu, if not a hero, then a demon of our time, are present in the articles, poems, . . . and conversations of many of our young writers" ("Puteshestvie v glub' nochi," 210).

These ingredients were indeed in gestation in *Chisla*, where Adamovich alluded to Proust's "comfortable suffering" to criticize the anxiety of French writers as too dry and their depiction of human tragedy as not tragic enough. Thus, shortly after the appearance of *Voyage*, Terapiano called on younger writers to "turn their everyday life into tragedy."[32]

The credo of existential pessimism found justification in the émigré-Soviet clash. Soviet ideologues insisted on the spiritual disintegration of Western art, which contrasted with the optimism of Soviet literature by "promoting pessimism as the basis of art."[33] Céline was singled out

as a prominent example of this "literature of disintegration." Soviet critics extended the same qualities to émigré literature, stressing the spiritual decay of the "émigré young man." "The literature of disintegration
is alien to us, but it is good that our enemy is disintegrating," proclaimed
Radek at the first congress of Soviet writers.[34] In this context émigrés
could view the esthetics of disintegration as artistically and spiritually
valuable.[35] Exiles greeted the merger of Western and émigré letters in the
Soviet opinion as a confirmation that their art faithfully recorded the
modern human condition.[36] But only a fine line separated this recording from indulgence in disintegration. This line was crossed by the Paris
School, in part out of desire to keep up with the French, in part owing
to the role of the Russian literary tradition in émigré poetics.

Describing two main models of the universe in nineteenth-century
Russian literature—binary and ternary—Lotman showed that the
binary model was split into two domains (positive-negative, sinful-
saintly) and treated earthly life as entirely sinful, while the ternary included an axiologically neutral domain, where human life needed no external justification and evil was a deviation from the norm.[37] The binary
model shaped the literary master plot of salvation through suffering,
whereby the hero's road to good ran through evil, followed by repen-
tance, spiritual transformation, and religious rebirth. The bigger the sin,
the harsher the trial and the closer salvation. Gogol wanted to use this
script in *Dead Souls* but did not go beyond earthly hell. Dostoevsky had
a similar project in *The Brothers Karamazov* but also cut it short. Both
found that transformation was beyond art and concentrated on evil as
a starting point on the road to good. Unlike the ternary model, the binary follows the logical progression from concepts to life: Dostoevsky
illustrates ideology with imagined reality, while in Tolstoy's work life often conflicts with and is richer than concepts.

Since claims to artistic "truthfulness" and to the primacy of content
in émigré letters rested on the assumption that one could impose ideological models upon reality, the Paris School drifted toward Dostoevsky.
Adamovich used Dostoevsky's favorite evangelical aphorism to express
his idea that émigré literature was doomed to artistic disintegration because only by dying could a seed engender new life.[38] Orientation toward the religious vantage point on the human condition was encouraged by the suppression of religion and mysticism in Soviet art. Soviet
critics argued that the tradition of religious ethics and mysticism in Russian literature survived only in emigration, while Soviet letters drew on
the positivist tradition embodied by Belinskii and Chernyshevskii.[39]

Spiritual and physical disintegration became a preferred subject of the Paris School, whose adepts argued that the demise of religious faith and fragmentation of the individual left poetry with only one topic—death.[40] The editor of *Chisla* mused in a poem:

> Не только в наш последний час
> Смерть—главное для нас. . . .
> Но если бы со всех сторон
> Мир этот не был окружен
> Ее дыханьем,—может быть,
> Не стоило бы жить.[41]

> [Not only in our last hour
> Death is the most important for us. . . .
> But if from all sides
> This world were not surrounded
> By its breath—maybe
> Life would not be worth living.]

The road to salvation ran through suffering, and the attention of "émigré Hamlets" turned to trial by crudeness (*ispytanie grubost'iu*).[42] The first issues of *Chisla* hardly contained a story or a poem that did not mention or describe death. "Funereal candor" became a trait of émigré modernism.[43] Not surprisingly, émigré critics of the "new malady" treated this "literature à la Père-Lachaise" as an artistic fad.[44]

In 1935 Adamovich perfected the Paris School esthetics with the tale of Mme Granier, in whose honor the society "Les Dames du Calvaire" had been founded in 1842. The young and rich woman suddenly lost her husband to cancer. Her two children died a week later. She wanted to kill herself but changed her mind, gave away her money, and tended to the desperately ill. Once she found an old woman suffering from face cancer (there follows a graphic description), but terrified doctors refused to treat the patient. To convince them, Mme Granier kissed the woman's ulcers. According to Adamovich, art had to resemble the exploit of Mme Granier, depicting "victory over matter, liberation" ("Kommentarii," *SZ* 58: 323–24). This variation on the master plot of salvation through suffering recalls Ivan Karamazov's story of a saint who warmed up a stranger by breathing into his mouth, "pus-filled and malodorous from some terrible disease." But Ivan questions the saint's sincerity, while there is not a shadow of a doubt in Adamovich's words.[45] The projection of a cancerous kiss upon literary activity summarized so well the esthetics of disintegration that years later "émigré Hamlets" recalled "that French woman who bandaged someone's wounds" as a symbol of their art and one of the most important texts in Russian literature.[46]

Victory over matter is a mirror reflection of the form-content dichotomy in émigré poetics. The Christian contrast of flesh and soul is functionally equivalent to the ideal of esthetic asceticism with the primacy of content over form and opposes Marxist thought, in which consciousness is a product of socioeconomic relations. Adhering to the view of the "Catholic renewal" that the postwar crisis could be overcome in a religious renaissance, "émigré Hamlets" echoed the view that Céline's novels depicted a Christian search for God.[47] "A journey to the end of the night is our path," wrote Terapiano ("Puteshestvie v glub' nochi," 210). A "Russian Céline" was eagerly awaited to replace *prustiantsy* under the banner of Mme Granier.

Dr. Ianovskii and Deus ex Machina

The "Russian Céline," however, appeared as early as 1930 in the persona of Vasilii Semenovich Ianovskii (1906–89). But before Céline's success, most émigré critics, even those associated with the Paris School, had refused to recognize Ianovskii's writings as artistically sound. *Voyage* legitimized Ianovskii's esthetics and created for him a place in émigré letters—that of a "Russian Céline." Postwar French literature and cultural mythology were crucial to Ianovskii's artistic identity. Launching his literary career in 1930, he was immersed in the esthetics of disintegration and demonstrated no interest in Proust as a literary model. A physician by occupation, Ianovskii made his debut with a story, "Trinadtsatye" (The thirteenth). The story's crude naturalism shocked the readers. An émigré critic saw it as an "insult to emigration as a whole" because its "unprecedented impudence and repugnance" surpassed the "indecent and depraved" Soviet literature (L'vov, "Belletristika 'Chisel,'" 3).

The story alluded to Blok's *Dvenadtsat'* (*The Twelve*) and described the fate of those excluded from and by the twelve Red Guards in the *poema*. Besides "antiartistic" crudeness and "antiliterary" language, "Trinadtsatye" contained such key traits of the "new malady" esthetics as the war-shock motivation and a young disoriented hero—an émigré poet and Parisian pimp haunted by war memories. This story within a story is built to confuse the reader, who cannot distinguish between the tale written by the protagonist and its narrative frame. The story sports the "Soviet" technique of montage; shocking vocabulary, marked as "obscene" in the Russian literary tradition: *semia* (semen), *matka* (uterus), *podmyvat'sia* (to bathe genitals), and *sif* (a slang word for syphilis); and graphic depiction of violence, sex, and disease. Ianovskii described the streets of Paris: "A policeman whistled next to a blood-covered prostitute; a coachman yelled in a coarse voice at a fallen horse; a porter with badge number 216 collapsed into snowy mud. He was seized by epileptic contortions. . . . Barber's shops were already spitting out people with bloody massaged napes" ("Trinadtsatye," 129–30).

The imagery in this passage reflects the writer's debt to Dostoevsky: prostitution, the collapse of a horse, and epilepsy are major topoi in *Crime and Punishment* and *The Idiot*. But Ianovskii exploits their potential for violence and naturalism, stressing those elements that Dostoevsky glossed over.[48] While Dostoevsky's "noble prostitutes" are never shown exercising their profession, Ianovskii's whores "break through the police barrage and their dense flock of rotten uteri flows into the city" (141). The writer combines crude expressionistic descriptions with the exclusive treatment of the dirty side of the urban environment and of war. The story became a symbol of the esthetic split in émigré literary Paris. It provoked a generational clash at a meeting devoted to *Chisla* and sparked a brawl in Soiuz Molodykh Poetov i Pisatelei, where Poplavskii praised Ianovskii's story for crudeness that brought it closer to life.[49]

In his own novels Poplavskii used taboo words—*nasrat'* (to shit), *konchat'* (to "come"), *bliad'* (whore), *onanizm* (masturbation)—and described genitals, semen, and sexual intercourse.[50] He even accused Ianovskii of plagiarism, for Ianovskii's novel *Mir* (The world, 1931) contained a joke that had appeared in *Apollon Bezobrazov*. In this joke the resurrected Lazarus says, "Merde!" This coincidence was the result of the writers' immersion in the same intellectual atmosphere; the joke attracted them by combining Christian thematics with naturalistic violation of taboos.[51] Émigré critics found this combination reflective of a general "taste for such things" among *Chisla*'s contributors. Recalled Ianovskii: "For some reason, lavatories played a great role in our Parisian life. . . . There, European tramps cuddled on ledges and grates, uncannily resembling evangelical paupers. . . . In the early hours, after a wasted night, one felt there an urge to pray heartily."[52]

Initially, critics found trite Ianovskii's conflation of Christian thematics with the esthetics of disintegration.[53] But Céline's success changed Ianovskii's artistic position. When Nikolai Berdiaev suggested that *Mir* had been written under the influence of *Voyage*, Ianovskii replied that he was a Parisian doctor like Céline and was naturally inclined to treat the same themes and use the same devices (*Polia Eliseiskie*, 162). Projecting his text upon a later model, Ianovskii committed an anachronism that revealed his determination to become a "Russian Céline." This was a feasible task, since he had already been regarded as a "new child of the century" whose "malady" surpassed that of his French peers.[54] Thus, if in early 1932 Otsup considered Ianovskii's propensity for the filth of life as an esthetic whim, in 1933 he argued that one could not write otherwise. Having read *Voyage*, émigré critics discerned in Ianovskii's oeuvre true sensation of suffering and an attempt to speak about the "most important" following the traditionally Russian path of Dostoevsky.[55]

Prophesying the advent of a "Russian Céline," Terapiano divided writers into the conformists interested in "formal" literary devices and the nonconformists "submerged in the night"; a "Russian Céline" would reject "literary pretension" in language and composition ("Puteshestvie v glub' nochi," 210). Indeed, Ianovskii resolved to become simpler and to cast himself in the persona of a doctor-writer à la Céline. His story "Rozovye deti" (Pink children), begun in late 1932, shows how fast was his reaction to *Voyage*. His narrator is an émigré doctor practicing in a suburban hospital for children, a detail that recalls Bardamu's suburban practice and the attention he paid to the suffering of young patients. In 1933 Ianovskii wrote another, "Rasskaz medika" (A doctor's story). Like "Rozovye deti," this first-person narrative has a strikingly simpler composition than Ianovskii's earlier works. Its plot is linear, with no montage or intentional incoherence. Emphatically short sentences have disappeared along with ellipses, formerly his favorite syntactic mark. Obscenities have given way to medical terms, also shocking but more justifiable in "Rasskaz medika."

"Rasskaz medika" builds the semantic opposition of flesh and spirit. Its hospital setting exposes the reader to repellent physiological scenes; the contrast is crude and straightforward. A graphic examination of patients with syphilis, tuberculosis, and cancer is followed by the view of the hospital chapel with an evangelical inscription, "I am the true path and life." Another round of physiological horrors, this time in a morgue, is once more paired with the view of the chapel, whose inscription reads, "He who believes in me has eternal life." The story implements the program of salvation through suffering: the dirtier and more painful life becomes, the more evident is the spiritual ideal beyond it.

Thanks to the recent experience of Ianovskii's readers, "Rasskaz medika" was projected on Céline's world of suffering and death, where people were divided into those obsessed with death and those who never thought about it (*V*, 388). Situational parallels in Ianovskii's post-1932 works and in *Voyage* are obvious. His hospital and morgue scenes hark back to Bardamu's depiction of physical suffering (*V*, 262–63, 299–302, 373–75). The autopsy in "Rasskaz medika" draws on Bardamu's anticipation of a "beautiful autopsy" for a living patient (*V*, 374) and on the autopsies in the Institut Bioduret (*V*, 280). Following Céline's example (*V*, 17–18), Ianovskii depicts people and animals entangled in their own intestines and resorts to animalistic metaphors (rats, bedbugs) to describe the human condition. He borrows from Céline (*V*, 280–82, 387) such details as pickled corpses and body parts next to which medical personnel have lunch. He sends his hero on a tour of Parisian lavatories, recalling Bardamu's visit to a New York "fecal cavern" (*V*, 195–96).[56]

A split in the émigré perception of linguistic simplicity in French and Russian texts forced Ianovskii to diverge from Céline's linguistic program. Selecting a limited number of forms marked as popular or slang, Céline integrated them into literary language. In *Voyage*, as in Ianovskii's early writings, popular language and slang are limited in the number of occurrences and in the choice of words. But their very presence implies the same quality in any expression that does not conform to the norms of literary language.[57] In syntax Céline was more radical than Ianovskii. His phonetic transcriptions produced sequences that violated basic principles of written French;[58] he reduced the verbal negation to its second element and omitted *il* in impersonal constructions;[59] he used the particle *que* expletively with no inversion of elements in the verbal syntagma;[60] and he created syntactic doubling.[61] Echoing French debates, the émigré critics of "human documents" saw Céline's language as skillful stylization, while "émigré Hamlets" treated his texts as the acme of linguistic simplicity.[62]

The Paris School expected the depiction of disintegration in literature to coincide with the disintegration of literature in ascetic language.[63] But the high concentration of bright and graphic metaphors in Ianovskii's texts, as in those of his peers, did not live up to the ideal of ascetic simplicity.[64] His emphatically short periods and bulky metaphors harked back to Isaac Babel's *Konarmiia* (Red cavalry).[65] Like Ianovskii, Céline created an atmosphere of tragedy with the help of metaphors steeped in the semantics of death, night, mud, and decomposing matter.[66] But to become a "Russian Céline," Ianovskii had to distance himself from Céline's stylistic program and "cleanse" his language, because it had too much in common with Soviet prose. The critics who lauded Céline's stylistic simplicity saw Ianovskii's language as an aberration.[67] Becoming "simpler," Ianovskii reintroduced normative syntax, reduced the importance of metaphors, and replaced slang and obscene vocabulary with medical terms. The narrator of his 1935 novel, *Liubov' vtoraia* (Second love), would speak elliptically about menstruation, for the subject is "inappropriate" (*Liubov' vtoraia*, 53)

Another point of contention was in the fact that for Céline disintegration had intrinsic value and led to the conclusion that all hope must be abandoned. Ianovskii, on the contrary, was intent on implementing the religious program ascribed to *Voyage* by those who saw disintegration as a prerequisite for spiritual salvation. In 1935 the émigré group Krug, frequented by Ianovskii, debated the place of solitude and death in the modern human condition. The discussants stressed the importance of overcoming death (*preodolenie smerti*) as a proof of spirit's primacy over matter. They refused to consider the value of disintegration and solitude as intrinsic, reproaching Adamovich for estheticizing these notions. They also agreed that the acceptance of life was possible though Christian love ("Krug: Beseda piataia 16 dekabria 1935 goda," 138–39). This vantage point on the human condition separated Ianovskii's and Céline's approaches to the esthetics of disintegration. As a "Russian Céline," Ianovskii was to lead Bardamu out of his impasse according to the model of spiritual salvation through suffering.

The writer put together all the elements of this program in his novel *Liubov' vtoraia*, where an émigré doctor publishes the notes of a woman who died under his care and which he calls a "human document" (129). This émigré woman fails to find employment and ends up homeless in Paris. Her physical and moral degradation—rats, refuse, street violence, prostitution, rape, panhandling—closely follows the menu of Céline's Paris, as duly noted by Ianovskii's émigré critics.[68] When the heroine finds a job, she enters another circle of hell reminiscent of Bardamu's experience at the Ford plant. She is unhappy because she cannot live "by bread alone" (34). Dismissing traditional protection from existential emptiness, she is reluctant to fight for "ideas" (40), indifferent to carnal love, and rejects literature as "unsubstantial" (44). Losing her job, sick and desperate, she decides to commit suicide. Death terrifies her until she realizes that her suffering is limited to a "monstrous heap of matter" (112) and that, as a Christian, she can transcend her body and overcome death, which concerns the flesh only (118–19). As a result of her "miraculous rebirth" (122), she finds Christian love, hence the title of the novel.

The heroine reads chapter 16 of the Gospel according to John, which speaks about earthly suffering as a test of spiritual strength. At this point, her narrative is interrupted by the doctor informing us that she died giving birth to the child she had conceived by her rapist (126). In the last scene Ianovskii shows that flesh is indeed irrelevant to the heroine's spiritual self. This graphic scene is modeled on two situations in *Voyage:* a woman's death during a premature delivery (*V*, 299–302) and a failed clandestine abortion (*V*, 262–63). But Ianovskii's picture surpasses those of Céline in naturalistic detail, including a baby on a tray with a skull cracked open, the heroine's chopped up and scattered organs, and the process of stuffing her emptied corpse with these organs and "lacing it up" from chest to genitals (127). All this is supposed to contrast flesh to the woman's serene facial expression, which symbolizes spirituality and forces observers to envy her death (128).

Simplified in language and composition, *Liubov' vtoraia* showed considerable artistic refinement in comparison with Ianovskii's earlier texts. Its reception followed the convention by which "émigré Hamlets" reconciled the ideal of "sincerity" with artistic creativity. Everybody saw that the "human document" published by the émigré physician was pure fiction. Yet critics praised the author's "truthfulness," "sincerity," and desire to treat an "important" subject in the tradition of the Russian psychological novel.[69]

The heroine's spiritual rebirth appeared implausible and unmotivated. "Where Ianovskii's heroine sees God, his reader sees only deus ex machina," wrote Khodasevich.[70] The reader is indeed unprepared for the heroine's Christian catharsis among the gargoyles of the Notre Dame de Paris, where she goes before her planned suicide. The description of her spiritual transformation gives the impression that an extraneous object forces its way into the heroine's body, echoing the manner in which Ianovskii forced his ideological program on the text of the novel: "I was engulfed by a torrent that hit me in the chest. Bending, grappling for support . . . I fell on the floor. . . . A storm resounded above me, noisily announcing and breaking many things. Fire raged all over my body. A whistling tornado pierced me; I felt: if its pressure increased or lasted a little longer, I would be squashed. . . . Mighty spirit was pouring into me" (109–10).

In another cultural context one could mock this mechanical representation of a spiritual rebirth, but "émigré Hamlets" saw its primitivism and naiveté (most certainly intentional) as more valuable than any artistic sophistication, because Ianovskii's artistic failure was "sincere," "simple," and "faithful" to reality.[71]

Ianovskii's artistic and philosophical contest with Céline coincided with an attempt to rival his émigré peers. By making his protagonist a woman, he provoked comparisons with Bakunina's novel *Telo* (The body), whose heroine closed her "human document" on a note of utter despair.[72] Bakunina's émigré protagonist "trudged through life for and because of her body," tormented by physical labor and squalor, divorced from her spiritual self. She sees sex as "revolting humiliation"; there is neither love nor God in her life; her condition comes from the shock of "Russia's terrible years."[73] The characters have so much in common that it looks as if Ianovskii wanted to correct and complete Bakunina's partial realization of the master plot of salvation through suffering, taking over where Bakunina's narrator abandoned her story, at the phrase, "I must forget that something better exists."

Discussing religious renaissance, Georgii Fedotov argued that by forcing Christian concepts upon art one transformed it into a utilitarian tool. "Such religious art would hardly differ from communist art," warned the philosopher. Indeed, the master plot of salvation through suffering recalled the master plot of the socialist realist novel, the tempering of the elemental forces of the individual by the party.[74] Communist ideology was informed by the Christian concept of historical time; the proletariat had the messianic function of redeeming humanity through suffering; the universal proletarian revolution, which would bring the end of history, echoed the apocalyptic conflict of Christ and the anti-Christ.[75] In both cases evil was a necessary element indicating future deliverance. Ironically, Ianovskii was first to point out the affinities of the two master plots. Reviewing Iurii German's novel *Nashi znakomye* (Our acquaintances), he echoed the critical views of *Liubov' vtoraia*. German's protagonist, Antonina, suffered various privations and contemplated suicide until the sudden arrival of commissars provided her life with meaning—social service and a five-year plan. Ianovskii mocks the miraculous apparition of the commissars, laughs at Antonina's rebirth as a Soviet cliché, but praises the realistic depiction of her torment ("Iurii German," 158–59). One wonders if he noticed that mocking German's commissars, he ridiculed his own deus ex machina.

Ianovskii's artistic program received a new stimulus with the publication of *Mort à crédit*, seen by Adamovich as more religious than the elegant "Catholic" novels of François Mauriac, whose inevitable light of hope at the end was unconvincing in contrast to Céline's despair. Ianovskii could apply this comment to his heroine's programmatic and implausible "victory over matter" in *Liubov' vtoraia*. The implementation of Mme Granier's exploit in art consisted of kissing cancerous sores as long as possible because, Adamovich argued, "sensitivity to and understanding of suffering was the only key to religion" ("'Smert' v razsrochku,'" 3). From that point on, like Dostoevsky, Ianovskii eschewed the resurrection finale of the master plot, concentrating on what he did the best—the creation of a literary hell.

This evolution is evident in his 1937 story "Vol'no-amerikanskaia" (Loosely American), praised by émigré critics for artistic merits despite its forced ideological agenda.[76] The émigré businessman Valerian B. swindles his associates and receives a splash of acid in the face. In a hospital he witnesses death and anguish that deepen his suffering. He realizes that he cannot live as he used to, but this realization and the ensuing spiritual catharsis take place in a public lavatory. The place of his transformation and its tongue-in-cheek description as a short but intense physical suffering evocative of abdominal cramps introduce bitterly ironic double entendre.[77] Criticized as too programmatic and histrionic, this scene clearly mocks the deus ex machina episode in *Liubov' vtoraia*. The reader does not know whether Valerian's deliverance is a spiritual transformation or if he goes mad, mistaking the relief of an urgent physiological function for divine intervention. This irony, so uncharacteristic in an émigré "human document," brought Ianovskii closer to Céline's bitter laughter in *Mort à crédit*, where, in contrast to *Voyage*, Ferdinand Bardamu was no longer afraid to comment ironically on the narrative's "legendary" nature (*M*, 533) and partiality for the esthetics of disintegration (*M*, 515). "Merde" was the most frequent word in the novel and not a single event went unmarked by it. This punch of negative liberation helped Ianovskii tear off the straightjacket of "truthful" literature in his novel *Portativnoe bessmertie* (Portable immortality), whose title may indicate that it was conceived as an answer to *Mort à crédit*.

Several chapters of *Portativnoe bessmertie* were serialized in 1938, but in its entirety the text appeared after the war. This novel is the closest Dr. Ianovskii ever approached Dr. Destouches as a follower and a rival. Critics remarked that by his circumstances Ianovskii's protagonist-narrator was practically identical to Céline's heroes.[78] He lives in a Parisian working-class suburb and practices in a clinic for poor patients. The physical and moral degradation of his milieu evokes Bardamu's experience, as do his disenchantment with medicine and recourse to nontraditional treatments. In *Portativnoe bessmertie* patients are prescribed silence, water jumping, and letter copying (38–42, 186, 211, 223); in *Mort à crédit* they are treated with cinema and pure water (*M*, 510–11).

Ianovskii followed Céline's narrative decomposition of the novelistic canon.[79] Narrative causality in *Voyage* is full of holes, such as Bardamu's unexplained escape from the front. Critical situations constitute the narrative skeleton of *Voyage*, but neither danger nor escape rely on cause-effect sequences. Céline voids the traditional mechanism of crises and resolutions of all substance by multiple ellipses. If the structure of *Voyage* seems amorphous and chapter divisions random, in *Mort à crédit* Céline does not mark chapters, simply leaving space between rather arbitrary segments. Ianovskii was no novice at elaborate plot construction (cf. "Trinadtsatye"). A similar effect of shapelessness in *Portativnoe bessmertie* conveyed the idea that this was not a novel but a confession whose author-narrator had no intermediary in the form of a fictional protagonist.[80]

The initiated discerned the novel's parti pris as a "human document" in its epigraph, "He had a vision" ("On imel odno viden'e"), which referred to the narrator's vision of ideal harmony between humans and their earthly habitat. The epigraph came from a poem by Pushkin ("Zhil na svete rytsar' bednyi") that described a "poor knight" who chose Virgin Mary as his lady. As a symbol of striving for the unattainable, the image of a poor knight had been used in Dostoevsky's *The Idiot* to metaphorize Prince Myshkin, a simpleminded Christ figure who scandalized society with idealism and lack of social grace. "Émigré Hamlets" used this metaphor as synonymous with the concepts of "émigré young man" and "man of the thirties." Playing on both senses of the word "poor," Terapiano insisted that the image of a "New Poor Knight" was an omnipresent ideal among younger émigrés ("Rytsar' bednyi," 10).

Céline's and Ianovskii's narrators are marked by the shock of war. Ferdinand's war experience "runs after" him (*M*, 525–26) in the form of a neurological disorder. The narrator of *Portativnoe bessmertie* traces his present condition to civil war experiences: his medical career began with picking up decomposing corpses (18); his aversion to stability springs from the apprehension of death acquired in southern Russia in 1919 (152, 200); silence recalls hand-to-hand combat during a cavalry charge (155). Ferdinand and his colleague examine each other for terminal illnesses and bet who will die first (*M*, 517). Ianovskii's doctor sees his job as a "preparation for the external attributes of death" (*Portativnoe bessmertie*, 216) and furnishes numerous graphic descriptions of corpses (167–69, 173, 194, 234). The odor of a recently deceased woman triggers the mechanism of memory in Ianovskii's hero, and he recalls all the corpses he saw in his lifetime (92). It is the same smell of a "freshly dead" concierge (*M*, 501) that inaugurates *Mort à crédit*. Both writers implicitly oppose death odors and the retrospective associations they trigger to Proust's involuntary memory, often initiated by odors, like the smell of mold in *A l'Ombre des jeunes filles en fleurs* (65).

Ianovskii's narrator stops short of realizing his necrophilia. He feels "happy, grateful, and eternal" in a morgue, thanks to his "sudden tenderness for and affinity to" the corpse of a virgin. As he swore to serve her ideal of purity in the dirty world, medical students around him chatted about sexual intercourse with corpses (*Portativnoe bessmertie*, 168). This necrophiliac version of purity evokes the "poor knight's" adoration of the Virgin and recalls the ironic double entendre of "Vol'no-amerikanskaia." It also introduces the first point of contention between *Mort à crédit* and *Portativnoe bessmertie*. The affection that the dead stirs in Ianovskii's protagonist is capable of defeating his apprehension of death. "She continued to live in me," he says, coming close to calling this affection "love." Moving away from Céline's heroes, Ianovskii's hero realizes the program of Mme Granier. His love is directly proportional to the physical degradation of its object. Getting involved with Nicole, who suffers from breast cancer, he proudly announces: "A miserable woman with severed breasts visits me once in a while; she is horrifying and repulsive, and I caress her" (*Portativnoe bessmertie*, 214).

Céline classified love as a myth that protected one from the fear of death and was but sexual desire. To prove him wrong, Ianovskii's hero finds objects of affection in the very depths of life but eschews carnal love. An exception is made for Nicole, a perfect specimen of misery, whose autopsy he imagines long before she dies (218). *Portativnoe bessmertie* is informed by the same ethos as *Liubov' vtoraia*: only Christian love can remedy the fact that humans are steadfastly marching toward death. Ianovskii did not renounce the master plot of salvation through suffering, although its denouement remained problematic. Excelling in the dark grotesque of disintegration, the writer could not stop the narrative once his hero concluded that suffering was necessary: life continued because living was difficult; without resistance it would succumb to death even faster (*Portativnoe bessmertie*, 97–98). Stopping at this point meant capitulating to Céline. The end of suffering lay in spiritual transformation from within. Proposing his version of salvation, Ianovskii persisted in his dialogue with Céline by creating Jean Doute, a spiritual double of his own hero and a ghost of Céline's narrator. The theme of doubles runs through *Voyage* and *Mort à crédit*. Bardamu's double is Léon Robinson, Ferdinand's is his mentor Courtial de Pereires. Bardamu meets Robinson at every stage of his transcontinental vagrancy. If Ferdinand's doubling in Courtial becomes obvious only by the end of *Mort à crédit,* Bardamu's fantastic and unmotivated doubling is evident from the outset. Like Céline, Ianovskii introduced a purely fantastic element into his "documentary" narrative, shaking off the straightjacket of "truthful" literature. His narrator's double is reminiscent of Courtial de Pereires in Céline's *Mort à crédit* and of Apollon in Poplavskii's *Apollon Bezobrazov.* Dr. Jean Doute, the hero's colleague at the clinic, has the appearance of Apollon, also ascribed to Poplavskii himself. He wears a sailor's shirt under a jacket; he is an athlete boasting his physical strength in public; he is a rude and straightforward preacher and the spiritual guide of a group of international adepts, whose picturesque past recalls the group of Apollon's followers (*Portativnoe bessmertie,* 31–32, 45–46). Ianovskii calls this group *Krug* (47, 50), alluding to the émigré philosophical circle Krug of which he was a member.[81]

Jean Doute's uncertain origin and fluent French and Spanish link him to the Franco-Spanish name of Courcial de Pereires—a dreamer, engineer-inventor, and international quack. Jean Doute is a medical quack. His very name phonetically alludes to his nature of a skeptical agent-provocateur (*j'en doute,* I doubt) that contrasts with the Christian idealism of Ianovskii's protagonist and evokes the opposition of Poplavskii's demonic Apollon and his disciple, the Christian mystic Vasilii. In addition, Jean is invested with many features of Céline's protagonist—transatlantic escapades, crudeness of expression, cynicism, a penchant for long diatribes, and an obsession with death. Thus, Ferdinand's own ghost is called to defeat despair, which triumphs in *Mort à crédit,* as he mourns Courtial's suicide.

In the last chapter of *Portativnoe bessmertie,* Jean returns from a trip to Asia with an invention—the Ω-rays. People exposed to these rays begin to love their neighbor and lose the fear of death (254). The group of adepts starts using Jean's "love machine." As they witness a Biblical scene in a zoo, where a lion lies beside an antelope and a wolf leaves a lamb alone (263; cf. Isaiah 65: 25), it seems that the arrival of God's kingdom on earth is imminent. The group goes to a political rally in order to sprinkle the crowd with the Ω-rays, but several adepts rebel against Jean's mechanical way of making humans happy. They prefer to join the violent crowd and preach Christian love. The novel ends abruptly with this confrontation between the teacher and his disciples. The vacillating narrator does not inform the reader which side he endorses.

The magic Ω-rays function as mocking equivalents of both deus ex machina in *Liubov' vtoraia* and of the communist and fascist hope to effect paradise on earth by material means. The fact that the ghost of Céline's narrator tries to impose this paradise upon humanity puts in question Céline's suggested potential for spiritual transformation. By 1938 Ianovskii knew of Céline's involvement in the French extreme right, his virulent antisemitism, and his advocacy of the Nazi regime.[82] The note of hope at the end of *Portativnoe bessmertie* and the narrator's skepticism regarding Jean's "love machine" may well be political and philosophical answers to Céline.[83]

It appears that Ianovskii realized the impossibility of accomplishing his program without resorting to a miracle. Although the narrator of *Portativnoe bessmertie* was not delivered from existential angst, his creator was definitely freed from the fetters of "truthful" literature. The last, antiutopian chapter of *Portativnoe bessmertie* is a compromise between artistic imagination and the requirement of "truthfulness." It runs counter to the intentionally unimaginative, uneventful, and monotonous "human documents" like Ianovskii's own *Liubov' vtoraia*, Bakunina's *Telo,* Sharshun's *Put' pravyi* (Righteous path, 1934), and Poplavskii's *Domoi s nebes.* In an open challenge to the requirement of "truthfulness," Ianovskii skipped the third and fourth chapters of *Portativnoe bessmertie* and hurried to publish the last one in *Russkie zapiski* (no. 17, 1939), which had serialized the novel's first two chapters in October 1938. The absence of critical responses from the Paris School adepts may indicate that Ianovskii's rebellion against the artistic conventions of the "human document" was not well received. But it may also have gone unnoticed in the wave of the most recent literary developments in the Russian Montparnasse.

By 1939 the Paris School esthetics, especially its vision of realism in art, was questioned by the very people who had promoted it earlier. In 1938 Georgii Ivanov published *Raspad atoma* (The disintegration of an atom), classified by Khodasevich as a lyrical poem in prose ("Raspad atoma," 9). Along with Ianovskii's novel, this publication heralded the disenchantment of the Paris School writers with the "human document" doctrine and its vision of the relationship between literature and reality.

The End of the "Human Document": *Raspad atoma*

In 1939 a group of Paris School writers published a collection titled *Literaturnyi smotr* (Literary audit). Adamovich contributed an article "O 'samom vazhnom'" (On the "most important"), questioning the last ten years of his own activity as a critic. He doubted the very possibility of speaking truthfully about the "most important" in literature. These doubts were brought about by the fact that many émigrés now wrote artistically convincing but similar pieces "about the most important." As a result, Adamovich was no longer sure what that "most important" really was because its literary displays were self-parodying in their cliché similarity. Now, to ensure their "sincerity," émigré writers had to separate altogether the "most important" from literary discourse. "As I write this, I am fully aware that I do not know how to unite the two," finished the critic in a gasp of mannered despair ("O 'samom vazhnom,'" in *Smotr*, 19).

Adamovich's esthetic foes had long observed that the Paris School rhetoric, which subordinated art to reality and cultivated antiliterary elements in literature, contradicted the school's desire to create art.[84] The impossibility of "truthful" literature was pointed out more and more often in the late 1930s. The sheer number of "human documents" in poetry and prose revealed the birth of just another literary model with its own conventions.[85] Riding the wave of self-flagellation, Terapiano declared the "human document" a misunderstanding, for its antiformalism was artistically motivated ("O novykh knigakh stikhov," 171–72). This was a logical development in the esthetics of disintegration—the negation of the negation of art. "Estheticizing" art was unacceptable, but "antiestheticizing" art had proven equally deceptive. One could now indulge in this vicious circle and write literature about the impossibility of literature. The war aborted this esthetic evolution manifest in Ianovskii's turn to imaginative literature and Ivanov's "poem in prose" about its own impossibility.

Raspad atoma is a monologue whose first-person narrative and the link of the hero's circumstances to those of the author fit the requirements of a "human document." Yet the autobiographical link is not complete. Ivanov's wife, Irina Odoevseva, never left her husband, whereas Ivanov's hero, a Parisian émigré writer, is abandoned by his beloved and this event initiates his monologue. The monologue revolves around all-consuming universal ugliness and all the elements of the "new malady." Like Céline's texts, it presents a chain of loosely linked and (seemingly) arbitrarily arranged scenes and observations, whose lyrical undercurrent springs from the fact that it is a reflection of an abandoned and lonely man. With the loss of love, Ivanov's protagonist is deprived of protection from the absurdity of life and the abomination of the modern human condition. It is the last in a series of losses he, as an émigré writer, experiences. Having lost his country, culture, and beloved, the hero is existentially "naked" and keen on noticing the disintegration of European culture. He is a "man of the thirties" (28, 34), whose God is dead (10) and whose everyday life is earthly hell: "I want order. It is not my fault that order has been destroyed. I want peace for my soul. But my soul is like a stirred-up refuse bucket—a herring tail, a dead rat, food leftovers, cigarette stubs dive into turbid depths and resurface, racing each other. I want clean air. Sweetish decay—the breath of universal ugliness—haunts me like fear" (8–9).

The smell of decomposition haunting the narrator is conveyed in the opening lines of his monologue: "I am breathing. Maybe this air is poisoned? But this is the only air I have" (5). These lines hark back to Ferdinand's opening monologue in *Mort à crédit*, which, as discussed earlier in this chapter, was also exploited by Ianovskii because of its anti-Proustian potential. But Ivanov's earthly hell is even more literary than Ianovskii's, no matter how much the writer tries to scandalize his reader with such words as *onanizm* (masturbation, *Raspad atoma*, 12, 66), *matka* (uterus, 26), *podmyvat'sia* (to wash genitals, 14), *konchat'* (to "come," 66), and *semia* (semen, 83). In 1938 Bem opined that émigré readers had gotten so used to "antiliterature" that few of them were actually scandalized by Ivanov.[86] The literariness of Ivanov's hell is reinforced by the contrast of obscenities with the refined language of his narrative. His style is free from the occasional awkwardness of Ianovskii's language, his vocabulary is richer, and his command of Russian is more sophisticated. Khodasevich and Nabokov, getting back at their artistic foe, described Ivanov's text as too pretty and literary.[87]

Instead of shocking the reader, the images of death and disintegration in Ivanov's "poem in prose" evoke similar details in contemporary Russian and French texts. *Raspad atoma* was published almost simultaneously with first chapters of *Portativnoe bessmertie*, and the striking coincidences of "dirty" details suggest that Ivanov and Ianovskii resorted to common topoi in the milieu of the Paris School. Both writers describe the life and death of a rat as a metaphor for the human condition; this metaphor is also present in Céline.[88] Both dwell on the depiction of public lavatories as the harbor of human refuse. In Ivanov's text a tramp soaks a piece of bread in a stream of urine to enjoy it with red wine (*Raspad atoma*, 65). Ianovskii's hero watches homeless and drunk philosophers who sleep to the sound of urinating and defecating visitors (*Portativnoe bessmertie*, 172, 174). And in both cases one recalls Bardamu's visit to a New York pubic lavatory (*V*, 195–96). Ivanov's description of cancer-ridden body parts in glass jars recalls similarly pickled corpses and body parts in *Portativnoe bessmertie* and *Voyage;* all three writers like to paint human beings and animals entangled in their own intestines and spare no sensibilities in graphic scenes of agony.[89]

The very title of Ivanov's text calls up literary associations by virtue of exploiting a trope from the Paris School critical discourse—the disintegration (*raspad, droblenie*) of human identity in the postwar spiritual crisis. Ivanov previously had used this cliché to compare the effects of Proust's analytical method to the disintegration of radium, which "could be both extraordinarily destructive and beneficial," for it "destroyed as mysteriously as it cured" ("Anketa o Pruste," 272). His ambiguous attitude toward disintegration echoed Adamovich's valorization of the esthetics of disintegration as artistically and existentially fruitful because only by dying could a seed engender life. Ivanov aired the same opinion, glorifying Poplavskii's self-destructive esthetics: "The poet's deed is to create a 'piece of eternity' at the price of seeing everything temporal die; this often includes his own death" ("Boris Poplavskii," 233). These words were written at a time when the Paris School was just developing its attitude toward the esthetics of disintegration in literature. By 1938 Ivanov's views underwent considerable evolution.

It is instructive to read the reviews of *Raspad atoma* that defend the crudeness of this highly sophisticated literary text as realistic in that it has nothing to do with the art of letters. Anachronistic at a time when the "human document" came to be seen by its former proponents as a hackneyed model, these reviews insisted that anyone walking in Paris could observe scenes from Ivanov's book and that the text was "a confession of our poor contemporary."[90] But the closer one reads Ivanov's "poem in prose," the stronger one feels its lack of originality with regard to contemporary texts that espouse the same esthetics. Why would an advocate of antiliterary simplicity and a weathered poet fill his narrative with the literary clichés of the day? If he indeed wanted to write a "human document," he should have played down its conventional side. In fact, Ivanov's narrator is torn between his wish to "confess" and his inability to believe any word in a literary work, forcing the reader to conclude that truthful literature is an oxymoron.

After the loss of his beloved, Ivanov's hero finds himself in an existential void. But rather than stimulating his art—as Adamovich earlier suggested, valorizing the esthetic function of solitude and death in the "new malady"—this situation deprived his artistic expression of all meaning and made the writer-protagonist infertile. This was a radical shift from Ivanov's earlier position, when he agreed with Adamovich that solitude liberated the writer's consciousness and turned his attention to the most important questions of existence. Ivanov wrote in 1930:

> Хорошо, что нет Царя.
> Хорошо, что нет России.
> Хорошо, что Бога нет.
> Только желтая заря,
> Только звезды ледяные,
> Только миллионы лет.
> Хорошо—что никого,
> Хорошо—что ничего,
> Так черно и так мертво,
> Что мертвее быть не может
> И чернее не бывать,
> Что никто нам не поможет
> И не надо помогать.

> ⟶

> [It is good that there is no Tsar.
> It is good that there is no Russia.
> It is good that there is no God.
> There is only yellow dawn,
> There are only icy stars,
> There are only millions of years.
> It is good that there is nobody,
> It is good that there is nothing,
> (And that) it is so dark and dead,
> That it could not be deader
> And will never get darker,
> (And) that nobody will help us,
> Besides, we do not need any help.]
>   (*Sobranie sochinenii*, 1:276)

Echoing both thematically and stylistically the eulogy of absolute solitude in Adamovich's poem "Za vse, za vse spasibo" (Thank you for everything; see chapter 1), this poem confirmed Ivanov's parti pris of a disoriented and desperate "European Hamlet," who used his existential crisis as material for "documentary" and confessional literature, plain and unpretentious in language and composition. But by 1938 Ivanov's view of the "new malady" must have changed.

An émigré critic pointed out that, while publicly decrying the fragmentation of the modern individual, "émigré Hamlets" despised the integrity of consciousness as antiquated. This spite led to the demise of the "human document": once all values were compromised, truth became relative as well, devaluing that "most important" stuff of existence to be treated in art. Any attempt to write literature in this state of mind, argued the critic, resembled a rape of dead poetry.[91] This metaphor was suggested by a necrophiliac scene in *Raspad atoma*, which metaphorized the hero's infertility in life and art: "Copulation with a dead girl. Her body was completely soft but somewhat coldish, as if after a bath. With tension, with special delight. She lay as if asleep. I did not do her any harm. On the contrary, these several impulsive minutes life was still continuing around her, if not for her. A star was paling in the window, jasmine was in late bloom. Semen flowed out and I wiped it with a handkerchief" (25).

This scene evokes *Portativnoe bessmertie*, where medics marvel at the corpse of a virgin. Although Ianovskii's hero did not rape the virgin, his adoration verged on lust (167). This necrophiliac motif harks back to Proust's *Recherche*. Marcel stops going to a bordello after giving its owner the sofa of his deceased aunt. The idea that whores entertained visitors on the sofa from Combray, a symbol of pure childhood, made Marcel "suffer more than the idea of raping a dead woman" (*Jeunes filles*, 148). The anti-Proustians à la Céline, for whom there was no pure past, were naturally tempted to exploit this image.[92]

Sexual intercourse with a dead girl implies more than mere hunger for a literary scandal. If the naked corpse of a virgin on a dissecting table inspires in Ianovskii's narrator the resolution to seek Christian love, in Ivanov's text it is a metaphor of artistic and spiritual impotence. The protagonist seeks love as the only protection from solitude but enters a vicious circle: solitude splits his personality like an atom (*Raspad atoma*, 58) and makes him infertile in love and art (62). As a "new child of the century" with fragmented consciousness he is unable to believe in anything. He cannot inspire love because he does not believe in its existence. Like Céline's Bardamu, he sees love as a myth that rationalizes the physiological nature of sex. He cannot write poetry because he regards literature as a medium in which truth is impossible and discards all belles-lettres as make-believe (28).

In search of a literary identity, Ivanov's protagonist turns to major traditions and trends in both nineteenth-century Russian literature and in émigré letters: Pushkin's artistic harmony, the metaphysical tradition of Dostoevsky, Tolstoy's ethically preoccupied art, the "estheticizing" camp of Nabokov and Khodasevich, and the "human document" doctrine. As a "man of the thirties," he discards them one by one, for they

cannot help his artistic infertility and existential absurdity. He sub-
scribes to the favorite Paris School opinion that Pushkin embodies "old
sensibility," in which the artist finds himself in harmony with his world
and art and believes in the necessity and emotive power of art. Ivanov's
hero and his contemporaries are alienated from Pushkin's art and world-
view because of their "modern" consciousness (*Raspad atoma*, 80). Even
if they tried to emulate Pushkin, contemporary poets could produce
only the "metaphysical heights of foul language," such as the trans-
sense poetry of Russian futurism (41–42). A far cry from Pushkin's
art, the trans-sense poetry is, for Ivanov's hero, proof of the decline of
Pushkin's artistic tradition.

Discarding Pushkin, he also rejects Pushkin's admirers among the
"formalists," who lay emphasis on style and composition, revealing
their belief in the intrinsic value of art and in its primacy over extra-
artistic reality. Implying, first and foremost, Nabokov and Khodasevich,
Ivanov's protagonist envies those who believe that the artistic reflection
of life is a victory over life, provided that one has a creative gift ("byl by
tol'ko talant") to transform existential absurdity, solitude, and suffering
through artistic harmony (*Raspad atoma*, 34–35). The condition that only
an artistic gift is necessary to vanquish life is a transparent allusion to
Nabokov's novel *Dar* (translated as *The Gift*), whose serialization began
in 1937. *Dar* contained critical attacks against the Paris School esthetics
and its view of Pushkin and mocked Ivanov personally. The dismal nature of the modern human condition precludes Ivanov's protagonist
from admiring estheticized pictures of existence. He experiences a "tormenting desire to save and console" his contemporaries instead of portraying them in a "sentimentally heartless" way that affirms the primacy
of art over its subject matter (35–36).

But art itself could "save and console," as in the case of Tolstoy's ethically preoccupied art. The problem is that "modern" consciousness is
deaf to all artistic expression—the lie of art cannot pass for truth. And
if so, "one cannot create new ingenious consolations, in fact, it is almost
impossible to find consolation in the old ones" (*Raspad atoma*, 30). The
narrator illustrates his point by Anna Karenina's tragic fate, which until recently moved the readers to tears but seems to have lost its pathos
in the tragic age, whose contemporaries lead tormented existences
and see the artistic representation of suffering as redundant and fake.
Ivanov's hero sums up his verdict on Tolstoy: "Soon everything will fade
away forever, leaving only the game of intellect and gift, curious reading that does not oblige one to believe in itself and does not inspire any

faith. . . . Tolstoy himself felt it before anyone, that line, the border, beyond which there was no consolation with invented beauty, not a tear shed over invented life" (30).

The association of tears with literary fiction is an allusion to Pushkin's art. The line, "I will shed tears over fiction" ("nad vymyslom slezami obol'ius'"), from Pushkin's 1830 elegy, had long been a proverbial expression in Russian culture.

In the Paris School opposition to Pushkin, modern sensibility could be embodied by either Dostoevsky or Lermontov. Ivanov's narrator chooses Dostoevsky as Pushkin's antipode. The protagonist draws parallels between his own existential situation and that of Akakii Akakievich from Gogol's story "The Overcoat." But the persona of his spiritual predecessor is, in fact, an amalgam of literary reminiscences. It includes Gogol's hero from "The Madman's Diary," Dostoevsky's Makar Devushkin from *The Poor Folk*, and the protagonist of *Notes from the Underground*. Whether writing literature or thinking about love, Ivanov's narrator ends up in a state of disillusionment. Such a state, he imagines, would be provoked in Gogol's and Dostoevsky's "little people" if they discovered that the object of their adoration, the "general's daughter" and "little angel," had smelly feet:

> Naked little fingers of a child are pressed against ossified lips. They smell like innocence, tenderness, and rose water. But no, no—you will not fool me. . . . Tell me, through innocence and rose water, what do your white little feet smell like, Psyche? In the very essence of things, what do they smell like, answer me? They smell just like mine, my little angel [*angel'chik*]. . . . Therefore, there is no difference between you and me, and you should not snub me: I kissed your noble little feet, I gave my soul for them, and you should now bend down and kiss my rotten socks. . . . What am I to do with you, Psyche? Shall I kill you? You will come to me all the same—even dead. (*Raspad atoma*, 78–80)

The situational parallelism of this passage with the scene of raping a dead girl is obvious. The "little angel," the Muse of Gogol's and Dostoevsky's "little people," is dead. The wretched and pitiful Akakii Akakievich and Makar Devushkin, who have been stirring compassion in the Russian reader for almost a century, become murderous monsters who make love to their dead Muse, kissing her ossified lips. They are as infertile in life as Ivanov's narrator, and their image as murderous necrophiles compromises just another literary trend, which used to move readers to tears, "saving and consoling" human spirit.

The hero's skepticism does not leave intact the myths of his own time. He asserts the false nature of the "new malady." Since modern men cannot believe in the lie of art, no one can now admire or repeat Werther's suicide (*Raspad atoma*, 28–29). By the same token, since truth is gone along with religious faith, "reality has become unreliable: a photographic picture lies and any human document is, in advance, a counterfeit" (37). Looking through photographs of suicide and murder victims, the protagonist remains unmoved by the violence and suffering they present. Suddenly, he remembers that his beloved is living at this very moment somewhere not far from him. His own suffering immediately brings him closer to the suffering of others, and he is emotionally overwhelmed by the images that previously left him indifferent (39). This proves his thesis that a "human document," whose goal is to photograph reality, is a lie. One cannot rely on reality alone to understand it: "To come closer to something one needs to distort it" (36–37), the way he distorts the photographs by personal reminiscences. This distortion constitutes artistic activity. The logical cycle is closed: one cannot find truth either in art or in extra-artistic reality.

Only one solution is left. "Our repulsive, hapless, solitary souls have merged into one and, like corkscrews . . . force their way toward God as best they can," says the narrator. But the road toward God and Truth runs through the "chaos of contradictions," where nothing is certain. One must walk along "the ugly, disheveled, contradictory stenogram of life" in order to find them (*Raspad atoma*, 37). This is a summary of the salvation-through-suffering master plot. The word "stenogram" cannot but evoke the concept of the "human document," placing the narrator into a vicious circle because "any human document is, in advance, a counterfeit." Nevertheless, he looks for love and tries to write literature.

Since he cannot "fertilize anything," his poetry resembles a stillborn child (*Raspad atoma*, 37). His discourse constantly shifts between his artistic and emotional quests. Making love to a prostitute, the narrator imagines that he makes love to Psyche (78); having written a poem, he feels that he has raped a corpse—"sperm flows out" (34), symbolizing artistic infertility. His artistic and emotional states finally merge in another naturalistic metaphor: a soldier masturbates in a latrine and his semen falls into the brown mass of excrement (66). Ivanov thus argues against Adamovich's and his own formerly held idea, which justified the artistic valorization of the esthetics of disintegration. The dying seed will no longer engender new life. This reversed metaphor summarizes the desperation of his hero.[93]

As we have seen, Ianovskii tried to do away with the contradictions of the "human document." He conjured up synthesizing Christian love by means of deus ex machina. But as this procedure proved unconvincing, he drifted away from the genre altogether. Unlike Ianovskii, Ivanov left all contradictions unresolved, alluding to the suicide of his hero. But even this denouement is uncertain; at least it is not clearly stated. This ending symbolizes the narrator's inner chaos. He is caught in the vicious circle of love and solitude and in the vicious circle of his own text as a work of art. The latter is especially important, for its solipsistic nature opens the text to several interpretations.

Claiming that he is incapable of taking art seriously, the protagonist envies writers-"esthetes" who believe that art can help them cope with reality. But the text we hold in front of us is exactly that type of stylistically refined literature capable of provoking esthetic pleasure even in places that are supposed to shock. Khodasevich and Nabokov stopped at the first possible interpretation, classifying *Raspad atoma* as a failed "human document" marred by literary clichés.

The second interpretation, aired by Zlobin and Gippius, envisions the text as a successfully realized "human document" that reflects the deepening disintegration in the consciousness of a "European Hamlet." The newly fashionable reflection on the relativity of the "most important" and on the impossibility of the "human document" as an alternative to art supported this interpretation. It enhanced the sensation of the narrator's fragmented consciousness, whose contradictions marked his text: he writes a "human document," being aware of its impossibility; he seeks God and truth, knowing that both concepts have become relative and dead; convinced of his own infertility, he, nonetheless, persists in attempts to fertilize his art and life, engendering stillborn poems and emotions.

But there is also another possible interpretation. One could consider Ivanov's "poem in prose" as the gesture of an agent provocateur. Ivanov's supreme artistic self-affirmation may have consisted of presenting the tropes and topoi from the writings of "émigré Hamlets" in a markedly literary and estheticized way, mocking everything and everybody around him. His narrator devalues all the main concepts of the Paris School esthetics: the "human document," the "new malady," salvation in religious rebirth, and the Christian basis of the esthetics of disintegration—the fertilizing and self-sacrificial death. The images used by Ivanov's peers to create the effect of antiliterary crudeness acquire in his text conspicuous esthetic value. As a result, the truth of life, which "émigré Hamlets" advocated in contrast to the estheticism of art, lost its meaning, appearing as a literary convention. By ridiculing the esthetics to which he had subscribed, Ivanov turned his weapon upon himself and his oeuvre of the last ten years. The universal skepticism of his narrator could be the best manifestation of a "European Hamlet's" spiritual disintegration.

Adamovich did not comment in writing on *Raspad atoma*. His significant silence and subsequent article "O 'samom vazhnom'" may illustrate that Ivanov's "poem in prose" made ever more evident the contradictions in the Paris School's concept of "truthful" literature and in its view of art as a "responsible" copy of life. Thus on the eve of the war that put a forceful end to Russian literary life in France, the Paris School's esthetic doctrine of the "human document" was as good as dead.

5

The Art of Writing a Novel

The "Pure Novel": From André Gide to Vladimir Nabokov

On July 24, 1934, Vladimir Nabokov, hard at work on what would be his last Russian novel, *Dar* (1937; translated as *The Gift*, 1963), wrote from Berlin to Vladislav Khodasevich, his literary mentor and ally in the fight against the Paris School esthetics:

> One should avoid the terrible odor of the émigré milieu (certainly, it is easy for me to say, since I live far from it all, in almost idyllic backwoods), the best thing—applicable, by the way, to all times and smells—is to lock oneself up in a room . . . and do one's meaningless, innocent, intoxicating job, apropos justifying everything that does not essentially require justification: the strangeness of such existence, inconveniences, solitude . . . and some quiet inner joy. That is why I find unbearable both intelligent and stupid speeches about "modern times," "inquiétude," "religious renaissance" and, really, any phrase containing the word "postwar." . . . I wish neither to be "anxious" nor to be "reborn."[1]

One recognizes in this passage major topoi of the "new malady." Nabokov's conspicuous aloofness from Parisian literary life seems to make his oeuvre inappropriate for the present study. Yet, the writer's removal is deceptive. The same letter informs Khodasevich that his correspondent regularly reads *Chisla;* and Nabokov's scathing diatribe shows familiarity with Parisian critical debates. What may look like disengagement from the issues haunting the capital of émigré letters is, in fact, an artistic stance dictated by Nabokov's strong opinions about these issues, which could not but mark his novel in progress.

French influence was a hot topic in Russian Paris. Nabokov was charged with "un-Russianness" by the Paris School critics, who exercised a double standard—for "émigré Hamlets," French influence was a marker of difference from the fathers (see chapter 1). Nabokov's denials of foreign influence served both to disprove his foes and to transform the issue of literary influence into a point of esthetic contention.[2] It is, therefore, logical that conspicuous evocations of French authors appeared in his novels only when he was no longer a Russian writer, as in *Lolita* (1955), which testifies to Nabokov's good knowledge of André Gide's oeuvre and contains a clear reference to the French *maître*.

In his flight across the United States, the scholar of French literature Humbert Humbert finds temporary abode in the town of Beardsley, inhabited by one Gaston Godin, a professor of French and "old fraud" hailed as a "French genius." According to Humbert, Gaston is a mediocre teacher, bad scholar, and pedophile who entertains small boys "in the privacy of an orientally furnished den" decorated with images of famous homosexuals: Chaikovsky, Gide, Nizhinsky, and Proust. The conjunction of Oriental tastes and homosexuality is emphasized by Gaston's gift that "a little lad of his" brings to Humbert. It is a money box with an Oriental design of the type one finds in Algiers (*Lolita*, 183–84, 217). This geographic index singles out Gide from the portraits in Gaston's studio. Obsession with boys permeates Gide's *L'Immoraliste* (1901), whose protagonist, Michel, is smitten by Algerian boys and brings his ailing wife to the unfavorable African climate to pursue his sexual reveries. The same motif marks *Les Faux-Monnayeurs* (1925; translated as *The Counterfeiters*), whose hero has an affair with his teenage nephew and buys a guide to Algeria for another, still younger, nephew.

It is tempting to see Gide's shadow in *Lolita* as that of a fake genius, especially since the problem of fake art is at the heart of *Les Faux-Monnayeurs*. But the text of *Lolita* provides no motivation for such an attack. As often happens in Nabokov's art, readily available explanatory keys are misleading. Humbert taunts Gaston's competence as a scholar, but his own competence proves faulty, for he fails to see that he is closer to Gide's heroes than Gaston is: like Michel, he hurries his wife's demise and pursues an underage sexual object. Gaston, who uses Humbert's textbook of French literature, only repeats Humbert's utterances in life and scholarship. Humbert turns out to be an intellectual counterfeiter—a crucial conclusion to which Nabokov leads us using Gidean subtexts.

This evocation of Gide acquires particular importance in light of the striking similarities in the conception and composition, narrative devices, imagery, and thematics of *Dar* and *Les Faux-Monnayeurs*. Yet, little effort has been made to confront Nabokov and Gide in a comparative study.[3] This is despite the fact that in émigré circles Gide was the most discussed French writer after Proust. Nabokov could not afford to ignore a writer like Gide, embroiled as he was in French and émigré artistic debates. Indeed, in 1933, the year *Dar* was begun, Nabokov wrote the story "Korolek" ("The Leonardo"), whose very title echoed that of Gide's novel—"korolek" is a slang term for "counterfeiter" (*Vesna v Fial'te i drugie rasskazy*, 71). The story frustrates the traditional juxtaposition of "true artists" and their philistine environment. The hero and would-be artist Romantovskii (a conflation of "romanticism" and "roman" [novel]) is persecuted by vulgar neighbors. But just as we get ready to bemoan the plight of the lonely genius, we learn that Romantovskii is merely a con artist, a counterfeiter recently released from jail. The suffering artist cliché is deconstructed by the godlike narrator along with other "decorations" conspicuously brought in to make a good story. It is in Gidean terms that "Korolek" prefigures *Dar*'s subversion of traditional poetics.

In this chapter I will argue that Nabokov used *Les Faux-Monnayeurs* as a springboard in refining his novelistic esthetics, which he opposed to the writings of his Parisian peers. It is the revolutionary novelty of Gide's magnum opus that brought Nabokov to Gide's literary lab. This thesis runs counter to Greenleaf's view of *"The Gift'*s determined russocentrism [that] suggests the genealogical omission not only of rival contemporary poets but also of European modernists" ("Fathers, Sons and Impostors," 144). I contend that—like Gazdanov, Fel'zen, Ianovskii, and Poplavskii—Nabokov creatively reworked his French source, but unlike his esthetic rivals, he did not use it as a conspicuous textual marker. He dissimulated his indebtedness to Gide in "the abundance . . . of false trails carefully prepared for the reader" (*G*, 172 [*D*, 193]).[4] Thus, filled with allusions to Proust, *Dar* seems to follow Gide's way out of Proustian circularity, fighting many esthetic notions commonly ascribed to Proust by his French and émigré interpreters.

Nabokov's motivation for turning to Gide could not coincide with that of Fel'zen's deferent and faithful "Proustianism," since Nabokov saw the issue of artistic borrowing as a bone of contention in his clash with the Paris School and did not accept Gide's esthetics in its entirety. Neither could he long to establish a clear kinship with a fashionable French author, as did Gazdanov, or to "outdo" his French model for the benefit of the émigré reader, as did Ianovskii, considering that Nabokov had to fight off constant accusations of "un-Russianness." The writer's interest in *Les Faux-Monnayeurs* must have originated in a genuine conviction that Gide's novel offered compositional, narrative, and thematic vistas that could revolutionize the genre and help Nabokov fight what he saw as adverse esthetics in contemporary art.

Gide's artistic persona contained features that were unacceptable to Nabokov—the estheticization of homosexuality, infatuation with Dostoevsky, and communist sympathies. But these divergences were not enough to prevent Nabokov from capitalizing on Gide's literary praxis. As Nabokov stated later on, "if you hate a book, you still may derive artistic delight from imagining other and better ways of looking at things, or, what is the same, expressing things, than the author you hate does" ("Fyodor Dostoevski," in his *Lectures on Russian Literature*, 105). To be sure, *Dar* owes too much to *Les Faux-Monnayeurs* to justify a claim that "Nabokov hates Gide," but the émigré's attitude to the French *maître* and his novel is not that of unequivocal acceptance. As I will show, Nabokov not only capitalizes on many compositional and thematic elements of *Les Faux-Monnayeurs* but strives to rework and go beyond his French model; learning much from Gide's esthetics, he exorcises its hostile features in his own art of the novel.

Les Faux-Monnayeurs is the story of a writer, Édouard, who nurtures the idea of a "pure novel" that would describe the process of artistic creation, codifying the rules of the genre as a kind of *Art of Novel* (*FM*, 990, 1082–84).[5] Édouard calls his novel *Les Faux-Monnayeurs*. He envisions it both as a project of conservation and a challenge to the naive realism and limitations of the nineteenth-century novel. His goal is narrative infinity (*FM*, 1201). Édouard records his progress and theories in notebooks that are part of Gide's text. They contain criticism of Édouard's ideal novel, foreshadowing many points raised against Gide's own novel. Considering the story of the book as more important than the book itself (*FM*,1083), Édouard does not complete his project. His last diary entry and the last words of Gide's novel indicate Édouard's intention to meet a new subject of observation: "We are supposed to meet tomorrow night. . . . I am eager to make Caloub's acquaintance" (*FM*, 1248). This equivalent of "to be continued" indicates that Édouard's story and the story of his novel transcend the physical boundary of Gide's *Les Faux-Monnayeurs*. In 1927 Gide published *Journal des Faux-Monnayeurs* (The journal of the counterfeiters), a record of his work on the novel and of his artistic agenda.

In the dedication to *Les Faux-Monnayeurs* and in *Journal des Faux-Monnayeurs*, Gide stated that this was his first novel, underscoring the importance of generic identity for a text that comprised, like Édouard's pure novel, the sum total of Gide's experience (*JFM*, 35; *FM*, 1081). The common perception that the novel was in crisis sparked lively debates in French literary circles about the genre's possible demise (see chapter 3). Gide's attempt to present the entirety of his novelistic and existential experience in a pure novel, that is, to encode the artistic principles and human significance of the genre (*JFM*, 13, 64, 66), was interpreted as a defensive response.[6] But his project was not artistically conservative: *Les Faux-Monnayeurs* combined classical language with radically new conception and composition.[7]

Dar describes the artistic maturation of an émigré writer Fedor Godunov-Cherdyntsev. Through a series of experiments in poetry and prose, Fedor comes to the conception of an ideal novel that echoes the universalist ethos of Édouard's project, "corresponding fully to the gift which he felt like a burden inside himself" (*G*, 94 [*D*, 108]). Fedor's novel will convey the role of fate in his life, his feeling of existence, and his esthetics, both drawing on the classical Russian novel and departing from it.[8] Although Fedor's ideal novel has no title, it could be titled *Dar*, because describing his life in exile Fedor will depict the maturation of his talent. Like Édouard, he dreams of narrative infinity (*G*, 329, 337 [*D*, 369, 378]). Nabokov's novel ends with a functional equivalent of "to be continued"—an Onegin stanza that states the unfinished nature of the narrative.[9] *Dar* contains samples of Fedor's literary experiments, which, like Édouard's diary, show a writer's evolution. Invoking the main vestiges of Russian literary history, Fedor surpasses Édouard's preoccupation with a genre and codifies the Russian literary tradition as a whole.

The fact that *Dar* addresses a greater scope of esthetic problems than does *Les Faux-Monnayeurs* follows from Nabokov's status as an émigré writer.[10] If Gide responds to the crisis of the novel in French literature, Nabokov is preoccupied with the fate of Russian letters in general. Despite differences in scope, both texts were esthetically ahead of their time, as testified by the reactions they elicited. Édouard feels that his work will be misunderstood by contemporaries, because he orients his art toward future readers (*FM*, 990–91). Echoing him, Gide wrote in *Journal des Faux-Monnayeurs*: "I am not interested in *urgent* issues, and, remaining myself, I would rather work for the *future*" (*JFM*, 17). Neither does Fedor expect much from his immediate audience, for "the real writer should ignore all readers but one, that of the future" (*G*, 340 [*D*, 381]).

Gide's rejection of the realist novel's mimetic conventions earned *Les*

Faux-Monnayeurs its most vocal foes. At the time when the new generation of writers was engaged in the renewal of realist conventions, Gide's metafiction exposed the artifice of literature and mocked naive realism. *Les Faux-Monnayeurs* proved too radical for both younger and older literati who remained under the spell of the "mimesis of product," as Hutcheon has described realist esthetics (*Narcissistic Narrative: the Metafictional Paradox*, 5). *Les Faux-Monnayeurs'* "mimesis of process" irritated the average reader and the average writer alike. Consequently, the reaction to Gide's "novel for critics" was often that of hostility.[11] On March 5, 1927, Gide wrote in his diary: "They insist that *Les Faux-Monnayeurs* is a failure. In less than twenty years they will see that the very things my book is blamed for constitute its merit" (*J*, 832). As critics aired hesitation and frustration vis-à-vis Gide's text, few commentators ventured to charge contemporaries with the misunderstanding of the novel's purpose and significance.[12] To make matters worse, many readers were annoyed with overt homosexuality in *Les Faux-Monnayeurs*. Some critics were scandalized to the point of refusing to discuss the novel.[13]

Dar's critical reception was also that of misunderstanding and embarrassment. Although Khodasevich hailed the novel as the summit of Nabokov's artistic evolution, *Dar* elicited few responses, failing to spark the critical debate Nabokov had expected.[14] Like Gide, Nabokov realized that his novel would irritate and even be inaccessible to the average reader.[15] Yet even professional literati withheld judgment. Throughout the novel's serialization, both friendly and hostile critics claimed to reserve their opinion until the text appeared in full; but when the publication was completed, they used the suppression of chapter 4 as a pretext not to discuss *Dar* until the definitive text was published.[16] Although an excerpt from chapter 4 did appear in the émigré press in late 1939, this status quo persisted through the demise of émigré literary life in Europe.[17]

Khodasevich predicted such critical reception. Echoing Jaloux's verdict on *Les Faux-Monnayeurs*, he suggested that to describe a writer at work Nabokov would have to create a plot too challenging for those unfamiliar with literary craft. Later he argued that *Dar* could not be duly appreciated by average readers and writers, because "the complexity of [Nabokov's] craft and the level of his artistic culture are head and shoulders above our literary epoch."[18] Indeed, the serialization of *Dar* had hardly begun when Pil'skii castigated the novel as written "not for readers but for and about literature," a reproach commonly leveled against *Les Faux-Monnayeurs*. The critic refused to consider *Dar* as a novel because of its departure from the nineteenth-century realist canon. This was a common view among Gide's critics as well. Some of them, however, gave *Les Faux-Monnayeurs* the benefit of the doubt, admitting that it could be a radically new kind of novel.[19] As for Nabokov, such critical attacks only reinforced his resolve to break the canon, for "every original novel was 'anti-' because it did not resemble the genre or kind of its predecessor" (*Strong Opinions*, 173).

The Novel as a Hall of Mirrors

Discussing his project with Roger Martin du Gard, Gide described the difference between the nineteenth-century realist esthetics and that of *Les Faux-Monnayeurs:*

> He took a white sheet of paper and drew a straight horizontal line. Then, with the luminous point of my flashlight, he slowly traced the line from one end to another: "This is your *Thibault.* . . . And here is how I want to compose my *Faux-Monnayeurs.*" He flipped the sheet, drew a large semicircle, placed the flashlight in the middle, and keeping it in one place, spun the flashlight, leading the ray along the curve: "Those are two different esthetics. . . . There exists a subtle science of illumination [science subtile des éclairages]; to vary illumination infinitely is an art in itself."[20]

Gide implemented his science of illumination by the compositional principle of the *mise en abyme,* a term he had coined some twenty years earlier, and by the introduction of multiple narrative voices that recount the same story from different viewpoints.

In his diary, Gide defined the *mise en abyme* technique as "a transposition of the work's subject matter on the level of its characters."[21] This technique consists of inserting one discourse within another, whereby the incorporated text "mirrors," in Gide's terms, the incorporating one, emphasizing the formal structure of the work as a whole and drawing attention to the relationship between the author and his creation.[22] *Les Faux-Monnayeurs* is a system of textual mirrors placed in front of each other and reflecting each other to infinity. Gide's attempt to compose a pure novel, as described in *Journal des Faux-Monnayeurs,* is mirrored in the activity of the novel's anonymous author-narrator, who keeps a similar journal (*FM,* 1109). The project of this narrator is mirrored in Édouard's attempt to write a pure novel, related through Édouard's diary and notebooks. Édouard's project is mirrored in his ideal novel because its protagonist is also a novelist in quest of a pure novel and will write a novel about writing a novel, which will be reflected in another novel, and so forth.

Journal des Faux-Monnayeurs mirrors Gide's intimate *Journal*, in which the writer discussed his project. The insertion of Édouard's notebooks devoted to his novel into his intimate diary mirrors the relationship between Gide's *Journal* and *Journal des Faux-Monnayeurs*. Gide intended to incorporate his *Journal des Faux-Monnayeurs* into *Les Faux-Monnayeurs* (*JFM*, 52), but they form one text even as separate publications. *Les Faux-Monnayeurs* mirrors the narrative in *Journal des Faux-Monnayeurs*, which tells two simultaneous stories: that of a book and that of a man writing a book. By calling *Journal des Faux-Monnayeurs* "l'histoire même du livre" (*JFM*, 52), whereby "histoire" is both history and story, Gide endows it with the value of fiction, reinforced by *Journal des Faux-Monnayeurs*'s literary language. Édouard also gives equal narrative value to his novel and to its record: he says that if there existed the journals of *Education Sentimentale* and *The Brothers Karamazov*, they could be more interesting than the novels themselves (*FM*, 1083). Édouard's and Gide's novels are in a mirror relationship with each other and with their respective journals, which are in a mirror relationship with the writers' intimate diaries. All these novels, journals, and diaries are complementary and self-perpetuating. Our progress in *Les Faux-Monnayeurs* is not linear or unidirectional—we are caught in a system of texts, shuttling from one text to another.[23]

Dar includes texts that function like Édouard's journal and diary: Fedor's poems, the stories of Fedor's father, Iasha, and Nikolai Chernyshevskii. They punctuate the progress of Fedor's artistic search. For Édouard narrative infinity is contingent on his ignorance of the novel's finale (*FM*, 1200); his novel is a mystical undertaking and its realization is mostly intuitive (*FM*, 1097, 1185). Fedor also feels that only intuition can help "transfer" his text from another dimension where it already exists (*G*,138, 171, 194 [*D*, 156, 192, 218]). Both writers think that fate will reveal the denouement of their novels: the role of fate in their lives is their novelistic material (*FM*, 1082; *G*, 363 [*D*, 407]). Fedor's method of trial and error is consistent with Édouard's cult of process. Neither *Les Faux-Monnayeurs* nor *Dar* present the fruit of the heroes' quests. Instead, they offer experiments that mirror both the ideal and the incorporating novels (we hold the latter in our hands).

However, Fedor's belief in his text's otherworldly life goes beyond Édouard's art of novel. The French novelist is unsure whether his project is feasible. Symptomatically, Édouard's friend suggests that he will never write his novel (*FM*, 1083). Fedor, on the other hand, implicitly profits from and capitalizes on Édouard's pioneering travail. As a result, he is more comfortable with regard both to his project and to his own ability (gift) to see it through. Thus, his mother is convinced that her son will realize his novel (*G*, 139 [*D*, 157]).

Building on Gide's literary praxis, Nabokov crosses its boundaries as outlined in *Les Faux-Monnayeurs*. Gide stresses the mirror relationship of incorporated and incorporating texts; Nabokov obfuscates it. He does so not only to veil his indebtedness to Gide but also to pursue his program of deliberately confusing the reader, manifest throughout *Dar*. The story of Iasha Chernyshevskii is said to have "remained unused by the writer" (*G*, 41 [*D*, 49]) because its banal nature "would never have permitted [Fedor] to make it into a short story or novel" (*G*, 43 [*D*, 51]). The story of Fedor's father is dismissed as "disjointed and inchoate extracts" (*G*, 138 [*D*, 156]). Yet both stories are fully told and reflect Fedor's own story. In his father's biography Fedor elaborates on the theme of a liberating journey away from home. His father is a natural scientist whose trips toward "Asiatic freedom" (*G*, 335 [*D*, 375]) evoke Fedor's journey into Pushkin's art and his own liberating exile. Iasha's story also mirrors Fedor's life in art. They belong to the same age group, share physical traits, live in Berlin, attend the same university, write poetry; Fedor wears Iasha's tie. Although the semblance is deceptive—articulating Iasha's esthetics, Fedor frees himself from its flaws (*G*, 40, 44 [*D*, 48, 53])—Iasha's "typical" and "classical" story evokes Fedor's ideal "classical novel with 'types,' love, fate, conversations" (*G*, 349 [*D*, 392]).

Besides the main narrative (Fedor's story), incorporated texts reflect each other. The stories of Iasha and Fedor's father anticipate that of Nikolai Chernyshevskii. Iasha is related to the critic by family heritage and esthetics (*G*, 43 [*D*, 51]); Chernyshevskii the exile repeats the eastward journey of Fedor's father (*G*, 284 [*D*, 316]). But his trip does not spell out freedom after he is released from forced labor, because he has no appreciation of nature. Being a philistine in art and life, this fighter for freedom fails Fedor's test by freedom.[24] Posterior to the stories of Iasha and Fedor's father in *Dar*, the life of the nineteenth-century critic anticipates them chronologically; mirrored and foreshadowed by the preceding stories, it reflects back—we return to the stories of Iasha and Fedor's father, which acquire additional meaning in the rearview mirror of Chernyshevskii's life and esthetics.

Paraphrasing Stendhal, Édouard says about his own diary: "This is a mirror that I carry with me. Nothing that I meet becomes real to me until I see it reflected in it [the mirror]" (*FM*, 1057). Critics seized on Gide's subversive use of the mirror metaphor, commonly applied to describe the realist view of art as a "mirror of life." Wrote Arland: "He appropriated Stendhal's epigraph: 'A novel is a mirror that walks along a road.' But at least Stendhal chose his road carefully, and, besides, the mirror Gide is holding is held badly, for it reflects Gide himself and only him."[25] Arland assailed Gide's violation of the "mimesis of product." For Gide, however, the very meaning of reality was different. What appears real is actually deceptive and must be filtered through the lens of writing. Even when reflected, a life utterance cannot be trusted. The plaque Bernard Profitendieu removes to access his mother's letters is alternately characterized as onyx and as marble. In a polished state both materials have a reflective surface in which Bernard can see himself. This mirror surface conceals the true Bernard, for the letters reveal that he is the fruit of an extramarital affair. What Gide presents as a *direct* reflection of inherently deceptive reality is perceived by Arland as a *distorted* reflection of life appearances taken at face value.

Fedor also finds that mirror surfaces hide the true state of things. He places money on glass counters in exchange for overpriced goods; his new shoes are unfitting but have a polished and shiny surface (*G*, 5–7, 69 [*D*, 12–13, 79]). This recalls the central image of Gide's novel—fake coins that reveal crystal surface under gold coating. In a mocking response to the naive realism of Marcel Arland and Nikolai Chernyshevskii, who view art as an inferior reflection of life, Nabokov's mirror reflections show how life imitates art: the wallpaper in Fedor's room matches the pattern of Frau Stoboy's dress; Iasha's parents share the same name and patronymic. Reality even cheats in front of a mirror. Fedor's landlady stands before a mirror with an "oddly altered expression (as if she were dimming and coaxing her reflection)" (*G*, 357 [*D*, 401]). But the ultimate slap in the face of realism comes in *Dar*'s opening scene, which realizes Stendhal's metaphor. Engaging with Gide's text, Nabokov manipulates the vocabulary of the critical debate around it. In this scene, movers carry a wardrobe with a mirror that reflects boughs "sliding and swaying not arboreally, but with a human vacillation, produced by the nature of those who were carrying this sky, these boughs" (*G*, 6 [*D*, 12]). The walking mirror from Stendhal's phrase is carried by humans who determine its angle of reflection the way a writer manipulates his literary "mirrors."

The poet with a "mirrory heart" (*G*, 65 [*D*, 76]), Fedor is haunted by mirrors from childhood.[26] He considers his own prose as "mirror-like" and akin to that of the émigré writer Vladimirov—Nabokov's alter ego in the novel (*G*, 321 [*D*, 359]). This detail elevates the mirror theme to the metaliterary level. Like the author and hero of *Les Faux-Monnayeurs*, the author and hero of *Dar* write "mirror" prose. Following the *mise en abyme* technique, the mirror composition of *Dar* is reflected in Fedor's texts, whose mirror composition will be reflected in his future novel. Fedor's writings and Nabokov's novel are in a mirror relationship that forces the reader to become a (re-)creator who shuttles from the incorporated to the incorporating texts (re)establishing *Dar*'s larger meaning.

The Novel as an Apple Peel

Fedor conceives his biography of Nikolai Chernyshevskii as "a single un-interrupted progression of thought. I must peel my apple in a single strip," he says (*G*, 200 [*D*, 225]). At first it seems that the circular structure of his *Chernyshevskii*, which opens with two tercets and closes with two quatrains of a sonnet, encouraging readers to return to its beginning, is in keeping with Fedor's artistic intent. But this is not quite what he longs for. Instead of following the never-ending spiral of an apple peel, the story is delimited by its closed circularity and is therefore finite, only caricaturing Fedor's ideal of narrative infinity. This camouflaged compositional discrepancy is mirrored in the deceptive similarity of Fedor's and Chernyshevskii's quests. Chernyshevskii dreams of a *perpetuum mobile*—utilitarian "infinity with a minus sign" (*G*, 218 [*D*, 245]), which distorts and caricatures Fedor's idea of infinity as otherworldly transcendence.[27] Such distorted mirroring on the compositional and thematic levels is in keeping with Fedor's larger conception of *Chernyshevskii* as a walk along the "narrow ridge between my own truth and a caricature of it" (*G*, 200 [*D*, 225]), a conception he borrows from *Les Faux-Monnayeurs* along with devices that help realize it.

A sonnet as a marker of infinity haunts *Journal des Faux-Monnayeurs*, whose narrator sees his own novel as a sonnet, with quatrains opening and tercets closing it, and wants "attentive readers" to heed his device ("J'aime à donner à mes livres l'aspect du sonnet qui commence en quatrains et finit en tercets. Il me paraît toujours inutile d'expliquer tout au long ce que le lecteur attentif a compris" [I like to give my books the appearance of a sonnet that opens with quatrains and closes with tercets. It always seems to me unnecessary to keep explaining what the attentive reader has understood], *JFM*, 97). By reversing the normal stanzaic order, Fedor capitalizes on Gide's device and attempts to create narrative infinity through circularity. His failure does not diminish the credit due to a disciple's courage to try and outdo his teacher before reaching full artistic maturity, which at any rate comes through the experience of trial and error. As could already be expected, the parodic mirroring of Fedor's artistic ideal in Chernyshevskii harks back to Édouard's position vis-à-vis his antagonist, the count of Passavant, who brags about his own future novel in which he will fully realize himself (*FM*, 1044). In this distorting but revelatory mirror relationship, Passavant's brilliance is as deceptive as that of fake coins (*FM*, 1167).

The distorted mirroring of Édouard's and Fedor's quests bears on their esthetics. When textual mirrors face one another, each text both caricatures and complements its counterpart. The common traits of Fedor's and Chernyshevskii's endeavors are both ridiculed and used to Fedor's ends. Fedor's and Édouard's antagonists are shadows that give an additional dimension to the heroes' personae. Fedor writes about Chernyshevskii:

> Any genuinely new trend is a knight's move, a change of shadows, shift that displaces the mirror. . . . Chernyshevskii, who like the majority of revolutionaries was a complete bourgeois in his artistic and scientific tastes, . . . wrote to his sons from Siberia in the seventies, "all Kazan was of the unanimous opinion that the man [Lobachevskii] was a complete fool. . . . What on earth is the curvature of a ray or curved space? What is geometry without the axiom of parallel lines"? (*G*, 239 [*D*, 268])

This passage recalls Gide's description of his science of illumination to Martin du Gard, whereby the chronological line of events, illuminated by a light source that moves parallel to it, yields to an oblique line (cf. "the curvature of a ray" and "curved space") illuminated unevenly by a stationary source. Debating with Martin du Gard, Gide wrote:

> Sa lanterne de romancier éclaire toujours de face les événements qu'il considère. . . . Jamais leurs lignes ne se mêlent [cf. geometry without the axiom of parallel lines] et, pas plus qu'il n'y a d'ombre, il n'y a de perspective [cf. curved space]. Étudier d'abord le point d'où doit affluer la lumière; toutes les ombres en dépendent. Chaque figure repose et s'appuie sur son ombre [cf. change of shadows].
>
> ⤸
>
> [His novelistic lantern always illuminates the contemplated events from the front. . . . Their lines never mix and there is nei-

ther shadow nor perspective. One must first study the source of
light; all shadows depend on it. Each figure is based upon and
relies on its shadow.] (*JFM*, 34)

For Fedor a glimpse into the otherworldly dimension, whose angle
is tilted, requires tilted mirrors and a play of shadows: direct reflection
produces a (vicious) circle, multiplication of deceitful appearances (*G*,
328, 341 [*D*, 368, 382]). When Fedor finds himself in a stairwell with a
glass door, an automatic light switch helps him momentarily transcend
everyday life. It is dark outside, the light is on, and the glass door reflects
life on the inside—Fedor's meeting with Zina. But when the switch
turns off the light, the door reveals the world on the outside and trans-
forms the light of a street lamp into a prismatic rainbow on the wall
of the stairwell. Fedor "suddenly felt—in this glassy darkness—the
strangeness of life, the strangeness of its magic, as if a corner of it had
been turned back for an instant and he had glimpsed its unusual lining"
(*G*, 183 [*D*, 205]). This experience is significant in its description of the
texture of space, which Fedor conveys by giving his ideal novel the spiral structure of an apple peel, whose twists reveal the inside as well as
the outside surface.

Much has been said about the composition of *Dar*. Tammi finds that
it "is organized in the form of a circle" (*Problems of Nabokov's Poetics*, 96).
Johnson sees it as a "ring structure with self-contained spiralling thematic nodes" and argues that "like the Chernyshevskii biography, *The
Gift* displays the form of the legendary snake swallowing its own tail"
(*Worlds in Regression*, 95). I. and O. Ronen have described it as a "Möbius
strip-like structure," whereby "the novel being read is at the same time
the novel to be written by its protagonist after the narrative's end" and
"the latter novel shows, as it were, through the texture of the former"
("Diabolically Evocative," 378). These views have been contested by
scholars such as Levin and Dolinin, who pointed out discrepancies between Fedor's description of his future novel and the text of *Dar*.[28] Taking to task the notion of *Dar*'s narrative as a circle, Toker dubbed the
novel's composition "a receding spiral," while Waite spoke about *Dar*'s
"tripartite linear structure which may provide 'a way out' of the circular structure."[29]

In the context of Gide's praxis, the conception of Chernyshevskii's
story as a spiral apple peel and its realization as a circle appears to be a
trap for the reader. Misled by the distorting mirror relationship of incorporating and incorporated texts, one projects the circular narrative
of the story upon *Dar*, which also ends with a poem that suggests nar-

rative infinity. But unlike the sonnet, *Dar*'s Onegin stanza does not necessarily send the reader to the novel's beginning, contrary to Boyd's suggestion (*Vladimir Nabokov*, 462). If we succumb to the temptation of circularity and reread *Dar* as Fedor's creation, we will violate his clearly articulated esthetics. *Dar* cannot be Fedor's *auto*biography in art: this would contradict his cult of imagination ("To fiction be as to your country true" [*G*, 156 (*D*, 176)]) and intention to rework life to the point "that nothing remains of the autobiography but dust" (*G*, 364 [*D*, 409]). Nabokov learns this compositional trap from Gide, who conditions us to become rereaders ("Je n'écris que pour être *relu*" [I write to be *reread* only], *JFM*, 47), while a rereading shows that Édouard's and Gide's novels do not coincide.[30] Shuttling in a system of textual mirrors, Gide's reader is engaged in a spiral rather than a circular motion, because he is not bound to the same text. He moves between the mutually reflective texts within *Les Faux-Monnayeurs* and between different textual levels—the novel, its *Journal*, and Gide's *Journal*. The goal is not to become a rereader but to rise above the existing levels and create Édouard's unwritten novel, which, like a never-ending spiral, engenders new texts about texts.

The reader easily succumbs to temptation by circularity, thanks to "the circular nature of everything in existence" (*G*, 204 [*D*, 230]). Fedor comes to see circularity as a vicious circle, "a diabolical semblance of space" that appears in a stereoscope (*G*, 17 [*D*, 24]). "In our straining toward asymmetry, toward inequality," says Koncheev in Fedor's imaginary dialogue with the émigré poet, "I can detect a howl for genuine freedom, an urge to break out of the circle" (*G*, 343 [*D*, 384]). This is why, having realized that the death of Iasha's father ends a chapter in his own life, Fedor does not want his recollections of this chapter "to close [zamknut'sia] and get lost"; "there is a way—the only way" to save them from deformation by circularity: Fedor must "apply all this to himself, to his eternity, to his truth, so as to enable it to sprout up in a new way" (*G*, 337 [*D*, 378]). This procedure undoubtedly refers to his future novel, which will eschew the temptation of circularity.

The temptation of universal symmetry and circularity is conveyed in Gide's and, subsequently, in Nabokov's novels by recurring numbers. In *Les Faux-Monnayeurs* this number is thirteen—an allusion to the supreme tempter who helps Bernard steal his mothers' letters and Édouard's suitcase; oversees Vincent Molinier's affair with Lady Griffith; attends to the distribution of fake coins by the pupils of the Azaïs pension; and assists their plot to drive their comrade Boris to suicide (*FM*,

934, 974, 996, 1045, 1233). There are thirteen letters in the batch stolen by Bernard; thirteen letters are written by characters in the novel, each punctuating the development of the plot.[31] The number symbolizes the novel's tendency to tempt the reader with (vicious) circularity.

In *Dar* the symbolic number is five. Fedor conceives six texts—his book of poetry; the poem to Zina; the stories of his father, Iasha, and Chernyshevskii; and, finally, the ideal novel—but realizes only five. Capitalizing on Gide's praxis, Nabokov sets up an additional trap. It is no longer enough to notice recurring numbers and link them to the pitfall of circularity. The symmetry of recurring numbers is deceptive. Fedor wants to buy five *pirozhki* but cannot afford the fifth (*G*, 30 [*D*, 37]); he thinks of five reviewers of his book, but the fifth is imaginary (*G*, 30 [*D*, 37]); Vasil'ev speaks about five Kremlin bosses who have four Western antipodes (*G*, 36 [*D*, 43]); Zina has five reasons not to kiss Fedor but kisses him after the fourth (*G*, 183 [*D*, 206]); Fedor passes five lines of rails on his way to the park (*G*, 328 [*D*, 367]), where he sees five nuns (*G*, 344 [*D*, 386]); and Koncheev exposes five weak points of his art (*G*, 339 [*D*, 380]). The break in symmetry, whereby five becomes four, alludes to Fedor's fifth text: as Blackwell has shown, the poem to Zina does not appear as a coherent text at the novel's first reading.[32] But if we ignore the break in symmetry and miss the camouflaged poem, we may assume, further encouraged by the obvious analogy with *Dar*'s five chapters, that Fedor's fifth text has been realized as *Dar* itself.

The web of deception in *Les Faux-Monnayeurs* and *Dar* reveals tension between the authors' desire to control textual interpretation and their desire to elevate the reader to the status of an artist. Falling into the trap of circularity, we will reread *Dar* as Fedor's novel and *Les Faux-Monnayeurs* as Édouard's creation. Seeing narrative infinity as a spiral, we will take over Fedor's and Édouard's ideal novels. According to Gide's *Journal*, the ending of *Les Faux-Monnayeurs* is supposed to give the impression of a limitless narrative, while the lack of a future plot outline (*l'érosion de contours*) encourages the reader to write his or her own story (*JFM*, 83, 94, 96). This creative freedom confirms the text's premise of esthetic pluralism ("Rien n'est bon pour tous" [Nothing is good for all], *FM*, 1089) and epitomizes Gide's rejection of the nineteenth-century novel as the authoritative account of an event. *Les Faux-Monnayeurs* thus appear as a "modèle maximale" of the novelistic narrative and one of many possible constructions of a story.[33]

Yet, *Journal des Faux-Monnayeurs* and Gide's *Journal* explicate the novel authoritatively by giving the creator's point of view on his creation. His *Journal* even suggests that *Les Faux-Monnayeurs* controls its readers by letting them believe that they are "more intelligent than the author, more moral, more perspicacious, and discover numerous things in the characters and numerous truths in the course of the narrative despite the author and, so to speak, without the author's knowledge" (*JFM*, 72).[34] This dialectic between the authorial desire to guard the text from unintended interpretation and to offer it as material for the reader cum artist is endemic to *Les Faux-Monnayeurs* and, through its mediation, to *Dar.* Along with the mirror composition, it marks another major device of Gide's science of illumination (assiduously studied by Nabokov)—the multiplicity of narrative voices.

The Novel as Puppet Theater

The use of multiple narrative voices both allows creative interpretation and channels reading in a direction projected by the author. Gide's reader sorts out narrative voices, evaluates their credibility, and decides how faithfully each conveys a given event (*JFM*, 33). Most characters in *Les Faux-Monnayeurs* are storytellers. There are four mature novelists: the author-narrator, Édouard, his friend X, and Robert de Passavant. There is also a group of Parisian teenagers, most of whom are aspiring writers. Lilian Griffith and Vincent Molinier are artists in their own right, for their interest in natural history has a strong storytelling bent. The author-narrator and characters offer their own, artistically stylized interpretations of events used by the reader to reconstruct a "truthful" rendition of a given event.

A case in point is the affair of Vincent Molinier and Laura Douviers. First, we learn about it from Vincent's brother Olivier, as he tells Bernard Profitendieu of eavesdropping on Vincent and Laura. The same story is related differently by Vincent to his lover, Lilian Griffith, who reinterprets it for her confidant, Robert de Passavant. Then we learn more contradictory information from Laura's letter to Édouard. Next Édouard interprets this liaison in his diary, stolen and read by Bernard. Bernard reinterprets Édouard's and Olivier's versions and tells his own to Laura. Later he proposes another view in his letter to Olivier. The narrator also gives his take on the matter "for the edification of the reader" (*FM*, 1045). Finally, Laura's husband exposes his understanding of the situation. This technique of multiple expositions echoes on the narrative level the novel's composition—numerous versions of one event function as mutually reflecting and distorting mirrors.

Gide reinforces the effect of multiple expositions by obfuscating the relationship between the narrator and his text. The narrative "I" seems to belong to the omniscient author-narrator, who places the discourse of characters in quotation marks as distinct from his own and stresses his control by commenting on the text's stylistic and compositional aspects.[35] Yet the tension between his presumed omniscience and lack thereof runs through the book. His lack of omniscience ranges from remarks that pass for stylistic idiosyncrasy to the ignorance of details and to statements implying that characters act independently from the author, as in chapter 7 of "Saas-Fée," where protagonists are discussed as agents of free will.[36] The reader vacillates between the narrative "I" as the property of an omniscient author-narrator and that of a subjective observer, whose exposition of events holds no more truth than the viewpoints of the novel's characters.

Nabokov successfully radicalized Gide's praxis by removing quotation marks around Fedor's discourse and by eliminating all graphic distinction between the voices of his author-narrator and Fedor, a distinction that runs through Gide's novel, where graphic and syntactic markers always separate the speech of the author-narrator from that of Édouard. In the context of Gide's narrative experiments, one is inclined to favor the second of the three possible approaches to the problem of narrative voices in *Dar*, outlined by Tammi as follows: 1) all voices belong to Fedor, who relates the story of his artistic maturation from the distanced position of a mature artist, in which case *Dar* is his creation; 2) the voices are divided between the author-narrator and Fedor, in which case Fedor's novel cannot coincide with *Dar* (a view first expressed by Davydov); 3) all voices belong to Fedor but he does not control them, for they constitute his "stream of consciousness" (a view elaborated by Levin).[37] Fedor imagines the inner life of others and assumes their identities. In the imaginary review of his poetry he speaks of himself in third person; he conducts imaginary dialogues with Koncheev, invents inner monologues for Iasha's father, and assumes the "I" of his own father.[38] *Dar's* narrator blurs the lines between narrative voices, mixing "I" and "we," as in the description of Fedor's trip home: "He was walking along streets. . . . Here at last is the square where we dined" (*G*, 53 [*D*, 62]). Prepared by previous alternation in narrative voices, one thinks that it is Fedor who says "we." This assumption is broken several lines later: "Accustomed to subjection we everywhere appoint over ourselves the shadow of supervision. Fedor understood perfectly well . . ." (*G*, 54 [*D*, 63]). The pronoun may include Fedor, but it is uttered by the author-narrator.[39] As Dolinin points out, this pronominal alternation sets up a compositional trap. In *Dar*'s closing scene (Fedor and Zina dine in a restaurant on a square), Fedor's passage by "the square where we dined" can serve as a proleptic allusion to the book's finale and proof that all voices belong to Fedor.[40] This interpretation (no. 1 in Tammi's classification) makes Fedor the author-narrator of *Dar*. But a rereader will notice that the square Fedor passes in chapter 1 differs from the square where he and Zina dine.

Gide used puppet theater imagery to symbolize his "technique of false authorship," which tricks the reader into assuming that he is more intelligent than the author and can produce an authoritative interpretation of events in the novel.[41] These images appear in the last part of *Les Faux-Monnayeurs*, when the old La Pérouse confesses that he contemplates suicide as the act of a puppet quitting the stage on its own, for he sees himself as a string puppet controlled by God's will (*FM*, 1132–33). The metaphor is developed in *Journal des Faux-Monnayeurs*, where the entire novel is likened to a theater and its characters to puppets (*JFM*, 27, 65), a comparison that can be extended to the reader who falls prey to authorial manipulation. The reader may think that, having assimilated the know-how of Édouard's craft, he can continue both Édouard's story and his unfinished novel. But the composition of *Les Faux-Monnayeurs* will not allow him to be more creative than Gide wants him to be, filtering the reader's imagination through the corrective lenses of *Journal des Faux-Monnayeurs* and Gide's *Journal*.

Authorial striving for control transpires with equal strength in *Dar*. The novel's narrator makes fun of the inattentive critic Linev, who in his reviews "provides books with his own ending—usually exactly opposite to the author's intention" (*G*, 169 [*D*, 190]). One feels here a desire to discipline those who do not follow the author's guidelines. Nabokov leaves little room for freedom in his text, as echoed in Fedor's own wish to "reach a final dictatorship over words," cutting short unintended interpretation, since presently his words "are still trying to vote" (*G*, 364 [*D*, 409]). Paperno sees in such a dictatorial attitude not only a desire to organize everything in the text proper but to determine its reading and the process of its literary investigation ("How Nabokov's *Gift* Is Made," 313). One could thus agree with Adamovich's view that *Dar* is "ironic by its very conception" ("'Sovremennye zapiski,' kniga 63," 3): it is indeed ironic that, suggesting to his reader that he is an equal partner in the process of creation, Nabokov ensnares him in the net of authorial control. But he is only successfully developing the lessons of *Les Faux-*

Monnayeurs, which was, equally ironically (and unlike *Dar*), among Adamovich's favorite books.

Nabokov adopted Gide's use of the puppet theater metaphor to describe this effect of authorial control. Puppet theater imagery first appears in chapter 1, when, interrupting the review of his poetry, Fedor exclaims: "Why doesn't the epithet 'quivering' quite satisfy me? Or does the puppeteer's colossal hand appear here for an instant among the creatures whose size the eye had come to accept (so that the spectator's first reaction at the end of the show is 'How big I have grown!')?" (*G*, 10 [*D*, 17]).[42] The same imagery describes Fedor's entire life as a theatrical convention ("the treaty with reason—the theater of earthly habit, the livery of temporary substance" [*G*, 355 (*D*, 399)]), emphasizing both his control over his texts and the reign of *Dar*'s author-narrator over his characters. Following Gide's example, *Dar*'s mirror composition and multiple narrative voices set a series of traps in order to make the reader "the author reflected in time" (*G*, 340 [*D*, 381]) by predetermining the way in which we assign narrative voices and move between textual mirrors.

Thus, if Fedor's attempt to exploit Gidean praxis in the composition of *Chernyshevskii* fails because of his artistic immaturity, Fedor's creator is more successful in drawing on the same lessons. It is Nabokov who, like Gide, completes his novel, while Fedor, similarly to Édouard, has yet much to learn before he can "transfer" his text from imagination to paper.

The Novel as a Bunch of False Keys

Setting up its traps, *Dar* played on the esthetic expectation of contemporaries whose memory bore a fresh impression of Proust's *La Recherche*, a circular narrative with the protagonist-narrator as its author. Proust is a decoy luring us into Nabokov's snares. Throwing in the false key of Proustian circularity, Nabokov makes his reader go back to the beginning and reread *Dar* only to discover that Fedor is not its author.[43] Buks has suggested that *Dar* may be a parody of the metanovel (*Eshafot v khrustal'nom dvortse*, 143). Indeed, thanks to elaborate structural deception, it appears both as a parody and as a new kind of metanovel, but only if one considers *La Recherche* as the paradigmatic metanovel of Nabokov's time.

Fedor's imaginary poetry review evokes Proust's art of memory through long sentences with multiple subordinate clauses and parenthetic digressions.[44] But these "Proustian" references are self-subversive.

In the course of his review, Fedor realizes the impossibility of recapturing the lost time of childhood. Objects, sounds, and smells that are pregnant with suggestive power for Marcel refuse to yield their secrets to Fedor (*G*, 5 [*D*, 11]); his recollections are suspiciously "wax-like" and "pretty" (*G*, 17 [*D*, 24]). Proust's steadfast linguistic articulation irritates Fedor, who is unable to express himself adequately: "What, then, compels me to compose poems about my childhood if in spite of everything my words go wide of the mark, or else slay both the pard and the hart with the exploding bullet of an 'accurate' epithet?" (*G*, 18, [*D*, 25]). Concluding that childhood cannot be recovered by means of art ("recollections either melt away, or else acquire a deathly gloss" [*G*, 17 (*D*, 24)]), Fedor concedes that it can only serve as literary material (*G*, 26 [*D*, 32]). Hence his skepticism about the documentary value of the art of memory. He sees Proust's method of amassing seemingly insignificant details as a device that creates the effect of "truthfulness" (*G*, 27 [*D*, 33]), which does not interest Fedor because of his cult of imagination. Alluding to the titles of Proust's novels, Fedor dismisses Proustianism as a fashion that interferes with more important aspects of his poems: "Did he [the reader] simply skim over them, like them and praise them, calling attention to the significance of their sequence, a feature fashionable in our time, when time is in fashion: if a collection opens with a poem about 'A Lost Ball,' it must close with 'The Found Ball'" (*G*, 28 [*D*, 35]).

Fedor's skepticism vis-à-vis Proust's art of memory harks back to Édouard's rejection of Proustian analysis and its satellite in the minds of his contemporaries, Freudian psychoanalysis (Nabokov's favorite punching bag), as products of imagination that only simulate "truthfulness." Writes Édouard: "I lost all interest in psychological analysis ever since I realized that one feels what he imagines that he feels. Consequently, it is possible that one imagines that he feels what he feels" (*FM*, 988). Édouard expresses the same doubts with regard to Mme Sophroniska's psychoanalytical treatment of Boris de La Pérouse, discarding the boy's confessions as fiction (*FM*, 1074). Supporting his criticism of Proustian analysis, Gide refused to follow Proust's novelistic metanarrative. Thanks to his close ties to the *Nouvelle revue française*, he was familiar with *La Recherche* in its entirety during his work on *Les Faux-Monnayeurs*, unlike the average reader, who saw the last volume of Proust's novel in 1927. Proposing a metanovel that confronted the Proustian model, Gide oriented his text toward the future reader rather than the reader of 1925. *Journal des Faux-Monnayeurs* appeared as a separate volume concurrently with *Le Temps retrouvé*, as if, by stressing the formal side of *Les Faux-Monnayeurs,* Gide also wanted to emphasize its difference from *La Recherche.*

Gide excluded Édouard's novel from *Les Faux-Monnayeurs,* freed the reader from the hegemony of one narrator; and offered three separate texts (*Les Faux-Monnayeurs, Journal des Faux-Monnayeurs,* and his *Journal*) to Proust's reader, who circled in a single text with one narrator.[45] But in doing so, Gide offered his reader false clues: *Journal des Faux-Monnayeurs* suggests that rereading is the only possible key to the reading of *Les Faux-Monnayeurs.* The image of a fake coin metaphorizes this trap. The rereading of *Les Faux-Monnayeurs* resembles the multiple use of a coin whose coating disappears with each touch, ultimately leaving the user with a piece of crystal. Upon rereading the novel, one understands that one has been swindled.

Russian émigrés' attention was drawn to Gide's rejection of Proustian esthetics as early as 1926, when the review *Zveno* published in translation an excerpt from *Journal des Faux-Monnayeurs,* which was being serialized by the *Nouvelle revue française.* The choice of excerpt was doubly significant ("Son o Marsele Pruste," 8; *JFM,* 72–75). First of all, this was the entry of March 5, 1923, relating Gide's (probably fictional) dream about a confrontation with Proust, whereby Gide dropped and damaged several rare volumes of Proust's favorite book—the memoirs of Saint-Simon which had served as the inspiration for *La Recherche*—but assured Proust that he did not do it on purpose. Secondly, when Gide confessed to Proust's butler that he had dropped the books intentionally, the butler consoled him by giving Gide a tap on the shoulder "in a Russian way" ("de petites tapes sur l'épaule, à la russe," *JFM,* 75). The latter detail could have had special significance for Nabokov as he was getting ready to tap into Gide's anti-Proustian revolt and to rewrite it *à la russe.*

The fact that Édouard does not realize his novel in *Les Faux-Monnayeurs* establishes such a realization as an ideal horizon; the impossible becomes a paradoxical figure of the possible. Here again Nabokov follows Gide but throws in false cues to point in Proust's direction. Leading an ascetic life, Fedor at once fantasizes about a chance sexual encounter and is aware of the gap between ideal and reality. He extends his wariness of realized dreams to his relationship with Zina (*G,* 329, 360 [*D,* 369, 404]), echoing the quixotic conflict of Proust's heroes. But the similarity is deceptive. Zina makes her father resemble Swann, casting herself as Swann's daughter, Gilberte, Marcel's first love (*G,* 187 [*D,* 210]), while Fedor distances himself from Marcel by rejecting his art of memory. During his infatuation with Gilberte, Marcel still believes in the objective existence of love (*Swann*, 393) and is subsequently disillusioned. Fedor's love for Zina is, on the contrary, internalized in art— Zina is his Muse. When she asks Fedor if he loves her, he answers that he has declared his love by sharing with her the conception of his future novel (*G*, 364 [*D*, 409]). This divergence leads Fedor and Marcel to different conclusions with regard to their quixotic complexes. Marcel distinguishes between art and life, completing his novel as a "truer than life" alternative to deceptive reality. Fedor prefers to view artistic activity through the prism of his quixotic conflict. Playing on the polysemy of *roman* (affair vs. novel—this double entendre is lost in the English translation), *Dar*'s narrator says:

> Когда он заглядывался на прохожую, он купно переживал и потрясающую возможность счастья, и отвращение к его неизбежному несовершенству,—вкладывая в это одно мгновение образ романа, но на среднюю часть сокращая его триптих. (*D*, 186)

☙

> When he looked at a passing girl, he imagined simultaneously both the stupendous possibility of happiness and repugnance for its inevitable imperfection—charging this one instant with a romantic image [the image of a novel], but diminishing its triptych by the middle section. (*G*, 165)

Like the consummation of erotic passion, the fulfillment of an artistic ideal leads to disappointment. Hence Fedor's evocation of the post-coital syndrome after a night of writing (*G*, 158 [*D*, 177]). A written text cannot correspond to its ideal: says Fedor, "[D]efinition is always finite, but I keep straining for the faraway; I search beyond the barricades (of words, of senses, of the world) for infinity, where all, all the lines meet" (*G*, 329 [*D*, 369]). Fedor refuses to complete the story of his father—his emotional investment is frustrated by the story's realization: "I am so much afraid I might dirty it with a flashy phrase, or wear it out in the course of transfer onto paper, that I already doubt whether the book will be written at all" (*G*, 138 [*D*, 156]). *Chernyshevskii* is finished because its hero receives little empathy from Fedor. Unlike Marcel, Fedor does not realize his ideal novel, having learnt from Édouard that the impossible can be a paradoxical figure of the possible.

The traps of Gide's and Nabokov's science of illumination are laid bare in the leitmotif of a key that is either hidden, or lost, or does not work, or opens a wrong door. In *Les Faux-Monnayeurs,* Bernard breaks

into his mother's chest, to which he has no key, and steals Édouard's suitcase, whose key is lost. Olivier uses a secret duplicate of the key with
which he is locked up to circumvent his parents. Lilian slips Vincent
her house key, which he uses to betray Laura. Armand Vedel acts as a
tempter, locking his sister Sarah in one room with Bernard. When he lets
Bernard out, the latter must wait until the front door of the Azaïs pension is unlocked. Punning on the phrase "clés de voûte du livre" (*JFM*,
37; the book's cornerstones vs. keys to the book's vault), the narrator of
Journal des Faux-Monnayeurs claims to have keys to *Les Faux-Monnayeurs*,
but the keys he offers are false.

Gidean imagery becomes a pivotal leitmotif in *Dar*. A number of
scholars have treated the novel's key imagery.[46] The most comprehensive
account belongs to Johnson, who elaborated on three metaphorical uses
of the key motif: as keys to Russia that Fedor preserves through art; as
a paronomastic allusion (*kliuch* as a spring/fountain) to the inspiration
he draws from Pushkin's writings; and as a shift to the world of chess,
whose discussion echoes fate's moves that bring together Fedor and
Zina and alludes to Fedor's artistic method (*Worlds in Regression*, 95–
106). Since Fedor's keys are more often than not misplaced, stolen, or
wrong, keys to *Dar* may not be more reliable: this technique of false clues
is laid bare in a chess puzzle whose key is disguised in "the fine fabric
of deceit" and "false trails carefully prepared for the reader" (*G*, 172 [*D*,
193]). Against the backdrop of *Les Faux-Monnayeurs*, the words of Fedor's
mother after her move to Paris acquire additional meaning: "She had
written that she just could not get used to being liberated from the perpetual fetters that chain a Berliner to the door lock" (*G*, 29 [*D*, 36]). Not
that in Paris one does not need keys because of the institution of the
concierge—one merely has other, less honest ways of getting in.

But it takes a good student to learn those ways. Conveying his impression that Nabokov's keys opened wrong doors, Adamovich wrote:
"The author tells us what he considers as true. But we do not have the
key to this truth, Sirin does not give it to us" ("Russkie zapiski," 3). In
the same year, Khodasevich suggested that, instead of disguising his
devices, Nabokov laid them bare like a prestidigitator who revealed to
the audience the laboratory of his miracles. In this practice Khodasevich saw "the key to Sirin" ("O Sirine," 249). These critical views are
complementary. Nabokov's keys lead the reader away from truth and
subjugate him to the authorial will, a technique that had been successfully tested by Gide a decade earlier.

The Novel against Realism

Among the salient features of *Les Faux-Monnayeurs* is its antirealist and antinaturalist ethos, expressed in the rejection of the novel as "a slice of life" and "a facsimile of reality" (*FM*, 1080). The narrator of *Journal des Faux-Monnayeurs* wants "to liberate the novel from its realist rut" (*JFM*, 61) and treats the imitation of extraliterary reality as futile because apparent reality is deceptive, while its photographic reproduction lies outside the genre of the novel (*FM*, 990). "The spirit of the novel is about having the possible come to life instead of making one relive the real" (*JFM*, 98), states the narrator. Cultivating artistic imagination, he claims that the best parts of his book are "pure fiction" (*JFM*, 75). For Gide, imagination constitutes not only the essence of the novelist's craft but also of his relation to extraliterary reality.

Wary of apparent reality, Édouard regards tension between imagination and reality as the main problem of his novel (*FM*, 1082). He borrows from life his novel's plot by following the adventures of several Parisian teenagers. His view of the novel as a sum total of his artistic and life experience requires that he take into account every utterance of extraliterary reality (*FM*, 1081). But his cult of imagination does not permit the use of this material as is. In this struggle Édouard's authorial task consists of pushing his writer-protagonist closer to reality despite the hero's intentions (*FM*, 1082). The same procedure is performed by Édouard's own creator. Édouard sets up a situation to be incorporated into his novel: he lets Georges Molinier read his drafts describing Édouard's meeting with the official who investigates the distribution of fake coins by Georges and his friends. Georges's reaction disappoints Édouard, for he had another reaction in mind. The novelist decides not to go with reality and rewrites the part he had shown, since it reproduces reality too faithfully, ruining the effect he expected. He crowns his decision with a verdict: "Let us leave to realist novelists the preoccupation with naturalness" (*FM*, 1225).

Criticizing realist esthetics, Gide used the nineteenth-century Russian novel to illustrate the "self-imposed slavery of verisimilitude" (*FM*, 1080; *JFM*, 34). Incidentally, *Dar*'s opening sentence comments on the Russian novel's peculiar truthfulness, which "a foreign critic once remarked" (*G*, 3 [*D*, 9]). This observation is stylized as a nineteenth-century novelistic exposition with a characteristic ellipsis in place of a year; the arrival of a movers' van recalls the arrival of Chichikov's cart in *Dead Souls*.[47] It is April 1, Gogol's birthday and April Fool's Day—not

a good day for a "true story." Ironic allusions to nineteenth-century
clichés abound in *Dar*, indicating that Fedor's resolve to draw on classical heritage is far from indiscriminate deference.[48] Like Édouard, he is
torn between his desire to borrow from life (*G*, 363 [*D*, 407]) and belief
in the superiority of imagination. As he distances himself from life by
imagining how he would artistically rework it (*G*, 363–65 [*D*, 407–9]),
Nabokov pushes him closer to reality, following Gide's recipe for treating the writer-protagonist. Fedor is unaware of the surprise fate has in
stock: neither he nor Zina have keys to the apartment where they will
consummate their love on the first night of freedom from Zina's family.

In their antirealist quests, Gide and Nabokov blur their novels' historical setting. But if Gide is openly ahistorical, Nabokov constructs a
time puzzle. The narrator of *Journal des Faux-Monnayeurs* strives to free
his novel from "historical preoccupations" (*JFM*, 17–18) by "melting in
one and the same intrigue" (*JFM*, 23) the events marking the fin de siècle and interwar France. He eschews all mention of the war so as to confuse even the general outlines of historical time. The story of teenage
counterfeiters harks back to 1906, as pointed out in *Journal des Faux-
Monnayeurs;* so does Barrès's election to the academy, which the heroes
discuss; the circulation of golden coins in France stopped in 1914; the
staging of Alfred Jarry's *Ubu roi*, mentioned as recent, took place in 1896;
the reading of *Action française* would have been impossible before 1908;
the project of a new review evokes the first steps of Dada and surrealism after the war;[49] Marcel Duchamp's "Joconda," published in the review, dates from 1919; Mme Sophroniska's interest in psychoanalysis
marks the early 1920s in France.

Nabokov's reader is similarly confused by the lack of temporal markers and needs to conduct a virtual archeological search to place the
novel's historical time span between 1926 and 1929.[50] But even this time
bracket is compromised by chronologically posterior events. This ahistoricity is especially evident in Fedor's treatment of the Germans, depicted as people of a totalitarian culture. Nabokov's letter of September
4, 1937, repeats verbatim passages from *Dar*, confirming that this ahistorical effect is intentional. In 1937 he was still working on *Dar*, and his
view of Nazism spilled into the novel.[51] Nabokov's ahistoricism, to be
sure, did not make its debut in *Dar*. As Dolinin has noted, the writer's
career in exile was, from the outset, characterized by a negative attitude
vis-à-vis historical determinism and secular eschatology in its Marxist
and Spenglerian guises.[52] But it might not have found its fullest artistic
expression in *Dar* without Gide's mediation.

Given Nabokov's historical imprecision, the omission of a date in the beginning of *Dar* is hardly a sign of "truthfulness." It indicates the author's refusal to be a slave to extraliterary reality in its most distinct aspect—historical time. Like Zina, who was "completely unconcerned whether or not the author clung assiduously to historical truth" as long as he expressed "a deeper truth" (*G*, 205 [*D*, 230]), the reader is invited to leave the peculiarly realist engagement with history. Zina considers Chernyshevskii's real life "as something of a plagiarism" (*G*, 204 [*D*, 230]), inferior to the artistic reality of Fedor's *Chernyshevskii*. The positivist belief in the linearity of time runs counter both to the "the circular nature of everything in existence" (*G*, 204 [*D*, 230]) and to Gide's and Nabokov's science of illumination. Their rejection of historical rootedness and chronological exposition of events in the realist novel is also a philosophical rejection of the positivist concept of time. The antipositivist ethos of *Les Faux-Monnayeurs* is passed on to *Dar*, which castigates the "rough-hewn materialism" (*G*, 221 [*D*, 249]) of those who deny mystical experience while being ignorant of deception in nature and of natural history in general.

A case in point is Vincent Molinier, an amateur of natural history whose accounts of marine fauna strike his listeners as novelistic material (*FM*, 1049, 1053). Vincent mocks the Goncourt brothers, who deplored the paucity of imagination in nature on their visit to the Paris Zoo, revealing the "stupidity and dimness of their little minds" (*FM*, 1051). Criticizing the naturalist writers' positivist blindness, Vincent condemns their esthetics, because "a novelist cannot, with impunity, take pride in being a psychologist, all the while turning away from the spectacle of nature and remaining ignorant of its laws" (*FM*, 1051). Fedor, like Vincent, derives esthetic pleasure and inspiration from natural history (*G*, 109, 115, 139 [*D*, 124, 131, 157]) and castigates vulgar materialists, "from Belinskii to Mikhailovskii," who reason about nature to substantiate their esthetics but know nothing of Russian flora and fauna. Their materialism is abstract and their positivist esthetics removed from positive knowledge (*G*, 200 [*D*, 225]). Chernyshevskii, for instance, uses botanical examples to prove the superiority of life to art but cannot distinguish between two kinds of trees and thinks that Siberian and European flora are identical (*G*, 243 [*D*, 273]).

Vincent illustrates his point with the example of deep-sea fish, considered blind until a closer examination reveals that they possess eyes and emit their own light. Passavant appropriates this story as an esthetic parable. So does Nabokov's narrator, when he describes a Russian writer

Shirin as blind and devoid of inner light. Like the Goncourt brothers in the Paris Zoo, Shirin does not heed animals in the Berlin Zoo, while discoursing "about the intellectual's alienation from nature" (*G*, 316 [*D*, 353]). Emphasizing the connection with Vincent's fish story, Nabokov puts on Shirin's nose

> large spectacles behind which, as in two aquariums, swam two tiny, transparent eyes—which were completely impervious to visual impressions. He was blind like Milton, deaf like Beethoven, and a blockhead to boot. A blissful incapacity for observation (and hence complete uninformedness about the surrounding world . . .). It happens, of course, that such a benighted person has some little lamp of his own glimmering inside him—not to speak of those known instances in which, through the caprice of resourceful nature that loves startling adjustments and substitutions, such an inner light is astonishingly bright. (*G*, 315–16 [*D*, 353])

As it happens, the resourceful nature that gave deep-sea fish their eyes and inner light refused these qualities not only to Shirin but also to Vincent, whose "positive culture" (*FM*, 1045) is his undoing. Vincent believes that humans merely imitate nature, especially as concerns natural selection. For Vincent, the novelist must both learn from nature and imitate it in art.[53] Thus he unwittingly becomes a predator, first with Laura, whom he uses and abandons, then with Lilian, whom he kills after a lucrative relationship. But despite his belief in the survival of the fittest, he is punished by insanity and will spend the rest of his life in African exile. Vincent's positivism contradicts the views of his creator. The narrator of *Journal des Faux-Monnayeurs* adheres to Oscar Wilde's paradoxical formula that "nature mimics art and, instead of limiting himself to nature's suggestions, the artist should present nature with nothing but that which it can or must soon imitate" (*JFM*, 33). This statement explains Édouard's conviction that it is not enough to be a good natural historian to become a good novelist (*FM*, 1076). A novelist must study nature but should not emulate it because, like all apparent reality, nature deceives those who take it at face value.

Dar's narrator and Fedor support this view. Fedor concludes that nature is full of deception that cannot be explained by mimicry to the end of natural selection—it is too unmotivated and refined for the crude perceptive abilities of animal predators, as if "invented by some waggish artist precisely for the intelligent eyes of man (a hypothesis that may lead far an evolutionist who observes apes feeding on butterflies)"

(*G,* 110, 330 [*D,* 126, 370]). Despite vulgar interpretations of Darwin's theory, apes differ from humans in evolutionary terms because they cannot relate to nature esthetically.[54] In its gratuitous imagination nature approaches and imitates art. A student of natural history, Fedor sees that "the most enchanting things in nature and art are based on deception" (*G,* 364 [*D,* 408–9]). Art must learn from nature but cannot imitate it, for it will be imitating deceptive appearances. The claim of nineteenth-century realists and their progeny to faithfully reproduce reality is rooted in the ignorance of the very nature to which they appeal. This issue was so important to Nabokov that in "Vtoroe dobavlenie k 'Daru'" (1939; translated as "Father's Butterflies: Second Addendum to *The Gift*") he allowed Fedor to expound on his entomological views and to debunk once more those evolutionists who ignore what nature, "our intelligent accomplice and witty mother wanted to achieve, and did."[55]

Both *Les Faux-Monnayeurs* and *Dar* have been called antinovels, thanks to their break with nineteenth-century realist conventions.[56] Gide's is a parodic counterfeit of the realist novel. It presents all apparent peculiarities of the genre concealing different conceptions of novelistic narrative, composition, and the relationship of art to life. The title of the novel refers both to counterfeiters in life, those insisting on the validity of appearances, and in art, those naive realists who claim that art mirrors life. The same tension between hidden and apparent reality runs through *Dar.* It is evident in the inscription on a van in "blue letters, each of which (including a square dot) was shaded laterally with black paint: a dishonest attempt to climb into another dimension" (*G,* 3 [*D,* 9)]. Fedor, in turn, cheats daily life by using the same tram ticket for a round trip. "Knowing the routes, one could turn a straight journey imperceptibly into an arc, bending back to the point of departure"; ultimately, he swindles the transport department out of a ticket to Russia, for the tram trip stimulates his imagination and gets him closer to his desk (*G,* 84 [*D,* 97]). Daily life is "pocket money, farthings clinking in the dark," whose value is "ephemeral" (counterfeit) vis-à-vis "real wealth, from which life should know how to get dividends in the shape of dreams, tears of happiness, distant mountains" (*G,* 164 [*D,* 183]). Earthly existence is "a mere reflection of the material metamorphoses taking place within us" (*G,* 342 [*D,* 384]). Just as coins can be counterfeit, reflections can be distorted—something realists are loath to admit.

Instead, the French reviewers of *Les Faux-Monnayeurs* and the Russian critics of *Dar* expressed frustration at the lack of realism, as they saw it, in the novels. They asserted that Gide failed to achieve either verisimilitude or plausibility.[57] *Dar*'s breach of realist conventions was likened to a wooden bust draped in a beautiful dress and exposed in a store window.[58] This was an unwitting self-commentary, since in *Dar*'s unpublished chapter 4 Chernyshevskii argued for the superiority of life to art, basing his judgment on the pictures of female models in art store windows. In the context of interwar esthetic debates, one must reassess the suggestion of I. and O. Ronen that Gide's novel "is a failure in terms of Nabokov's poetics, because Gide never achieved the illusion of reality . . . operating as he did with a set of clichés" ("Diabolically Evocative," 378). Gide's rejection of realist illusion and manipulation of realist clichés appear instrumental to the elaboration of Nabokov's antirealist stance. The differences in their treatment of the issue of realism in art hardly imply an esthetic split between the *maître* and his disciple, but rather stem from Nabokov's status of a good pupil who can capitalize on Gide's lessons and move beyond them.

Both novelists found their harshest critics in the postwar generation of writers. The "Hamlets" of both literatures were scandalized by Gide's and Nabokov's refusal to play along the ongoing renewal of realist conventions. Following the vogue of confessional literature with fluid borderlines between author and hero, critics identified Édouard's esthetics with that of Gide and Fedor's with that of Nabokov. The technique of multiple narrative voices only reinforced this conflation. As a result, the novelists were attacked for the esthetics of their protagonists.[59] Although, with Adamovich's exception, no Paris School associate reviewed *Dar*, Khodasevich saw "émigré Hamlets'" post-1937 attacks on Nabokov as motivated by the derisive treatment of their esthetics in the novel ("Sovremennye zapiski, kn. 65," 9).

The Novel as Target Practice

Les Faux-Monnayeurs attacked the notion of literary sincerity, widespread in the postwar critical discourse. Édouard finds the notion irritating, for it is too crude to account for the multitude of aspects in which a given event may appear (*FM*, 987). Sincerity is pointless when it comes to the replication of inherently deceptive extraliterary reality. Suggesting the hypocritical nature of the discourse of sincerity, Gide makes all his heroes act out roles and hide behind the mask of false appearances (*FM*, 934–35). For his part, Nabokov likens artistic "sincerity" to a monetary transaction that evokes the notions of corruption and false currency. Fedor says in the imaginary review of his poetry, punning on the polysemy of the verb *podkupat'*, which can mean "to bribe," "to pay off," and "to seduce":

В целом ряде подкупающих искренностью . . . нет, вздор, кого подкупаешь? Кто этот продажный читатель? не надо его. (*D*, 18)

⤜

[In a whole set of poems, seducing by their sincerity . . . no, that's nonsense, Who is being paid off? Who is this corrupt reader? We do not need him.][60]

A monetary transaction is a convention between seller and buyer. Fedor considers such transactions as disguised deception. Literary "sincerity" is also a convention, whereby author and reader, like a store clerk and his customer, engage in the "nasty imitation of good" and "grow intoxicated from the wine of honesty" (*G*, 5 [*D*, 11–12]).

Nabokov linked his Paris School antagonists to nineteenth-century positivism, which subordinated art to extra-artistic considerations and divided it into form and content (*G*, 222, 239 [*D*, 250, 268]). Chernyshevskii's utilitarian sermons to writers—"Speak of life, and only of life" (*G*, 237 [*D*, 266])—rang familiar to Nabokov's contemporaries acquainted with Adamovich's demand that one write "sincerely," "responsibly," and "truthfully," reject imagination and treat the most urgent problems of existence.[61] In his review of Fedor's *Chernyshevskii*, Christopher Mortus, a thinly veiled parody of Adamovich, says that positivists were often mistaken in their literary opinions but "in the general 'intonation' of their criticism there transpired a certain kind of truth" so that "in some final and infallible sense their and our needs coincide" (*G*, 304 [*D*, 340]). Although Adamovich's agenda is more sophisticated than Chernyshevskii's, its affinities with Russian utilitarianism make "émigré Hamlets," by Mortus's own admission, Chernyshevskii's grandchildren (*G*, 304 [*D*, 340]). But even in his esthetic scuffle with Chernyshevskii's Russian grandchildren, Nabokov drew on the topoi, polemical devices, and imagery of Gide's attack against "European Hamlets."

Reflecting on postwar literary life, Gide placed the conflict of fathers and sons at the center of his novel. Learning that he is an illegitimate child, Bernard likens himself to Hamlet (*FM*, 977). Chapter 6, which narrates his flight from home, has as an epigraph Hamlet's lines: "We are all bastards; and that most venerable man which I did call my father, was I know not where when I was stamp'd" (*FM*, 975). Translating *Hamlet* concurrently with his work on *Les Faux-Monnayeurs* and using it as a model for the *mise en abyme,* Gide endowed Bernard with traits evocative of Hamlet and of "European Hamlets." Both men are students. Hamlet is obsessed with the idea of his mother's infidelity. *Les Faux-Monnayeurs* starts with Bernard's discovery of his mother's affair, accompanied by his bookish desire to hear steps in the hall: "C'est le moment de croire que j'entends des pas dans le corridor" (The moment has come to hear steps in the passage), he says in the first line of the novel (*FM,* 933), paraphrasing Bernardo's opening remark in *Hamlet:* "Who's there?"[62] But Bernard is an illegitimate son reared by his adoptive father, while Hamlet is a legitimate son whose stepfather plots his demise. Unlike Hamlet, who follows paternal instructions, Bernard rebels against parental authority. "Ignorance of one's father cures the fear of resembling him," he says (*FM,* 933).

But there was one crucial uniting trait which overshadowed all the differences between Bernard the "European Hamlet" and prince Hamlet: both men grounded their approaches to art in that very referential illusion which was debunked in *Les Faux-Monnayeurs* and in *Dar.* Long before Stendhal coined his aphorism about the novel as a mirror of life, Hamlet had discoursed before a group of itinerant actors about "the purpose of playing, whose end, both at the first and now, was and is, to hold, as 'twere, the mirror up to nature" (*Hamlet,* 1090). Nabokov was surely no less aware than Gide of the esthetic "aberration" which prince Hamlet had passed on to his modern progeny, for just like the French *maître,* Nabokov had attempted to translate *Hamlet* not long before he began his work on his magnum opus. Three excerpts from Nabokov's translation of *Hamlet* were published in the émigré press in October–November 1930 as the writer was preparing to translate the entire play— a project that never materialized (Boyd, *Vladimir Nabokov,* 362).

Fedor has much in common with Bernard. They are of the same age: Fedor is born in 1900 (*G,* 12 [*D,* 19]); Bernard passes his *bac* exam (taken at eighteen or nineteen) in the year of Dada's Parisian debut, 1919. Bernard's last name means "he who wrestles with God," the name given to Jacob after his struggle with the angel, who wrestles Bernard too. Fedor means "God given." Fedor appears to represent a more mature continuation of Gide's rebellious teenager, as if Nabokov were engaging in a covert dialogue with Gide. The story of a literary-beginner Bernard, who eventually makes peace with his parents, finds a sequel in the story of Fedor, who venerates his father as an artistic model (*G,* 109, 115 [*D,* 124, 131]). Bernard is unsure whether to write poetry or prose and

whether "writing does not impede living"—a properly dadaist preoccupation (*FM*, 1088, 1096, 1150). For his part, after an early fling with
symbolism (*G*, 149 [*D*, 168]), Fedor outgrows the avant-garde passion for
turning life into art and is confident about his own artistic calling.

Explaining Bernard's disappearance, Albéric Profitendieu invents a
story about an uncle, the brother of his "real mother," who had arranged
for the boy's adoption (*FM*, 947). Bernard's friend Olivier lives with his
own uncle, Édouard, his mentor and lover. This father-uncle alternative
played into Nabokov's infatuation with Viktor Shklovskii's description
of art as a knight's move, whereby each generation chose as a model an
uncle over a father.[63] Fedor first uses the metaphor to describe Chernyshevskii's youthful diary: "The drolly circumstantial style, the meticulously inserted adverbs, the passion for semicolons, the bogging down
of thought in midsentence, . . . the knight-moves of sense in the trivial
commentary on his minutest actions, . . . the seriousness, the limpness,
the honesty, the poverty—all this pleased Fedor so much, he was so
amazed and tickled by the fact that an author with such a mental and
verbal style was considered to have influenced the literary destiny of
Russia" (*G*, 194–95 [*D*, 219]).

This description recalls Paris School ideals—"the seriousness,
the limpness, the honesty, the poverty" of style and the self-absorbed
"commentary on minutest actions" marked the writings of Gazdanov
and Fel'zen, famous for their "passion for semicolons." Nabokov thus
throws into one basket of hostile esthetics Chernyshevskii's socially engaged art; Russian formalism, compromised by its affiliation with the
pro-Soviet avant-garde; and the "émigré Hamlets," whose rejection of
the fathers was advertised as part of their esthetics.

And yet Fedor applies the formula "We are all bastards" to his own
art as well, once again using Shklovskii's metaphor: "Any genuinely new
trend is a knight's move" (*G*, 239 [*D*, 268]). This use of formalist phrase-
ology rests on a double standard: Nabokov changes connotations to suit
his purposes. The traits he denounces in "émigré Hamlets" reappear as
positive in Fedor's own esthetics. The very fact of drawing on Gide's
legacy indicates that Nabokov practices a knight's move, choosing as
his model the French counterpart ("uncle") of a Bunin or a Zaitsev
("émigré fathers"). Bashing his peers for similar practices, Nabokov
stresses his disagreement with the way in which they go about artistic
borrowing but not with their choice of models. Thus, like Hamlet, Fedor is both a legitimate son who does not renounce his father and a bas-
tard in his artistic praxis.

In the early 1920s "European Hamlets" used Gide's name to justify their opposition to literary elders. Furthermore, *Les Faux-Monnayeurs* drew on the "new malady" by virtue of describing anxious and disoriented young men. Thérive saw Gide's "spiritual role among young postwar writers" in that Gide "set the tone for a literary trend and may have received his own tone from it. Not counting Alfred Jarry, not a single detail of the mores suggests that the scene [of *Les Faux-Monnayeurs*] is not laid in 1924," thought the critic.[64] Nabokov could not miss Gide's popularity among "European Hamlets," whom he scolded in a late 1920s speech, deploring the "multitude of bad French novels about *jeunes gens d'après guerre.*"[65] But as former admirers rebuked Gide's magnum opus, they encouraged Nabokov's recourse to it: writing a novel "removed from life" (Arland, Fernandez), Gide "deceived" young writers (Malraux), who no longer "saw any use in this corpse save for his anxiety" (Maxence).[66] Now Nabokov could side with Gide against the *jeunes gens d'après guerre,* provided he exorcised "their" Gide from Fedor's art, including the latest French literary fads—homosexuality, Dostoevskophilia, and communist sympathies.

Reviewing *Chernyshevskii,* Mortus contrasts Fedor's art to another type of émigré writing, which was "plainer, more serious, drier—at the expense of art, perhaps, but in compensation producing (in certain poems by Tsypovich and Boris Barski and in the prose of Koridonov) sounds of such sorrow, such music" (*G,* 303 [*D,* 339]). Tsypovich and Boris Barski evoke the Paris School poets Otsup, Zakovich, and Poplavskii. Koridonov recalls Gide's treatise *Corydon* (1924), an apology of homosexuality whose scandalous aura, fused with that of *Les Faux-Monnayeurs,* convinced many writers that it was "a matter of good taste to practice *corydonisme* or pretend that one practiced it."[67] Homosexuality became part of French literary dandyism (cf. Jean Cocteau, René Crevel, and Raymond Radiguet). Besides Adamovich, a homosexual promoter of Gide, the best-known "Gidean" among Nabokov's foes was Vladimir Varshavskii, the author of a manifesto about the "émigré young man's" affinity to Gide and a rumored homosexual.[68] His "plain, serious, and dry" prose exemplified Paris School ideals and could serve as Nabokov's target, especially since Varshavskii attacked Nabokov from the standpoint of "sincere" and "ascetic" art ("V. Sirin," 266–67).

Varshavskii's stress on both the spiritual and the artistic affinity of a young male with an older and experienced male echoed the typical plot of homosexual liaisons in Gide's writings.[69] In *Les Faux-Monnayeurs,* the easily influenced Olivier becomes both a pupil and a lover to his uncle, but only after Édouard parts ways with the heterosexual Bernard, who preceded Olivier in Édouard's literary lab but gradually decided to follow an independent artistic course. In this context Nabokov's opposition to the *corydonisme* of his Parisian peers is not so much a mockery of the fad of homosexuality as a denunciation of a certain type of literary borrowing, whereby a writer confuses necessary artistic apprenticeship with spirituality, something that is profoundly individual and cannot be borrowed. Purging the unacceptable features of Gide's esthetics, Nabokov used Gide's own novel as a subtextual basis for this exorcism. Such praxis may seem paradoxical, but it also suggests Nabokov's intent to save "his" Gide from that of his foes by reworking the legacy of the *maître* to whom he owed too much to relegate him entirely to the opposite camp.

Thus, following the example of *Les Faux-Monnayeurs*, *Dar* places the estheticization of homosexuality and suicide at the center of literary life.[70] Describing the gestation of a radical antiesthetic movement, Gide drew on the dadaist-surrealist suicide myth, to which he had unwittingly contributed the concept of a gratuitous act (see chapter 2). This group sees writing as an obstacle to living (*FM*, 1198, 1229). In a conversation with Olivier, an editor of the review *Avant-Garde*, Bernard cites Rimbaud as his model and muses about suicide as a means of self-expression (*FM*, 1150). Combining the cult of suicide with eccentric ("gratuitous") conduct, the teenagers of the Azaïs pension take as their motto "Strong man does not value life" (*FM*, 1238). Homosexuality and suicide are inseparable in *Les Faux-Monnayeurs*. Olivier attempts suicide after making love to Édouard, following Bernard's maxim that one can commit suicide "out of enthusiasm" (*FM*, 1151). Boris de La Pérouse's suicide is also laden with homoeroticism. Boris arrives in the Azaïs pension after therapy targeting his masturbation habit. Suicide is the last resort in his effort to gain acceptance in the "Strong Men's" club. He longs for the affection of his peers, falling prey to their deadly game. Unlike Boris, the "strong men" who set up his death as gratuitous and spontaneous do not live up to their motto.

The fact that the wrong people try to kill themselves—not the preachers of suicide but their victims—makes suicide, unlike homosexuality, a negative value in Gide's novel. Olivier and Boris are pushed to self-destruction by spiritual counterfeiters. Incidentally, the "strong men" traffic in false coins under the supervision of adults who pose as avant-garde artists (a detail that is echoed in Nabokov's story "Korolek," discussed earlier in this chapter). Even Rimbaud's artistic and existential renunciation is travestied in Vincent's persona: having killed Lilian, Vincent goes mad in a remote corner of Africa. Gide presents the dadaist-surrealist suicide myth as false rhetoric. Édouard is so anguished by Olivier's suicidal attempt and Boris's death that he refuses to estheticize these events as novelistic material (*FM*, 1246). Gide brought the issue of suicide close to Nabokov's agenda. Boris was born in Warsaw when it was part of the Russian empire, and his primary education was thus marked by Russian culture; the boy even wore a "Russian shirt" in the photograph kept by the old La Pérouse (*FM*, 1028–30). In addition, Bernard credits Dostoevsky's Dmitrii Karamazov with inspiring his own suicide theory (*FM*, 1151, 1180). Given his status as one of Fedor's whipping boys (*G*, 341 [*D*, 382]) and the butt of many jokes in Nabokov's novel *Otchaianie* (1932), Dostoevsky's association with a homoerotically connoted suicidal attempt was quite opportune for Nabokov's esthetic exorcism.

    Dar's version of a "modern" suicide—the story of Iasha Chernyshevskii—stigmatizes the esthetic cult of homosexuality, Symbolist and Decadent artistic praxis, the French and Soviet avant-garde, the Paris School of émigré letters, the myth of the Russian writer as a prophet-martyr, and all affirmation of life's preeminence over art. Fedor uses suicide as a unifying trait that brings diverse cultural phenomena to a common denominator.[71] Boris Poplavskii's widely advertised "accidental suicide," which occurred midway into Nabokov's work on *Dar*, combined a kinship to the dadaist-surrealist suicide myth with a homoerotic enigma about Poplavskii's ties to his fellow victim, Sergei Iarko. The case also recalled the prominence of homosexuality and suicide in the Symbolist and Decadent praxis of "life-creation."[72] Drawing on Symbolist legacy, Poplavskii was a former Soviet sympathizer and avant-garde poet, who fashioned himself as a prophet-martyr. Several critics have argued convincingly that it is, first and foremost, with Symbolist praxis that Nabokov associated the estheticization of homosexuality.[73] Thus, as a prominent "émigré Hamlet," Poplavskii's persona conveniently amalgamated many esthetic features unacceptable to Nabokov and could be used as a model for Iasha.[74]

    One discerns in Fedor's treatment of Iasha's life and death a mocking echo of the "new malady," which Fedor exposes as "vulgar and humorless drivel about the 'symptoms of the age' and the 'tragedy of youth'" (*G*, 40 [*D*, 48]). Similarly to Édouard, Fedor discards these theories as false rhetoric that produces senseless victims like Iasha, in whose story "any 'serious' novelist in horn-rimmed glasses—the family doctor of

Europe and the seismographer of its social tremors—would no doubt have found . . . something highly characteristic of the 'frame of mind of young people in the post-war years'" (*G*, 40 [*D*, 48]). However, Fedor's ruthless treatment of the "new malady" is tainted by a double standard, because Gide must be included among the artistic exploiters of Europe's doubtful malady. Although Édouard refuses to use Boris's story in his novel, this story is included in *Les Faux-Monnayeurs*, as Gide capitalizes on the elements of the fashionable malaise. Furthermore, Nabokov follows Gide's example: Fedor refuses to use Iasha's story as novelistic material (*G*, 41 [*D*, 49]), yet it is fully narrated and is part of *Dar*.

Both Fedor and Édouard turn to suicide stories for esthetic "target practice," to apply Fedor's own term, which he used to describe his *Life of Chernyshevskii* (*G*, 196 [*D*, 221]). Fedor says about his father, who was a very good shot: "My father not only taught me a great deal but also trained my very thoughts, as a voice or hand is trained, to the rules of his school. Thus I was rather indifferent to the cruelty of war; I even conceded that one could take a certain delight in the accuracy of a shot, in the danger of a reconnaissance or in the delicacy of a maneuver; but these little pleasures (which are better represented moreover in other special branches of sport . . .) in no way compensated for that touch of dismal idiocy which is inherent in any war" (*G*, 127–28 [*D*, 145]).

Viewing art as akin to sport (chess) and applying shooting metaphors to describe his own poetry (*G*, 18–19 [*D*, 25]), Fedor turns his texts into a firing range for settling esthetic scores. Target practice belongs in sport and in art but not in war or any other man-slaughtering enterprise, where shooting is part of extra-artistic reality and kills literally. The esthetic treatment of suicide is foreign to Fedor's universe because it is alien to art proper.

Iasha Chernyshevskii is lost in intellectual counterfeit, and his drama sounds "in the context of the epoch . . . like an unbearably typical, and therefore false, note" (*G*, 44 [*D*, 53]). The émigré reader could see in this detail a reference to the Paris School and Poplavskii, rumored to have coined the expression "Paris note." Iasha's "anxiety" over Spengler recalls the *inquiétude* of European and émigré "Hamlets"; his indebtedness to Alexander Blok echoes Poplavskii's return to Blok after 1927; his inability to see the triteness of the word "rose," to follow stress rules, to count the number of syllables in the word "October," and to avoid such fashionable clichés as sailors, gin, and jazz merely reiterate Nabokov's review of Poplavskii's *Flagi*. Compare Nabokov's and Fedor's respective opinions.

Fedor: "Эпитеты, у него жившие в гортани. . . . употребляемые молодыми поэтами его поколения, обманутыми тем, что архаизм, прозаизм, или просто обедневшие некогда слова вроде 'роза', совершив полный круг жизни, получали теперь в стихах как бы неожиданную свежесть." (*D*, 46)

⤜⤛

[Those epithets inhabiting his larynx. . . . Young poets of his generation used them, fooled by the fact that an archaism, a prosaism, or simply a long impoverished word like "rose," having completed a full life cycle, now seemed to acquire unexpected freshness in poetry.] (my translation)

Nabokov: "Поплавский не избежал модных образов: мореходства и роз у него хоть отбавляй. Любопытная вещь: после нескольких лет, в течение коих поэты оставили розу в покое, считая, что упоминание о ней стало банальщиной и признаком дурного вкуса, явились молодые поэты и рассудили так: 'Э, да она совсем новенькая, отдохнула, пошлость выветрилась, теперь роза в стихах звучит даже изысканно.'"

⤜⤛

[Poplavskii has not been spared by the epidemic of fashionable images: he has more than his share of navigation and roses. A curious thing: after some years, during which poets left the rose alone, considering its evocation banal and in bad taste, fledgling poets have reasoned as follows: 'Hey, it is brand new and rested, its banality has disappeared, now the rose sounds even exquisite in poetry.'] ("B. Poplavskii. 'Flagi'," in *BP*, 168)

Fedor: "И все это было выражено бледно, кое-как, со множеством неправильностей в ударениях. . . . 'октябрь' занимал три места в стихотворной строке, заплатив лишь за два." (*D*, 47)

⤜⤛

[All of this was expressed insipidly, just anyhow, with a multitude of incorrect stresses. . . . "October" occupied three spaces in a line, having paid only for two.] (my translation)

Nabokov: "Ударения попадаются невыносимые. . . . Неряшливость слуха, которая, удваивая последний слог в слове, оканчивающийся на две согласных, занимает под него два места в стихе: 'октябер.'"

⤜⤛

[One finds intolerable stresses. . . . (His) slovenly ear doubles the last syllable in a word that ends with two consonants, allotting it two spaces in a verse: "October (*oktiaber*)."] ("B. Poplavskii. 'Flagi'," in *BP*, 168)

Drawing attention to "roses," Nabokov shoots through his primary target to hit another one—Georgii Ivanov, his bitter enemy who authored a poetic collection *Roses* (1931) and a eulogy of Poplavskii's *Flagi*. (It is telling that Nabokov purged "roses" and "October" from *Dar*'s English version [*G*, 39], since only émigrés could see their referents.) Iasha's "adventurous sailors" (*G*, 39 [*D*, 47]) evoke not only poetic clichés of the day and Poplavskii's dress mannerisms (he wore a sailor's shirt), but images of homosexuality in Jean Cocteau's drawings of sailors.[75] At the same time, his homosexuality recalls the sensibility of Chernyshevskii and the "men of the sixties," albeit filtered through Symbolist esthetics.[76] The poet's homoerotic passion is "akin to that of many a Russian youth in the middle of the last century, trembling with happiness, when, raising his silky eyelashes, his pale-browed teacher, a future leader, a future martyr, would turn to him" (*G*, 43 [*D*, 51]).

Fedor stresses the estheticized nature of Iasha's demise. Iasha and his friends, Rudolf and Olia, form "a banal triangle of tragedy" with a "suspiciously neat structure, to say nothing of the fashionable counterpoint of its development" (*G*, 42 [*D*, 51]). Rudolf is in love with Olia; Iasha is attracted to Rudolf (this "incorrigible deviation" makes "Rudolf's squeamishness understandable" to Fedor); Olia is a femme fatale with "all the proper literary associations" (*G*, 43 [*D*, 51]). They resemble dramatis personae of the classical French theater (*G*, 44 [*D*, 52]) and, let us add, of modern French literary life, given their recourse to a group suicide à la Jacques Vaché and Boris Poplavskii. But if suicide comes to Gide's Olivier and Boris as a negative and extraneous element that is smuggled in dishonestly and threatens to destroy the creative force of homoeroticism, Iasha's "incorrigible deviation" is a prerequisite for his self-destruction. Nabokov could not be clearer in his negation of *corydonisme*. According to *Dar*'s logic and contrary to that of Gide, Bernard is not the only one culpable for Olivier's suicidal attempt—Édouard is equally to blame, for he sexually exploits a young pupil, taking advantage of his spiritual and esthetic control over Olivier.

The circumstances of Iasha's suicide illustrate the falsity of the esthetics underlying his death. Like Gide's Boris, Iasha is encouraged to pull the trigger by friends who do not follow suit. The "strong men" draw prearranged lots to make Boris shoot first. Iasha is also doomed by taking the enterprise seriously: he wants to shoot first and refuses to draw lots, but "the stroke of drawn lots . . . in its coarse blindness, would probably have fallen on him anyway" (*G*, 47 [*D*, 56]). After Iasha's death, Rudolf emulates Gide's teenagers and hides the gun. But at this point

Nabokov departs from Gide's scenario. The rumor has it that, in the time between Iasha's death and the arrival of the police, Rudolf and Olia engaged in a sexual act. This detail, once again, serves to condemn *corydonisme*. While Gide's teenagers keep an all-male company after Boris's demise and Olivier stays attached to Édouard, Nabokov's heroes find heterosexual license in Iasha's death, as if homoeroticism had been merely a ruse that helped Rudolf get rid of his rival.

Similarities between Boris and Iasha do not stop at the circumstances of their death. Iasha is five years younger than Fedor (*G*34 [*D*, 41]); the same age difference exists between Bernard and Boris. But if Bernard toys with esthetically valuable suicide, Fedor has covered the distance separating Bernard and Édouard. His vantage point on Iasha's story coincides with Édouard's view of Boris's tragedy. Like Édouard, he debunks suicidal esthetics and frequents the family of the deceased. Iasha's father furnishes material for Fedor's artistic imagination, just as Boris's grandfather feeds that of Édouard.

Among other things, Iasha falls victim to the Russian tradition of martyrs who, "if they did not meet with some kind of more or less heroic death—having nothing to do with Russian letters . . . subsequently abandoned literature altogether" (*G*, 38 [*D*, 46]). One of his models is Chernyshevskii, about whom Iasha's father says, "There are, after all, cases where the fascinating beauty of a good man's dedicated life fully redeems the falsity of his literary views" (*G*, 40 [*D*, 48]). Yet Iasha's artistic incompetence cannot be remedied by a tragic life whose memory will not outlast his poetry. Fedor undermines the myth of the writer-martyr by projecting it on Soviet art, which claims Chernyshevskii as a precursor. Mocking Jakobson's view of Maiakovskii as a martyr who walked the "poetic Golgotha" crowned by a "thorny wreath of revolution,"[77] he says about Chernyshevskii: "His biographers mark his thorny path with evangelical signposts (it is well known that the more leftist the Russian commentator the greater is his weakness for expressions like 'the Golgotha of the revolution')" (*G*, 215 [*D*, 242]). Recalling that the writing of *Dar* concurred with Gide's communist fling (presented in terms of Christian symbolism), we need not limit Nabokov's allusions to Western-based apologetics of Soviet culture to Russian writers only.

Chernyshevskii toyed with the idea of suicide (*G*, 235 [*D*, 263]) but was too pragmatic to implement it; Maiakovskii compromised himself by collaborating with the Soviets. Fedor links the Paris School to Chernyshevskii, to Soviet writers, and to their émigré apologists. Mortus, Chernyshevskii's self-proclaimed grandson, contrasts Koncheev, Fedor's favorite émigré poet, to Soviet writers, whose art appeals to Mortus's peers. Koncheev's "little pieces about dreamy visions are incapable of seducing anyone," writes Mortus. "And in truth it is with a kind of joyous relief that one passes from them to any kind of 'human document,' to what one can read 'between the words' in certain Soviet writers (granted even without talent), to an artless and sorrowful confession, to a private letter dictated by emotion and despair" (*G*, 168 [*D*, 189]). Mortus subordinates the gift of creativity, which Fedor values above all, to extra-artistic concerns. Like the nineteenth-century positivists and their Soviet heirs, the Paris School esthetics lies outside art, as far as Fedor is concerned.

Iasha's story is a force field amalgamating diverse cultural phenomena that bring about the death of a Russian poet. Using Gide's novel as a model, a subtext, and a butt of esthetic exorcism, Nabokov marks for Fedor's target practice the intelligentsia myth of the Russian writer, nineteenth-century positivism and utilitarianism in art, Symbolist and Decadent esthetics, the artistic cult of homosexuality, the Paris School of émigré letters, the Russian and French avant-garde esthetics, and Soviet literature. These targets are united by their common claim to life's preeminence over art, a precept that is as potentially destructive to the future of Russian literature as to Iasha's tragic life. But insofar as Gide the writer betrays, according to Nabokov, the very esthetic principles of *Les Faux-Monnayeurs* that Nabokov admires, the French *maître* is included among the "'serious' novelists in horn-rimmed glasses" derided by Fedor as intellectual counterfeiters.

Discarding dominant esthetic trends, both Gide and Nabokov wrote metanovels that preserved previous novelistic experience from the attacks of the postwar writers and provided a matrix for "modern" texts in contrast to the nineteenth-century realist novel. Their texts differ from prior metaliterary narratives, namely, from that of Proust, by inciting the reader to create his own text according to sets of rules articulated in the novels. Both novels belong to what Segal has called "literature as a safe-conduct"—an attempt to preserve threatened esthetic norms through their codification in art ("Literatura kak okhrannaia gramota," 151–244). Composing his *Art of Novel* with Gide's unacknowledged help, Nabokov gave Fedor an artistic and existential safe-conduct. Unlike Iasha's, Fedor's art will endure and transport the memory of his life back to Russia (*G*, 350 [*D*, 394]). This safe-conduct will also guarantee the future of Russian letters, which Nabokov views as threatened on all sides of their political and esthetic divide.

Conclusion

Discussing the poetry of Joseph Brodsky, David Bethea argued that Brodsky's poetic vision incorporated both the West and Russia, "implanting a Russian source within a Western source so that each source commented on the other, implicating a third source—Brodsky himself." This interpretive mechanism served as a frame for various notions of exile—ethnic, geographical, cultural, and personal. "In essence," wrote Bethea, "Brodsky constantly 'outflanked' his own marginal status through cultural triangulation" (*Joseph Brodsky and the Creation of Exile*, 49–50). But in the case of Brodsky's predecessors who had gone into exile some fifty years earlier, the cultural translation of exilic experience did not follow the same principles, because the East-West force field in their creative activity had a different structure. Maturing as artists only abroad, many younger émigrés felt equally at home in the French and the Russian literary traditions. Their artistic self-definition in the triangulated relationship of older émigré, Soviet, and French literatures entailed a rejection of contemporary Russian models both in the USSR and in emigration. Following Bethea's terminology, such artistic vision could be considered "quadrangular" in that the clash of three literary sources informed a fourth vantage point—that of the second generation of émigré writers.

The careers of Poplavskii, Gazdanov, Fel'zen, and Ianovskii reveal the same mechanism that came into play when each writer tried to define his artistic identity in the émigré-French-Soviet triangle. Their self-identification as "émigré" writers was a more complex process than the older émigrés' opposition to French and Soviet literary esthetics. With the exception of Fel'zen, all of them went through a period of interest in Soviet art; their coming of age was steeped in French literary life; quite naturally for a budding generation, they opposed the "fathers" represented by older émigré writers. The logic of their artistic evolution in many ways echoed Shklovskii's description of literary history as a knight's move. Rejecting the art of the immediate predecessors, young writers created their own Russian tradition by filtering a French literary "uncle" through the prism of a more remote Russian ancestor. Fel'zen chose Proust and Lermontov; Poplavskii opted for the surrealists, Blok, and Dostoevsky; Ianovskii drew on Dostoevsky and Céline; and Gazdanov exploited Blok's and Proust's legacies.

The case of Nabokov, who fancied so much Shklovskii's arresting metaphor, is the exception that confirms the rule. Although the writer spent most of his interwar career in Berlin, he had been drawn into Parisian literary life long before moving to France. From his artificial and affected seclusion, Nabokov lent an attentive ear to both émigré and French artistic developments, which left an indelible mark on his Russian magnum opus. The analysis of *Dar* shows that Nabokov was caught in the same triangulated esthetic opposition as his Parisian peers, forging a "fourth" stance that contradicted the major features of Soviet and émigré literary discourses. The difference of Nabokov's position, however, resides in his relentless desire to assure his own originality. Asserting his full artistic independence, the writer did not subscribe to the generational division in émigré art, lumping together the negative esthetic features of both older and younger writers. In addition, he disguised his indebtedness to Gide, partly to differ from his Parisian peers who programmatically brandished their French models and partly to fend off the accusations of "un-Russianness," commonly leveled by his artistic foes.

By virtue of such close literary relations with the host culture, the second generation and its émigré mentors followed suit in the artistic decline of all main branches of literary modernism. Surrealism ceased to exist as a viable artistic force by the early 1930s, when Breton's group split into several factions. With the exception of Aragon's uninspired "socialist realist" novels and Éluard's poetic work, the group's original members drifted away from literature.[1] After *Les Faux-Monnayeurs*, Gide's literary career went downhill, and he entered the 1930s as a social thinker rather than as a writer. Proust's popularity reached its nadir in the early 1930s, and his artistic method lost its former importance. Céline abandoned novelistic work in 1936 to resume it only after the war, becoming in the meantime a political journalist and commentator.

The flurry of émigré literary activity between 1930 and 1940 can be explained by a time lag rather than a greater artistic vitality of émigré modernism, since most younger writers—the driving force of émigré literature in the 1930s—became artistically active only circa 1925. Their mentors and organizers fell silent as creative writers almost simultaneously with their French peers. After 1927 Khodasevich stopped publishing poetry and devoted himself to literary criticism and scholarship. By 1930 Adamovich's ongoing poetic work was completely overshadowed by his position as a critic. Ivanov stopped publishing his literary works almost immediately after the appearance of *Raspad atoma* and resumed literary activity only in the mid-1940s.

Younger émigrés followed suit. In the 1930s the volume of Poplavskii's poetry dropped considerably, as he grew more interested in critical and philosophical discourse. His second novel showed a penchant for nonfictional genres. Leaving France in 1940, Nabokov abandoned Russian literature. Gazdanov's novel *Istoriia odnogo puteshestviia* (1938) was received as a testimony of artistic impasse.[2] By 1940 Fel'zen and Ianovskii entered a new phase in their careers. Fel'zen reached the logical end of his novelistic project in the story "Kompozitsiia." Had he survived the war, the writer's esthetics could have changed radically. Ianovskii's rebellion against "truthfulness" in *Portativnoe bessmertie* suggests a similar sense of artistic completion and of impending esthetic change. The general disenchantment with the "human document" doctrine marked the end of an artistic epoch in émigré art and the decline of émigré modernism. The war interrupted the normal development of French and émigré letters. But the simultaneous appearance of *Raspad atoma* and Sartre's first novel, *La Nausée,* with which Ivanov's text has many thematic and compositional affinities, seems to confirm Otsup's retrospective suggestion that the Paris School went neck and neck with nascent French existentialism.[3]

Considering the key role of French literary sources for the younger generation of émigré writers, one wonders how fruitful French literary and cultural influence turned out to be for Russian artistic activity abroad. Although this influence defined in more than one way the artistic identities of younger émigrés, it is clear that it was not limited to imitation of French models. Recoding various elements of French literary discourse, Russian expatriates fully integrated them into émigré poetics. But they seem to have developed only those features of the French models that fit their own artistic and existential needs, ultimately rivaling with their French teachers. The very fact that these exiles drew such a significant part of their artistic identity from French sources speaks for their cultural flexibility and capacity to transcend the initial shock of cultural and national loss. Reflecting on the ways of the artistic modeling of exilic experience, Guillén wrote:

> A certain kind of writer speaks of exile, while another learns from it. . . . Writings of the former sort can be rightly regarded as examples of the literature of exile. Instances of the latter compose what I shall call the literature of counter-exile, that is to say, of those responses which incorporate the separation from place, class, language or native community, insofar as they triumph over the separation and thus can offer wide dimensions of meaning that transcend the earlier attachment to place or native origin. ("On the Literature of Exile and Counter-Exile," 271–72)

The literary activity of younger émigrés represents such a literature of counter-exile, for they strove to shed the "confining skin of uninationality," to use Fel'zen's terminology (*Pis'ma o Lermontove*, 30), transforming exilic loss into esthetic gain. They did not mourn the lost paradise of prerevolutionary Russia, which they hardly considered paradisiac. Unlike older Russian writers, who never completely came to terms with indefinite expatriation which imposed on them the need to forge a new life and a new cultural identity, younger émigrés knew how to drink the vodka of exile, to paraphrase Babel's aphorism. And so they "took pleasure in misery and in joy," while their older colleagues kept lamenting the bygone days in a country that was no more and "suffered for all those who drank vodka without knowing how to drink it." Younger writers used the experience of expatriation as material for the construction of their artistic identities in a new homeland that was, as in Andersen's tale, "just as beautiful" as the one they left behind ("Wild Swans," in *Andersen's Fairy Tales*, 199). They took as their motto one of Adamovich's favorite sayings: "Every human being has two native lands: his own and France" ("Druz'ia i vragi," 3). Exile was an artistic blessing because it freed these "modernists" from the fetters of geographical attachment, national origin, and ideological control. Contrary to the paradigmatic examples of literary exile, in which civilization covers the space from which the writer is banished, emigration placed young émigrés at the center of European cultural life and away from Soviet Russia, which they commonly perceived as hopelessly "provincial."

In conclusion, I hope to have illustrated that both the history of Russian émigré letters and the study thereof are inseparable from the story of French modernist literature between the two World Wars.

Abbreviations

Notes

Bibliography

Index

_____

Abbreviations

Archives

Amherst.	Amherst Center for Russian Culture.
Bakhmeteff.	Bakhmeteff Archive of Russian and East European History and Culture.
Beinecke.	The General Collection, Russian Literature. Beinecke Rare Book and Manuscript Library.
Doucet.	Bibliothèque littéraire Jacques Doucet.
Hoover.	Hoover Institution Archives.

Collections of Sources

AGC.	*André Gide: Les Contemporains* (Paris, 1928).
Berega.	*Dal'nie berega: Portrety pisatelei emigratsii. Memuary,* ed. V. Kreid (Moscow, 1994).
BP.	*Boris Poplavskii v otsenkakh i vospominaniiakh sovremennikov,* ed. L. Allen and O. Griz (SPb-Düsseldorf, 1993).
CNTG.	*Les Critiques de notre temps et Gide,* ed. M. Raimond (Paris, 1971).
Enquête.	*Enquête sur les maîtres de la jeune littérature,* ed. H. Rambaud and P. Varillon (Paris, 1923).
HMP.	*Hommage à Marcel Proust,* ed. J. Rivière (Paris, 1927).
Rajeunissement.	*Le Rajeunissement de la politique,* ed. H. Daniel-Rops (Paris, 1932).
Réflexions.	*Dix ans après: Réflexions sur la littérature d'après guerre,* ed. H. Massis (Paris, 1932).
Rencontres.	*Rencontres: Soirées franco-russes,* ed. R. Sébastien and W. de Vogt (Paris, 1930).
RP.	*Recherche de Proust,* ed. G. Genette and T. Todorov (Paris, 1980).
RLE.	*Russkaia literatura v emigratsii: Sbornik statei,* ed. N. Poltoratskii (Pittsburgh, 1972).

70 critiques.	*70 critiques de Voyage au bout de la nuit 1932–1935,* ed. A. Derval, (Paris, 1993).
S'ezd.	*Stenograficheskii otchet pervogo vsesoiuznogo s'ezda sovetskikh pisatelei,* ed. I. Luppol (Moscow, 1934).
Smotr.	*Literaturnyi smotr: Svobodnyi sbornik,* ed. Z. Gippius and D. Merezhkovskii (Paris, 1939).

Periodicals

CQ.	*Cahiers de la Quinzaine.*
IIR.	*Illiustrirovannaia Rossiia.*
NLAS.	*Nouvelles littéraires, artistiques, et scientifiques.*
NRF.	*Nouvelle revue française.*
PN.	*Poslednie novosti.*
RS.	*La Révolution surréaliste.*
SSR.	*Le Surréalisme au service de la révolution.*
SZ.	*Sovremennye zapiski.*
VR.	*Volia Rossii.*
Vz.	*Vozrozhdenie.*

Notes

Introduction

1. Levin, "Literature and Exile," in *Refractions*, 68, 74.

2. See Eiseley, "Cosmic Orphan," 16–19; Said, "Mind of Winter," 49–55; Wichs, "Onlyman," 21–31.

3. Steiner, "Extraterritorial," in *Extraterritorial: Papers on Literature and the Language Revolution*, 11.

4. Gul', *"Ia unes Rossiiu,"* 1: 169, 170, 178. On the modeling of the Russian revolution according to French paradigms, see Furet, *Le Passé d'une illusion*, 108–34; Jelen, *L'Aveuglement*, 14, 55–59; Kondrat'eva, *Bolcheviks et Jacobins;* Shlapentok, "Images of the French Revolution in the February and Bolshevik Revolutions," 31–54.

5. In late 1923 the militant literary groups LEF and *Na postu*, which acted as the watchdogs of "proletarian" art, struck an alliance against *Krasnaia Nov'*, the review of fellow travelers. 1924 gave reason to believe in the imminent dictatorship of "proletarian" writers. On July 1, 1925, *Pravda* published the resolution "On the Policy of the Party in the Area of Belles-Lettres," which regulated Soviet literary life, showing the party's intention and capacity to control literary expression. See Fleishman, *Boris Pasternak v dvadtsatye gody*, 39, 48; Maguire, *Red Virgin Soil*, 150, 159–60, 170–75.

6. For the émigré poet and critic Terapiano, "the inter-war emigration was a miraculously preserved fragment of Petersburg transported to the banks of the Seine. . . . I have always felt that the start of the war, 1939, was the end of this 'fragment of Petersburg.'" (Feb. 27, 1962, Aleksis Rannit Papers, box 29, folder "Iurii Terapiano," Beinecke). The same view of the outbreak of hostilities in Europe as a symbolic end of Russian literature in exile was expressed by the émigré poet Anatolii Shteiger and critic Al'fred Bem. See Shteiger's letters to Iurii Ivask (Dec. 22, 1939, and Feb. 8, 1940, in Livak, "K istorii 'Parizhskoi shkoly.' Pis'ma Anatoliia Shteigera, 1937–1943," 105–10) and Bem's letter to Aleksei Remizov (June 4, 1941, Alexei Remizov Papers, box 8, folder 2, Amherst).

7. "Problems in the Study of Language and Literature," in Jakobson, *Language in Literature*, 47–49.

8. Boldt, Segal, and Fleishman, "Problemy izucheniia literatury russkoi emigratsii pervoi treti XX veka," 75.

9. See Geertz, *Interpretation of Cultures,* 3–30; Lotman and Uspenskii, "O semioticheskom mekhanizme kul'tury," in Lotman, *Izbrannye stat'i v trekh tomakh,* 3: 329–30; Ricoeur, "Model of the Text," 82, 85.

10. See Geertz, *Interpretation of Cultures,* 44–46; Lotman and Uspenskii, "O semioticheskom mekhanizme kul'tury," 328–29; Ricoeur, "Model of the Text," 98–99.

11. See Lotman, "The Poetics of Everyday Behavior in Eighteenth-Century Russian Culture," in *Semiotics of Russian Cultural History,* 67–94; "The Decembrist in Daily Life (Everyday Behavior as a Historical-Psychological Category)," in *Semiotics of Russian Cultural History,* 95–149; "Literaturnaia biografiia v istoriko-kul'turnom kontekste (K tipologicheskomu sootnosheniiu teksta i lichnosti avtora)," *Izbrannye stat'i v trekh tomakh,* 1: 365–76.

12. See Boym, *Death in Quotation Marks;* Freidin, *Coat of Many Colors;* Paperno, *Suicide as a Cultural Institution in Dostoevsky's Russia.*

13. See Eliade, *Aspects du mythe,* 12; Ricoeur, "Model of the Text," 100.

14. See Barthes, *Mythologies,* 215; Eliade, *Aspects du mythe,* 16, 18–19, 32.

15. See Bakhrakh, "Berlinskii 'Klub Pisatelei,'" 5.

16. See Adamovich, *Odinochestvo i svoboda,* 300; Raeff, *Russia Abroad,* 5.

17. Adamovich, *Odinochestvo i svoboda,* 35, 37.

18. See Berberova, *Italics Are Mine,* 226, 354–55; Damanskaia, "Na ekrane moei pamiati," 171–72; Struve, "Russian Writers in Exile," 598; idem, *Russkaia literatura v izgnanii,* 239; Terapiano, *Vstrechi,* 148.

19. See Terapiano, "Chelovek 1930-kh godov," 210; idem, "Iu. Fel'zen: 'Schast'e,'" 268; Varshavskii, "Neskol'ko rassuzhdenii ob Andre Zhide i emigrantskom molodom cheloveke," 220–21; idem, "O 'geroe' emigrantskoi molodoi literatury," 164–65.

20. Varshavskii, *Nezamechennoe pokolenie,* 165.

21. This similarity has been noticed by Struve, *Russkaia literatura v izgnanii,* 235–36. Cf. the term "lost generation," which described American literary exiles in Paris in the interwar period. See also Calinescu, *Five Faces of Modernity,* 147; Otsup, "Klim Samgin," 181; idem, "Personalizm kak iavlenie literatury," *Literaturnye ocherki,* 131; Poggioli, *Theory of the Avant-Garde,* 96–97.

22. See Adamovich, "Zhizn' i 'zhizn',''' 2; Gazdanov, "O molodoi emigrantskoi literature," 404–8; Poplavskii, "Chelovek i ego znakomye," 135–38; Terapiano, "Chelovek 1930-kh godov," 210–12; Varshavskii, "Neskol'ko rassuzhdenii ob Andre Zhide," 216–22; idem, "O proze mladshikh emigrantskikh pisatelei," 410–13.

23. Sonya Yetter's dissertation, "The Orphic Theme in the Poetry of Boris Julianovic Poplavskij" (University of Wisconsin, 1992), is limited to the immanent analysis of one theme in Poplavskii's poetry. Igor' Savel'ev's master's thesis, "Boris Poplavsky: 'The Unknown Soldier' of Russian Literature" (University of Iowa, 1991), is strictly biographical and does not analyze Poplavskii's writings.

24. See, for instance, O. N. Mikhailov, ed., *Literatura russkogo zarubezh'ia: 1920–1940.*

Chapter 1. Exilic Experience as a Cultural Construct

1. See Aldanov, "Novye knigi," 3; Levinson, "Siuares," 357; Shletser, "Zhizn' slova," 308–9.
2. Shletser, "Novoe v zapadnoi literature," 2.
3. Adamovich, "O frantsuzskoi 'inquiétude' i o russkoi trevoge," 2; idem, "Literaturnye besedy," *Zveno* 133: 2.
4. Adamovich, "Literaturnye besedy," *Zveno* 1: 8; idem, "André Gide," 22. For conflicting evaluations, see also the émigré debate on Gide's oeuvre in Adamovich, "André Gide," 21–30; Kirill Zaitsev, "Fal'shivomonetchiki," 3; idem, "Les Débats," 40–41; Varshavskii, "Neskol'ko rassuzhdenii ob Andre Zhide."
5. K. Zaitsev, "Fal'shivomonetchiki," 3. Shmelev thought that Marcel Proust could not satiate exigent spirit, unlike Dostoevsky—a "saturator" whose depth emphasized Proust's superficiality and whose writings were too unpolished in comparison with Proust's refined art ("Anketa o Pruste," 277). See also Sushchev's [Veidle] review of Georges Bernanos's *Sous le soleil de Satan* and Pierre Benois's *Alberte*, which failed the "Dostoevsky test" as "too brilliantly polished" and "too elaborate" while containing "no living soul" ("Novoe vo frantsuzskoi literature," 5).
6. See the polemics surrounding Tamanin's *Otechestvo* (1933). This artistically unsound *roman à thèse* was greeted as a continuation of Dostoevsky's "spiritual" approach to art (Struve, *Russkaia literatura v izgnanii,* 277).
7. Slonim, "Literatura v emigratsii," 1. Cf. Adamovich's eulogy of Gide, credited with "Russian" ("high") qualities: Gide "did not play and did not want to entertain anyone"; he took personal responsibility for what he wrote; and the import of his work lay in the existential questions it raised ("André Gide," 26, 30).
8. See Boym, *Death in Quotation Marks,* 120; Freidin, *Coat of Many Colors,* x; Lotman, "Literaturnaia biografiia v istoriko-kul'turnom kontekste," 369–74; idem, "Russkaia literatura poslepetrovskoi epokhi i khristianskaia traditsiia," in *Iu. M. Lotman i tartussko-moskovskaia semioticheskaia shkola,* 365–69. For a striking manifestation of this model in the émigré critical discourse, see Fedotov, "Jean Maxence et Nadejda Gorodetzky," 99–100.
9. See Berberova et al., "Ot redaktsii," 2; Bibikov, "V poiskakh literaturnogo napravleniia," 4; B. Poplavskii, "O smerti i zhalosti v 'Chislakh,'" 3; Reznikov, "Chto budet s nashei literaturoi?" 4.
It is in these familiar terms that Anatolii Shteiger, a poet from Adamovich's circle, described his ideal vision of the Russian writer in a letter to another émigré poet, Iurii Ivask: "Reading Proust (and Gide), I am ever more shocked by the difference between Russian and Western literatures: a great Russian writer is always a *good* person, whereas for a great Western writer this requirement is waived. Gide and Proust are wonderful writers—but are they good people?" (Feb. 8, 1940, George Ivask Papers, box 1, folder 30 "Shteiger, Anatolii 1937–1941," Beinecke).
10. See Kelli, "Andre Morua o russkoi literature," 1; Lanoë, "Le Corps, par Catherine Bakounine," 919; Marcel, "Souvenirs de ma vie littéraire, de Maxime

Gorki," 253–54; P.-H.-S., "Catherine Bakounine: Le Corps," 969; Travérsey, "Les Débats," 63.

11. Writing about Nabokov's novel *Otchaianie* (1932–33; translated as *Despair*), Arland argued that fantasy, game, and taste for pure story—French qualities in the émigré opinion—were inherent in the Russian tradition ("Essais Critiques," 1042). Cf. the view of these same qualities in Nabokov's novels as "un-Russian" in Adamovich, "Sirin," 3; idem, "Sovremennye zapiski: Kn. 55-ia," 2; idem, "Sovremennye zapiski: Kn. 56," 3; idem, "Perechityvaia 'Otchaianie,'" 3; Ivanov, "V. Sirin," 233–35.

12. See Mochul'skii, "Novoe vo frantsuzskoi literature," 3; Pozner, "L'âme slave et l'esprit gaulois," 6; Sazonova, "Slavianskaia dusha," 3.

13. Adamovich, "O frantsuzskoi 'inquiétude' i o russkoi trevoge," 2. See also B. Poplavskii, "Molodaia russkaia zhivopis' v Parizhe," 195–96.

14. N. Andreev, "Sovremennye zapiski: Kniga 49, 1932," 184. See also Osorgin, "Podvig," 3.

15. See Golenishchev-Kutuzov, "Sovremennye zapiski: Kniga 49," 4. See also Struve, "Double Life of Russian Literature," 403.

16. Ivanov, "V. Sirin," 234. On Nabokov's feud with Ivanov and Parisian émigré literati, see Boyd, *Vladimir Nabokov: The Russian Years,* 350, 374; Davydov, *"Teksty-matreshki" Vladimira Nabokova,* 10–51; Dolinin, "Dve zametki o romane 'Dar,'" 173–80; Mel'nikov, "'Do poslednei kapli chernil . . .'," 73–82.

17. Adamovich, "Chisla: Kniga desiataia," 2; Bitsilli, "Neskol'ko zamechanii o sovremennoi zarubezhnoi literature," 132; K. Zaitsev, "'Vecher u Kler' Gaito Gazdanova," 3.

18. Adamovich, "Literaturnye besedy," *Zveno* 203: 2; idem, "Sovremennye zapiski," *PN* 3144: 2.

19. Troyat, *Un si long chemin,* 77.

20. See Iurii Mandel'shtam, "Dnevnik pisatelia," 9; Osorgin, "Anri Truaia," 3.

21. See Adamovich, "Zhizn' i 'zhizn','" 2; Khodasevich, "Podvig," 3.

22. See Adamovich, "Otkliki," 3; idem, "Iz mira literatury," 194; Khodasevich, "O zadachakh molodoi literatury," 4.

23. See Aldanov, "O polozhenii emigrantskoi literatury," 409; Berberova, *Italics Are Mine,* 354; Damanskaia (Merich), "Privilegirovannyi klass," 3; "Literatura ne kormit," 3. Troyat wrote in his memoirs that despite public success, his books sold badly and the idea of living on literary income alone seemed absurd (*Un si long chemin,* 67, 74).

24. See Gippius, "Nashi ankety," 3; Boris Zaitsev, "Nashi ankety," 2.

25. On the cultural rigidity and insularity of older writers, see Aldanov, "Nashi ankety," 2; Levinson, "Svoe i chuzhoe," 247; Vasilevskii, "My," 2; Tsetlin, "Emigrantskoe," 435–41.

26. In her plan for *A History of the Émigré Intelligentsia,* Gippius described the years 1920–25 as marked by "constant interaction": "[M]any [émigrés] socialized with French circles, with high society women, and with writers" (Pachmuss, "Zinaida Gippius," 3). See also Veidle, "Angliiskaia kniga o sovetskoi literature," 3.

27. See Adamovich, "Literaturnye besedy," *Zveno* 2: 74–75; Avksent'ev et al., "Ot redaktsii," 7; Gippius, "Polet v Evropu," 138; Levinson, "Svoe i chuzhoe,"

248; "Ot redaktsii," *Lloid-zhurnal* 1 (1931): 3–4; Tsetlin, "Emigrantskoe," 437; idem, "Anketa o Pruste," 277; Veidle, "O frantsuzskoi literature," 501; B. Zaitsev, "Dnevnik pisatelia," 3.

Dmitrii Merezhkovskii's correspondence with the eminent French critic Édmond Jaloux furnishes a telling example of émigré attitudes vis-à-vis Russian-French interaction. Replying to Jaloux's initiative to organize a society in support of émigré writers, "Amis des Lettres Russes," Merezhkovskii stipulated a need for reciprocity rather than "philanthropy," because Russians had much to give to the French. He wrote: "*Moral* support should be as much of a goal for the 'Amis' as material assistance; the former may be even of bigger importance. Russian writers in France must not become the *objects* of philanthropy in the vulgar and humiliating sense of this word. . . . We represent a great spiritual force of Russian Literature, Art, and Thought—things that are rather badly known in France, and so we could help you learn them better. This is the principle of *mutual aid*, if not equality, of the unity of interests which is the minimal prerequisite for the small circle of the 'Amis des Lettres Russes'" (Dec. 6, 1922, MS 6851, Doucet.) See a similar opinion in Dashkov [Veidle], "Ob odnoi popytke franko-russkogo sblizheniia," 3.

28. Regarding the "situation de gêneurs et de gênés," see Drieu La Rochelle, "Paris, ville d'exilés," 1. See also Beucler, "Les Russes de France," 866–96; Delage, *La Russie en exil;* Charles Ledré, *Les Émigrés russes en France;* and idem, *Trois romanciers russes.*

29. The following is a selective list of émigrés who collaborated in French periodicals and collections: Aldanov (*France et monde, Illustration, Revue de France*); Bal'mont (*Candide, Mercure de France*); Berdiaev (*CQ, Esprit, Les Iles, Roseau d'Or, NRF*); Bunin (*Illustration, NRF*); Fokht (*CQ, France et Monde, L'Intransigeant*); Gorodetskaia (*CQ, France et monde, Les Iles*); Izvol'skaia (*Courrier des Iles, Esprit, Les Iles, Revue de France*); Ladinskii (*Cahiers 1929*); Knut (*Cahiers 1930*); Kuznetsova (*Cahiers 1930, France et monde*); Levinson (*NLAS*); Lukash (*Mercure de France*); Mandel'shtam (*Revue de France*); Merezhkovskii (*Revue de Paris*); Mochul'skii (*Le Mois*); Nabokov (*Le Mois, NRF*); Osorgin (*Figaro, Revue des Vivants*); Remizov (*Cahiers du Sud, Esprit, Europe, Figaro, Mesures, NLAS, NRF, Paris-Soir, Revue bleue, Revue de Genève, Revue Européenne, Revue Hebdomadaire, Revue nouvelle, Roseau d'Or*); Shestov (*Cahiers Verts, NRF, Mercure de France*); Shletser (*Courrier des Iles, Mercure de France, NRF, Revue Musicale*); Shmelev (*Revue Bleue, Revue Hébdomadaire*); G. Struve (*Le Mois*); Veidle (*Courrier des Iles, Les Iles, Le Mois, NRF, NLAS, Temps Présent*); Zaitsev (*Cahiers de l'Etoile, France et Monde, Roseau d'Or*).

30. Bal'mont called Édmond Jaloux "a true friend of Russian Letters," while Merezhkovskii wrote that in Jaloux's persona, "a great French writer greets us [Russian writers] fraternally and we will never forget this." Remizov hailed Jaloux's support, for the critic's voice was "one of the few that count in France." Expressing his gratitude to Gide, Bunin assured the writer that his friendship and professional assistance compensated for an exile's grief ("I hope to benefit from your gracious friendship and to forget in your company the grief that comes to us from Russia"). Shletser repeatedly conveyed to Charles Du Bos the émigrés' appreciation for the attention of a figure of his standing and claimed

that the critic should take credit for Lev Shestov's success in France. See Bal'mont to Jaloux, March 5, 1923, MS 6781a; Merezhkovskii to Jaloux, n.d. 1923, MS 6854; Remizov to Jaloux, Nov. 5, 1936, MS 68652; Bunin to Gide, Aug. 13, 1922, MS Y 99–1; Shletser to Du Bos, July 25, 1922, and May 26, 1923, MS 26685, Doucet.

Veidle enjoyed the "protection" of the eminent poet and critic Paul Valéry and of Jean Paulhan, the editor-in-chief of the *Nouvelle revue française*. See Veidle's letter to Ivask (April 26, 1972, Iurii Ivask Papers, series 1, correspondence, box 6, folder 64, Amherst); Valéry's letter to Paul Hazard (Collection Weidle, box 1, folder "Valéry, Paul. Paris, 5 Oct. 1939 to Paul Hazard t. l., lp.," Bakhmeteff); and Paulhan's letters to Veidle (Collection Weidle, box 1, folders "Paulhan, Jean. Mirande par Sartilly, France, 1939–1940. To Wladimir Weidle 2 a. l. s. 2 t. l. s.," "Paulhan, Jean. Paris & n. p., n. d. To [Wladimir Weidle] 14 a. l. s.," "Paulhan, Jean. Paris, 1941–1942. To Wladimir Weidle 4 a. l. s.," Bakhmeteff).

31. See Chuzeville, "Lettres russes," 518; Gippius, "Polet v Evropu," 137; Osorgin, "Sud'ba zarubezhnoi knigi," 387.

Even a cursory examination of catalogs disproves claims that French publishers ignored émigré writers and intellectuals. According to the catalog *Livres Imprimés* (Bibliothèque Nationale de France), which lists books only, in the interwar period Aldanov published at least nine novels and collections of stories and essays; Berdiaev, nineteen; Bunin, ten; Gippius, two; Gorodetskaia, five; Kuprin, ten; Levinson, fourteen; Merezhkovskii, eighteen; Nabokov, four; Remizov, seven; Shestov, ten; Shmelev, one; B. Zaitsev, four. Thus, Aldanov could write to Merezhkovskii as early as 1925: "Do you have a list of all your translated works (and those of Zinaida Nikolaevna [Gippius])? . . . It will be necessary to publish this data on ten or twelve [émigré] writers, especially in light of the Soviet press' insistence that there is no interest for émigré literature in the West" (Oct. 27, 1925, Z. Gippius and D. Merezhkovsky Papers, series 2, box 4, folder 3, Amherst).

32. Vladimir Veidle's studies appeared in the collection *Courrier des Iles*, directed by Jacques Maritain for the Plon publishing house. Maritain wrote to Veidle: "It is possible that I will run into problems of commercial nature. . . . But I really hope that if such difficulties arise I will be able to surmount them; and, at any rate, be assured that I will do my best in this regard" (Collection Weidle, box 1, folder "Maritain, Jacques, Meudon, France, Dec. 9, 1937, to Wladimir Weidle t. l. s., lp.," Bakhmeteff).

33. There were some exceptions among younger émigrés. Vasilii Ianovskii's first novel, *Koleso* (1930), appeared in 1932 as *Sachka: L'Enfant qui a faim*. This is the only known translation of his writings into French, but there must exist others, for Ianovskii wrote to Shakhovskaia, who collaborated in French-language periodicals: "Time to time they translate me and publish here in French,—would it be possible to place one of these stories in your [journal]?" (Nov. 15, 1934, Schakovskoy Family Papers, series 1, Zinaida Schakovskoy Papers, box 1, folder 26, Amherst). Ekaterina Bakunina's first novel, *Telo* (1933), was available to the French reader (*Le Corps*) in 1934. Ivan Lukash had two novels translated: *Le Loulou de l'Empereur* (1929) and *Le Pauvre amour de Moussorgsky* (1939). Four of Nabokov's novels appeared in French: *Chambre Obscure* (1934), *La Course du fou* (1934), *Désespoir* (1938), and *La Méprise* (1939). Before she began writing in

French, Nadezhda Gorodetskaia saw four of her novels published in translation: *Les ailes blanches* (1931), *Les mains vides* (1931), *Chimère* (1932), and *L'Étoile du berger* (1933). The translation of Veidle's monograph, *Les Abeilles d'Aristée* (1936), preceded in print the Russian original (*Umiranie iskusstva*, 1937).

34. On the significance of Pontigny in émigré-French cultural commerce, see the 1923 letters of Lev Shestov, in Baranoff-Chestov, *Vie de Léon Chestov*, 1: 296; Berdiaev, "Essai d'autobiographie spirituelle," in Heurgon-Desjardins, *Paul Desjardins et les Décades de Pontigny*, 388–90. On the history of the debates, see François Chaubet, *Paul Desjardins et les décades de Pontigny* (Paris: Presses Universitaires du Septentrion, 2000).

35. See Martin-Chauffier, "Besedy v Pontigny," 253–54; D. Leis [Veidle], "Pontin'i," 2–3.

36. As per Gleb Struve's informed estimate (*Russkaia literatura v izgnanii*, 191).

37. See Lukash, "Zametki na poliakh," 3; Slonim, "Russkii Parizh dvadtsatykh godov," 6.

38. Fel'zen, "Parizhskie vstrechi russkikh i frantsuzskikh pisatelei," 5.

39. In addition, *France et Monde, Cahiers de la Quinzaine*, and *Cahiers 1929* (later *Cahiers 1930* and *Cahiers mensuels*) promoted émigré writing. Beginning in 1929, they published in translation works by Aldanov, Gorodetskaia, Knut, Kuznetsova, Remizov, Teffi, Tsvetaeva, and B. Zaitsev.

40. See Fel'zen, "Parizhskie vstrechi," 5; Golenishchev-Kutuzov, "Frankorusskaia studiia," 4; Sazonova, "Vstrecha frantsuzskikh i russkikh pisatelei," 5; Veidle, "Franko-russkie vstrechi," 399; B. Zaitsev, "Dnevnik pisatelia," 3.

41. Never reprinted, full transcripts of the meetings are available in the following issues of the *Cahiers de la Quinzaine: Rencontres*, ed. R. Sébastien and W. de Vogt (hors série, 1930); nos. 5, 6, 8, 9 (série 20, 1930); nos. 1, 2 (série 21, 1930); nos. 4, 5, 6 (série 21, 1931); no. 1 (série 22, 1931). The review *Chisla* (1929–34), initially sponsored by the French review *Cahiers de l'Étoile*, organized similar debates attended by French intellectuals of all convictions. See "Vechera 'Chisel,'" 253; "Po literaturnym sobraniiam," 199.

42. Influenced by the French Orthodox priest Lev Gillet, whom he met at the Studio, Fokht underwent a religious conversion, embarked on a pilgrimage to Jerusalem, and became a monk and a secretary to the patriarch of Antioch in Damascus (Behr-Sigel, *Un Moine de l'Église d'Orient*, 265).

43. Veidle gained access to prestigious French periodicals thanks to the acquaintances he made at the Studio. Among these was Du Bos, who introduced Veidle, Adamovich, and Fel'zen to the Parisian literary salons (Veidle, "Frankorusskie vstrechi," 397, 399). Some twenty years later, Adamovich still fondly recalled his exposure to French intellectuals in correspondence with friends, all the while deploring émigré cultural isolation in his memoirs. See his letter to Terapiano (May 22, 1956): "I've just received R[usskaia] M[ysl'] and read your review of my book. Thank you for your attention. As Paul Valéry put it (at one of the meetings organized by Fokht)—'Ce n'est pas l'admiration que je cherche, mais l'attention.' This is both quite true and the only attitude worthy of a writer." "Adamovich, Georgii Viktorovich (1931–1960)," Iurii Konstantinovich Terapiano, Correspondence and Other Papers, box 1, folder 1, Beinecke.

44. See in the transcripts of the Studio franco-russe the reaction of René Lalou, Jean Maxence, and Marcel Péguy to Iuliia Sazonova's exposé (*Rencontres*, 73–75); the altercation between J.-V. Bréchignac, Lalou, and Tsvetaeva (*Rencontres*, 87); and Valéry's response to Veidle's speech "Paul Valéry et la poésie pure" ("Les Débats," 65).

45. Adamovich, "Literaturnye besedy," *Zveno* 125: 2; idem, "Literaturnye besedy," *Zveno* 2: 74–75; Veidle, "O frantsuzskoi literature," 499–501; idem, "Les Débats," 42.

46. Adamovich, "André Gide," 25–26, 30; B. Zaitsev, "Les Débats," 41.

47. Fel'zen, "Marc Chadourne, 278; and idem, "Fransua Moriak," 33.

48. See Levinson, "Siuares," 357; Shletser, "Novoe v zapadnoi literature," 2.

49. See Adamovich, "Literaturnye besedy," *Zveno* 5: 247–48; Terapiano, *Vstrechi*, 130–32.

50. See B. Zaitsev, "Nashi ankety," 2; idem, "Les Débats," 36.

51. See Crémieux, "Le roman depuis 1918," 6; Berge, *L'Esprit de la littérature moderne*, 117–19; Fel'zen, "My v Evrope," 154–55, 159.

52. Valéry, "La Crise de l'esprit," in *Oeuvres*, 1: 992–93, 1000.

53. See *Enquête*: Louis Aragon (17), Gérard Bauer (237–39), Benjamin Crémieux (52–54), Raymond Escholier (75), Henri Massis (332–33), and Philippe Soupault (195–96). See also Bancquart and Cahné, *Littérature française du XX siècle*, 134–36; Crémieux, "Le roman depuis 1918," 9; Crevel, "Pour la liberté de l'esprit," in *Détours*, 171–72, 175; André Glucksmann, preface to *La Guerre comme expérience intérieure*, by Ernst Jünger, 14–15; Massis, *Réflexions sur l'art du roman*, xi–xiv; Pourtalès, "Note sur Marcel Proust et John Ruskin," in *De Hamlet à Swann*, 10–11. The sense of a spiritual and cultural crisis permeated not only French literature but the postwar European literature in general. See, for example, T. S. Eliot's *Waste Land* or the poetry of Ezra Pound.

54. See Bauer, in *Enquête*, 238; Crémieux, "Le Bilan d'une enquête," 293.

55. See Arland, *Essais et nouveaux essais critiques*, 11–37. See also his "Chroniques: Sur un nouveau mal du siècle," 49.

56. See Rivière, "La Crise du concepte de littérature," 159–60.

57. See Arland, "Chronique: Sur un Nouveau mal du siècle," 26; idem, "Témoignage," in *Réflexions*, 117–21. For an exemplary "examen de conscience," see Arland, "Examen de conscience," 12. On the use and abuse of the concept of the "new malady" and its constituents, see Aragon, *Traité du style*, 124–27; Beauvoir, *Mémoires d'une jeune fille rangée*, 318; Breton, *Les Pas perdus*, 9; Chaumeix, "Les Jeunes et les littératures étrangères (1)," 708; Daniel-Rops, "Enquête sur l'inquiétude contemporaine," 1073; idem, "Un bilan de dix ans," 178; Massis, "Rencontre," in *Réflexions*, 76; idem, "Reconstruction," in *Réflexions*, 91–98; Soupault, "Déposition," 161.

58. See Mauriac, "Le Bon apôtre, par Philippe Soupault," 610–11. The drive for the "new malady" in literature was so overwhelming that even Proust's hero Marcel was interpreted as one of these disoriented young men, although he did not fit chronologically into the postwar malady (Crémieux, *Inquiétude et reconstruction*, 69).

59. See the disdainful treatment of Gide by young French writers in the Studio franco-russe. Quoting Mauriac, Maxence said that Gide's *inquiétude* was the

only reason to be interested in this "corpse"—an allusion to the pamphlet *Un Cadavre* published by the surrealists on the occasion of Anatole France's death ("Les Débat," *CQ* 20, no. 6, [1930], 44).

60. See Michel Leiris's preface to his 1939 novel: "Being one of so many autobiographical novels, intimate diaries, memoirs, and confessions which have been, for several years, extraordinarily fashionable (as if one despised the *creative* side of literary work . . .), *L'Âge d'homme* proposes no more than its author's attempt to speak of himself with maximum lucidity and sincerity" (*L'Âge d'homme*, 10). See also Magny, *Histoire du roman français depuis 1918*, 1: 73.

61. See Berge, *L'Esprit de la littérature moderne*, 17–19.

62. See Léonard, *La Crise du concept de littérature en France au XXe siècle*, 66–67.

63. See "Iskusstvo i politika," 3; Adamovich, "Pis'ma o Lermontove," 2.

64. See Adamovich, "Literaturnye besedy," *Zveno* 94: 2.

65. Adamovich, "O frantsuzskoi 'inquiétude' i o russkoi trevoge," 2. See also Fedotov, "Rossiia, Evropa i my," 4; Gorodetskaia, "Spor pokolenii," 5; Leis [Veidle], "Bolezn' veka," 5–6; Mochul'skii, "Nishchie dukhom," 3–4.

66. See N. Dashkov [Veidle], "Iz evropeiskoi literatury," 4; Fel'zen, "My v Evrope," 154–60; Raevskii, "O russkoi trevoge i nemetskoi Sensucht," 4; Reznikov, "Chto budet s nashei literaturoi?" 4.

67. Adamovich, "Sovremennye zapiski," *PN* 3144 (Oct. 31, 1929): 2; idem, "Parizhskie vpechatleniia," 2.

68. See Adamovich, "Eshche o 'zdes'' i 'tam'," 3; Terapiano, "Zhurnal i chitatel'," 26.

69. See Fokht, "Quelques aspects du roman russe depuis 1918," 15–26; Terapiano, "Chelovek 1930-kh godov," 210–12; Varshavskii, "Neskol'ko rassuzhdenii ob Andre Zhide i emigrantskom molodom cheloveke," 216–22; and idem, "O 'geroe' emigrantskoi molodoi literatury," 164–72.

70. Arland, "Chroniques: Sur un Nouveau mal du siècle," 18; B. Poplavskii, "Vokrug 'Chisel'," 205.

71. See B. Poplavskii, "O misticheskoi atmosfere molodoi literatury v emigratsii," 310–11. Cf. Daniel-Rops's description of the esthetics of the "new malady": "The rejection of anything that pertains to a gratuitous game in art. . . . The innermost feeling that the explanation of one's own role in the world resides in that *individual, rare and pure note* which everyone brings to the great concert of the universe [cette *note individuelle, pure et rare*, que chacun apporte au grand concert de l'univers]. These are the most noble among all the peculiar traits of 'inquiétude'" ("Un bilan de dix ans," 180; emphasis added).

Describing the main ingredients of his peers' literary esthetics, Terapiano wrote: "The main things are the anxiety and the feeling of distress which, ever since Pushkin, Lermontov, and Tiutchev, constitute the 'letters of nobility' of Russian poetry" (Aug. 24, 1962, Aleksis Rannit Papers, box 29, folder "Iurii Terapiano," Beinecke).

72. See Varshavskii, "O proze mladshikh emigrantskikh pisatelei," 410.

73. "Krug: Beseda piataia 16 dekabria 1935 goda," 138.

74. See Adamovich's "Nachalo," 502; idem, "O literature v emigratsii," *SZ* 50 (1932): 337. Later Adamovich expressed his dislike of this poem due to its programmatic nature and lack of nuance. At the time of its publication, however,

the text served as an artistic and philosophical manifesto. See Adamovich's letter to Ivask, who had solicited a contribution from Adamovich for a poetic anthology: "About your anthology and the choice of my poems: Do as you please and choose anything you like. . . . I have only one request—*do not* choose 'Za vse, za vse spasibo . . .' Z. N. Gippius liked this poem very much. . . . But it jars me. There is something too *direct* in it, not incarnated in poetry but left in the form of naked thought or feeling" (July 26, 1952, Iurii Ivask Papers, series 1, correspondence, box 1, folder 2, Amherst).

75. Adamovich, "Na raznye temy," 3. The case of Charles Péguy is another example of Russification. Fedotov assimilated the French poet to the "righteous men of the Russian intelligentsia," finding in his career such "Russian" qualities as "full absence of literariness, even of literary self-definition, complete unity of life and art, writing as socioreligious service, unconditional self-sacrifice to the idea, and sacred poverty assumed as a form of vocation" ("Jean Maxence et Nadejda Gorodetzky," 99–100).

76. Adamovich, "Literaturnye zametki," *PN* 6088: 3; see also his "Zhizn' i 'zhizn'," 2.

77. See Khodasevich, "Krizis poezii," 3; idem, "Zhalost' i 'zhalost'," 4. Berberova suggests that Khodasevich, trapped in the esthetics of symbolism, missed much in contemporary French letters, whose young "fought for . . . confession rather than fiction" (*Italics Are Mine*, 219, 226; cf. idem, "Borolis' . . . za 'ispoved'" protiv 'romana,'" in *Kursiv moi*, 262). See also Hagglund, "Adamovich-Xodasevich Polemics," 250.

78. See Izvol'skaia, "Twenty-Five Years of Russian Émigré Literature," 70; Iu. Mandel'shtam, "Dnevnik obmanutogo cheloveka," 4; idem, "Dnevnik pisatelia," 9; Mochul'skii, "Krizis voobrazheniia," 76, 79; idem, "Novyi chelovek," 3; idem, "Romantizm i my," 3; Pikel'nyi, "Na temu 'iskusstvo i byt,'" 187; Raevskii, "O 'kontse' iskusstva," 3–4; Slonim, "Gibel' literatury,"61; Sushchev [Veidle], "Novoe vo frantsuzskoi belletristike," 7; Veidle, "Pol' Moran," 3; idem, "Chelovek protiv pisatelia," 139–45.

79. Adamovich, "Pis'ma o Lermontove," 2.

80. See Shklovskii, "Serapionovy brat'ia," 20–21.

81. Clark, "La Prose des années vingt," in Etkind et al., *Histoire de la littérature russe: Le XX-e siècle*, 2: 379.

82. Cf. Bem's view of Soviet literature as based on a system of pseudo-values (*sistema psevdo-tsennostei*) and Petrov-Skitalets's description of émigré literature as produced by "savages who consider themselves cultured" ("literatura etikh dikarei, mniashchikh sebia kul'turnymi"). Bem, "O proshlom i nastoiashchem" (*Mech* 1–2, May 20, 1934), in his *Pis'ma o literature*, 169; S. Petrov (Skitalets), "Zasedanie dvadtsat' tret'e. 30 avgusta 1934 g., vechernee," in *S'ezd*, 610. I borrow the term "esthetics of opposition" from Lotman, *Lektsii po struktural'noi poetike*, in *Iu. M. Lotman i tartussko-moskovskaia semioticheskaia shkola*, 226.

83. See Lotman and Uspenskii, "O semioticheskom mekhanizme kul'tury," in Lotman, *Izbrannye stat'i v trekh tomakh*, 3: 326.

84. Terapiano opposed the cultural continuity of the interwar émigré literature to the uprootedness in the writings of new expatriates after WWII, implying that Soviet education severed them from prerevolutionary traditions: "One

can easily define the contemporary 'note' and style—there is no natural, organic continuation of the old cultural line but rather an attempt (after a *break* and *disruption*) to appropriate and fill with one's own meaning *disparate fragments of a broken whole*" (Feb. 27, 1962, Aleksis Rannit Papers, box 29, folder "Iurii Terapiano," Beinecke).

85. Khodasevich, "Letuchie listy," 3. See also Adamovich on futurism and "Soviet experimentalism" in "Nikolai Ushakov—sovetskie prozaiki," 188–94; and idem, "Parizhskie vpechatleniia," 2.

86. Struve, *Russkaia literatura v izgnanii*, 274–76.

87. See his undated letter to Zdanevich in B. Poplavskii, *Pokushenie s negodnymi sredstvami*, 94–95.

88. Terapiano, *Vstrechi*, 150–51.

89. Berberova et al., "Ot redaktsii," 2.

90. On February 11, 1928, Gippius wrote to Berberova about the esthetic program of *Novyi dom* and its heir journal, *Novyi korabl'* (The new ship): "As concerns 'influences' in general: I greet them, have always sought and happily accepted them" (Nina Berberova Papers, box 8, folder 199 "Gippius, Zinaida Nikolaevna / 1926–30, n. d.," Beinecke).

91. Adamovich, "Nesostoiavshaiasia progulka," 290–91. Boris Zaitsev expressed the same opinion in the Studio franco-russe ("Les Débats," 36).

92. Kul'man, "Novyi dom: 3-ia kniga," 3.

93. See Gazdanov, "Literaturnye priznaniia," 259. The artificiality of this simplicity was so evident that émigré critics labeled it the temptation and the myth of simplicity. See Bem, "Soblazn prostoty" (*Mech* 11–12, July 22, 1934), in his *Pis'ma o literature*, 177–81; Gomolitskii, *Arion*, 34–35; Veidle, "G. Gazdanov," 200–201. Ivask wrote to Veidle: "I've been thinking about émigré poetry. Between us—is it not too dressed up [*nariadnaia*]? I mean the verse of G. Ivanov, Adamovich. . . . The same old melodious rhythms, refinement in expression, logic in the narrative! Adamovich kept writing about simplicity, even poverty, but his own poems are often rhetorical and always in a lofty tone. . . . The best émigré poets preserved good acmeist manners of 1913" (Jan. 18, 1965, Collection Weidle, box 2, folder "Ivask Iurii Pavlovich, 1965," Bakhmeteff).

94. See Terapiano "O zarubezhnoi poezii 1920–1960 godov," 7; idem, *Vstrechi*, 151.

95. See Terapiano, "O novykh knigakh stikhov," 172.

96. Maguire, *Red Virgin Soil*, 418–21.

97. Fleishman, *Boris Pasternak v tridtsatye gody*, 2–3, 124.

98. Exiles promptly sensed the importance of these events in émigré-Soviet dynamics. See Berberova, *Italics Are Mine*, 227–28; Slonim, "Russkii Parizh dvadtsatykh godov," 6.

99. Blium, "Pechat' russkogo zarubezh'ia glazami Glavlita i GPU," 265–68.

100. Raskol'nikov, "Pis'mo v redaktsiiu," 1. See also "Protiv burzhuaznykh tribunov pod maskoi sovetskogo pisatelia. Protiv pereklichki s beloi emigratsiei," 1; Volin, "Nedopustimye iavleniia," 1; Petrunkevich, "S. F. Platonov," 72–95.

101. Sazonova, "V zashchitu . . . tsenzury," 3.

102. See Knut, "Zelenaia lampa," 42; Petrov (Skitalets), "Zasedanie dvadtsat' tret'e," in *S'ezd*, 608–9; Smirnov, "Solntse mertvykh," 250–67; idem, "Na tom

beregu," 141–50; Volin, "Emigrantskaia poeziia," 20–23; Zelinskii, "Rubaki na sene," 10. See also Terapiano's letter to Berberova. Writes Terapiano: "A letter has arrived from a poet . . . who returned to Russia a year and a half ago. . . . His letter is a cri de coeur. Material conditions are much better there than in emigration, but spiritually—it's a desert. Words like 'idealism,' 'personality,' 'romanticism,' 'mysticism' are invectives. Poetry is written to socio-political directives, the atmosphere in groups and associations is unbearable. The *unpublished* texts are as bad, dull and untalented as the *published* ones; and, most importantly, plunging into that atmosphere one understands why no poetry can come out of there. . . . 'Now, having seen it, I am telling you: neither Moscow, nor Leningrad but Paris alone is the center of Russian literature. Quit quarreling, do not by any means return to Russia and dissuade those who would like to return: spiritually this place is worse than a cemetery' (I quote my source who read the letter.)" (Sept. 9, 1927, Boris I. Nikolaevsky Collection, box 402, series 233 "Berberova N. N.," folder 34 "Terapiano, Iurii," Hoover).

103. Slonim, "Literaturnyi dnevnik," *VR* 7 (1928), 62; idem, "Molodye pisateli za rubezhom," 100; idem, "Zametki ob emigrantskoi literature," 616–27.

104. Toying with the idea of return, Gazdanov denied the possibility of young émigré literature, nullifying his own literary career ("O molodoi emigrantskoi literature," 406–8). On Gazdanov's desire to end his exile, see his letters in Dienes, *Russian Literature in Exile*, 78, 80. For the émigré interpretation of Gazdanov's words as a pro-Soviet manifesto, see Khodasevich, "'Sovremennye zapiski,'" *Vz* 3935, 3. See Nabokov's description of Gazdanov's "prancing" (*vzdyblennaia*) article as a sign that he would soon return to Russia (Correspondence with Zinaida Shakhovskaia, Letter 19 [n. d.], Vladimir Nabokov Archive, Library of Congress; I am grateful to Alexander Dolinin for sharing this document with me).

Back in the USSR, the critic and poet German Khokhlov wrote that émigré letters disintegrated morally and artistically and neared their death ("Da byl li mal'chik?" 2).

After publishing his *Panorama de la littérature russe contemporaine* (1929), which denied the existence of émigré literature, Vladimir Pozner "defected" to French communists (see Struve, *Russkaia literatura v izgnanii*, 8). Composing an anthology of émigré poetry, Adamovich rejected Pozner's candidacy as "Soviet" even though the writer lived in Paris: "I am relishing the pronouncements Vova Pozner has made in Moscow. . . . 'As a member of the French Communist Party, I. . . .' Thus all doubts about his participation in our anthology have been resolved. Or else we would have to include Erenburg as well" (in Struve, "K istorii russkoi zarubezhnoi literatury," 234). Characteristically, Adamovich insisted on calling the texts in the anthology "émigré" in contrast to "poetry abroad" (*zarubezhnaia poeziia*, 254).

105. Aldanov, "O polozhenii emigrantskoi literatury," 401; Khodasevich, "'Sovremennye zapiski,'" *Vz* 3935, 3; Osorgin, "O 'molodykh pisateliakh,'" 3.

106. Khodasevich, "Rossica," 3.

107. See Adamovich, "O literature v emigratsii," *PN* 3732: 2; idem, "O literature v emigratsii," *SZ* 50: 339. See also Bem, "O kritike i kritikakh" (*Rul'* 3168, April 29, 1931, 2) in his *Pis'ma o literature*, 34–36.

108. The following excerpt from Adamovich's letter to Gide is illustrative of the émigré position vis-à-vis French writers turned communist sympathizers: "A gathering devoted to 'André Gide and the USSR,' organized by the Russian review *Chisla,* will take place on Tuesday. I know that you have been informed. I am to open the debate. There is, however, one point that bothers me. You might decide, I am afraid, that this is something *against* you. . . . Not at all. We were surprised to read your 'Pages du journal,' we are trying to understand you. But, really, we owe you too much ever to debunk you,—no matter what political or social orientation you adopted" (March 24, 1933, Y. 868.1, Doucet).

109. See Berdiaev, "Vérité et mensonge du communisme," 104; idem, "Iskaniia sotsial'noi pravdy molodoi Frantsiei," 58; Dashkov [Veidle], "Komsnobizm," 3; Khodasevich, "Poeticheskaia beseda," 3; Kostrov, "Lui Aragon," 3; Odoevtseva, *Na beregakh Seny,* 140; Tsetlin, "Ob Anatole Franse," 438.

110. See Berdiaev, "Iskaniia sotsial'noi pravdy molodoi Frantsiei," 58; idem, "O profeticheskoi missii slova i mysli (k ponimaniiu svobody)," 60; Fedotov, "Rossiia, Evropa i my," 6; idem, "Zachem my zdes'?" 443; Fel'zen, "My v Evrope," 155; idem, "Vozvrashchenie iz Rossii," 120, 124.

Shteiger wrote to Ivask: "Adamovich read a very intelligent paper on Gide's recent book. . . . I found this paper particularly important, because I am keenly following trends in French social life and its treatment in French intellectual circles. France may be today the *purest* country in the world, and I am trying to decide whether the very fate of Christianity might not be at stake in France today" (Jan. 30, 1937, in Livak, "K istorii 'Parizhskoi shkoly.' Pis'ma Anatoliia Shteigera, 1937–1943," 91–92).

111. See Struve, *Russkaia literatura v izgnanii,* 239; Berberova, *Italics Are Mine,* 226–27, 354–55.

112. See Dashkov [Veidle], "Komsnobizm," 3; Merezhkovskii, "O svobode i Rossii," 20–21; Mogilianskii, "Mir iskusstva," 2; Osorgin, "Bez kliukvy," 3; Rudnev, "W. Ch. Huntington," 449–51.

After reading Berdiaev's "Vérité et mensonge du communisme," Gide was eager to meet the émigré philosopher and discuss the links between communism and Christianity. The writers and communist sympathizers Paul Nizan, André Malraux, and Jean-Richard Bloch repeatedly met with Berdiaev to discuss the same issue. See Berdiaev, "Essai d'autobiographie spirituelle," in Heurgon-Desjardins, *Paul Desjardins et les Décades de Pontigny,* 391. Gide heeded the émigré opinion throughout his flirtation with communism. See his letter to Alexander Kerenskii: "While arranging my papers, I have found your kind letter of December 16 containing your reflections on my book, *Retour de l'URSS,* which I am now rereading with great interest. Have I thanked you? I do not think so; and you may have interpreted my silence as a sign of indifference or ungratefulness? . . . I ask belatedly for your forgiveness; for a long time I have been submerged by the wave of reactions to the publication of my book. And yes, your reflections are of great interest for me; they have even moved me. On the other hand, I hope that the book I am finishing now, conceived as an appendix to my *Retour de l'URSS,* will address and answer some of your questions" (Feb. 19, 1937, Y. 1246.2, Doucet).

113. Liubimov, "Skandal na sobranii 'Chisel,'" 3. In a letter to Struve, Slonim

gave a different account of this event: "Merezhkovskii spoke there and a scandal ensued after I had warned the audience—in French, naturally, that they should not rejoice at the writer's 'defection' into the camp of the friends of the Soviet Union and advised that instead of making loud pronouncement they had better read Gide's oeuvre. There was shouting, banging, some thugs rushed to the rostrum but I refused to step down, so that the frightened [Paul] Vaillant-Couturier [the editor-in-chief of the communist newspaper *L'Humanité*] restored calm and they listened to the rest of my speech. He said to me—quite irate, 'You can rejoice, now that you have ruined our meeting'" (March 29, 1972, Gleb Struve Collection, box 137, folder 1 "Slonim, Mark. Correspondence," Hoover).

114. See Veidle, "O tekh, kogo uzhe net," 397. For the émigré press coverage of the incident, see "Drug Maiakovskogo," 4; Adamovich, "Literaturnaia nedelia," *IlR* 30 (271): 22. Levinson's "beating" was invented by the French communist press. See a reprint from *L'Humanité*: "Un insulteur de Majakowsky reçoit une visite désagréable," *SSR* 1 (1930): 21–22.

115. See this letter and Levinson's reply in *NLAS* 400, June 14 (1930): 6. See also Adamovich, "Literaturnaia nedelia," *IlR* 30 (271): 22; Fel'zen, "Na odnom strannom raute v Parizhe," 4.

116. Adamovich et al., "Autour de Maïakovsky," 6.

117. Furthermore, Berberova, who later put such an unfavorable spin on this incident, personally collected signatures for the open letter in the *Nouvelles Littéraires*. See some responses to her query: Vsevolod Fokht (July 1, 1930), Dovid Knut (June 30, 1930), and Iurii Terapiano (June 28, 1930) in Boris I. Nikolaevsky Collection, box 401, series 233 "Berberova, N. N.," folders 13 "Fokht, V." and 34 "Knut, Dovid"; and box 402, series 233 "Berberova, N. N.," folder 34 "Terapiano, Iu.," Hoover. It is quite telling that Berberova "forgot" to mention this public climax of the "Maiakovskii affair" in her memoirs, since it did not fit her interpretation of the émigré-French ideological dynamics.

118. See Crémieux, *Inquiétude et reconstruction,* 154, 157–59; Furet, *Le Passé d'une illusion,* 165–211, 233–35, 468–74; Drieu La Rochelle "Gide et le communisme," 135–39; "Littérature communisante," 129–32; and "Littérature de front commun," 132–34 in his *Sur les écrivains.*

119. Gide, *Retour de l'U.R.S.S. suivi de Retouches à mon Retour de l'U.R.S.S.,* 71–81. See also Brousson, "Témoignages russes et littéraires," 3; Drieu La Rochelle, "La véritable erreur des surréalistes," 166–71; idem, "Gide et le communisme," 135–38; Gerbod et al., *Introduction à la vie littéraire du XX siècle,* 142; Kelli, "Andre Morua o russkoi literature," 1.

In the Studio franco-russe, Maxence confronted Pozner's claim that Soviet writers represented the only viable Russian literature. Defending émigré letters, he stressed the case of French émigrés, who proved to be "infinitely greater than many of those who propelled them into exile." See his "Les Débat," *CQ* 20, no. 8: 33, 37.

120. See Berdiaev, "Iskaniia sotsial'noi pravdy molodoi Frantsiei," 58; Fel'zen, "Parizhskie vstrechi russkikh i frantsuzskikh pisatelei," 5; Izvol'skaia, "Frantsuzskaia molodezh' i problemy sovremennosti," 130–31.

121. See Aymé et al., "Un appel des écrivains français," 9; Montherlant, "Partageons la liberté," 9. See similar evaluations of the Soviet-émigré literary

opposition in Delage, *La Russie en exile*, 106–11; Ledré, *Les émigrés russes en France*, 199–202; idem, *Trois romanciers russe*, 10–11.

122. Iu. Mandel'shtam, "Frantsuzskie pisateli o russkikh," 9. Berberova wrote in her memoir: "At that time in the entire Western world there was not *one single* writer of renown who would have been *for us*, who would have lifted up his voice against the persecution of the intelligentsia in the USSR, against repressions, Soviet censorship, arrests of writers, trials, the closing of periodicals, against the iron law of socialist realism" (*Italics Are Mine*, 226).

123. See Terapiano's description of the initial hostility of the editors of *Sovremennye zapiski* to "apolitical" poetry by younger émigrés ("V pamiati eta epokha zapechatlelas' navsegda," 278).

124. See Fedotov, "Zachem my zdes'?" 436–37; Rappoport, "Konets zarubezh'ia," 380–81.

125. See Fleishman, *Boris Pasternak v dvadtsatye gody*, 124; Shklovskii, "Pamiatnik nauchnoi oshibke," 1.

126. See Clark, *Soviet Novel*, 32; idem, "La Prose des années vingt," 393, 401.

127. See Fleishman, *Boris Pasternak v tridtsatye gody*, 158–60. See also *S'ezd:* Gladkov, "Zasedanie shestoe: 21 avgusta 1934 g., utrennee," 151; Iudin, "Doklad ob ustave Soiuza Sovetskikh Pisatelei," 663; Zhdanov, "Rech' sekretaria TsK VKP(b)," 5.

128. Averbakh, "My stroim sotsialisticheskuiu literaturu," 2. See also *S'ezd:* Braun, "Zasedanie dvadtsat' piatoe: 31 avgusta 1934 g., vechernee," 648; Lezhnev, "Zasedanie sed'moe: 21 avgusta 1934 g., vechernee," 177.

129. See Fleishman, *Boris Pasternak v tridtsatye gody*, 323–52, 376; Romashov, "Unichtozhit' vragov, pokhoronit' manilovshchinu," 4. Rozental' and Usievich, "Zadachi literaturnoi kritiki," 4; "O bditel'nosti i otvetstvennosti," 1.

130. See *S'ezd:* Chumandrin, "Zasedanie shestoe: 21 avgusta 1934 g., utrennee," 167–69; Erenburg, "Zasedanie sed'moe: 21 avgusta 1934 g., vechernee," 185; Gor'kii, "Zasedanie pervoe: 17 avgusta 1934 g., vechernee," 1; Iudin, "Doklad ob ustave Soiuza Sovetskikh Pisatelei," 663, 665; Luppol, "Zasedanie desiatoe: 23 avgusta 1934 g., utrennee," 259; Radek, "Sovremennaia mirovaia literatura i zadachi proletarskogo iskusstva," 317; Shklovskii, "Zasedanie shestoe: 21 avgusta 1934 g., utrennee," 154–55; Zhdanov, "Rech' sekretaria TsK VKP(b)," 5. See also Clark, *Soviet Novel*, 27–29, 46; Strada, "Le réalisme socialiste," in Etkind et al., *Histoire de la littérature russe: Le XX-e siècle*, 2: 26, 29–31.

131. See "Proletarskaia poeziia na pod'eme," 1. *S'ezd:* Erenburg, "Zasedanie sed'moe," 185; Iudin, "Doklad ob ustave," 662; Radek, "Sovremennaia mirovaia literatura," 317; Seifullina, "Zasedanie deviatoe: 22 avgusta 1934 g., vechernee," 236; Zhdanov, "Rech' sekretaria TsK VKP(b)," 4.

132. See Adamovich, "O literature v emigratsii," *PN* 3732, 2; idem, "O literature v emigratsii," *SZ* 50, 335–39; idem, "Parizhskie vpechatleniia," 2; Berdiaev, "O profeticheskoi missii slova," 59–61; Fel'zen, "Mal'ro. (Frantsuzskie 'Tridtsatye gody')," 30–32; idem, "My v Evrope," 154–55, 159; B. Poplavskii, "Chelovek i ego znakomye," 135–36; idem, "Vokrug 'Chisel,'" 205, 209; Sazonova, "K. Fedin," 239; Varshavskii, "Neskol'ko rassuzhdenii ob Andre Zhide," 216–22; "Lichnost' i obshchestvo. Anketa," 129–33.

133. "Ot redaktsii," *Chisla* 1: 6. See also B. Poplavskii, "Vokrug 'Chisel,'" 204.

Adamovich's esthetic theories gave a boost to this departure from "politics." See his letter to Gippius: "What about 'the most important'? Don't you think it concerns exclusively *the personality and soul of the individual, not the humankind*, i.e., neither democracy versus monarchy, nor the fate of the white and yellow races, the end of the world or the meaning of crusades etc., etc.—not all this secondary stuff" (Sept. 10, 1928, Z. Gippius and D. Merezhkovsky Papers, series 1, incoming correspondence, box 1, folder 11, Amherst). But there can be no doubt that his theories were in large part a reaction to Soviet art. A year earlier he wrote to Gippius: "I am now reading a rare nastiness—[Il'ia] Erenburg's new novel, hoping that it may beat sense into me better than Pushkin, i.e., according to the 'principle of contrast' [*kak teorema—'ot obratnogo'*]" (July 1927 [no date], folder 7).

134. See Bakunina, "Bagrovoe solntse gliadelo kak glaz raz'iarennyi byka," 5; Fel'zen, "Vozvrashchenie," 167; Gazdanov, *Vecher u Kler*, in *Sobranie sochinenii v trekh tomakh*, 1: 111; B. Poplavskii, *Apollon Bezobrazov*, in his *Domoi s nebes: Romany*, 24.

135. In her *History of the Émigré Intelligentsia*, Gippius notes that starting in 1930 "the feeling of émigré 'mission' is replaced by *arrivisme*," "the young are no longer united by 'ideas,'" "they lose interest in general questions," and "escape into private life" (Pachmuss, "Zinaida Gippius," 6, 8).

136. See B. Poplavskii, "Chelovek i ego znakomye," 137; "Iskusstvo i politika," 3.

137. Khodasevich, "O zadachakh molodoi literatury," 3. See Stepun, "Porevoliutsionnoe soznanie i zadacha emigrantskoi literatury," 12–28.

138. The term "émigré poetics" was first suggested in Boldt, Segal, and Fleishman, "Problemy izucheniia literatury russkoi emigratsii pervoi treti XX veka," 85.

139. Adamovich, "O frantsuzskoi 'inquiétude' i o russkoi trevoge," 2. See also Adamovich, "Literaturnye besedy," *Zveno* 203: 2; idem, "O literature v emigratsii," *PN* 3732: 2; Gippius, "Polet v Evropu," 138; Tsetlin, "Emigrantskoe," 439; Varshavskii, "Neskol'ko rassuzhdenii ob Andre Zhide," 221–22; Veidle, "O frantsuzskoi literature," 501.

140. Berberova, "Zelenaia lampa," 42–43.

141. Osorgin, "Kniga Chisel," 3. See also Adamovich, "Literaturnye besedy," *Zveno* 5: 246; idem, "Literaturnye zametki," *PN* 4257: 2; Bitsilli, "Iakor'," 463, 465; idem, "Vozrozhdenie allegorii," 191–92; Khodasevich, "'Chisla,'" 3; Osorgin, "Chisla," 508; Postnikov, "O molodoi emigrantskoi literature," 216, 218–19; Remizov, "Samoe znachitel'noe proizvedenie russkoi literatury poslednego piatiletiia," 1; B. Zaitsev, "Dnevnik pisatelia," 3.

142. See Varshavskii, "Neskol'ko rassuzhdenii ob Andre Zhide," 221; Shletser, "Marsel' Prust," 2. See a similar recoding procedure involving the names of Gide and Dostoevsky in Adamovich, "Andre Zhid i SSSR," 2.

143. Fel'zen came to the same conclusion in his description of younger émigrés' "romance with the West," which distinguished them from older émigré and Soviet writers ("My v Evrope," 155–56, 169).

144. See Fel'zen, "Avtobiografiia," 121; B. Poplavskii, "Sredi somnenii i ochevidnostei," 96–105; idem, "O misticheskoi atmosfere," 308–11; idem, "O

smerti i zhalosti v 'Chislakh,'" 3; idem, "Chelovek i ego znakomye," 135–38; idem, "Vokrug 'Chisel,'" 204–9; Terapiano, "Chelovek 1930-kh godov," 210–12; idem, "'Rytsar' bednyi," 9–10; Sharshun, "Magicheskii realizm," 229–31; Varshavskii, "Neskol'ko rassuzhdenii ob Andre Zhide," 216–22; idem, "O 'geroe' emigrantskoi molodoi literatury," 164–72; idem, "O proze mladshikh emigrantskikh pisatelei," 409–14.

145. See Fedotov, "O parizhskoi poezii," 189; Otsup, "Personalizm kak iavlenie literatury," in his *Literaturnye ocherki*, 131. Adamovich's reaction to Berberova's claim that it was not his critical influence but that of Khodasevich that attracted "everything gifted" in émigré letters confirms the Paris School's self-conception as the most talented and original émigré artistic event. Adamovich wrote: "Khodasevich and his new book, that is, the collection of old articles with an introduction by Ninon. . . . That idiot Berb[erova]. She is writing in the introduction that 'everything gifted grouped around Khodasevich.' Actually, the only people who grouped were herself and Smolenskii" (Nov. 14, 1954, Collection Bacherac, folder 7 "Adamovich to Bakhrakh 1954–55," Bakhmeteff).

146. See Gorodetskaia, "Les Débats," 55; Fel'zen, "My v Evrope," 160; Otsup, "Klim Samgin," 181; Terapiano, "Chelovek 1930-kh godov," 210; Varshavskii, "Neskol'ko rassuzhdenii ob Andre Zhide," 220; idem, "O 'geroe' emigrantskoi molodoi literatury," 165.

147. See Balakshin, "Emigrantskaia literatura," 135. Bem agreed with this estimate but included among these "truly émigré" writers: Adamovich, Bunin, G. Ivanov, Khodasevich, Remizov, Shmelev, and Tsvetaeva. See "Russkaia literatura v emigratsii" (*Mech* 4 [241], Jan. 22, 1939) in his *Pis'ma o literature*, 334–36.

148. See Adamovich, "'Sovremennye zapiski' kn. 50-ia," *PN* 4236: 3; Otsup, "Gaito Gazdanov," 232.

149. On the European modernist worldview, see Calinescu, *Five Faces of Modernity*, 147; Poggioli, *Theory of the Avant-Garde*, 96–97; Russell, *Poets, Prophets, and Revolutionaries*, 39.

150. Terapiano, "'Na Balkanakh,'" 140. For some examples of this mythology, see Adamovich, "Novye pisateli," 3; Berberova, *Italics Are Mine*, 215, 220; Gazdanov, "O molodoi emigrantskoi literature," 408; Khodasevich, "Podvig," 3; idem, "O smerti Poplavskogo," 3; Terapiano, "O zarubezhnoi poezii 1920–1960 godov," 3; Varshavskii, *Nezamechennoe pokolenie*, 165, 167, 170.

151. See Slonim, "Nezamechennoe pokolenie," 8; Struve, "O molodykh poetakh," 3; Zeeler, "Neobkhodimye popravki," 2. Gippius wrote in reaction to Khodasevich's obituary of Poplavskii, which alleged that older writers shunned and isolated their younger colleagues: "I will not dwell on the well-known fact that the so-called young literature have been gathering for years every Sunday at our place, at full freedom: those who did not come did so because they did not feel like it and once they changed their mind, they were welcome back. Poplavskii was among the most faithful *habitués*: this year he has not missed a single Sunday, even in the summer, including the last one, almost on the eve of his death. I repeat, you must be aware of this and so you certainly did not mean us, emphasizing the general 'indifferent and scornful' attitude on the part of the older [writers] vis-à-vis the younger ones (but who could actually fit [this de-

scription]? Shmelev? Bunin? Remizov? Zaitsev? Teffi?)" (Nov. 14, 1935, Nina Berberova Papers, Series VIII: Vladislav Khodasevich Papers, box 57, folder 1289 "Gippius, Zinaida / 1925–39, n. d.," Beinecke).

152. See Aldanov, "O polozhenii emigrantskoi literatury," 404, 408; Bakunina, "Dlia kogo i dlia chego pisat'," 254–55; Damanskaia, "Na ekrane moei pamiati," 206; Ianovskii, *Polia Eliseiskie,* 112–13; Ivask, "Chudaki," 183–87; Osorgin, "Sud'ba zarubezhnoi knigi," 385, 388–89; Slonim, "Novye zarubezhnye zhurnaly," 892.

153. See Kovalevskii, *Zarubezhnaia Rossiia,* 28; Slovtsov (Nikolai Kalishevich), "Russkie vo Frantsii," 2.

154. Knut, "Russkii Monparnass," 3.

155. See Aleksinskaia, "Emigrantskaia pechat'," 53; Berberova, *Italics Are Mine,* 273; Dienes, *Russian Literature in Exile,* 36, 41–42, 80; Ianovskii, *Polia Eliseiskie,* 150; Knut, "Materialy Soiuza Russkikh Pisatelei," 19; Osorgin, Letter to Gor'kii (Feb. 9, 1930) in Nikonenko, "Neskol'ko slov o Gaito Gazdanove," 272; B. Poplavskii, "Pis'ma Iu. P. Ivasku," 205, 207; Iu. Poplavskii, "Boris Poplavskii," 146; Terapiano, *Vstrechi,* 122. See also Varshavskii's stories "Iz zapisok besstydnogo molodogo cheloveka," 55–70, and "Uedinenie i prazdnost'," 51–76.

156. A. B., "Sud'ba russkikh bezhentsev vo Frantsii," 1; Oualid, "Pour une politique de l'immigration en France," 558–59; Racine, "La main-d'oeuvre étrangère en France," 622; Kovalevskii, *Zarubezhnaia Rossiia,* 18–19; Lilienfeld, "Le problème international des réfugiés et apatrides," 588; Vishniak, *Legal Status of Stateless Persons,* 47.

157. See Dienes, *Russian Literature in Exile,* 36–37; Bakhrakh, "Gazdanych," 9; Knut, "Materialy Soiuza Russkikh Pisatelei," 19; Terapiano, "Po povodu nezamechennogo pokoleniia," 5.

Terapiano wrote to Berberova: "In July my life took a bad turn. . . . I got a job at Hachette's control office, i.e., I start at eight in the morning and finish at six thirty" (Dec. 2, 1928, Boris I. Nikolaevsky Collection, box 402, series 233 "Berberova N. N.," folder 34 "Terapiano, Iu.," Hoover). Later he wrote to Lidiia Ivannikova, who lived in the United States: "What a hard life you are leading in the country of comfort and material success! What exhausting work! My generation also had to work much, but life is structured differently here so that work-employment does not squeeze one dry; we always had time for other things" (April 12, 1962, Aleksis Rannit Papers, box 29, folder "Iurii Terapiano," Beinecke).

158. See Aleksinskaia, "Emigrantskaia pechat'," 53; Berberova, *Italics Are Mine,* 273; Bakhrakh, "Po pamiati, po zapisiam . . . II," 350; Fel'zen, "Avtobiografiia," 121; Gul', *"Ia unes Rossiu": Apologiia emigratsii,* 2: 135; N. Stoliarova, "Otvety N. I. Stoliarovoi na voprosy, zadannye A. N. Bogoslovskim," in B. Poplavskii, *Neizdannoe,* 75–76; Ianovskii, *Polia Eliseiskie,* 35; Smolenskii, "Materialy Soiuza Russkikh Pisatelei," 19; Terapiano, *Vstrechi,* 122; Troyat, *Un si long chemin,* 74; Veidle, "O tekh, kogo uzhe net," 377.

159. Adamovich, "Nesostoiavshaiasia progulka," 291; Ianovskii, *Polia Eliseiskie,* 61. See also Gazdanov, "Literaturnye priznaniia," 261; idem, "O Poplavskom," in *Berega,* 288.

Vladimir Smolenskii, who happened to be an accountant, did his best to dramatize his life, clearly juxtaposing material security and poetry writing. One reads in his undated letter to Berberova: "I think you are wrong when you say that fate did us a disservice and we should have come to America thirty years ago. . . . Had we left for America thirty years ago we could be now living like well-to-do and untroubled American petty bourgeois with cars and fridges, but the world would probably not have either your or my poetry. . . . Poets perish, while their poetry contributes to the goodness and beauty of the world. . . . All things considered, you and I will be able to say on our deathbed that we have not lived in vain. How many people can say the same thing?" (Nina Berberova Papers, box 19, folder 522 "Smolenskii, Vladimir/1951–58," Beinecke).

160. Bakhrakh, "Gazdanych," 9; Dienes, *Russian Literature in Exile*, 80; Gazdanov, "Literaturnye priznaniia," 260–61; idem, "O molodoi emigrantskoi literature," 408.

161. See Knut, "Marginalii k istorii literatury," in his *Sobranie sochinenii v dvukh tomakh*, 1: 258. See also Knut, "Materialy Soiuza Russkikh Pisatelei," 18–19; Terapiano, "Po povodu nezamechennogo pokoleniia," 5.

162. Daniel-Rops, "Un bilan de dix ans," 179; Varshavskii, "O 'geroe' emigrantskoi molodoi literatury," 164.

163. Terapiano, "Rytsar' bednyi," 9–10. See also Bakunina, "Dlia kogo i dlia chego pisat'," 254–55; Gazdanov, "Literaturnye priznaniia," 261–62. On the rejection of the value of recognition and success in French literature, see also Aragon, *Traité du style*, 194; Arland, "Examen de conscience," 12; Breton, *Les Pas perdus*, 9; Datz, "Examen de conscience," 68.

164. See Bakunina, "Dlia kogo i dlia chego pisat'," 254–55; Fel'zen, "Propisi," in *Smotr*, 146–47; Gazdanov, "Literaturnye priznaniia," 260; Ianovskii, "Mimo nezamechennogo pokoleniia," 2, 5; Terapiano, "'Na Balkanakh,'" 139; idem, "Po povodu nezamechennogo pokoleniia," 5; Varshavskii, *Nezamechennoe pokolenie*, 165, 170.

Later, and in private, they idealized the interwar émigré readership. See Ianovskii's letter of 1953 (no date): "There was a time when we complained about a 'crisis' in the book market in Paris, but actually it is only now that things are really nearing the denouement: there are no publishing venues, no readers. . . . I'd like to try an American journal—writing for a Russian one makes no sense: the reader-'*intelligent*' is gone. What a wonderful émigré crowd we used to have: one could express anything—and they would always understand. Where did it all go?" (Fedor Stepun Papers, box 15, folder 496 "Ianowsky, V. S. 1953–58," Beinecke).

165. See N. Andreev, "Ob osobennostiakh i osnovnykh etapakh razvitiia russkoi literatury za rubezhom," *RLE*, 26; Dienes, *Russian Literature in Exile*, 68; Mirskii, "Zametki ob emigrantskoi literature," 6; Slonim, "Novye zarubezhnye zhurnaly," 892; idem, "Volia Rossii," *RLE*, 299; Struve, "O molodykh poetakh," 3; Veidle, "O tekh, kogo uzhe net," 372, 376; Vishniak, "Sovremennye zapiski," *RLE*, 355.

On July 14, 1946, Dovid Knut mused in a letter about the beneficial publishing circumstances he enjoyed before the war: "As for Paris, the local 'audience' has shrunk so much that my publisher, who had offered me a very good contract for [the book of poetry] *Nasushchnaia Liubov'* and implored me before the war to publish a book of collected poems, would not even hear about it today" (Collection Chekver, folder "Knut D. M. Paris & Boulogne 1946–49," Bakhmeteff).

166. See Adamovich, "Literaturnye besedy," *Zveno* 167: 1–2; idem, "Literaturnye besedy," *Zveno* 200: 1; idem, "Literaturnye besedy," *Zveno* 5: 246; idem, "Vadim Andreev," 521; "Novye pisateli," 3; Mochul'skii, "Molodye poety," 2; Osorgin, "'Sovremennye zapiski,'" 2; Slonim, "Molodye pisateli za rubezhom," 106; idem, "Nezamechennoe pokolenie," 8; Struve, "K istorii zarubezhnoi literatury," 219, 234, 239.

167. See Gippius's successful lobbying in *Sovremennye zapiski* on behalf of younger writers as related in her letters to Berberova (July 13, 1926, and Aug. 27, 1926, Nina Berberova Papers, box 8, folder 199 "Gippius, Zinaida Nikolaevna/1926–30, n. d.," Beinecke). An editor of *Sovremennye zapiski*, Il'ia Bunakov-Fondaminskii, informed Gippius several times that the review was actively recruiting younger contributors (Knut, Ladinskii, Gornyi among others). On one occasion he wrote to Gippius: "No 'master key' is necessary to unlock the doors of *Sovremennye zapiski*. We crave for *young poets*. Therefore, would you please send me all those poems you approve of and *send as many as you can*. Solicit poems from those poets you find not without gift, pick whatever you deem worth publishing, and send to me. By all means, do this and do this quickly. I promise success. I beg you to take charge of this and I am impatiently waiting for the first installment" (March 1, 1926, Z. Gippius and D. Merezhkovsky Papers, series 1, incoming correspondence, box 1, folder 77, Amherst. See also in the same folder letters of March 29, 1926, and Aug. 27, 1926).

168. See Ianovskii, *Polia Eliseiskie*, 37–38; Khodasevich, "Knigi i liudi," *Vz* 3732: 3; Struve, "Zametki o stikhakh," 3; idem, *Russkaia literatura v izgnanii*, 295.

169. See Aldanov, "'Vstrechi': Kniga 1 i 2," 3; N. Andreev, "Sovremennye zapiski," 183; Avksent'ev et al., "Ot redaktsii," 6; Fel'zen, "Literaturnaia molodezh' iz 'Kochev'ia,'" 4.

170. See Adamovich, "Literaturnye besedy," *Zveno* 5: 246; idem, "Vadim Andreev," 521; idem, "Novye pisateli," 3; idem, "Pis'ma o Lermontove," 2; Berberova, "Zelenaia lampa," 42–43; Knut, "Zelenaia lampa," 42; Khodasevich, "Knigi i liudi," *Vz* 2781: 3; idem, "Novye stikhi," 3–4; Varshavskii, *Nezamechennoe pokolenie*, 177–78, 184. In a 1936 letter Khodasevich discouraged Berberova from contributing to *Sovremennye zapiski* so as not to end up among less-known writers and because he wanted to "get under the skin" (*nasolit'*) of the editor, who solicited her contribution (Bethea, "Pis'ma V. Khodasevicha k N. Berberovoi," 309). One finds similar advice against *Chisla* as a venue for publication in Khodasevich's letter to Veidle, based on his view of the journal as "a nest of scoundrels" (Collection Weidle, folder "Khodasevich, Boulogne, France Oct. 31, 1929," Bakhmeteff). The contrast between Khodasevich's eulogy of young émigrés who write despite the fact that they cannot publish and his practical sobriety in literary politics is striking. See a similar contrast between Shteiger's public and private pronouncements. The poet wrote to Shakhovskaia regarding the possibility of collaborating in an émigré journal based in Finland: "I have been invited to contribute to '[Zhurnal] Sodruzhestva,' but I will refuse, for who needs a journal published at the end of the world and which will never

reach our 'capitals'?" (Aug. 16, 1935, Schakovskoy Family Papers, series 1, Zinaida Schakovskoy Papers, box 1, folder 41, Amherst).

171. See Kuskova, "O nezamechennom pokolenii," 2; Kantor, "Nado Pomnit'," 2; Nabokov, "Literaturnyi smotr," 283; Osorgin, "Pozhelaniia," 3; Slonim, "Molodye pisateli za rubezhom," 106; Struve, "O molodykh poetakh," 3; Vishniak, "Sovremennye zapiski,"355; Zeeler, "Neobkhodimye popravki," 2.

See Aldanov's letter, written in the heat of the debate around Varshavskii's *Nezamechennoe pokolenie:* "There has never been any unnoticed generation. Why would the editors be hostile to any writers whatsoever? Especially such people as Rudnev and Fondaminskii? After all, Sirin [V. Nabokov] was 'noticed' ever since his first book. The late Vadim Viktorovich [Rudnev] told me many times that publishing young writers was all he wanted to do because the older ones were too few and kind of boring. But he also told me that young prose seemed to him of little interest. Miliukov offered the young and then unknown Adamovich the foremost literary 'spot' in 'Posl[ednie] Nov[osti].' Besides, the young had their own reviews, which, as far as I recall, did not reach out to old [writers]. As for living conditions, they were equally difficult for *everybody,* and this was not because of the ill will of our journals but the result of their poverty and the readers' reluctance to *buy* books" (Oct. 30, 1955, Collection Aldanov, box 5, folder "Kuskova E. D. Carbon copies of letters to E. D. Kuskova Feb. 51–57," Bakhmeteff). One finds a similar opinion in Slonim's correspondence. Reacting to the pronouncements of the former "émigré Hamlet" Vasilii Ianovskii, Slonim wrote to Struve: "Ianovskii should know better than anyone how much labor, care and material effort went into my support of the 'young' in Prague and Paris" (Oct. 12, 1955, Gleb Struve Collection, box 137, folder 1 "Slonim, Mark," Hoover).

Chapter 2. The Surrealist Adventure of Boris Poplavskii

1. See the cursory treatment of this period in Struve, *Russkaia literatura v izgnanii,* 161–63.

2. See Knut, "Russkii Monparnass," 3.

3. See Beaujour, *Alien Tongues,* 140; Gibson, *Russian Poetry and Criticism in Paris from 1920 to 1940,* 116–17; Karlinsky, "Surrealism in Twentieth-Century Russian Poetry," 606; Terapiano, *Vstrechi,* 114. L. Foster criticized such indiscriminate use of the term "surrealism" in "K voprosu o siurrealizme v russkoi literature," 199–201. Menegaldo suggested affinities between Poplavskii's poetry and that of Breton's group but did not elaborate on her thesis ("L'Univers imaginaire de Boris Poplavsky [1903–1935]," 439); idem, "Boris Poplavskii—ot futurizma k siurrealizmu," in B. Poplavskii, *Avtomaticheskie stikhi,* 20.

4. See Breton, *Les Pas perdus,* 138; Léonard, *La Crise du concept de littérature,* 49; Nadeau, *Histoire du surréalisme,* 67.

5. See Breton, "Manifeste du surréalisme," in *Manifestes du surréalisme,* 50; Rimbaud, "Une saison en enfer," in *Poésie: Une saison en enfer,* 131.

6. See Berge, "A propos du surréalisme," 32; Fondane, *Faux Traité d'ésthétique,* 47; Russell, *Poets, Prophets, and Revolutionaries,* 127.

7. See Breton, "Second manifeste du surréalisme," in *Manifestes,* 86. Cf. B. Poplavskii, "Dnevnik T.," 179–80, 192.

8. Rivière, "Reconnaissance à Dada," 228.

9. Breton, "Manifeste du surréalisme," 38; idem, *Les Pas perdus*, 137. See also Éluard, "L'évidence poétique," in *Oeuvres complètes*, 1: 114.

10. See Aragon, *Traité du style*, 188–89; Breton, "Manifeste du surréalisme," 39; idem, *Les Pas perdus*, 138; Nadeau, *Histoire du surréalisme*, 59, 61–62. On "lived poems" (artificially created situations) that supplemented written poetry, see Soupault, *Mémoires de l'Oubli: 1914–1923*, 146–48.

11. B. Poplavskii, "Literaturnaia anketa," 287. Symptomatically, in a letter to Zdanevich (February 4, 1928), he argued that "literature must be essentially a slightly disguised fact of life. . . . Whereas life must be constructed so that, having failed to give happiness, it becomes a literary event, that is, material for the realization of various charming inventions" (*Pokushenie*, 104).

12. See Adamovich, "Pamiati Poplavskogo," 2; Bakhrakh, "Po pamiati, po zapisiam . . . II," 338; Bitsilli, "Iakor'," 463; Gazdanov, "O Poplavskom," in *Berega*, 287; Odoevtseva, *Na beregakh Seny*, 150; Osokin, "Boris Poplavskii," 197; Terapiano, "Boris Poplavskii," 143. Adamovich wrote to Ivask: "One had to *know* P[oplavskii] fully to appreciate his extraordinary persona. He left behind mere reflections, although these reflections are also extraordinary" (July 23, 1964, Iurii Ivask Papers, series 1, correspondence, box 1, folder 3, Amherst).

13. Quoting Rimbaud in an epigraph to his novel *Apollon Bezobrazov*, which described the life of the Russian avant-garde, Poplavskii chose a passage that dealt with lifestyle: "Oisive jeunesse / A tout asservie, / Par délicatesse / J'ai perdu ma vie" (*Domoi s nebes: Romany*, 82).

14. Ginzburg, *On Psychological Prose*, 20. See also Mints, "Poniatie teksta i simvolistskaia estetika," 134–41; Khodasevich, "Konets Renaty," in *Koleblemyi trenozhnik*, 270–72.

15. See Paperno, "The Meaning of Art: Symbolist Theories," in Paperno and Grossman, *Creating Life*, 22–23.

16. See Chertkov, "Debiut Borisa Poplavskogo," 377.

17. See Irina Gutkin, "The Legacy of the Symbolist Aesthetic Utopia: From Futurism to Socialist Realism," in Paperno and Grossman, *Creating Life*, 167–96.

18. In the dedication to the poem "Pokushenie s negodnymi sredstvami" (1926) Poplavskii called himself Zdanevich's disciple. See his *Pokushenie*, 86.

19. For a detailed treatment of Russian literary life in Paris in the early 1920s, see Livak, "Histoire de la littérature russe en exil," 133–50.

20. On Poplavskii's participation in the meetings of "Palata poetov" and "Gatarapak," see his diary of 1921 (August 1, September 20, 28, 30) in *Neizdannoe*. See also Iulius, "Russkii literaturnyi Parizh 20-kh godov," 88; Mamchenko, "Pis'ma N. P. Smirnovu," in B. Poplavskii, *Neizdannoe*, 83–84.

21. See Zdanevich (Iliazd), "En approchant Éluard," 41.

22. See Beyssac, *La Vie culturelle de l'émigration russe en France*, 19; Josephson, *Life among the Surrealists*, 132; Sanouillet, *Dada à Paris*, 303; Sharshun, "Moe uchastie vo frantsuzskom dadaisticheskom dvizhenii," 170, 173. On Poplavskii's participation in this event, see Menegaldo, "La jeune génération des avant-gardistes russes à Paris, 1921–1930," 249–60.

23. V. Andreev, *Istoriia odnogo puteshestviia*, 304. See also B. Poplavskii, "Pis'ma Iu. P. Ivasku," 207.

24. Contrary to Menegaldo's suggestion that Poplavskii lived in Berlin for two years ("L'Univers imaginaire de Boris Poplavsky," 37; "Chastnoe pis'mo Borisa Poplavskogo," in B. Poplavskii, *Neizdannoe*, 38), the poet's visit was short. See Iu. Poplavskii, "Boris Poplavskii," 146; V. Andreev, *Istoriia odnogo puteshestviia*, 304. Most probably, he returned to Paris in the fall of 1922, when artistic life in the capital resumed after the traditionally dead summer season. Mamchenko recalls meeting him at literary gatherings in January 1923 ("Pis'ma N. P. Smirnovu," in B. Poplavskii, *Neizdannoe*, 83–84); Iulius cites him among the participants of a joint Dada-Cherez venture in April 1923 ("Russkii literaturnyi Parizh 20-kh godov," 89–90).

25. See Zdanevich, "Boris Poplavskii," 165–67.

26. Zdanevich, "En approchant Éluard," 46. Tzara's show was organized by Cherez in return for the dadaist participation in the Cherez soirée of April 29, 1923, devoted the poet Boris Bozhnev (Livak, "Histoire de la littérature russe en exil," 143). Poplavskii attended this soirée and read his poems alongside French dadaists (Iulius, "Russkii literaturnyi Parizh 20-kh godov," 89–90; Menegaldo, "Boris Poplavski. Rencontres à Montparnasse," 125). Although no documentary evidence is available, it is almost certain that Poplavskii attended *Le Coeur à Barbe*.

27. See Zdanevich, "En approchant Éluard," 48; Gayraud, "Iz arkhiva Il'i Zdanevicha," 137, 140; idem, "Promenade autour de Ledentu le Phare," in Zdanevich (Iliazd), *Ledentu le Phare*, 154.

28. On Poplavskii's personal contacts in the milieu of the French avant-garde, see Sosinskii, "Konurka," 176.

29. See Adamovich, "Parizhskie vpechatleniia," 2; idem, "Poeziia v emigratsii," 50; V. Andreev, *Istoriia odnogo puteshestviia*, 329–30.

30. See Terapiano, *Vstrechi*, 150–51.

31. See Fleishman, *Boris Pasternak: The Poet and His Politics*, 140.

32. From a letter to Sosinskii in B. Poplavskii, *Neizdannoe*, 246–47. In 1930 he told Ivask that he had been "an ardent futurist and had not published" ("Pis'ma Iu. P. Ivasku," 207).

33. See also Khodasevich's letter of September 3, 1925: "The Club of Young Poets has talked me into editing their collections" (Collection Boris Zaitsev, box 1, folder "Khodasevich Vl. F. 1924–27," Bakhmeteff).

34. See Gayraud, "Iz arkhiva Il'i Zdanevicha," 152; idem, "Tvoia druzhba ko mne—odno iz samykh tsennykh iavlenii moei zhizni," in B. Poplavskii, *Pokushenie*, 15–16; Zdanevich, "Boris Poplavskii," 168.

35. About Nikolai Tatishchev's editing of Poplavskii's poems, see Menegaldo, "Boris Poplavskii—ot futurizma k siurrealizmu," in B. Poplavskii, *Avtomaticheskie stikhi*, 6–7. *Dirizhabl'* poems analyzed here conform to their manuscript versions in B. Poplavskii, *Dadafoniia*.

36. See Aragon, *Une vague de rêves*, 15; Breton, "Manifeste du surréalisme," 33; Éluard, "Donner à voir," in *Oeuvres complètes*, 1: 981.

37. See Tatishchev, "Poet v izgnanii," 199–205.

38. See Breton, "Du surréalisme en ses oeuvres vives," in *Manifestes*, 166; B. Poplavskii, "Po povodu," 173.

39. References to poems from Poplavskii's collections will be given in the

text with abbreviations: *G* for *Grammofon, D* for *Dirizhabl',* and *F* for *Flagi.*
Grammofon can be found in B. Poplavskii, *Pokushenie; Dirizhabl'* in vol. 3 of
B. Poplavskii, *Sobranie sochinenii;* and *Flagi* in vol. 1 of *Sobranie sochinenii.* French
texts will be cited by the first word of the collection title and by page from the
following sources (see Bibliography for full citations): Aragon, *Le Paysan de Paris;*
Breton, *Clair de terre;* idem, *Poisson soluble;* Breton and Soupault, *Les Champs magnétiques;* Desnos, *Destinée arbitraire* (containing *Peine perdue* and *C'est les bottes de
7 lieues*—abbreviated as *Bottes*); Éluard, *Capitale de la douleur* (including *Répétitions, Mourir de ne pas mourir,* and *Nouveaux poèmes*).

40. See a possible pun: "d'une façon inexplicable" can also mean "an inex-
plicably cut/tailored torso."

The reader should be aware of my conviction that no translation of surrealist poetry can be adequate, although for the sake of those who do not read
French or Russian I have attempted to provide translations throughout this
chapter.

41. Cf. Éluard: "Il fait un triste temps, il fait une nuit noire / À ne pas mettre
un aveugle dehors" (The weather is sad [possible pun: time is sad], night is
dark / So dark a blind man should not be left outside [a pun on the idioms "un
temps de chien" and "il fait un temps à ne pas mettre un chien dehors"—bad
weather—and "chien d'aveugle"—a guide dog]," *Mourir,* 70); Desnos: "Qu'on
me fiche la guerre" (Leave me at war [a pun on the idiom "fiche mois la paix"—
leave me in peace]," *Bottes,* 53).

42. See Winspur, "Ethical Loops in Eluard," 182–83.

43. See Riffaterre, "La Métaphore filée," 221–22.

44. Éluard, "Premières vues anciennes," in *Oeuvres complètes,* 1: 539; idem,
"Poésie involontaire," in *Oeuvres complètes,* 2: 1133–34.

45. B. Poplavskii, *Pokushenie,* 133. Cf. the same procedure in Éluard:

Je ramasse les débris de toutes mes merveilles . . .
Je les jette aux ruisseaux vivaces et pleins d'oiseaux.
La mer, la calme mer est entre eux comme le ciel dans la lumière . . .
Je m'endors et je mène la grande vie

⸙

[I collect the debris of all my marvels. . . .
I throw them into streams, hardy [possibly: persistent] and full of birds
The sea, the calm sea is among them like the sky in the light. . . .
I fall asleep and live large]

(*Mourir,* 55)

See also Desnos: "Par la fenêtre fermée les oiseaux s'obstinent à parler comme
les poissons d'aquarium" (Through a closed window birds speak obstinately
like fish in an aquarium, *Bottes,* 49); Breton: "Quand on lève la tête on découvre
les grands parterres qui n'en sont plus et les oiseaux tenant comme d'ordinaire
leur rôle entre sol et ciel. Les *parciels* se reflètent légèrement dans la rivière où se
désaltèrent les oiseaux" (Looking up one discovers the large stalls [a possible
pun: flower beds, borders] which are no longer [that] and the birds playing their
usual roles between earth and sky. The *parciels* [a pun on "parterre," literally, what

lies on the sky; a possible phonetic pun on "partiel"—partial] are slightly reflected in the stream where the birds are quenching their thirst, *Poisson*, 47).

46. See Alexandrian, *Le surréalisme et le Rêve*, 131; Aragon, *Une vague de rêves*,
18.

47. See Aragon, *Une vague de rêves*, 14; idem, *Le Paysan de Paris*, 81; Boiffard
et al., "Préface," 1; Breton, "Manifeste du surréalisme," 48.

48. Aragon, *Une vague de rêves*, 19.

49. See Éluard's *Nouveaux poèmes*:

Au soir de la folie, nu et clair,
L'espace entre les choses a la forme de mes paroles . . .
Le monde se détache de mon univers . . .
Je distingue le jour de cette clarté d'homme . . .
Le sommeil du rêve

            ☙

[During the night of madness, naked and clear,
Space between things has the form of my words . . .
The world detaches itself from my universe . . .
I distinguish (the light of) day from this clarity of man . . .
(I distinguish) Sleep from dream]

            (89–90)

Lumières de précision, je ne cligne pas des yeux,
Je ne bouge pas,
Je parle
Et quand je dors
Ma gorge est une bague à l'enseigne de tulle

            ☙

[The lights of precision, I do not blink,
I do not move,
I speak
And when I sleep. . . .]

            (91)

C'est ici que la clarté livre sa dernière bataille.
Si je m'endors, c'est pour ne plus rêver

            ☙

[It is here that light [possibly: brightness, clarity] makes its last stand
If I fall asleep, it is in order to stop dreaming]

            (92)

50. Cf. also Breton, "Du surréalisme en ses oeuvres vives," 166.

51. See Aragon, *Une vague de rêves*, 13; Breton, *Poisson*, 27–31, 47–50; idem,
Clair, 63, 78; Desnos, *Bottes*, 50, 52–53, 55–56; idem, *Peine*, 41, 42; Éluard, *Mourir*,
57, 66; idem, *Répétitions*, 23, 26; idem, *Nouveaux poèmes*, 91. The image of a freely

flowing river also evokes the facility of expression acquired through "automatic writing." Cf. Éluard's poem "J'ai la beauté facile est c'est heureux" (My beauty is light [other possible meanings: simple, elegant, effortless] and this is lucky, *Répétitions*, 21). The expression "la beauté facile" recalls the standard definition of eloquence—"une facilité de la parole." Contemporary parodies of automatic writing testify to the establishment of surrealist clichés. A dadaist review published a parody containing the following lines: "Raid sous-marin—Le rêveur fait pointer le périscope. Le somnambule plonge et regarde par les hublots. Le délirant touche le fond" ([An] Underwater raid—The dreamer sets [possible pun: punches through] his periscope. The somnambulist submerges and looks into portholes. The delirious reaches the bottom [possible pun: the bottom of his delirium], Malespine, "Côté doublure," 77).

52. Surrealists used death as a metaphor for dreaming (cf. *Mourir de ne pas mourir*). Breton wrote in *Manifestes du surréalisme:* "C'est vivre et cesser de vivre qui sont des solutions imaginaires" (To live and to stop living these are some imaginary solutions, 60). Dreams are a trip into the "Dead Sea" (Boiffard et al., "Préface," 1).

53. See Rimbaud, "Une saison en enfer," in *Poésie: Une saison en enfer*, 131.

54. Cf. "Ma tombe, après la fermeture du cimetière, prend la forme d'une barque tenant bien la mer . . . la barque s'élève sans bruit. Elle glisse à faible hauteur au-dessus des terres labourées" (My grave, after the closing of the cemetery, takes shape of a sea barque . . . the barque lifts up without noise. It glides at low altitude over the plowed soil [possible reading: dug up earth], *Poisson*, 66–67). "Tout un cimetière navigue sur le canal. . . . Gardes célestes vous dressez contravention aux ballons captifs ces forçats du paradis" ([The population of] the entire cemetery navigates in the canal. . . . Celestial guards, you fine the captive balloons [another meaning: a dirigible attached to the ground by ropes], these convicts of paradise, *Peine*, 35).

55. Boiffard et al., "Préface," 1.

56. See Aragon, *Paysan*, 44; Breton, *Clair*, 61–62; idem, *Nadja*, 18; Desnos, *Peine*, 35, 38.

57. See Breton, *Les Pas perdus*, 96. See also Carrouges, *André Breton et les données fondamentales du surréalisme*, 133.

58. Gibson, *Russian Poetry and Criticism in Paris*, 117; Menegaldo, "L'Univers imaginaire de Boris Poplavsky," 124.

59. See Aragon, *Traité du style*, 182–83, 188–89; Béhar and Carassou, *Le Surréalisme*, 386–87; Breton, "Manifeste du surréalisme," 37–38; Kostrov, "Lui Aragon," 3; Nadeau, *Histoire du surréalisme*, 50; Ribemond-Dessaigne, *Déjà jadis*, 116.

60. See B. Poplavskii, *Avtomaticheskie stikhi*, 6.

61. Rimbaud, "Ophélie," in *Poésie: Une saison en enfer*, 29.

62. See Gayraud, "Tvoia druzhba ko mne," 10; Zdanevich, "Boris Poplavskii," 168.

63. See Tatishchev, "Boris Poplavskii," 37.

64. From an undated letter in Poplavskii, *Pokushenie*, 94–95.

65. See Chénieux, *Surrealism*, 39; Josephson, *Life among the Surrealists*, 119; Nadeau, *Histoire du surréalisme*, 104.

66. On August 11, 1927, Adamovich wrote to Gippius: "Speaking of [poetry that is] *'sobre'* and 'without images': I *exterminate* and *purge* 'picturesque' expressions in my [writings]. . . . Let us adopt the office style or that of a legal codex. . . . You will never convince me that 'there is a limit' in this respect. There is no limit and the only things I want are precision and purity" (Z. Gippius and D. Merezhkovsky Papers, series 1, incoming correspondence, box 1, folder 10, Amherst).

67. See Adamovich, "Literaturnye besedy," *Zveno* 109: 2; Izvol'skaia, "Commerce," 2–3; E. Rais, "O Borise Poplavskom," in *Berega*, 302; Sharshun, "Magicheskii realizm," 229; Terapiano, "Zhurnal i chitatel'," 26; Varshavskii, "O proze mladshikh emigrantskikh pisatelei," 413; Veidle, "Zhivopis' siurrealistov," 6–7; idem, "Monparnasskie mechtaniia," 461; idem, "Mekhanizatsiia bessoznatel'nogo," 463–64, 469; Vering, "O 'novom gumanizme' v zhivopisi," 14.

68. A. E., "Molodye zarubezhnye poety," 119–20.

69. See Bakhrakh, "Po pamiati, po zapisiam," 337–38; Gomolitskii, *Arion*, 25; Slonim, "Molodye pisateli za rubezhom," 108; Terapiano, "Boris Poplavskii," 144.

70. See Karlinsky, "In Search of Poplavsky: A Collage," 328; Beaujour, *Alien Tongues*, 143; Struve, *Russkaia literatura v izgnanii*, 339.

71. See Éluard's "Max Ernst" (*Répétitions*, 13), "Paul Klee," "Joan Miró" (*Nouveaux poèmes*, 106, 129). See also Passeron, *Histoire de la peinture surréaliste*, 63–64.

72. See Menegaldo, "L'Univers imaginaire de Boris Poplavsky," 150–51.

73. Adamovich, "Literaturnye besedy," *Zveno* 4: 190.

74. See Berberova, *Italics Are Mine*, 269; Nabokov, "B. Poplavskii, *Flagi*," in *BP*, 168; Struve, "Zametki o stikhakh," 3.

75. See B. Poplavskii, "Zametki o poezii," 28; idem, "Doklad o knige Georgiia Ivanova 'Peterburgskie zimy,'" in *Neizdannoe*, 253.

76. See Adamovich, "Literaturnye besedy," *Zveno* 4: 190; idem, "Vadim Andreev," 522; Ivask, "Chudaki," 185; Slonim, "Kniga stikhov B. Poplavskogo," in *BP*, 169; Veidle, "Sovremennye zapiski XXXIX," 3.

77. Adamovich, "Literaturnye besedy," *Zveno* 4: 187–91; idem, "Vadim Andreev," 523; Ivanov, "Sovremennye zapiski," 3; idem, "Boris Poplavskii," 233. On April 20, 1928, Adamovich wrote to Gippius: "Has Poplavskii paid you a visit and how did you like him? He seems to me intelligent and talanted but he is also cunning, like Esenin who pretended to be a 'simpleton'" (Z. Gippius and D. Merezhkovsky Papers, series 1, incoming correspondence, box 1, folder 11, Amherst). Gippius wrote to Adamovich on April 21, 1928: "We have not seen Poplavskii at our place. He is waiting for you to introduce him" (Georgii Adamovich Papers, box 1, folder 8 "Gippius Z. N. 1926–1928," Beinecke). In the same year Adamovich informed Gippius: "Georges Iv[anov] tried to place Poplavskii's poetry in 'S[ovremennye] Zapiski' but it looks like he failed" (1928 [no date], folder 6).

78. See Mochul'skii, "Molodye poety," 2; Struve, "Zametki o stikhakh," 3.

79. See Adamovich, "Sovremennye zapiski," *PN* 3144: 2; Ianovskii, *Polia Eliseiskie*, 12–13; A. Leonidov, "Boris Poplavskii: *Flagi*," 5; Iu. Mandel'shtam, "Boris Poplavskii," in *BP*, 66; Slonim, "Kniga stikhov B. Poplavskogo," in *BP*, 169;

Struve, "Zametki o stikhakh," 3; Stoliarova, "Otvety N. I. Stoliarovoi," in B. Poplavskii, *Neizdannoe*, 77; Terapiano, "Pamiati Borisa Poplavskogo," 148.

80. See Adamovich, "Sovremennye zapiski," *PN* 3144: 2; Slonim, "Molodye pisateli za rubezhom," 108–9; idem, "Kniga stikhov B. Poplavskogo," 169–71.

81. See Veidle, "Sovremennye zapiski XXXIX," 3. Cf. Poplavskii's poems "Karliki i gnomy na skam'iakh sobora" and "Malen'kii sviashchennik igral na roiale," and Blok's poems "Devushka pela v tserkovnom khore" and "V goluboi dalekoi spalenke."

82. See B. Poplavskii, "O misticheskoi atmosfere molodoi literatury v emigratsii," 311; "Les Débats," *Rencontres*, 136. Cf. Dostoevsky, *Brat'ia Karamazovy*, in his *Sobranie sochinenii v dvenadtsati tomakh*, vol. 11 (Moscow: Pravda, 1982), 288.

83. See Gazdanov, "O Poplavskom," 288; Gomolitskii, *Arion*, 25; Karlinsky, "Surrealism in Twentieth-Century Russian Poetry," 616; Terapiano, "Boris Poplavskii," 144. In private, Terapiano provided a slightly different interpretation, identifying Khodasevich as the chief culprit. See his letters to Ivask: "Poplavskii promised much, he has many beautiful lines and images but *in general* he perished when he tried to curry favor with Khodasevich and began to write 'like everybody.'. . . *Flagi* . . . was his only striking book, whereas the two posthumous ones—alas! nothing special" (May 8, 1964); "[Poplavskii] wanted to follow Khodasevich's canons but that tradition was organically alien to him. What came out was *Flagi* mixed with 'classical' mishmash" (June 14, 1964) (Iurii Ivask Papers, series 1, correspondence, box 6, folder 41, Amherst).

84. See Adamovich, "Poeziia v emigratsii," 55–56.

85. See Poplavskii's French text in *Pokushenie*, 24–25. Placing a number of texts in 1933 under the title *Avtomaticheskie stikhi* (Automatic poems), Poplavskii joined this collection to the body of writings that were supposed to appear long after his death.

86. See B. Poplavskii, "O misticheskoi atmosfere molodoi literatury v emigratsii," 308–11; idem, "O smerti i zhalosti v 'Chislakh,'" 3.

87. Adamovich, "Pamiati Poplavskogo," 2; Fel'zen, "Poplavskii," in *Berega*, 297; Zdanevich, "Boris Poplavskii," 165–66; Varshavskii, "O proze 'mladshikh' emigrantskikh pisatelei," 412–13.

88. See Breton, "Manifeste du surréalisme," 16–17; Chénieux, *Le Surréalisme et le roman*, 12; Matthews, *Surrealism and the Novel*, 9–10.

89. See Carrouges, *André Breton et les données fondamentales du surréalisme*, 246.

90. Rais, "O Borise Poplavskom," 301.

91. Rovskaia, "Sergei Sharshun," 126.

92. Texts cited in *Apollon Bezobrazov* are from B. Poplavskii, *Domoi s nebes: Romany*.

93. The juxtaposition of Vasilii and Apollon harks back to Il'ia Erenburg's novel *Khulio Khurenito* (1921), in which Alexander Tishin, a Russian *intelligent* endowed with all the qualities of Vasilii, is the exact opposite of his demonic teacher, Khulio.

94. On Poplavskii's lifestyle and contradictory persona, see "Boris Poplavsky," 3; Adamovich, "Pamiati Poplavskogo," 2; idem, "Kommentarii," *Krug* 3: 133–34; Bakhrakh, "Po pamiati, po zapisiam," 336–37; Sedykh, "Monparnasskie teni," in *BP*, 85; Shakhovskaia, *Otrazheniia*, 52; Stoliarova, "Otvety N.

I. Stoliarovoi," in B. Poplavskii, *Neizdannoe,* 75; Terapiano, *Vstrechi,* 113; Tatishchev, "Poet v izgnanii," 201; idem, "O Poplavskom," in *BP,* 92; Varshavskii, *Nezamechennoe pokolenie,* 195.

95. In addition to *Khulio Khurenito,* this doubling of the alter ego may have been inspired by Philippe Soupault's 1923 novel *Le Bon Apôtre,* which had two protagonists: Jean X., Soupault's dadaist alter ego, and Philippe Soupault, the narrator. Describing his transition from Dada to surrealism as a compromise, Soupault sees its alternative in the unbending Jean X., who, like Apollon, "leaves" at the end.

96. "Oiseau enfermé dans son vol, il n'a jamais connu la terre, il n'a jamais eu d'ombre" ([A] Bird trapped in flight, he has never known earth, he has never had a shade [possible pun: he has never been in a shade, or he has never cast a shade], *Apollon,* 20).

97. Cf. "Moe letnee schast'e osvobozhdalos' ot vsiakoi nadezhdy" (My summer happiness liberated itself from all hope, *Apollon,* 25) and "Ochishchaetsia schast'e ot vsiakoi nadezhdy" (Happiness purges itself from all hope, *G,* 69).

98. Cf. Breton: "On publie pour chercher des hommes. Des hommes, je suis de jour en jour plus curieux d'en découvrir" (We publish [our writings] to seek out people. People, [—] with every passing day I am more and more curious about discovering them, *Les Pas perdus,* 9).

99. See Carrouges, *André Breton et les données fondamentales du surréalisme,* 21–26, 44.

100. In 1930 Poplavskii wrote: "I am neither a church man nor an admirer of clergy" ("Pis'ma Iu. P. Ivasku," 209). See also B. Poplavskii, "O smerti i zhalosti v 'Chislakh,'" 3.

101. See Poplavskii's diary of 1921: September 3 and 19, March 6, April 9 (in *Neizdannoe*). See also Menegaldo, "L'Univers imaginaire de Boris Poplavsky," 72–74.

102. See Tatishchev, "O Poplavskom," 97–98; Terapiano, *Vstrechi,* 117.

103. Karlinsky, "In Search of Poplavsky," 329. On the use of drugs by the surrealists, see Crespelle, *La Vie quotidienne à Montparnasse à la Grande Époque 1905–1930,* 143; Chénieux, *Surrealism,* 61–62.

104. See Adamovich, "Literaturnye zametki," *PN* 6485: 3; Gazdanov, "Krug: Al'manakh, Kniga tret'ia," 480.

105. On June 30, 1933, Poplavskii wrote about himself: "No one but the saints themselves know the meaning of sanctity. . . . My God, only You know how boring are the days of sanctity. . . . Only the saints know how boring sanctity can be" (*Neizdannoe,* 107–8).

106. See Menegaldo, "L'Univers imaginaire de Boris Poplavsky," 458; Tatishchev, "Siniaia tetrad'," in *Berega,* 290–93; Terapiano, *Vstrechi,* 113; Varshavskii, "Monparnasskie razgovory," in *BP,* 57.

107. Ianovskii, *Polia Eliseiskie,* 27.

108. See Bakhrakh, "Po pamiati, po zapisiam," 336–37; Sedykh, "Monparnasskie teni," 85–86.

109. On Poplavskii's refusal of gainful employment, see Gul', *"Ia unes Rossiu,"* 2: 135; Struve, *Russkaia literatura v izgnanii,* 314; Veidle, "O tekh, kogo uzhe net," 377. On his library, see Iu. Poplavskii, "Boris Poplavskii," 146. After Poplavskii's

death, a note in his own handwriting about "well-priced" heroin and cocaine was discovered ("Deux réfugiés russes s'adonnaient aux stupéfiants," 8; Sedykh, "Tragicheskaia smert' Borisa Poplavskogo," 4; idem, "Monparnasskie teni," 87). On Poplavskii's collection of paintings, see "Stikhi Borisa Poplavskogo," 3.

110. On October 10, 1932, Poplavskii wrote: "I march with one foot on water (the left soul drinks it), the right foot in fire (the right rubber shoe is warm), purposefully enhancing, exaggerating destitution in my face (I don't shave) and in my dress (I like rags). I have defeated all desires and doubted the happiness of Jesus" (*Neizdannoe*, 108).

111. Rimbaud's words actually refer to the Paris Commune and are not concerned with any antiwork ethics: "Je serai un travailleur: c'est l'idée qui me retient, quand les colères folles me poussent vers la bataille de Paris,—où tant de travailleurs meurent pourtant encore tandis qe je vous écris! Travailler maintenant, jamais, jamais; je suis en grève" (I will become a worker: this idea restrains me when I am pushed by mad rage toward the battle of Paris,—where so many workers are still dying even as I write you! Work now, [—] never, never; I am on strike, letter to George Izambard in his *Poésie: Une saison en enfer*, 200).

112. See Breton, *Nadja*, 68–69; Josephson, *Life among the Surrealists*, 120–21, 126. Cf. Poplavskii's 1927 diary: "She reproached me: you are good for nothing. You don't want to work. I answered: Someone must live like this. I am justified in my own eyes by my dreams" ("Dnevnik T.," 204).

113. See Aragon, *Une vague de rêves*, 25; Rigaut, "Roman d'un jeune homme pauvre," in *Écrits*, 25.

114. See a monocle as a symbol of the bygone avant-garde days in Bozhnev's letter to Zdanevich (Jan. 14, 1937, Boris Bozhnev Papers, box 2, Hoover), which included Zdanevich's portrait drawn by Bozhnev. Both artists were Poplavskii's colleagues and close friends in Cherez:

Илья Зданевич

Три пальца—кукиш и три пальца—крест.
И кукишем ты крестишь футуристов,
Через монокль читая манифест,
За кафедрой насмешлив и неистов . . .

Б. Божнев

[Il'ia Zdanevich

Three fingers—a *kukish* (insulting gesture) and three fingers—a cross.
And you cross the futurists with a *kukish*,
Reading a manifesto through a monocle,
Derisive and furious at your lectern . . .

B. Bozhnev]

Dear Il'ia Mikhailovich, arranging my old poems etc. I found my-your portrait-couplet. Since this portrait is yours-mine, I am sending it to you. It will remind you of the times when all of us, and especially you, were young. B. Bozhnev.

115. Ianovskii, *Polia Eliseiskie*, 25.

116. Sedykh, "Monparnasskie teni," 85; Tatishchev, "Poet v izgnanii," 201; idem, "O Poplavskom," 92.

117. Cravan, *Oeuvres*, 87–91.

118. Soupault, *En Joue!* 19, 23–24, 202, 204. Among other sources, Poplavskii's familiarity with this aspect of avant-garde mythology may have come from Sharshun, who met Cravan in 1916. Cravan introduced Sharshun to the "dadaist spirit" (Sharshun, "Moe uchastie vo frantsuzskom dadaisticheskom dvizhenii," 169).

119. For a detailed treatment of the suicide myth in French surrealism, see Livak, "The Place of Suicide in the French Avant-Garde of the Inter-War Period," 245–62.

120. "Enquête: Le suicide est-il une solution," *RS* 1 (1924): 2.

121. See Aragon, *Traité du style*, 88–90; Artaud and Crevel in "Enquête: Le suicide est-il une solution," *RS* 2 (1925): 12–13; Rigaut, "Jacques Rigaut," 57.

122. See Victor Crastre, "Sur le suicide de Jacques Rigaut," 253; Morand, *L'Art de mourir*, 11, 19–20, 23–24, 30, 34–38.

123. Breton, "Pour Dada," 210.

124. See Conover et al., *Four Dada Suicides*, 252; Crastre, "Trois héros surréalistes," 5; Soupault, *Mémoires de l'Oubli: 1914–1923*, 88.

125. Rigaut, "Jacques Rigaut," 57; idem, untitled article, *Littérature* 17: 5–8.

126. Crastre, "Sur le suicide de Jacques Rigaut," 253–55.

127. Jaloux, "Sur les 'Papiers posthumes,'" in Rigaut, *Écrits*, 213. See also Jaloux, "L'Esprit des Livres: L'Autre sommeil, par Julien Green," 3.

128. Crastre, "Trois héros surréalistes," 6–7; George Pomerand, "Trois suicides significatifs," 697–701.

129. See Desnos, "Jacques Rigaut," in Rigaut, *Écrits*, 186; Soupault, *Mémoires de l'Oubli: 1914–1923*, 199–202.

130. See Berdiaev, "Po povodu 'Dnevnikov' B. Poplavskogo," 441. See also Gippius's letter to Adamovich (April 17, 1930): "Last Sunday we had screaming and agitation, it was relatively interesting, although the gathering turned out to be . . . somewhat 'dull.' But your speech was not bad. Poplavskii spilt his decadent stuff, 'perish, you who are perishing'" (Georgii Adamovich Papers, box 1, folder 9 "Gippius Z. N. 1929–41," Beinecke).

131. See Adamovich, "Zhizn' i 'zhizn','" 2; Fedotov, "O smerti, kul'ture i 'Chislakh,'" 143–45; Khodasevich, "Zhalost' i 'zhalost','" 3–4.

132. The only surviving police record regarding their death can be found in the 1935 register of the Institut Médico-Légal in Paris. The autopsy showed that both men had died of "poisoning." But in the section "Presumed cause of death" both have "cause unknown," whereas in neighboring cases the register gives precise indications of death causes, indicating suicide, accident, or murder (Préfecture de Police, Institut Médico-Légal, Corps déposés, October 1935, 178, Archives de la Police, Paris).

133. Gazdanov, "Boris Poplavskii," 466; Gomolitskii, *Arion*, 27; Khodasevich, "O smerti Poplavskogo," 3–4. See also Shteiger's letter of November 5, 1935, in Shakhovskaia, *Otrazheniia*, 95–96.

134. See Breton, "Anthologie de l'humour noir," in Cravan, Rigaut, and Vaché, *Trois suicidés de la société*, 254.

135. Rais, "O Borise Poplavskom," 302–3. Cf. Poplavskii: "You know, all these books of ours are futile, I want to get rid of mine, I am looking for someone to take them" (Tatishchev, "Poet v izgnanii," 205). Julien: "Je te donne mes livres, tu peux faire d'eux tous ce que tu veux . . . Ils me dégoûtent tant. Quel poids dans ma vie!" (I give you my books, you may do with them what you please. . . . They disgust me so much. What a burden on my life!, Soupault, *En Joue!* 96).

136. On the experience of émigrés with esthetically connoted suicides, see Nesbet, "Suicide as Literary Fact in the 1920s," 827–35. The only surviving page of Poplavskii's 1922 diary reads: "Belief in my unlimited will power gave me a crazy idea—to realize the Gospels. The first thirty years will be the years of education of the sacrificial lamb" (*Neizdannoe,* 138). Whether this entry was made in 1922 or added later, the age at which he died makes Poplavskii seven months short of Christ's age at Golgotha.

137. See Lotman, "The Poetics of Everyday Behavior in Eighteenth-Century Russian Culture," in *Semiotics of Russian Cultural History,* 86.

138. See Lieberman, "Romanticism and the Culture of Suicide in Nineteenth-Century France," 611, 621; Paperno, *Suicide as a Cultural Institution in Dostoevsky's Russia,* 7–8; Thomas de Quincey, "On Suicide," in *Collected Writings,* 398–99.

139. See Lotman, "Literaturnaia biografiia v istoriko-kul'turnom kontekste," in his *Izbrannye stat'i* 1: 370.

140. Khodasevich, "O Maiakovskom," 3–4. See also Adamovich et al., "Autour de Maïakovsky," 6; Bem, "Spor o Maiakovskom" (*Rul'* 3220 [July 2, 1931]), in his *Pis'ma o literature,* 59–63; Levinson, "La poésie chez les Soviets," 6.

141. Jakobson, "O pokolenii, rastrativshem svoikh poetov," 9–10, 15, 20, 31–32. Cf. Berberova's account of the fate of Poplavskii and other émigré poets: "*Stalin also did away with them.* . . . With rare exceptions they are all dead. Poplavsky, Knut, Ladinsky, Smolensky . . . represent in the history of Russia a unique generation of deprived, broken, silenced, stripped, homeless, destitute" (*Italics Are Mine,* 268). The Russian text explicitly states that the poet "perished" rather than "died": "Gibel' Poplavskogo—imenno gibel', ne smert' i, veroiatno, ne samoubiistvo" (Berberova, *Kursiv moi,* 315). The emulation of Christ was indeed present in Maiakovskii's death style. See Fleishman, "O gibeli Maiakovskogo kak 'literaturnom fakte,'" 126–30.

142. Breton, "Liubovnaia lodka razbilas' o byt," 19.

143. On Yarko, see "Tragicheskaia smert' Borisa Poplavskogo," 3; "Tragicheskaia gibel' B. Poplavskogo," 4; Mamchenko, ""Pis'ma N. P. Smirnovu," 84. Poplavskii's parents suggested that he was murdered. They insisted that he had never used drugs before and that Yarko poisoned him. Apparently, they denied Poplavskii's drug use because the incident occurred in their apartment, where the police found more drugs and they, as *apatrides,* could have been prosecuted and even sent out of France ("'C'était la première fois que mon fils prenait un stupéfiant', nous dit la mère de Maurice Poplasky," 5). Poplavskii's father added more picturesqueness to the story, inventing a letter in which Yarko had told his fiancée that he wanted to die, taking someone with him (Iu. Poplavskii, "Boris Poplavskii," 147). This version was developed by memoirists who claimed to have seen this letter in the French press (Odoevtseva, *Na beregakh Seny,* 152; Ter-

apiano, *Vstrechi*, 116–17). But no French newspaper published anything on Poplavskii's or Yarko's deaths after announcing them on October 10. The November obituary in *NLAS* (631 [1935]: 3) still called their death an accident. Émigré newspapers closely followed the case but did not mention any letter to Yarko's fiancée. However, Yarko's mother told the police that he had written her a letter, informing her that he used drugs ("Tragicheskaia smert' Borisa Poplavskogo," 3). This letter must have been transformed into Yarko's confession to his fiancée.

144. See Chervinskaia, Letter to Bogoslovskii, in B. Poplavskii, *Neizdannoe*, 80; Ianovskii, *Polia Eliseiskie*, 30.

Chapter 3. The Prodigal Children of Marcel Proust

1. *Du côté de chez Swann* was published in 1913 and in 1917 (*Swann* in all references); *À l'ombre des jeunes filles en fleurs* appeared in 1919 (*Jeunes filles*); *Le Côté de Guermantes I* in 1920 (*Guermantes I*); *Le Côté de Guermantes II* and *Sodome et Gomorrhe I* in 1921 (*Guermantes II*; *Sodome I*); *Sodome et Gomorrhe II* in 1922 (*Sodome II*); *La Prisonnière* in 1923; *Albertine disparue* in 1925; *Le Temps retrouvé* in 1927.

2. Proust, "Préface," in Morand, *Tendres Stocks*, 29. See Gabory, *Essai sur Marcel Proust*, 15–16; Pierre-Quint, *Marcel Proust*, 132; Tadié, "Proust et le 'nouvel écrivain,'" 81.

3. Charpentier, "Les romans," 753.

4. Daniel-Rops opined that, to be noticed, a young writer had to make a bold statement about Proust ("Proust et ses quatre critiques," 70). See also Alden, *Marcel Proust and His French Critics*, 94.

5. On the widespread dismissal of Proust as a high-society novelist, see Alden, *Marcel Proust and His French Critics*, 35, 41, 46, 48; Crémieux, "Où en est Marcel Proust?" 3.

6. *Enquête*, 270. In 1921 *Littérature* 's contributors rated writers on a scale from -25 to 20. Proust had the average of 0 ("absolute indifference"). See *Littérature* 18 (March 1921): 6.

7. See *Enquête*: Aragon, 17; Bauer, 238–39; Béraud, 28; Billotey, 32; Crémieux, 52; Drieu, 71; Imann, 81; Massis, 332–33, 335; Soupault, 195–96.

8. Crémieux, "Le Bilan d'une enquête," 292–93.

9. See Crémieux, "Le Bilan d'une enquête," 292; Duhamel, *Essai sur le roman*, 114; Gabory, *Essai sur Marcel Proust*, 22; Jaloux, "Souvenirs du jardin détruit, par René Boylesve (Ferenczi)," 3; Lalou, *Défence de l'homme*, 244; Mauriac, *Proust*, 66–67; Montfort, "Chronique des romans," 301; Pourtalès, *De Hamlet à Swann*, 219–20; Rivière, "Les lettres françaises et la guerre," in *Quelques progrès dans l'étude du coeur humain*, 72–73; Robertfrance, "Freud ou l'opportunisme," 5. This appropriation did not heed many exposés of its delusional nature. See Cor, "Marcel Proust et la jeune littérature," 46; Ségur, "La Jeune littérature," 182–83.

10. See Alden, *Marcel Proust*, 108–9; Daniel-Rops, "Proust et ses quatre critiques," 71; Lalou, *Défence de l'homme*, 244; Mauriac, "Une heure avec M. François Mauriac," 1; Pierre-Quint, *Marcel Proust*, 142; Rivière, "Marcel Proust et l'esprit positif," 81–83, and "Quelques progrès dans l'étude du coeur humain,"

in *Quelques progrès,* 130; Robertfrance, "Freud ou l'opportunisme," 5; Sautel, "Découverte de Proust," 99.

11. See Bersani, "Proust et Dada," 261–66; Crémieux, "Sincérité et imagination," 545; idem, "Le Temps retrouvé," in *Du côté de Marcel Proust,* 62; Crevel, "Pour la liberté de l'esprit," in his *Détours,* 173; Dommartin, "Benjamin Crémieux et la littérature moderne," 73; Rambaud, "Sur la tombe de Marcel Proust," 3; Rivière, "Quelques progrès dans l'étude du coeur humain," 183–84; Saurat, *Tendances,* 200–201. Unlike the surrealists, Proust insisted on the cognitive control of material in the exploration of the unconscious. See *Albertine disparue,* 7; *Le Temps retrouvé,* 185, 218; *Contre Sainte-Beuve,* 49–50.

12. See *Enquête*: Crémieux, 54, 57; Drieu La Rochelle, 69; Martin-Chauffier, 94; Massis, 332.

13. See Bauer, 238, in *Enquête*; Crémieux, "Le Bilan d'une enquête," 293; Ségur, "La Jeune littérature," 181.

14. See Robertfrance, "Freud ou l'opportunisme," 5.

15. See Crémieux, 54; Escholier, 75, in *Enquête*; Crémieux, "Le roman depuis 1918," 9; Massis, *Réflexions sur l'art du roman,* xi, xiii–xiv.

16. Man, "Literary History and Literary Modernity," in *Blindness and Insight,* 148, 162. See also Habermas, "Modernity—An Incomplete Project," 143–44.

17. Eliade, *Le Mythe de l'éternel retour,* 173, 176.

18. See Ségur, "La Jeune littérature," 183.

19. Robertfrance, "Freud ou l'opportunisme," 5. See also Arland, "Chroniques: Sur un nouveau Mal du Siècle," 19–20; Crémieux, "L'Année littéraire 1924," 1.

20. See Arland, "Chroniques: Sur un nouveau Mal du Siècle," 28; Dommartin, "Benjamin Crémieux et la littérature moderne," 70.

21. See Barthes, "Proust et les noms," in *Le Degré zéro de l'écriture suivi de Nouveaux Essais critiques,* 134; Genette, "Proust et le langage indirect," in *Figures II,* 248.

22. See Berl, "Marcel Proust en jugement," 8; Du Bos, "Points de repère," in HMP, 159; Crémieux, *XX-e siècle,* 61, 95; idem, "Sincérité et imagination," 545–46; Gourmont, "Revue de la quinzaine," 179–80; Jaloux, "L'Oeuvre de Marcel Proust," 151–52, and "Sur la psychologie de Marcel Proust," in his *L'Esprit des livres,* 162; Rivière, "Les lettres françaises et la guerre," 73; idem, "Marcel Proust et l'esprit positif," 84–85; idem, "Quelques progrès dans l'étude du coeur humain," 129–30, 141–42.

23. Dommartin, "Benjamin Crémieux et la littérature moderne," 72. See also Pierre-Quint, *Marcel Proust,* 126.

24. See Alden, *Marcel Proust,* 72; Jaloux, "L'Oeuvre de Marcel Proust," 156; Rivière, "Marcel Proust et l'esprit positif," 85.

25. "'Elle disait: 'Mon' ou 'Mon chéri', suivis l'un ou l'autre de mon nom de baptême, ce qui, en donnant au narrateur le même prénom qu'à l'auteur de ce livre, eût fait: 'Mon Marcel', 'Mon chéri Marcel'" (She would say: "My" or "My dearest" followed by my Christian name, which, if we give the narrator the name of the author of this book, would be "My Marcel," "My dearest Marcel," *Prisonnière,* 67). See also *Prisonnière,* 147.

26. See Gaubert, "Le jeu de l'Alphabet," in *RP*, 86; Michihiko, "Le 'je' proustien," 73–74; Tadié, *Proust et le roman*, 7.

27. See Brée, *Du temps perdu au temps retrouvé*, 27; Genette, "Discours du récit," in *Figures III*, 255; Michihiko, "Le 'je' proustien," 79–80; Tadié, *Proust et le roman*, 130, 196.

28. See the literary opinions of such "philistines" as Bloch the son (*Swann*, 89), Bloch the father (*Jeunes filles*, 337), and Mme de Villeparisis (*Jeunes filles*, 289–90) and Marcel's meeting with the writer Bergotte, whose public persona "n'avait pas l'air d'être du Bergotte" (did not resemble the Bergotte, *Jeunes filles*, 120). See also *Contre Sainte-Beuve*, 127, 196.

29. See Boulenger, "Sur Marcel Proust," in HMP, 131; Crémieux, *XX-e siècle*, 81–82, 93–94; Gabory, *Essai sur Marcel Proust*, 15; Gide, "Billets à Angèle, III: A propos de Marcel Proust," in *Incidences*, 46–47; Jaloux, "L'Oeuvre de Marcel Proust," 153, 157; Maurois, "Attitude scientifique de Proust," in *HMP*, 152; Pierre-Quint, *Marcel Proust*, 131–33; Rivière, "L'Évolution du roman après le symbolisme," 38–41; idem, "Le Roman de Monsieur Marcel Proust," in his *Quelques progrès*, 43.

30. See Boylesve, "Premières réflexions sur l'oeuvre de Marcel Proust," in *HMP*, 97–98; Crémieux, *XX-e siècle*, 94; idem, "Albertine disparue," in *Du côté de Marcel Proust*, 50; Germain, "Regard sur l'oeuvre de Marcel Proust," in *De Proust à Dada*, 17, 27–28; Pierre-Quint, *Marcel Proust*, 132; Ségur, "La Jeune littérature," 183.

31. See Duhamel, *Essai sur le roman*, 128; Thibaudet, *Le Liseur de romans*, 37, 48.

32. See Boulenger, "Sur Marcel Proust," 130–31; Boylesve, "Premières réflexions," 99, 100–104; Crémieux, "Albertine disparue," 44; Honnert, "L'Apport humain de Marcel Proust," 22; Lalou, "Les Débats," 49–50; Montfort, "Chronique des romans," 301–2; Rivière, "L'Évolution du roman après le symbolisme," 39, 41.

33. See Crémieux, "Sincérité et imagination," 69–70, 76; idem, "Le Temps retrouvé," 54–55, 57–58; Dommartin, "Benjamin Crémieux et la littérature moderne," 67; Gabory, *Essai sur Marcel Proust*, 95.

34. Barthes, "Proust et les noms," 121–22; Tadié, *Proust et le roman*, 342–43, 348.

35. See Breton, "Manifeste du surréalisme," in *Manifestes*, 16–19, 43; Crémieux, "L'Année littéraire 1924," 1; Raimond, *La Crise du roman*, 128–35.

36. See Berl, "Marcel Proust en jugement," 8; Boulenger, "Sur Marcel Proust," 130; Crémieux, *XX-e siècle*, 96; idem, "Où en est Marcel Proust?" 3; Du Bos, "Points de repère," 158; Fernandez, "La Garantie des sentiments et les intermittences du coeur," in *Messages*, 147–48; Germain, "Regard sur l'oeuvre de Marcel Proust," 28; Jaloux, "L'Évolution de M. Henry Bernstein," 3; Lalou, *Défence de l'homme*, 236–37, 241, 243; Mauriac, "Sur la tombe de Marcel Proust," 5–9; idem, *Proust*, 67; Maurois, "Attitude scientifique de Proust," 151–53; Montfort, "Chronique des romans," 302; Rivière, "L'Évolution du roman après le symbolisme," 40; idem, "Marcel Proust et l'esprit positif," 181.

37. See Crémieux, "L'Année littéraire 1924," 1; Jaloux, "Souvenirs du jardin détruit," 3; Massis, *Réflexions sur l'art du roman*, 72, 74; idem, "Inventaire," in *Réflexions*, 87–89.

38. See Desjardins, "Un aspect de l'oeuvre de Marcel Proust: dissolution de l'individu," in *HMP*, 137; Dommartin, "Benjamin Crémieux et la littérature moderne," 70; Rivière, "Marcel Proust et l'esprit positif," 84–85; idem, "Quelques progrès dans l'étude du coeur humain," 165.

39. See Berl, "Marcel Proust en jugement," 8; Crémieux, "Le Temps retrouvé," 62–63; Germain, "Regard sur l'oeuvre de Marcel Proust," 28; idem, "Marcel Proust: La Prisonnière," in *De Proust à Dada*, 36; Mauriac, *Proust*, 27; Pièrre-Quint, *Marcel Proust*, 236–37, 241; Rivière, "Le Roman de Monsieur Marcel Proust," 45; idem, "Quelques progrès dans l'étude du coeur humain," 162, 176.

40. Crémieux, "Où en est Marcel Proust?" 3.

41. See Alden, *Marcel Proust*, 65, 106; Betz, "Sur une crise de la conscience artistique," 59; Crémieux, "Sincérité et imagination," 544–45; idem, "Les Livres," 324; Lalou, "Les Débats," 49–50; Ségur, "La Jeune littérature," 185; Suarès, "Anketa o Pruste," 275; Vandérém, "Les lettres et la vie," 603; "Feuillets de la Semaine: Ce qu'on lit. A la recherche du temps perdu," 581.

42. For one such attempt at neo-Proustian classification, see Crémieux, *XX-e siècle*, 231.

43. Germain, "Philippe Soupault: A la Dérive," in *De Proust à Dada*, 235; Soupault, *A la dérive*, 72. Cf. Lucien in Arland's 1923 novel *Terres étrangères*: "Les souvenirs sont pernicieux" (Memories are pernicious, 91).

44. Germain, "Philippe Soupault: A la dérive," 234–35.

45. Germain, "Philippe Soupault: Le Bon apôtre," in *De Proust à Dada*, 225.

46. Betz, "Sur une crise de la conscience artistique," 62, 70–71; Vandérém, "Les lettres et la vie," 603.

47. Crémieux, "Le Bilan d'une enquête," 293. See also Crevel, "Terres étrangères par Marcel Arland," in *Détours*, 141–42; Lalou, "Les Débats," 49–50.

48. See Bauer, 237–39; Crémieux, 54; and Lacretelle, 87 in *Enquête*. Lalou, *Histoire de la littérature contemporaine*, 572; Ségur, "La Jeune littérature," 183; Thibaudet, *Le Liseur de romans*, 197.

49. "Il lui semblait que ce temps passé ensemble était du temps perdu" (It seemed to him that the time they spent together was lost time, Cocteau, *Le grand écart* in his *Romans, poésies, oeuvres diverses*, 46). Cocteau's hero in *Thomas l'imposteur* runs away to the front from three mother figures at a time.

50. See Ehrhard, *Le roman français depuis Marcel Proust*, 155; Thibaudet, *Le Liseur de romans*, 197. Jaloux wrote: "It is quite clear that Marcel Proust's influence can be felt already. . . . One understands today that the main interest of the novel [as a genre] is precisely in the illumination of the complex elements of human consciousness and not in the combination of events" ("Souvenirs du jardin détruit," 3).

51. Lacretelle wrote: "There may be some people who think that minute details in character depiction undermine the work's dramatic action. They call such literature boring. I completely disagree with this sentiment. For me, the only boring literature is that which emphasizes primarily the exterior world of characters and their actions. . . . I owe a great deal to Proust" ("Une heure avec M. Jacques de Lacretelle," 2).

52. Charpentier, "Les romans," 754; Crémieux, *XX-e siècle*, 61; Jaloux,

"L'Évolution de M. Henry Bernstein," 3; idem, "Esprit des livres. Sur Jean Paul et sur Marcel Proust," 3; Massis, "Commerce et littérature," in *Réflexions*, 62.

53. See Proust, *Temps retrouvé*: "La souffrance que les autres lui cause-raient, ses efforts pour la prévenir, les conflits qu'elle et la seconde personne cruelle créeraient, tout cela, intérpété par l'intelligence, pourrait faire la ma-tière d'un livre non seulement aussi beau que s'il était imaginé, inventé, mais encore aussi extérieur à la rêverie de l'auteur . . . aussi accidentel qu'un caprice fortuit de l'imagination" (The suffering inflicted upon him by others, his efforts to ward it off, the conflicts between his unhappiness and the cruelty of another person, all this, interpreted by his intellect, could provide material for a book not just as beautiful as the one he could imagine, invent, but also as exterior to the dreams of the author . . . as accidental as a fortuitous caprice of his imagination, 208). Elsewhere in *Temps retrouvé* Marcel says: "Une femme dont nous avons besoin, qui nous fait souffrir, tire de nous des séries de senti-ments profonds. . . . Un écrivain peut se mettre sans crainte à un long travail" (A woman whom we need, who makes us suffer, elicits from us a series of pro-found feelings. . . . A writer can [now] embark upon a long labor without fear, 214). "Les oeuvres . . . montent d'autant plus haut que la souffrance a plus pro-fondément creusé le coeur" (Works of art . . . rise to a height proportional to the extent to which suffering has dug into the [writer's] heart, 215). "Les anées heureuses sont les années perdues, on attend une souffrance pour travailler" (The happy years are the lost years, one must wait for suffering before one can set to work, 216).

54. See *Albertine disparue*: "On n'est que par ce qu'on possède" (We exist solely through that which we possess, 70). "La possession totale d'Albertine, pos-session qui avait été mon but et ma chimère depuis le premier jour où je l'avais vue" (The complete possession of Albertine, the possession which had been my goal and my chimera from the day I first saw her, 79). *Swann*: "Depuis qu'il s'é-tait apperçu qu'à beaucoup d'hommes Odette semblait une femme ravissante et désirable, le charme qu'avait pour eux son corps avait éveillé en lui un besoin douloureux de la maîtriser entièrement" (Ever since he had observed that to many men Odette seemed a ravishing and desirable woman, the attraction which her body held for them had aroused in him a painful need for absolute mastery over her, 267). *La Prisonnière*: "On n'aime que ce qu'on ne possède pas, et je me remettais à me rendre compte que je ne possédais pas Albertine" (One loves only that which he does not possess, and I was beginning to understand that I did not possess Albertine, 370).

55. See also Chardonne's *Éva ou le journal interrompu*, whose hero uses his own wife as a mirror for a liberating self-study.

56. This is also true for Chardonne's *Éva*, whose hero projects the story of his marriage onto that of his literary vocation, abandoned out of revulsion for the "lie" of art (*Oeuvres complètes*, 3: 17–18).

57. See Adamovich, "Literaturnye zametki," *PN* 3515: 2; Bitsilli, "Paralleli," 341; Fel'zen, "Razroznennye mysli," 129; Muratov, "Iskusstvo prozy," 255; Tsetlin, "Anketa o Pruste," 277; K. Zaitsev, "'Vecher u Kler,'" 3.

58. "Anketa o Pruste," *Chisla* 1 (1930): 272.

59. See Bakhrakh, "Gazdanych," 8; Fel'zen, "O Pruste i Dzhoise," 217; Gole-

nishchev-Kutuzov, "Sovremennye Zapiski," 3; Gorodetskaia, "Les Débats," 55; Terapiano, "Zhurnal i chitatel'," 26.

60. See "Ot redaktsii," *Chisla* 1: 5; Fel'zen, "Mal'ro," 32; Khodasevich, "'Chisla,'" 3; Muratov, "Iskusstvo prozy," 254; Osorgin, "Kniga Chisel," 3; Pil'skii, "Novyi zhurnal—'Chisla' 1," 6; K. Zaitsev, "'Vecher u Kler,'" 3.

61. See Isdebsky-Pritchard, "Art for Philosophy's Sake: Vrubel against 'the Herd,'" in Rosenthal, *Nietzsche in Russia,* 241; Lane, "Nietzsche Comes to Russia: Popularization and Protest in the 1890s," in Rosenthal, *Nietzsche in Russia,* 60; Rosenthal, introduction to *Nietzsche in Russia,* 12, 20.

62. See Adamovich, "Nachalo," 503–4; idem, "Soiuz molodykh poetov v Parizhe,"240; idem, "Pis'ma o Lermontove," 2.

63. Aldanov, "Marcel Proust," 453; Fel'zen, "O Pruste i Dzhoise," 216; idem, "Umiranie iskusstva," 126; Muratov, "Iskusstvo prozy," 252; Shletser, "Zerkal'-noe tvorchestvo (Marsel' Prust)," 238; idem, "Marsel' Prust," 2; Terapiano, *Vstrechi,* 131–32; Veidle, "Odinochestvo khudozhnika," 55.

64. Fel'zen, "O Pruste i Dzhoise," 216, 218; Shmelev, "Anketa o Pruste," 277–78; Tsvetaeva, "Les Débats," 50–51; Vysheslavtsev, "Proust et la Tragédie objective," 28–30.

65. Adamovich, "O frantsuzskoi 'inquiétude' i o russkoi trevoge," 2; Slonim, "Bunin molodym pisateliam," 119–20.

66. See Aldanov, "Marcel Proust," 453–54; idem, "O romane," 436; Bitsilli, "Paralleli," 341–44; "Zhizn' i literatura," 278–80; D'Artan'ian, "Iurii Fel'zen: Obman," 31; Fedotov, "Bor'ba za iskusstvo," 34; Golenishchev-Kutuzov, "Sovremennye Zapiski," 3; Muratov, "Iskusstvo prozy," 255; Shenshin, "O Marsele Pruste," 28; Veidle, "Odinochestvo khudozhnika," 56; idem, "Mekhanizatsiia bessoznatel'nogo," 467; Vinaver, "Ugolovnyi roman," 257.

67. See Aldanov, "O romane," 437; Bitsilli, "Zhizn' i literatura," 277; idem, "Venok na grob romana," 166, 170–73; Iu. Mandel'shtam, "Poteriannoe bezrazlichie," 4; Mochul'skii, "Krizis voobrazheniia," 76; Veidle, "Kriticheskie zametki," 3; idem, "Odinochestvo khudozhnika," 55; Vinaver, "Ugolovnyi roman," 257.

68. See Lunts, "Na Zapad!" in *Rodina i drugie proizvedeniia,* 298, 302, 305; O. Mandel'shtam, "Konets romana," in *Sobranie sochinenii,* 2: 269.

69. See Adamovich, "O frantsuzskoi 'inquiétude,'" 2; Fel'zen, "Razroznennye mysli," 130; Khokhlov, "Iurii Fel'zen: Obman. Izd. Ia. Povolotskii i Ko, Parizh, 1930," 199; Terapiano, *Vstrechi,* 132; Fedotov, "Chetverodnevnyi Lazar'," 139. On externalized expressionistic descriptions as a reaction to the psychological novel in Soviet literature, see Chudakova, *Masterstvo Iuriia Oleshi,* 34–40; Maguire, *Red Virgin Soil,* 97–99. On the style of Soviet prose in the 1920s, especially the "abridged phrase," see Chudakova, *Masterstvo Iuriia Oleshi,* 25–34, 41–50.

70. Otsup, "Klim Samgin," 181, 183.

71. See *S'ezd:* Erenburg, "Zasedanie sed'moe," 182; Gor'kii, "Doklad o sovetskoi literature," 10–11; Radek, "Sovremennaia mirovaia literatura," 315; Tarasov-Rodionov, "Zasedanie trinadtsatoe. 25 avgusta 1934 g., utrennee," 326.

72. See "Krug: Beseda piataia 16 dekabria 1935 goda," 139; Adamovich, "Chelovecheskii dokument," 3; idem, "Eshche o 'zdes'' i 'tam,'" 3; idem, "Literaturnye zametki," *PN* 6088: 3; D'Artan'ian, "Iurii Fel'zen," 32.

73. See Adamovich, "Zhizn' i 'zhizn'," 2; Golenishchev-Kutuzov, "Sovremennye Zapiski," 3; Ivanov, "Anketa o Pruste," 272; Osorgin, "Kniga Chisel," 3.
74. See Bakhrakh, "Gazdanych," 8; Ianovskii, *Polia Eliseiskie*, 34.
75. See Adamovich, "Literaturnaia nedelia," 14; Bakhrakh, "Gazdanych," 8; Fokht, "Quelques aspects du roman russe depuis 1918," 26; Gorlin, "Pokhval'-noe slovo Gaito Gazdanovu," 8; Khokhlov, "Gaito Gazdanov," 25–26; Osorgin, "Vecher u Kler," 3; Otsup, "Gaito Gazdanov," 232–33; Pil'skii, "Gaito Gazdanov. Vecher u Kler," 6; A. Savel'ev, "G. Gazdanov," 5; Slonim, "Literaturnyi dnevnik: Dva Maiakovskikh," 456; Struve, *Russkaia literatura v izgnanii*, 293; Veidle, "Russkaia literatura v emigratsii," 4; K. Zaitsev, "'Vecher u Kler' Gaito Gazdanova," 3.
76. Gazdanov, "Zametki ob Edgare Po, Gogole i Mopassane," 97–99, 105–6. On Gazdanov's self-styled biographical myth, see Bakhrakh, "Gazdanych," 9.
77. Fel'zen, "Literaturnaia molodezh' iz 'Kochev'ia,'" 4.
78. See Khokhlov, "Gaito Gazdanov," 25–26; Osorgin, "Vecher u Kler," 3; idem, letter to Gor'kii, in Nikonenko, "Neskol'ko slov o Gaito Gazdanove," 727; Veidle, "Russkaia literatura v emigratsii," 4.
79. See Crémieux, *XX-e siècle*, 94; idem, "Albertine disparue," 49–50; Pierre-Quint, *Marcel Proust*, 132; Saurat, "Le judaïsme de Proust," in *Tendances*, 154–60.
80. See Milly, *La Phrase de Proust*, 5.
81. Proust, *Temps retrouvé*, 202. See also Genette, "Proust et le langage indirect," 294.
82. The Russian text (*Kler* in all references) is cited from *Sobranie sochinenii v trekh tomakh*, vol. 1. The English text (*Claire*) is cited from the 1988 translation, *An Evening with Claire*.
83. See Spitzer, "Le style de Marcel Proust," in *Études de style*, 411–12, 417, 420–21.
84. The translation is my own. In *An Evening with Claire* this period is divided into three separate sentences (*Claire*, 33).
85. See Boylesve, "Premières réflexions," 97–98; Germain, "Regard sur l'oeuvre de Marcel Proust," 17, 27–28; Terapiano, *Vstrechi*, 132.
86. K. Zaitsev, "'Vecher u Kler' Gaito Gazdanova," 3.
87. See Genette, "Vraisemblance et motivation," in *Figures II*, 79, 85; idem, "Discours du récit," 142.
88. See Khokhlov, "Gaito Gazdanov," 26; Otsup, "Gaito Gazdanov," 232–33; Pil'skii, "Gaito Gazdanov," 6; Savel'ev, "G. Gazdanov," 5; Slonim, "Literaturnyi dnevnik," 455.
89. See Houston, "Les structures temporelles dans 'A la recherche du temps perdu,'" in *RP*,ß88–90.
90. See Khokhlov, "Gaito Gazdanov," 25–26; Otsup, "Gaito Gazdanov," 233; Veidle, "Russkaia literatura v emigratsii," 4.
91. See Cocteau, *Thomas l'imposteur*, 26; Lacretelle, *La Vie inquiète de Jean Hermelin*, 235. Nikolai's use of a war and of an older married woman for spiritual deliverance recalls Radiguet's *Le Diable au corps*.
92. See Bakhrakh, "Gazdanych," 9; Fokht, "Quelques aspects du roman russe depuis 1918," 18, 26; Otsup, "Gaito Gazdanov," 233; Slonim, "Literaturnyi dnevnik," 456.

93. Gazdanov, "Rasskazy o svobodnom vremeni," in *Sobranie sochinenii v trekh tomakh*, 3: 30. See his speech in Rencontres, 141–42.

94. K. Zaitsev, "'Vecher u Kler' Gaito Gazdanova," 3. On the importance of books in Nikolai's adventures, see Gorlin, "Pokhval'noe slovo," 8; Pil'skii, "Gaito Gazdanov," 6.

95. An incongruity illustrates Gazdanov's intention to "isolate" his hero, who says: "I didn't know my father very well" (*Claire*, 34; *Kler*, 54); and later: "I thought about Mother, whom I knew less well than Father" (Claire, 42; Kler, 62).

96. "Ces similitudes mêmes du désir et du voyage firent que je me promis de serrer un jour d'un peu plus près la nature de cette force . . . qui portait si haut les cités, les femmes, tant que je ne les connaissais pas, et qui se dérobait sous elles dès que je les avais approchées" (But these very similarities between desire and travel made me promise that one day I would grasp a little closer the nature of this force . . . which exalted to such a height cities, women, so long as I did not know them, and slipped away from beneath them as soon as I approached them, *Prisonnière*, 161).

97. "Je me rendais compte de tout ce qu'une imagination humaine peut mettre derrière un petit morceau de visage comme était celui de cette femme, si c'est l'imagination qui l'a connue d'abord; et, inversement, en quels misérables éléments matériels et dénués de toute valeur pouvait se décomposer ce qui était le but de tant de rêveries, si, au contraire, cela avait été perçu d'une manière opposée" (I realized how much human imagination could put behind a tiny scrap of a face such as this woman's was, if it was imagination that came to know it first; and, conversely, into what miserable pieces, material and entirely valueless, something that had been the subject of so many dreams might be decomposed if, on the contrary, it was perceived in the opposite manner, *Guermantes I*, 151). See also *Jeunes filles*, 438; *Guermantes II*, 550–51; *Sodome et Gomorrhe II*, 401; *Prisonnière*, 5, 11.

98. Cf. the two scenes. Gazdanov writes: "When I kissed her hand at the door, she said irritably, 'Mais entrez donc, vous allez boire une tasse de thé.' . . . We drank tea in silence. I felt uneasy and, going up to her, said: 'Claire, don't be angry with me. I have waited to be with you like this for ten years.' . . . I noticed with horror—for I had waited far too long . . . that Claire had come right up to me and that her breast was pressing against my buttoned, double-breasted coat" (*Claire*, 25; *Kler*, 45). Proust writes in *Swann*: "Il n'entrait jamais chez elle. Deux fois seulement . . . il était allé participer à cette opération capitale pour elle: 'prendre le thé'" (He never entered her house. Twice only . . . had he gone in to partake in the rite which was of vital importance for her: "afternoon tea," 216). "Et ce fut Swann qui, avant qu'elle le laissât tomber, comme malgré elle, sur ses lèvres, le retint un instant, à quelque distance, entre ses deux mains. Il avait voulu laisser à sa pensée le temps d'accourir, de reconnaître le rêve qu'elle avait si longtemps caressé et d'assister à sa réalisation. . . . Peut-être aussi Swann attachait-il sur ce visage d'Odette non encore possédée, ni même encore embrassée par lui, qu'il voyait pour la dernière fois, ce regard avec lequel, un jour de départ, on voudrait emporter un paysage qu'on va quitter pour toujours" (And it was Swann who, before she let him fall, as though in spite of herself, upon her lips, held it [her face] back for a moment longer, at some distance, between his

hands. He had wanted to give his mind the time to catch up with him, to recognise the dream it had cherished for so long and to assist at its realisation. . . . Perhaps, too, Swann was fixing upon that face of an Odette not yet possessed, nor even kissed by him, [the face] he was seeing for the last time, the gaze with which, on the day of departure, one hopes to bear away with him a landscape he is leaving forever, 230).

99. Cf. Blok: "Ну, так с Богом! Вечер близок, / Быстрый лет касаток низок, / Надвигается гроза, / Ночь глядит в твои глаза." (Well, God speed! Evening is near, / The swift flight of swallows is low, / A thunderstorm is approaching, / Night is looking you in the eyes, *Sobranie sochinenii*, 2: 82). Pushkin: "С Богом, в дальнюю дорогу! / Путь найдешь ты, слава Богу. / Светит месяц; ночь ясна; / Чарка выпита до дна" (God speed, the trip is long! / You will find your way, thank God. / The moon is shining; the night is clear; / The cup is drunk to the dregs, *Polnoe sobranie sochinenii v desiati tomakh*, 3: 299).

100. "Вся жизнь моя была залогом / Свиданья верного с тобой; / Я знаю, ты мне послан Богом, / До гроба ты хранитель мой . . . / Ты в сновиденьях мне являлся" (My entire life has been the gage / Of a sure tryst with you; / I know, you have been sent to me by God, / You are my guardian till death . . . / You appeared to me in my dreams; Pushkin, *Evgenii Onegin* in *Polnoe sobranie sochinenii v desiati tomakh*, 5: 70–71).

101. See Adamovich, "'Sovremennye zapiski,' kniga 64," 3; idem, "Literatura v 'Russkikh zapiskakh,'" 3; Bitsilli, "Neskol'ko zamechanii o sovremennoi zarubezhnoi literature," 132; Golenishchev-Kutuzov, "Sovremennye Zapiski," 3–4; Khodasevich, "'Chisla,'" 3; Manziarly, "La soirée chez Claire, par Gaito Gazdanov," 306; Osorgin, "Kniga Chisel," 3; idem, "Vecher u Kler," 3; Savel'ev, "Chisla, no. 1," 3; Veidle, "G. Gazdanov" 200–201; K. Zaitsev, "Chisla," 3; idem, "'Vecher u Kler,'" 3.

102. Adamovich, "Na raznye temy," 3.

103. Fel'zen, "Probuzhdenie" (1933), "Vozvrashchenie" (1934), "Vecherinka" (1936), "Povtorenie proidennogo" (1938), "Kompozitsiia" (1939), and "Figuratsiia" (1940).

104. Many years later those who had known Fel'zen personally still used this title to speak about his novelistic project. See Adamovich, Odinochestvo i svoboda, 294; Ianovskii, Polia Eliseiskie, 46; Veidle, "O tekh, kogo uzhe net," 387–88.

105. See Gazdanov, "Literaturnye priznaniia," 260; Ivanov, "V. Sirin," 235; Varshavskii, "V. Sirin," 267. See also Golenishchev-Kutuzov, "Sovremennye Zapiski," 3–4; Otsup, "Gaito Gazdanov," 232–33; Veidle, "Russkaia literatura v emigratsii," 4.

106. Cf. Nabokov: "В приемной, где Герман сел у плетеного столика, на котором лежали, свесив холодные плавники, мертвые, белобрюхие журналы и где на камине стояли золотые часы под стеклянным колпаком, в котором изогнутым прямоугольником отражалось окно, за которым были сейчас душное солнце, блеск Средиземного моря, шаги, шуршащие по гравию,— ждало уже шестеро людей." (In a waiting room, where German sat down at a wicker table, on which lay dead white-bellied magazines, having lowered their

254 Notes to Pages 122–125

cold fins, and where a gold clock stood on a mantelpiece in the glass case, which reflected the bent rectangle of the window, beyond which there were now the stuffy sun, the glitter of the Mediterranean, steps rustling in the gravel,—six people were already waiting, *Kamera obskura*, 358).

107. See Slonim: "Pod Prusta napisannyi rasskaz Freidenshteina" (Freidenshtein's story written à la Proust, "Novyi korabl'," 121). On Fel'zen's suspected German descent, see Odoevtseva, *Na beregakh Seny*, 148; Struve, *Russkaia literatura v izgnanii*, 300.

108. Reviewing a Paris School collection, Nabokov called Fel'zen's contribution the collection's only "jewel" ("true, pure, and candid literature"), scolding the author for his lack of compositional rigor and excessive psychological discourse ("Literaturnyi smotr," 284).

109. See Adamovich, "Literaturnye besedy," *Zveno* 5: 248; idem, "Literaturnye zametki," *PN* 3515: 2; idem, *Odinochestvo i svoboda*, 294; Khokhlov, "Iurii Fel'zen: Obman," *VR* 1–2: 198; idem, "Iurii Fel'zen: Obman," *SZ* 46: 500–501; Pil'skii, "Iurii Fel'zen: Obman," 267; idem, "Tikhii gospodin s mikroskopom," 8; Savel'ev, "Iurii Fel'zen: Obman," 3; Struve, *Russkaia literatura v izgnanii*, 299; Terapiano, "Iu. Fel'zen: 'Schast'e,'" 268–69; Veidle, "O tekh, kogo uzhe net," 389.

110. "Vozmutitel'no-gorestno-lishnii" (outrageously-bitterly-superfluous), "dobrozhelatel'no-zabotlivo-shirok" (benevolently-caringly-magnanimous), "miagko-vrazumitel'no" (softly-persuasive), "trogatel'no-nezhno-poeticheskii" (touchingly-gently-poetic), (Fel'zen, "Vecherinka," 24, 28).

111. "Samozhertvennyi" (*Obman*, 25, 29, 218), "samopozhertvennyi" (*Pis'ma*, 62) instead of "samootverzhennyi" (selfless); "neprotivliaemost'" instead of "neprotivlenie" (non-resistance) (*Pis'ma*, 135); "oshchutitel'nyi" instead of "oshchutimyi" (palpable") (*Pis'ma*, 41); "golovnaia pravda" (head truth) as a notion opposed to psychological intuition (*Schast'e*, 73); "nedostizhenie" (unachievement) as a condition preceding failure (*Pis'ma*, 135); "otvetnost'" as "responsiveness" (*Obman*, 86, 93).

112. See Struve, "Dva romana o liubvi," 4; Veidle, "O tekh, kogo uzhe net," 389.

113. See Fel'zen, *Schast'e*, 59; "Razroznennye mysli," 130: Gazdanov, "Krug," 480.

114. Adamovich, "Literaturnye besedy," *Zveno* 5: 247; idem, "Literaturnye zametki," *PN* 3515: 2; idem, Odinochestvo i svoboda, 294; D'Artan'ian, "Iurii Fel'zen," 32; Osorgin, "Kniga Chisel," 3; Pil'skii, "Tikhii gospodin s mikroskopom," 8; Savel'ev, "Iurii Fel'zen: Obman," 3; Terapiano, Vstrechi, 130, 132.

115. See Adamovich, "Literaturnye besedy," *Zveno* 5: 248; Fel'zen, "Irène Némirovsky 'David Golder,'" 247; idem, "Fransua Moriak," 32; idem, *Pis'ma o Lermontove*, 99; Osorgin, "Kniga Chisel," 3; B. Poplavskii, "Vokrug 'Chisel,'" 206; Savel'ev, "Chisla, no. 1," 3; idem [S. Savel'ev], "Iu. Fel'zen: Pis'ma o Lermontove," 444–45; Struve, "Na vechere 'Perekrestka,'" 4; Terapiano, "Iu. Fel'zen," 268; idem, *Vstrechi*, 131; Varshavskii, "O proze mladshikh emigrantskikh pisatelei," 413; K. Zaitsev, "Chisla," 3.

116. See Adamovich, *Odinochestvo i svoboda*, 294; Struve, "Na vechere 'Perekrestka,'" 4.

117. Segments from *Pis'ma* were serialized in 1930–31. A reference to the events in *Pis'ma* confirms the posteriority of the episode narrated in *Schast'e* (65).

118. See Adamovich, "Literaturnye zametki," *PN* 3515: 2; Fel'zen, "Avtobiografiia," 121; idem, "Fransua Moriak," 32–33; idem, "Irène Némirovsky," 247; idem, "Marc Chadourne," 278; idem, "Eva ou le journal interrompu," 255–56; idem, "My v Evrope," 159; idem, "O sud'be emigrantskoi literatury," 18; Khokhlov, "Iurii Fel'zen: Obman," *VR*, 199, and *SZ*, 499; Pil'skii, "Iurii Fel'zen," 269; Struve, "Na vechere 'Perekrestka,'" 4.

119. Adamovich, *Odinochestvo i svoboda*, 293; Ianovskii, *Polia Eliseiskie*, 212.

120. Obman: "*Я* всегда как-то удивленно вспоминаю берлинские и первые парижские годы.... Очевидно, те, кого *мы* любим сейчас, *нам* представляются поэтизированными" (I always recall with some surprise [*my*] Berlin and first Parisian years.... Apparently, those *we* love now appear to *us* in a poetic light, 128); "Но даже если *я* и оказывался перед Зинкою прав ... в памяти оставалось ее приказание.... *Мы* нередко считаем ответственными перед собой тех, кого любим" (But even if *I* was right regarding Zinka ... *I* kept in mind her order.... Not infrequently, *we* hold those we love responsible for *our* [problems], 156; emphasis added). Jeunes filles: "*Je me* disais que c'était avec elle que *j'*aurais mon roman. L'état caractérisé par l'ensemble de signes auxquels *nous* reconnaissons d'habitude que *nous* sommes amoureux" (I was telling *myself* that it was with her that *I* was going to have *my* affair. This state is marked by a combination of signs which usually suggest to *us* that *we* are in love, 476; emphasis added).

121. See Fel'zen, "Sergei Sharshun," 285; Ianovskii, *Polia Eliseiskie*, 36, 277.

122. Kel'berin, "Iurii Fel'zen," 183; Khokhlov, "Iurii Fel'zen: Obman," *VR*, 198, and *SZ*, 500; Pil'skii, "Iurii Fel'zen," 268; Terapiano, "Iu. Fel'zen," 268; Tsetlin, "Iurii Fel'zen," 460.

123. See Fel'zen, "O literaturnoi molodezhi," 27; idem, "Mal'ro," 32; idem, "Avtobiografiia," 121; idem, *Pis'ma*, 51.

124. See Adamovich, "Pis'ma o Lermontove," 2; Khodasevich, "Pis'ma o Lermontove," 4; Otsup, "Iz dnevnika," *Chisla* 9: 134; Struve, "Na vechere 'Perekrestka,'" 4.

125. On the Paris School view of Pushkin and Lermontov, see Adamovich, "Kommentarii," *Chisla* 1: 142; idem, "Zhizn' i 'zhizn','" 2; Dolinin, "Tri zametki o romane Vladimira Nabokova 'Dar,'" 704–6; Fedotov, "O parizhskoi poezii," 197; Ivanov, *Raspad atoma*, 34–35, 79–80; Khodasevich, "Avtor, geroi, poet," 167–71; Otsup, "Iz dnevnika," *Chisla* 2–3: 163; B. Poplavskii, "Po povodu," 171. Bem wrote to Khodasevich on February 13, 1936: "I was told that our opinions of Fel'zen's book diverged considerably.... Maybe indeed I am not giving Fel'zen enough credit but what I find so irritating in his novel are his paraphrases of Adamovich's 'Kommentarii'" (Nina Berberova Papers, Series VIII: Vladislav Khodasivech Papers, box 57, folder 1278 "Bem, A. 1934–38," Beinecke). See also

Bem's review of *Pis'ma,* "Stolichnyi provintsializm" (*Mech* 3, Jan. 19, 1936) in his *Pis'ma o literature,* 242–46.

126. Cf. Drieu La Rochelle's description of Proust as the precursor and savior of his generation ("L'Exemple," 321).

127. See Arland, "Témoignage," in *Réflexions,* 119, 121–22; Crémieux, *Inquiétude et reconstruction,* 27, 177; Daniel-Rops, "Un bilan de dix ans," 178; Massis, "Commerce et littérature," 64, "Sur un nouveau poncif," 66–67, "Inventaire," 83–84, and "Reconstruction," 92–93, 98, in *Réflexions;* Maulnier, "Retour à l'essentiel," in *Réflexions,* 129, 131.

128. See Arland, "Témoignage," in *Réflexions,* 122; Crémieux, *Inquiétude et reconstruction,* 27–28, 33, 74; Daniel-Rops, "Notes sur le réalisme de Proust," in *Rouge et le noir,* 19; Maulnier, "Retour à l'essentiel," 128, 132; Maxence, "L'écrivain et l'action," in *Rajeunissement,* 116, 127.

129. See Daniel-Rops, "Carence," in *Rajeunissement,* 66–68; Fernandez, "Vie intellectuelle, vie politique," in *Rajeunissement,* 82–85; Frank, "A la recherche du temps perdu," 7; Péguy, "Les Débats," 54; Maxence, "L'écrivain et l'action," 116–19, 125–27.

130. See Adamovich, "Zhizn' i 'zhizn','" 2; Fedotov, "Bor'ba za iskusstvo," 34–35, 41; Golenishchev-Kutuzov, "Sovremennye Zapiski," 3–4; Muratov, "Iskusstvo prozy," 255–56; Veidle, "Odinochestvo khudozhnika," 57, 62; Vysheslavtsev, "Proust et la Tragédie objective," 28.

131. See Adamovich, "Chisla. Kniga desiataia," 2; D'Artan'ian, "Iurii Fel'zen," 31–32;

132. See Fel'zen, "My v Evrope," 154–58, 160; idem, "Umiranie iskusstva," 128. Cf. Crémieux, "Le Temps retrouvé," 61; idem, *Inquiétude et reconstruction,* 80.

133. See Crémieux, "Où en est Marcel Proust?" 3; idem, *Inquiétude et reconstruction,* 33, 75–76; Daniel-Rops, "Notes sur le réalisme de Proust," 19.

134. See Alden, *Marcel Proust,* 144; Daniel-Rops, "Proust, par Pierre Abraham," 97; Marcel, "Proust, alchimiste spirituel," 138; Saurat, "Lettres de Marcel Proust à la Comtesse de Noailles," 340–44.

135. Fel'zen, "My v Evrope," 155. See Fel'zen on Céline, "My v Evrope," 158.

136. See Fel'zen "Neravenstvo," 113; idem, *Schast'e,* 58–59, 69, 74, 158, 193.

137. Although never publicly articulated by émigré commentators, critical comparisons of exiled *prustiantsy* did take place. See, for instance, Veidle's letter to Ivask: "Fel'zen was . . . an unlucky gold-digger of true literature [neudachlivyi staratel' podlinnoi literatury]. Gazdanov was luckier in literary dealings [v literaturochke udachlivei] (I mean his first books), but he was unable even to imagine that which Fel'zen longed for and failed to attain" (Feb. 4, 1977, Iurii Ivask Papers, series 1, correspondence, box 6, folder 65, Amherst).

Chapter 4. The Esthetics of Disintegration

1. See Beauvoir, *Mémoires d'une jeune fille rangée,* 318; Chaumeix, "Les nouveaux enfants du siècle (1)," 701; idem, "Les Jeunes et les littératures étrangères (1)," 708.

2. See Décaudin, *Panorama du XX siècle français,* 151–52; Gomolitskii, *Arion,*

34. See also Arland, "Chroniques: Sur un Nouveau mal du siècle," 18, 28; Crevel, "Après Dada," 5; Daniel-Rops, "Un bilan de dix ans," 180; Léonard, *La Crise du concept de littérature*, 66–67.

3. See Arland, "Chroniques: Sur un Nouveau mal du siècle," 19–20; Berge, *L'Esprit de la littérature moderne*, 192–93; Faure, "D'un Voyage au bout de la nuit," in *70 critiques*, 189; Gluksmann, "Préface," in Jünger, *La Guerre comme expérience intérieure*, 10, 14; Soupault, *Mémoires de l'Oubli: 1923–1926*, 35, 62.

4. See Tsetlin, "Anri Barbius," 241–42.

5. Godard, *Voyage au bout de la nuit de Louis-Ferdinand Céline*, 180.

6. Morand's narrator is a "night traveler" and his journeys are "nights" (*Ouvert la nuit suivi de Fermé la nuit*, 13). See also Drieu La Rochelle: "Une nuit, c'est un chemin tournant qu'il faut parcourir de bout en bout" (A night, it is a winding path one has to travel from one end to another, *Le Feu follet*, 157–58).

7. *Voyage au bout de la nuit* (*V* in all references) and *Mort à crédit* (*M*) are cited from Céline, *Romans*, vol. 1.

8. See Arland, "Chronique des romans," 964–70; idem, "Céline et le 'Voyage au bout de la nuit,'" in *Essais et nouveaux essais critiques*, 228–31; *70 critiques*: Bataille, "Voyage au bout de la nuit," 117; Descave, "Voyage au bout de la nuit," 32; Laprade, "Le Cas Céline," 185; Rousseaux, "Le Cas Céline," 68–71.

9. Bataille, "Voyage au bout de la nuit," 117. See also Céline's interview in *Cahiers Céline 1: Céline et l'actualité littéraire 1932–1957*, 22; *70 critiques*: Planhol, "Autour de Bardamu," 123; Faure, "D'un Voyage au bout de la nuit," 188.

10. Chamson, "Voyage au bout de la nuit," in *70 critiques*, 59. See also Godard, *Voyage*, 37, 52–53.

11. *70 critiques*: Crespin, "Voyage au bout de la nuit," 109; Faure "D'un Voyage au bout de la nuit," 189; Fernandez, "Voyage au bout de la nuit," 33; Israël, "Voyage au bout de la nuit," 53–54; Pierrey, "Voyage au bout de la nuit," 91–92; Régnier, "Voyage au bout de la nuit," 140; Sabord, "Voyage au bout de la nuit," 26.

12. See Daudet, "Voyage au bout de la nuit," in *70 critiques*, 98. See also Godard, *Voyage*, 52–53.

13. Cf. Freud's suggestion that the death instinct (the desire to kill and to be killed) was as inherent to human psychology as the libido. Céline made public pronouncements about his debt to Freud (Godard, *Voyage*, 81–82) and treated Freudian allusions as a necessary bow to fashion (Céline, *Lettres à Joseph Garcin*, 30, 55).

14. See Latin, *Le "Voyage au bout de la nuit" de Céline*, 42; Rigaud, "L'Argot littéraire (II)," 54.

15. *70 critiques*: Altman, "Le goût âcre de la vie: Un livre neuf et fort," 17; Berge, "Encore des prix," 129–30; Lapierre, "Voyage au bout de la nuit," 43–44; Margueritte, "Voyage au bout de la nuit," 25; Pallu, "Voyage au bout de la nuit," 23–24; Régnier, "Voyage au bout de la nuit," 140; Thibaudet, "De Magny à Drouant," 154. See also Vitoux, *La Vie de Céline*, 240.

16. See Céline, *Cahiers Céline 1*, 22; idem, *Romans*, 1119–20.

17. See *Cyrano* of May 29, 1936, and *L'Intransigeant* of May 22, 1936. See also Céline, *Romans*, 1407–8.

18. See Arland, "Céline et le 'Voyage au bout de la nuit,'" 228–29, 231; *70 cri-*

tiques: Bernanos, "Au bout de la nuit," 74; Lambert, "Un livre," 149; and Pierrey, "Voyage au bout de la nuit," 92.

19. See *70 critiques:* Bernanos, "Au bout de la nuit," 74; Bourget-Pailleron, "Voyage au bout de la nuit," 82–83; Dabit, "Voyage au bout de la nuit," 56; Faure, "D'un Voyage au bout de la nuit," 192; Israël, "Voyage au bout de la nuit," 53; Lévi-Strauss, "Voyage au bout de la nuit," 119; Pallu, "Voyage au bout de la nuit," 22–24; Pierrey, "Voyage au bout de la nuit," 91; Rousseaux, "Le Cas Céline," 67–68.

20. Céline, *Cahiers Céline 1,* 21, 23, 26, 33; idem, *Romans,* 1107, 1262.

21. See Gibault, *Céline,* 1: 136; Vitoux, *La Vie de Céline,* 78.

22. Céline wrote to a friend that the job of a needy writer was to know what the reader wanted and to follow the fashion like a *midinette.* As an example he cited the topic of the Great War (*Lettres à Joseph Garcin,* 55). Incidentally, Drieu La Rochelle admitted in 1929 that the topic of war attracted him not because of his brief and quiet experience at the front, but thanks to its romantic and imaginative potential and its significance in postwar letters (*Sur les écrivains,* 147–48).

23. Arland, "Céline et le 'Voyage au bout de la nuit,'" 232; idem, "Chronique des romans," 967. For the older critics' reaction, see *70 critiques:* Ducasse, "Voyage au bout de la nuit," 183; Henriot, "Sur un écrivain pessimiste," 96–97. Also Jaloux, "Voyage au bout de la nuit," 3.

24. *70 critiques:* Fréville, "Voyage au bout de la nuit," 93–95; Lévi-Strauss, "Voyage au bout de la nuit," 121; Nizan, "Voyage au bout de la nuit," 61.

25. *70 critiques:* Bernanos, "Au bout de la nuit," 75; Schwob, "Lettre ouverte à L.-F. Céline," 180.

26. Faure, "D'un Voyage au bout de la nuit," in *70 critiques,* 193.

27. Adamovich, "Nachalo," 504; Fel'zen, "Sergei Sharshun," 285; Ianovskii, *Polia Eliseiskie,* 247, 277; Iu. Mandel'shtam, "Smert' v kredit," 5.

28. See Adamovich, "Na raznye temy," 3; Terapiano, "Chelovek 1930-kh godov," 268; Iu. Mandel'shtam, "Dnevnik obmanutogo cheloveka," 4; idem, "Smert' v kredit," 5.

29. Adamovich, "'Smert' v razsrochku,'" 3.

30. See Adamovich, "Na raznye temy," 3; idem, "Puteshestvie vglub' nochi," 3; idem, "'Smert' v razsrochku,'" 3; Kel'berin, "L. F. Céline," 223–24; Terapiano, "Puteshestvie v glub' nochi," 210.

31. Adamovich, "Puteshestvie vglub' nochi," 3; Kel'berin, "L. F. Céline," 223; Iu. Mandel'shtam, "Poteriannoe bezrazlichie," 4; B. Poplavskii, *Neizdannoe,* 222.

32. See Adamovich, "Kommentarii," *Chisla* 1: 136; Terapiano, "'Na Balkanakh,'" 140. See also Vysheslavtsev's opinion that émigrés found insufficiently tragic the self-analysis of Proust's protagonist ("Proust et la Tragédie objective," 26, 31). The notion of Proust's "comfortable suffering" largely relied on the myth of the corrections he brought to the scene of Bergotte's agony (*La Prisonnière*) from personal experience shortly before death. See Aldanov, "Marcel Proust," 453; Crémieux, "Où en est Marcel Proust?" 3.

33. See *S'ezd:* Gor'kii, "Doklad o sovetskoi literature," 11; Kirshon, "Za sotsialisticheskii realizm v dramaturgii," 400–401; Nikulin, "Zasedanie trinadtsatoe: 25 avgusta 1934 g., utrennee," 331; Radek, "Sovremennaia mirovaia literatura," 303; Zhdanov, "Rech' sekretaria TsK VKP(b)," 3–4.

34. Averbakh, "My stroim sotsialisticheskuiu literaturu," 2; Khokhlov, "Da byl li mal'chik?" 2; Radek, "Zakliuchitel'noe slovo," in *S'ezd*, 370; Smirnov, "Solntse mertvykh," 250–67; idem, "Na tom beregu," 141–50; Volin, "Emigrantskaia poeziia," 20–23; Zelinskii, "Rubaki na sene," 10.

35. See Adamovich, "O literature v emigratsii," *SZ* 50: 335.

36. See Adamovich, "Otsenki Pushkina," 2; idem, "Kommentarii," *SZ* 58: 321.

37. "O russkoi literature klassicheskogo perioda: Vvodnye zamechaniia," in *Iu. M. Lotman i tartussko-moskovskaia semioticheskaia shkola*, 382. On Russian cultural models of the universe, see also Lotman and Uspenskii, "Rol' dual'nykh modelei v dinamike russoi kul'tury," in Uspenskii, *Izbrannye trudy*, 1: 219–53.

38. See Adamovich, "O literature v emigratsii," *SZ* 50: 333; idem, "Zhizn' i 'zhizn','" 2. Gippius's letter to Adamovich (July 24, 1927) sheds light on the value of the esthetics of disintegration in émigré art: "You know, I kind of like the fact that you have lost 'the last remnants of values.' If one is to lose anyway, he might as well lose everything. In such cases (i.e., when it seems that one has lost *everything*) the necessary stuff, the indestructible roots still remain and they will sprout anew. But you have not yet reached a 'tabula rasa.' You are on the way. A good way, it seems to me, for it entails revolution and resurrection. . . . And do read Erenburg: there is [in this reading] a slim hope to become angry. No matter how much you lose—you will never reach the state of 'destitution' that befell Osorgin (who has just written the most tender review of Erenburg)" (Georgii Adamovich Papers, box 1, folder 8 "Gippius Z. N. 1926–1928," Beinecke). Adamovich wrote back on July 26: "I am flattered that you regard my loss of values and so forth in terms of 'it won't be resurrected if it does not perish' ['ne ozhivet, ashche ne umret']. . . . I am flattered,—but, personally, I am far from fooling myself,—and all my sympathy definitely and irrevocably goes to 'those who have not been resurrected'" (Z. Gippius and D. Merezhkovsky Papers, series 1, incoming correspondence, box 1, folder 10, Amherst).

39. Luppol, "Zasedanie desiatoe," in *S'ezd*, 259.

40. See Adamovich, "Nachalo," 505, 507; B. Poplavskii, "O smerti i zhalosti v 'Chislakh,'" 3; Terapiano, "Soprotivlenie smerti," 144.

41. See Otsup, "Ne tol'ko v nash poslednii chas," 23.

42. Otsup, "Iz dnevnika," *Chisla* 9: 134; Zakovich, "Vecher soiuza molodykh poetov," 259.

43. Otsup, "Personalizm kak iavlenie literatury," in his *Literaturnye ocherki*, 131.

44. See Bem, "'Chisla'" (*Rul'* 3244, July 30, 1931), in his *Pis'ma o literature*, 71–72; Khodasevich, "Novye stikhi," 3–4; Osorgin, "Chisla," 506, 508; Slonim, "O 'Chislakh,'" 3; Terapiano, "O smerti i umiranii," 3; K. Zaitsev, "Chisla," 3. Even Adamovich expressed doubts in private. He wrote to Gippius: "One dies alone, even while feasting one's eyes on death . . . but [dying] as a group, as the entire editorial office of *Chisla*—[this is] an extremely abominable sight. Blok wrote a poem about 'Death speaking' (by the way, it has a marvelous ending: S nego dovol'no slavit' Boga. / Uzh on ne golos—tol'ko ston. / Ia otvoriu . . . No pust' nemnogo / Eshche pomuchaetsia on [He has sung enough praise to God. / His is no longer a voice—just a groan. / I will open . . . But let him have just a little /

more suffering] i.e., he is knocking on her door). And so, she [Death] could say after reading *Chisla*—'I thought they would be frightened, and instead they started flirting with me [prinialis' so mnoi koketnichat'].' This is quite true and abominable" (April 16, 1930, Z. Gippius and D. Merezhkovsky Papers, series 1, incoming correspondence, box 1, folder 13, Amherst).

45. Dostoevskii, *Brat'ia Karamazovy,* 278. François Mauriac's "Catholic" novel *Le Baiser au lépreux* (1926) is a possible French subtext of Adamovich's story.

46. Ianovskii, *Polia Eliseiskie,* 118; Varshavskii, *Nezamechennoe pokolenie,* 182.

47. See Adamovich, "Na raznye temy," 3; idem, "Puteshestvie vglub' nochi," 3; idem, "'Smert' v razsrochku,'" 3; Iu. Mandel'shtam, "Evoliutsiia Selina," 9.

48. See Adamovich, "Russkie zapiski," 3.

49. Ianovskii, *Polia Eliseiskie,* 262; Zakovich, "Vecher soiuza molodykh poetov," 259.

50. See B. Poplavskii, *Neizdannoe,* 384, 470; idem, *Domoi s nebes,* 253, 275, 278–79, 293–94, 284, 288. See also Bakunina's first novel, which graphically described physiological functions, sexual acts, and genitals (*Telo,* 32–33, 44, 59).

51. See an early version of *Apollon Bezobrazov,* chapter 28, "In mare tenebrum," *Chisla* 5 (1931), 107 (excluded from the final version); Ianovskii, *Polia Eliseiskie,* 14.

52. Ianovskii, *Polia Eliseiskie,* 50. See also Balakshin, "Emigrantskaia literatura," 136, 138; Bem, "'Chisla,'" 73; Struve, "Na vechere 'Perekrestka,'" 4.

53. See Khodasevich, "Knigi i liudi," *Vz* 2431: 3–4; Nabokov, "'Volk, volk!'" in *Rasskazy,* 397–98; V. L., "Novye knigi," 3. Slonim wrote to Struve: "He [Ianovskii] hates me because I told him (or rather, reminded him) about the 'Artsybashev stuff' in his writings. Indeed, he was Artsybashev's disciple in Poland, in Warsaw, [and] his Russian is nasty. Afterwards he began to emulate Céline" (Oct. 12, 1955, Gleb Struve Collection, box 137, folder 1 "Slonim, Mark," Hoover).

54. See Izvol'skaia, "Affirmations," 1053; Otsup, "V. S. Ianovskii," 263–64. Characteristically, Ianovskii furnished the French translation of his first novel, *Koleso* (1930), with a dramatic and fictional autobiography that conflated the novel's author and hero, depicting the former as a product of social and cultural cataclysms (*Sachka: L'Enfant qui a faim,* 7–9).

55. See Adamovich, "V. Ianovskii," 457; Otsup, "V. S. Ianovskii," 263; idem, "Iz dnevnika," *Chisla* 9: 130–34.

56. Ianovskii, *Portativnoe bessmertie,* 167, 172–74, 177.

57. See Godard, *Voyage,* 131–33; Kristeva, *Pouvoirs de l'horreur,* 228–41; Latin, *Le "Voyage au bout de la nuit" de Céline,* 50–264; Rouayrenc, "Le Langage populaire et argotique dans le roman français de 1914 à 1939."

58. "T'as raison, Arthur, pour ça t'as raison" (You're right, Arthur, there you're right, *V,* 8); "J'pense plus à rien" (I don't think anything at all, *V,* 47).

59. "Y a pas plus communiste" (Nothing's more communist, *V,* 179); "Faut sortir" (Gotta get out, *V,* 199); "C'est pas la peine de se débattre" (There's no point in struggling, *V,* 357).

60. "Que je lui dis" (I say to him); "qu'il me répond" (He says to me). This is Céline's preferred device, used some nineteen hundred times (Godard, *Voyage,* 112; Rouayrenc, "Le Langage populaire," 457).

61. "J'ai cru longtemps qu'elle était sotte la petite Musine" (For a long time

I thought she was stupid the little Musyne, *V*, 78); "Il en eut assez l'enfant de mes doigts tripoteurs" (He'd had enough the child of my fiddling fingers, *V*, 273). See Spitzer, "Une habitude de style chez M. Céline," 193–208.

62. See Adamovich, "Puteshestvie vglub' nochi," 3; idem, "'Smert' v razs-rochku,'" 3; Iu. Mandel'shtam, "Smert' v kredit," 5; Veidle, "Chelovek protiv pisatelia," 144.

63. See Terapiano, "'Rytsar' bednyi,'" 10; idem, "Soprotivlenie smerti," 147.

64. Ianovskii described street lamps as the "pus-filled blisters of steamy swirling wounds" ("Trinadtsatye," 130); wind like "[s]omeone cold blew with a large mouth, dispersing clouds" (*Koleso*, 7); fog as "fat jelly chunks"; and snow as "shot down swans" (*Mir*, 203, 285). Cf. Bakunina's poem "Bagrovoe solntse" (5) and her novel *Telo* (84), and Poplavskii's *Apollon Bezobrazov* (22, 42).

65. In Babel's text, a street is "clean like the bald spot of a cadaver"; night is "torn to pieces by the moon's milk"; "the orange sun rolled in the sky like a sev-ered head"; and at sunset "tender blood flows from a toppled bottle up above, enveloping me with a light smell of decay" (*Konarmiia*, in his *Odesskie rasskazy: Konarmiia*, 88, 105, 108–9). Cf. Ianovskii: "The purple sun is rising like a blood filled louse" ("Ee zvali Rossiia," 60).

66. Earth is "that pulpy and granular thing in which they put the dead to rot" (*V*, 96); the city is "building refuse attached to the ground by black slime" (*V*, 238); the country is "night of the field of mud" (*V*, 495); and Africa is the place where "one sinks deeper into mud with each viscous rain" (*V*, 175). It suffices to com-pare the description of a New York public toilet in Georges Duhamel's *Scènes de la vie future* (210–11) to that in *Voyage* (195–96) to see that the naturalistic elements banned by Duhamel are hyperbolized by Céline.

67. See Adamovich, "V. Ianovskii," 457; idem, "'Sovremennye zapiski,' kniga 65," 3; Kel'berin, "V. Ianovskii," 251; Pil'skii, "Kniga," 6; V. L., "Novye knigi," 3; Zenzinov, "Ivan Boldyrev," 526–29.

68. Bem was probably the first to link *Liubov' vtoraia* to *Voyage*. See "O 'Liub-vi vtoroi' V. S. Ianovskogo" (*Mech* 38, Sept. 29, 1935) in Bem, *Pis'ma o litera-ture*, 232.

69. See Adamovich, "Liubov' vtoraia," 188; Bem, "Russkaia literatura v em-igratsii," in his *Pis'ma o literature*, 336; Osorgin, "Liubov' vtoraia," 3; Savel'ev [S. Savel'ev], "V. S. Ianovskii," 443–44; G. Voloshin, "V. S. Ianovskii," 477.

70. Khodasevich, "Knigi i liudi," *Vz* 3732, 3. See also Adamovich, "Liubov' vtoraia," 187; Osorgin, "Liubov' vtoraia," 3; Struve, *Russkaia literatura v izgnanii*, 296; Voloshin, "V. S. Ianovskii," 476–77.

71. Adamovich, "Liubov' vtoraia," 188; Voloshin, "V. S. Ianovskii," 477.

72. Regarding comparisons, see, for instance, Bem, "O 'Liubvi vtoroi' V. S. Ianovskogo," 232.

73. See Bakunina, *Telo*, 11–12, 16–17, 28, 33, 44, 46, 71–73, 84–86, 97, 100, 114.

74. Fedotov, "Bor'ba za iskusstvo," 43. On the master plot of the socialist re-alist novel, see Clark, *Soviet Novel*.

75. See Eliade, *Aspects du mythe*, 225; idem, *Le Mythe de l'éternel retour*, 167–68.

76. Adamovich, "'Sovremennye zapiski,' kniga 63," 3; Khodasevich, "'Sovre-mennye zapiski,' kn. 63-ia," 9; Pil'skii, "'Sovremennye zapiski,' kniga 63," 3.

77. Ianovskii, "Vol'no-amerikanskaia," 115, 118.
78. Adamovich, "Literatura v 'Russkikh zapiskakh,'" 3.
79. See Arland, "Céline et le 'Voyage au bout de la nuit,'" 228–29, 231; Jaloux, "Voyage au bout de la nuit," 3; *70 critiques:* Berge, "Encore des prix," 129; Descaves, "Voyage au bout de la nuit," 28.
80. Struve, "Double Life of Russian Literature," 404.
81. Poplavskii's candidacy to Krug was rejected in 1935 because of the poet's "dubious" religious philosophy. Ianovskii was among those who voted him down (*Polia Eliseiskie*, 80). The poet's subsequent death, which Ianovskii blamed largely on his isolation, may have invested the novelist with a sense of guilt.
82. Knut wrote on March 29, 1938: "Antisemitism in France is growing. . . . Recently the Club du Faubourg held a soirée devoted to Céline. Unfortunately, we were unable to attend, but those who went were surprised and horrified to discover the resurrection of elemental hatred and hostility toward Jews" (Shapiro, "Desiat' pisem Dovida Knuta," 201).
83. Shortly after the novel's publication in a separate book, Ianovskii wrote to Ivask: "Ianovskii is aware of the danger posed by the new form of violence— the Ω-rays and warns his contemporaries against it: this is the main subject of the novel!" (1953, no date); "I read the end of your review with sadness and disbelief. You give a sermon to the author, explaining that this 'machine' paradise is a form of tyranny etc. . . . However, the author is well aware of this: this is one of the novel's main subjects—there are two rival factions in the book. Sviftson's group represents a different approach (see, in particular, his Presentation which is the best of what I have ever written and I hope that one day someone will notice this. . . . Besides, Fedotov and Fondaminskii did take notice and published the excerpt in *Novyi Grad:* This was the best they could do). If you read the last paragraph of *Portativnoe bes[smertie]* attentively, you will see that in the finale there is a schism that initiates 'an epic struggle to the last' between these two tendencies of our history. That is why, to my mind, one would be more justified to say that 'the author knows about the danger' and uses his entire book to designate it" (May 1, 1953) (Iurii Ivask Papers, series 1, correspondence, box 7, folder 6, Amherst).
84. Ianovskii, *Polia Eliseiskie*, 119.
85. See Gomolitskii, *Arion*, 34–35, 39; Veidle, "Chelovek protiv pisatelia," 145.
86. Bem, "Literatura s kokainom" (*Mech* 31, Aug. 7, 1938) in his *Pis'ma o literature*, 334. For an example of a scandalized critic, see S. Iegulov, "Georgii Ivanov," 80. According to Gul', scandalized critics boycotted the text in "a conspiracy of silence" (*Odvukon'*, 68–69). However, it was reviewed and discussed by a number of émigré critics in periodicals belonging to different esthetic and ideological camps.
87. Khodasevich, "Raspad atoma," 9; Nabokov, "Literaturnyi smotr," 284.
88. Cf. Ianovskii, *Portativnoe bessmertie*, 181–82; Ivanov, *Raspad atoma*, 21–22; Céline, *Mort à crédit*, in *Romans*, 1: 517–18.
89. Cf. Ianovskii, *Portativnoe bessmertie*, 167, 173, 177, 234; Ivanov, *Raspad atoma*, 26, 38–40; Céline, *Voyage*, in *Romans*, 1: 17–18, 280–82, 299–302, 262–63, 373–75, 387.

90. Gippius, "Cherty liubvi," 147–49; Zlobin, "Chelovek v nashi dni," in *Smotr*, 158.

91. Gomolitskii, *Arion*, 35, 37–38.

92. See also Poplavskii's *Domoi s nebes*, whose narrator has sexual intercourse with a virgin "amid the icy hell of dead, tormented and corpselike white bodies" (193–94).

93. Cf. Khodasevich's poem "Pod zemlei" (1923), where the scene of masturbation in a Berlin underground toilet inverts the Biblical aphorism about the death of a seed and expresses the fear of artistic and emotional impotence. For a detailed analysis of this poem, see Bethea, *Khodasevich: His Life and Art*, 293–94.

Chapter 5. The Art of Writing a Novel

1. Nina Berberova Papers, box 15, folder 409 "Nabokov, Vladimir Vladimirovich/1934–1939, n.d.," Beinecke. Excerpts from this letter are cited in Boyd, *Vladimir Nabokov*, 409.

2. Nabokov challenged the fad of French influence in "Anketa o Pruste," 274. On Nabokov's denials of foreign influence, see Foster, *Nabokov's Art of Memory*, 15; Sedykh, "U V. V. Sirina," 2; Shakhovskaia, *V poiskakh Nabokova*, 119–20.

3. Critical comparisons of *Les Faux-Monnayeurs* and *Dar* have been limited to cursory remarks and footnote digressions. See Iu. Levin, "Ob osobennostiakh povestvovatel'noi struktury i obraznogo stroia romana V. Nabokova *Dar*," 219, 229 n. 41. I. and O. Ronen, "'Diabolically Evocative,'" 378; Tammi, *Problems of Nabokov's Poetics*, 195.

4. Russian and English texts are cited from *Dar* (*D* in all references) and *The Gift* (*G*), respectively.

5. Gide's texts are cited from *Les Faux-Monnayeurs* in *Romans* (*FM* in all references); *Journal des Faux-Monnayeurs* (*JFM*); *Journal, 1889–1939* (*J*).

6. See Décaudin, *Panorama du XX siècle français*, 98; Jaloux, "Les Faux-Monnayeurs, par André Gide (NRF)," 12–13; Léonard, *La Crise du concept de littérature*, 123; Raimond, *La Crise du roman*, 243.

7. See Arland, "Les Faux-Monnayeurs," 27; Crémieux, "André Gide et l'art du roman," in *AGC*, 126; Jaham-Desrivaux, "L'Esthétique des Faux-Monnayeurs," 9, 11; Jaloux, "Les Faux-Monnayeurs," 15; idem, "André Gide et le problème du roman," in *AGC*, 163, 167; Larnac, "Le Roman, d'après André Gide," 18–19; Martineau, "Les Faux-Monnayeurs," 31; Nadeau, "Un romancier contre le roman," in *CNTG*, 70: Thibaudet, "Roman pur et pure critique," in *CNTG*, 56.

8. On the subject matter of Fedor's novel, see *G*, 337, 350, 364 (*D*, 378, 394, 409); on its relation to the classical Russian novel, see *G*, 4, 9, 94, 327, 349, 364 (*D*, 10, 15, 108, 367, 392, 409).

9. "Good-by, my book! Like mortal eyes, imagined ones must close some day. Onegin from his knees will rise—but his creator strolls away. And yet the ear cannot right now part with the music and allow the tale to fade; the chords of fate itself continue to vibrate; and no obstruction for the sage exists where I have put The End: the shadows of my world extend beyond the skyline of the page,

blue as tomorrow's morning haze—nor does this terminate the phrase" (*G,* 366 [*D,* 411]).

10. See Boldt, Segal, and Fleishman, "Problemy izucheniia literatury russkoi emigratsii," 87.

11. See Arland, "Les Faux-Monnayeurs," 25–26; Du Bos, "L'échec esthétique des 'Faux-Monnayeurs,'" in *CNTG,* 49–50; Buenzod, "Les Faux-Monnayeurs," 13; Charpentier, "Les Faux-Monnayeurs," 22; Crémieux, "André Gide et l'art du roman," 134; Jaloux, "Les Faux-Monnayeurs," 10–11; Massis, "Faillite d'André Gide," 740–41; Nadeau, "Un romancier contre le roman," 70–71; André Thérive, "Les Faux-Monnayeurs," 41–49; Thibaudet, "Roman pur et pure critique," 55–56, 58.

12. See Du Bos, "L'échec esthétique," 48; Jaloux, "Les Faux-Monnayeurs," 9; Thibaudet, "Roman pur et pure critique," 58. Crémieux echoed Gide: "In twenty years one will be stupefied by the fact that, initially, critics could not see in the conscious accomplishment of *Les Faux-Monnayeurs* anything but a great failed experiment" ("André Gide et l'art du roman," 134).

13. See Arland, "Les Faux-Monnayeurs," 27; Billy, "Les Faux-Monnayeurs," 24; Du Bos, "L'échec esthétique," 50; Honnert, "Les Faux-Monnayeurs," 74–75; Marin, "André Gide, Les Faux-Monnayeurs," 124; Martineau, "Les Faux-Monnayeurs," 31; Massis, "Faillite d'André Gide," 743; Thérive, "Les Faux-Monnayeurs," 44; Thibaudet, "Roman pur et pure critique," 58.

14. Khodasevich, "'Sovremennye zapiski,' kn. 63-ia," 9. See also Aldanov, "Vechera 'Sovremennykh zapisok,'" 3.

15. See Nabokov's letter to Vadim Rudnev (February 11, 1935): "I have been working on my novel 'about Chernyshevskii' for two years, but it is quite unfinished, not to mention the fact that the range of readers who will find it accessible will, in all likelihood, be even narrower" (Alloi, "Iz arkhiva V. V. Nabokova," 278). Cf. Gide: "Ce cahier où j'écris l'histoire même du livre, je le vois versé tout entier dans le livre, en formant l'intérêt principal, pour la majeur irritation du lecteur" (I see this notebook in which I write the actual story of the book become part and parcel of the book itself, thereby shaping the book's principal interest to the major irritation of the reader, *JFM,* 52).

16. See Adamovich, "'Sovremennye zapiski,' kniga 64," 3; idem, "'Sovremennye zapiski,' kniga 65," 3; idem, "'Sovremennye zapiski,' kniga 67," 3; Khodasevich, "'Sovremennye zapiski,' kniga 64," 9; idem, "'Sovremennye zapiski,' kniga 66," 9; idem, "Knigi i liudi," *Vz* 4157: 9.

17. An excerpt from chapter 4 was published in a Parisian émigré newspaper *Bodrost',* which until the summer of 1939 had been a mouthpiece of the quasi-fascist Mladorossy movement. But following the Nazi-Soviet pact in August and the opening of hostilities in September 1939, *Bodrost'* changed its political orientation and courted many writers it had formerly barred from its pages: Berberova, Fel'zen, Mochul'skii, Veidle, among others. See Nabokov, "Arest Chernyshevskogo (iz neizdannoi glavy romana 'Dar')," 3–4.

18. Khodasevich, "'Sovremennye zapiski,' kn. 63-ia," 9. See also his "O Sirine," in *Literaturnye stat'i i vospominaniia,* 253. Cf. Jaloux: "André Gide failed only in that, after rising to the level which others had neither contemplated nor even conceived of, he did not stay there" ("Les Faux-Monnayeurs," 10, 12).

19. See Pil'skii, "'Sovremennye zapiski,' kniga 63," 3. Cf. Crémieux, "André Gide et l'art du roman," 126; Martineau, "Les Faux-Monnayeurs," 31; Veidle, "Andre Zhid," 3–4.

20. Martin du Gard, "A propos des 'Faux-Monnayeurs,'" in *CNTG*, 53–54. See also *JFM*, 34–35.

21. "J'aime assez qu'en une oeuvre d'art, on retrouve ainsi transposé, à l'échelle des personnages, le sujet même de cette oeuvre. Rien n'éclaire mieux et n'établit plus sûrement toutes les proportions de l'ensemble. Ainsi, dans les tableaux de Memling ou de Quentin Metzys, un petit miroir convexe et sombre reflète, à son tour, l'intérieur de la pièce où se joue la scène peinte. . . . Ce procédé du blason qui consiste, dans le premier, à en mettre un second 'en abyme'" (I truly like it when one finds in a work of art such a transposition of the work's subject matter on the level of its characters. Nothing illuminates better and establishes more firmly overall proportions. Thus, in Memling's or Quentin Metzys' paintings a little convex and somber mirror reflects, in its own turn, the interior of the room in which the painted scene is laid. . . . This [is a] heraldic device which consists of placing a second [element] "en abyme" within the first one, *J*, 41).

22. See Dällenbach, *Le récit spéculaire*, 16, 18, 25.

23. See Brosman, "Le Journal des Faux-Monnayeurs: oeuvre accessoire ou oeuvre autonome," 541; Marty, "Les Faux-Monnayeurs: Roman, mise-en-abyme, répétition," 105–6.

24. For another instance of this device, whereby surface resemblance conceals essential differences, see the coincidence of such "hygienic" circumstances in Fedor's and Nikolai Chernyshevskii's stories as pimple squeezing (*G*, 158, 220 [*D*, 177, 247]) and masturbation (*G*, 219, 325 [*D*, 247, 365]), both linked metaphorically to creativity by referring to ascetic inspiration, exhaustion after an act of creation (*G*, 158 [*D*, 177]), and the criticism of a created text (*G*, 34 [*D*, 41]). The deception of these coincidences lies in the profound esthetic and philosophical divide between the two writers.

25. Arland, "Les Faux-Monnayeurs," 25. See also Jaloux, "André Gide et le problème du roman," 158.

26. See his autobiographical poem: "You reload to the bottom the barrel, / With a creaking of springs / Resiliently pressing it down on the floor, / And you see, half concealed by the door / That your double has stopped in the mirror, / Rainbow feathers in head band / Standing on end" (*G*, 14 [*D*, 21]).

27. This distorting mirror relationship between Fedor and Chernyshevskii is further echoed in Fedor's caricature relationship with German Ivanovich Bush, a writer of comic esthetic blindness. Bush dreams of an ideal novel open to "absolute-infinity" (*G*, 210 [*D*, 236]).

28. Dolinin, "Gift," 164; Iu. Levin, "Ob osobennostiakh," 202–3.

29. Toker, *Nabokov*, 161; Waite, "On the Linear Structure of Nabokov's *Dar*," 55.

30. Iurii Levin suggested that the composition of *Les Faux-Monnayeurs* may have influences that of *Dar* but did not elaborate on this point ("Ob osobennostiakh," 219).

31. Bernard writes to his father (*FM*, 941); Édouard to Olivier's mother (959);

Laura to Édouard (984); Georges to Édouard (1003); Bernard to Olivier (1066); Félix Douviers to Laura (1092); Olivier to Bernard (1102); Rachel Vedel to Édouard (1120); Laura to Édouard (1183); Lady Griffith to Passavant (1193); Bronia to Boris (1212); Alexandre Vedel to his brother Armand (1233); Georges steals a letter written by his father's mistress (1147).

32. See the poem's reconstruction in Blackwell's "Boundaries of Art in Nabokov's *The Gift*," 617–20.

33. See Fernandez, "La figure de la vie dans les Faux-Monnayeurs," 101; Fokkema, "Semiotic Definition of Aesthetic Experience and the Period Code of Modernism," 72–74; Jaloux, "André Gide et le problème du roman," 164–65; Krysinski, "*Les Faux-Monnayeurs* et le paradigme du roman européen autour de 1925," 236; Léonard, *La Crise du concept de littérature*, 128; Thérive, "Les Faux-Monnayeurs," 43–44, 46, 49.

34. See Marty, "Les Faux-Monnayeurs," 108.

35. "Tout ce que j'ai dit ci-dessus n'est que pour mettre un peu d'air entre les pages de ce *journal*. A présent que Bernard a bien respiré, retournons-y" (All I have said on this [subject] is but to let a little air into the pages of this *journal*. Now that Bernard has had enough air, let us go back [to the story], *FM*, 1023); "Ici intervint un incident grotesque que j'hésite à raconter" (At this point occurs an incident so grotesque that I hesitate to recount it, *FM*, 1035); "A bien examiner l'évolution du caractère de Vincent dans cette intrigue, j'y distingue divers stades, que je veux indiquer, pour l'édification du lecteur" (At a closer examination, I distinguish different stages in the evolution of Vincent's character throughout this story, which I want to point out for the edification of the reader, *FM*, 1045).

36. "Je ne sais quelle secrète réserve" (I do not know what secret reservation, *FM*, 935); "Je ne sais trop quoi" (I do not really know what, *FM*, 960); "Je ne sais pas trop où il dîna ce soir" (I do not really know where he dined this evening, *FM*, 950); "Je ne sais pas trop comment Vincent et lui se sont connus" (I do not know much about the circumstances of their first meeting with Vincent, *FM*, 960); "J'aurais été curieux de savoir ce qu'Antoine a pu raconter à son amie" (I would be interested to learn what Antoine could have told his girlfriend, *FM*, 950); "Lilian m'agace un peu lorsqu'elle fait ainsi l'enfant" (Lilian irritates me a little when she acts this way like a child, *FM*, 973).

37. See Davydov, "*Teksty-matreshki*" *Vladimira Nabokova*, 188–96; Iu. Levin, "Ob osobennostiakh," 191–210; Tammi, *Problems of Nabokov's Poetics*, 84–85.

38. See *G*, 26–27 (*D*, 33); *G*, 34–35 (*D*, 42); *G*, 309–10 (*D*, 346–48); *G*, 122–24 (*D*, 139–41).

39. Characteristically, Nabokov wrote to Rudnev about the Chernyshevskii chapter: "My hero and I have worked on it for four years" (Alloi, "Iz arkhiva V. V. Nabokova," 278). For more examples of this procedure, see *G*, 62, 93, 143, 331/ *D*, 73, 106, 162–63, 370.

40. See Dolinin, "Gift," 164.

41. For more on Gide's technique of false authorship, see Prior, "Auteur et narrateur dans *Les Faux-Monnayeurs*," 44.

42. Cf. the comment of Gide's narrator: "Une sorte de contrainte étrange, inexplicable, pesait sur eux aussitôt qu'ils se trouvaient seuls. (Je n'aime pas ce mot

'inexplicable', et ne l'écris ici que par insuffisance provisoire)" (Some strange, inexplicable constraint burdened them once they found themselves alone. [I do not like this word "inexplicable" and use it here only due to temporary insufficiency], *FM*, 1106). See another instance of puppet imagery in *Dar:* "At the next corner his approach automatically triggered the doll-like mechanism of the prostitutes who always patrolled there" (*G*, 325 [*D*, 364]).

43. This false clue has proven effective. See Louria, "Nabokov and Proust," 471.

44. See *G*, 4–5 (*D*, 10–11); *G*, 11 (*D*, 17–18). See Pil'skii's criticism of Nabokov's style in "Sovremennye zapiski, kniga 63," 3. Characteristically, "Proustian" periods reoccur in chapter 2, when Fedor reminisces about his father (*G*, 79–80 [*D*, 91–92]).

45. Narrative differences between Gide's and Proust's novels were immediately remarked by critics. See Souday, "Les Faux-Monnayeurs," 36.

46. See Dolinin, "Gift," 139–40, 149; Johnson, "Key to Nabokov's *Gift*," 190–206; Waite, "On the Linear Structure of Nabokov's *Dar*," 51–72.

47. See Boyd's discussion of the parodic classical stylization in *Dar*'s opening scene (*Vladimir Nabokov*, 465–66).

48. Blackwell sees this facet of Nabokov's novel as ironic flag-waving, for while evoking Russian traditions, *Dar* breaks them "in order to flaunt their violation" ("Boundaries of Art," 608). Here are some examples of such "flag-waving." Fedor introduces digressions and ellipses: "None of the poems in the book alludes to a certain extraordinary thing that happened to me as I was recovering from a particularly severe case of pneumonia. When everyone had moved into the drawing room (to use a Victorian cliché), one of the guests who (to go on with it) had been silent all evening. . . . The fever had ebbed away, etc." (*G*, 22 [*D*, 28–29]); "Kaput on the first try,' as your stepfather would put it,' he said in reply to her question about the manuscript and (as they used to write in the old days) briefly recounted his conversation at the editorial office" (*G*, 208 [*D*, 234]). See also Nabokov's use of such nineteenth-century phraseological clichés, lost in translation, as "sumerki sgustilis'" (dusk gathered): "Он повернул выключатель, но в комнате нечему было сгуститься" (He turned the light switch off but there was nothing to gather in the room, *D*, 66); "zima vydalas'" (winter happened to be): "Зима, как большинство памятных зим, как и все зимы, вводимые в речь ради фразы, выдалась (они всегда 'выдаются' в таких случаях) холодная" (Winter, like most memorable winters, and like all the winters mentioned for the sake of a felicitous expression, happened to be [they always "happen to be" in such cases] cold, *D*, 229); "vo vremia etoi tirady" (during this tirade) and "mina" (a look): "'Ну, это не так интересно,'—сказал Федор Константинович, который во время этой тирады (как писали Тургенев, Гончаров, Граф Салиас, Григорович, Боборыкин), кивал головой с одобрительной миной" ("Well, this is not as interesting,"—said Fedor Konstantinovich, who during this tirade [as Turgenev, Goncharov, Count Salias, Grigorovich, Boborykin used to write] nodded with a look of approval, *D*, 381).

49. The name of the review, *Fer à repasser*, was recognizable to contemporaries. Sharshun claims that Gide borrowed it from the title of a drawing that ac-

companied his dadaist poem *La Foule immobile* ("Moe uchastie vo frantsuzskom dadaisticheskom dvizhenii," 173).

50. See Dolinin, "'Dvoinoe vremia' u Nabokova (ot 'Dara' k 'Lolite')," 283–322; Peterson, "Time in *The Gift*," 36–40.

51. Cf. *G*, 81, 336, 343, 350 (*D*, 93–94, 377, 385, 393) and especially the scene of Germans "returning from some civic orgy" (*G*, 362 [*D*, 406]) to a passage from this letter: "We are at a complete loss with regard to the future but, at any rate, we will *never* go back to Germany. It is a disgusting and terrible country. I've always hated Germans, their beastly spirit, and given their present political order (which fits them perfectly, by the way) life there has become unbearable for me—and not just because my wife is Jewish" (Leving, "Literaturnyi podtekst palestinskogo pis'ma Vladimira Nabokova," 123). Thus, a Russian Nazi reviewer fell prey to the novel's ahistoricism. Characterizing the depiction of the Germans in *Dar* as political propaganda against Hitler's regime, the critic stated that even though Nabokov intended to satirize "the contemporary, athletically tempered Germany," he unwittingly described the Weimar Republic period, when Germany suffered under the yoke of the Jews who had since been chased from Germany "to the banks of the Seine" (Garf, "Literaturnye pelenki," 6).

52. Dolinin, "Doklady Vladimira Nabokova v berlinskom literaturnom kruzhke," 9; and idem, "Clio Laughs Last," 211–12.

53. See Brosman, "Novelist as Natural Historian in 'Les Faux-Monnayeurs,'" 48–59.

54. For a detailed analysis of Nabokov's criticism of vulgar Darwinism, see Alexandrov, "Note on Nabokov's Anti-Darwinism," 239–44.

55. Nabokov, "Father's Butterflies: Second Addendum to *The Gift*," in *Nabokov's Butterflies*, 223. See the Russian version in Dolinin, "V. V. Nabokov: Vtoroe dobavlenie k 'Daru,'" 101.

56. Dolinin, "Gift," 140; Goux, "La Métaphore monétaire dans les Faux-Monnayeurs," 91–108; Rieder, "Les Faux-Monnayeurs," 97.

57. Charpentier, "Les Faux-Monnayeurs," 22; Du Bos, "L'échec esthétique des Faux-Monnayeurs," 49; Jaloux, "André Gide et le problème du roman," 163; Larnac, "Le Roman," 18–19.

58. Osorgin, "Literaturnye razmyshleniia," 2. Echoing Thérive's view of Gide as a counterfeiter of life ("Les Faux-Monnayeurs," 49), Pil'skii denounced Nabokov as a prestidigitator whose artificial verbal rain fell from the ceiling just like the real thing ("Sovremennye zapiski," 3).

59. On Gide, see Du Bos, "L'échec esthétique des Faux-Monnayeurs," 52; Jaloux, "Les Faux-Monnayeurs," 11; Larnac, "Le Roman," 16; Marin, "Le Roman: André Gide," 123; Massis, "Faillite d'André Gide," 743; Thibaudet, "Roman pur et pure critique," 55; idem, "Les Faux-Monnayeurs," 20. On Nabokov, see Adamovich, "Sovremennye zapiski, kniga 67," 3; Pil'skii, "Sovremennye zapiski," 3. Shteiger wrote on January 30, 1937: "Sirin read an excerpt from his new novel about Chernyshevskii; I have already heard other segments from it in Berlin. My impression from these excerpts and from his reading (exceptionally theatrical) is embarrassing and depressing, but it seems to me that the choice of episodes intentionally aimed at entertaining the audience, which

was indeed quite pleased. From my conversations with Sirin I know that his novel is more serious and intelligent. But Sirin's formalist juggling still puzzles me" (Livak, "K istorii 'Parizhskoi shkoly'. Pis'ma Anatoliia Shteigera, 1937–1943," 91).

60. My translation. The aspect of monetary transaction was lost in the published translation: "In a whole set of poems, disarming by their sincerity . . . no, that's nonsense—Why must one 'disarm' the reader? Is he dangerous?" (*G*, 11).

61. See, for instance, Adamovich, "Nachalo," 503–4; idem, "Zhizn' i 'zhizn','" 2.

62. *Hamlet*, in *The Complete Works of William Shakespeare*, 1071. For more links between Bernard and Hamlet, see Steel, "To be or not to be un personnage des Faux-Monnayeurs," 485–86.

63. See Shklovskii, "Khod konia," in *Khod konia*, 9–11.

64. Thérive, "Les Faux-Monnayeurs," 42. See also Jaloux's comment on the novel's overpopulation by "anxious young men" ("Les Faux-Monnayeurs," 11).

65. Nabokov, "On Generalities," in Dolinin, "Doklady Vladimira Nabokova," 14.

66. See Arland, "Les Faux-Monnayeurs," 25; Fernandez, "La figure de la vie," 103; Malraux, Maxence in "Les Débats," *CQ* 20: 6 (1930), 44, 50.

67. Billy, *L'époque contemporaine (1905–1930)*, 287. In a letter of February 8, 1940, Shteiger mentioned both books in one breath, mixing embarrassment with admiration: "Have you read Gide's *Faux-Monnayeurs*? What a marvelous but nasty book. I don't like *Corydon*—except for one tender and very fine scene in the introduction. The rest of it is too German" (Livak, "K istorii 'Parizhskoi shkoly'. Pis'ma Anatoliia Shteigera, 1937–1943," 111). Baron Anatolii Shteiger, a Gide aficionado and Adamovich's close friend, whose homosexual escapades were well known in Russian Paris (Ianovskii, *Polia Eliseiskie*, 252–53), may have been among the writers ridiculed in this passage. Dolinin has suggested that "Boris Barskii" was a contamination of *Bar*on (Shteiger) and *Boris* Poplav*skii*; but the critic missed the link to Gidean *corydonisme*, which allowed the assimilation of both poets in one persona (Dolinin, "Dar," in Nabokov, *Sobranie sochinenii russkogo perioda v piati tomakh*, 4: 758).

68. Adamovich wrote to Ianovskii on September 18, 1951: "Fourth—Ivask. Homosexual? He is very delicate, very sensitive: probably a homosexual. I may have heard something of this sort about him, but Volodia [Varshavskii] is lying when he says that this is 'common knowledge.' Whatever information he has must come from his personal experience" ("Pis'ma Vasiliiu Ianovskomu," 126). Adamovich's conversations with Ivask confirm the existence of rumors about Varshavskii's homosexuality and add another detail, namely that Varshavskii was rumored to be Adamovich's lover. See Adamovich's remark: "I was never in love with Varshavskii. We were strictly friends" (Iurii Ivask Papers, series 1, box 1, folder 6, "Besedy s Georgiem Adamovichem. Chast' vtoraia. Peterburgskie anekdoty," Amherst).

69. Promoting Varshavskii's argument in the émigré press, Adamovich unwittingly opened himself to Nabokov's attacks by describing younger writers as "émigré 'children'" ("emigrantskie 'deti'") who were attracted to Gide (i.e., Gide's writings), and turned a deaf ear to "their elders" (i.e., older émigré writ-

ers) (Adamovich, "Andre Zhid i SSSR," 2). Thus, on January 19, 1931, Nabokov mocked his esthetic foe in a letter to Struve by conflating "Adamovich" with "Sodom." One reads in this letter that the serialization of Nabokov's novel *Podvig* was "accompanied by the quiet whistling of Sodomovich and other Zhorzhiki" (Gleb Struve Collection, box 108, folder 17, Hoover). By "other Zhorzhiki" Nabokov meant Georgii (Georges) Ivanov, whose homosexual adventures were the stuff of hearsay in Russian literary circles. See, for instance, Adamovich's own confession to Ivask: "I had a thing with Zhorzhik Ivanov too. It was he who seduced me" (Iurii Ivask Papers, series 1, box 1, folder 6, "Besedy s Georgiem Adamovichem. Chast' vtoraia. Peterburgskie anekdoty," Amherst).

70. Thibaudet considered the suicidal atmosphere of *Les Faux-Monnayeurs* as a salient value in the axiological system of its protagonists ("Les Faux-Monnayeurs," 21–22).

71. Nabokov wrote to Aldanov, who found indecorous *Dar*'s attacks on the Paris School: "I was guided not by an urge to laugh at this or that person . . . but solely by a desire to show a certain order of literary ideas, typical at a given time—which is what the whole novel is about (its main heroine is literature)." Cited in Boyd, *Vladimir Nabokov*, 480. On Nabokov's parodic technique in *Dar*, see also Dolinin, "Dve zametki o romane 'Dar,'" 173–80.

72. On suicide esthetics in Russian Symbolist and Decadent circles, see Khodasevich, "Konets Renaty," in *Koleblemyi trenozhnik*, 270–72.

73. See Brodsky, "Homosexuality and the Aesthetic of Nabokov's *Dar*," 95–115; Skonechnaia, "'People of the Moonlight,'" 33–52.

74. Nesbet suggested another prototype for Iasha's story—a 1928 group suicide in the Berlin émigré community ("Suicide as Literary Fact," 828). While by no means mutually exclusive, the case of Boris Poplavskii, in my view, is considerably more important for Nabokov's agenda in *Dar* than that of Alexei Frenkel'.

75. Although Cocteau's drawings appear as Nabokov's immediate referents, the image of sailor also figured as a symbol of homosexuality in the stories of Adamovich's and Ivanov's sexual adventures as they were related in Russian literary circles. Nabokov's readership, for the most part, ignored these privately disseminated narratives but the novelist was most certainly privy to them. Adamovich told the following story: "One night an unusually pretty sailor paid me a visit. . . . I wrote to the editorial office of *Zveno* that I could not come next morning, [because I was] sick. . . . The next day the entire editorial office showed up at my place—M. L. Kantor, Mochul'skii. I opened the door just a little and said—I cannot let you in, I have a terrible headache. . . . Suddenly, Kantor, who was standing in the foyer, saw a sailor's cap with a pompon—it adorned the table in my room . . . the door was ajar. . . . Well, then—they all fell silent and quickly left" (Iurii Ivask Papers, series 1, box 1, folder 6, "Besedy s Georgiem Adamovichem. Chast' vtoraia," Amherst). One reads in the same interview (chapter "Peterburgskie anekdoty"): "[Once] In Paris, Georgii Ivanov let his guard down [zabylsia] and said to me in the presence of Odoevtseva: Georges, get a load of that pretty sailor [Zhorzh, smotri kakoi krasivyi matros]. Irina looked at him with pity: Feed the wolf all you like, he'll keep running off to the forest."

76. See Skonechnaia, "'People of the Moonlight,'" 40–49.

77. See Jakobson, "O pokolenii, rastrativshem svoikh poetov," 15, 20, 32.

Conclusion

1. Breton, Soupault, and Crevel devoted themselves to journalism, cultural and art criticism, philosophy, and politics. From 1930 to 1939, Desnos worked for the radio and, with one exception (*Sans cou*, 1934), stopped publishing poetry. In the same decade, Jean Cocteau, Breton's most hated rival, gave the bulk of his time to cinema, theater, and criticism.

2. See Adamovich, "G. Gazdanov," 3; Khodasevich, "Istoriia odnogo puteshestviia," 9; Veidle, "G. Gazdanov," 200–201.

3. Otsup, "Personalizm kak iavlenie literatury," in his *Literaturnye ocherki*, 131.

Bibliography

Primary sources

ARCHIVES
Amherst Center for Russian Culture. Amherst College. Amherst, Mass.
Archives de la Police. Paris, France.
Bakhmeteff Archive of Russian and East European History and Culture. Rare Book and Manuscript Library. Columbia University, New York.
Bibliothèque littéraire Jacques Doucet. Paris.
General Collection, Russian Literature. Beinecke Rare Book and Manuscript Library. Yale University, New Haven, Conn.
Hoover Institution on War, Revolution, and Peace. Archives. Stanford University, Stanford, Calif.
Manuscript Department. Library of Congress, Washington, D.C.

COLLECTIONS OF SOURCES
André Gide: Les Contemporains. Paris: Éditions du Capitole, 1928.
Allen, Louis, and Ol'ga Griz, eds. *Boris Poplavskii v otsenkakh i vospominaniiakh sovremennikov.* St. Petersburg and Düsseldorf: Logos-Goluboi vsadnik, 1993.
Daniel-Rops, Henri, ed. *Le Rajeunissement de la politique.* Paris: Éditions Roberto A. Corrêa, 1932.
Derval, André, ed. *70 critiques de Voyage au bout de la nuit 1932–1935.* Paris: IMEC Éditions, 1993.
Gippius, Zinaida, and Dmitrii Merezhkovskii, eds. *Literaturnyi smotr: Svobodnyi sbornik.* Paris: Dom knigi, 1939.
Kreid, Vadim, ed. *Dal'nie berega: Portrety pisatelei emigratsii. Memuary.* Moscow: Respublika, 1994.
Luppol, Ivan, ed. *Stenograficheskii otchet pervogo vsesoiuznogo s'ezda sovetskikh pisatelei.* Moscow: OGIZ RSFSR, 1934.
Massis, Henri, ed. *Dix ans après: Réflexions sur la littérature d'après guerre. Cahiers de la Quinzaine.* Paris: Desclée de Brouwer et Cie, 1932.
Raimond, Michel, ed. *Les Critiques de notre temps et Gide.* Paris: Éditions Garnier frères, 1971.

Rambaud, Henri, and Pierre Varillon, eds. *Enquête sur les maîtres de la jeune littérature*. Paris: Librairie Bloud & Gay, 1923.

Rivière, Jacques, ed. *Hommage à Marcel Proust: Cahiers Marcel Proust* 1. Paris: Gallimard, 1927.

Sébastien, Robert, and Wsevolod de Vogt, eds. *Rencontres: Soirées franco-russes*. Paris: Cahiers de la Quinzaine, v. 1 hors série, 1930.

INDIVIDUAL AUTHORS
(MULTIPLE ENTRIES ARE LISTED CHRONOLOGICALLY)

A. B. "Sud'ba russkikh bezhentsev vo Frantsii." *Poslednie novosti* 1370 (October 12, 1924): 1.

Adamovich, Georgii [Sizif]. "Literaturnye zametki." *Zveno* 68 (May 19, 1924): 2.

———. "Literaturnye besedy." *Zveno* 94 (November 17, 1924): 2.

———. "Literaturnye besedy." *Zveno* 109 (March 2, 1925): 2.

———. "Literaturnye besedy." *Zveno* 125 (June 22, 1925): 2.

———. "Literaturnye besedy." *Zveno* 133 (August 17, 1925): 2.

———. "Literaturnye besedy." *Zveno* 167 (April 11, 1926): 1–2.

———. "Literaturnye besedy." *Zveno* 200 (November 28, 1926): 1–2.

———. "Literaturnye besedy." *Zveno* 203 (December 19, 1926): 1–2.

———. "Literaturnye besedy." *Zveno* 1 (July 1, 1927): 3–8.

———. "Literaturnye besedy." *Zveno* 2 (August 1, 1927): 67–75.

———. "Nikolai Ushakov—sovetskie prozaiki." *Zveno* 4 (1927): 188–94.

———. "O frantsuzskoi 'inquiétude' i o russkoi trevoge." *Poslednie novosti* 2822 (December 13, 1928): 2.

———. "Dva stikhotvoreniia." *Novyi korabl'* 4 (1928): 3.

———. "Literaturnye besedy." *Zveno* 4 (1928): 187–91.

———. "Literaturnye besedy." *Zveno* 5 (1928): 243–48.

———. "Sovremennye zapiski." *Poslednie novosti* 3144 (October 31, 1929): 2.

———. "Vadim Andreev: Nedug bytiia. Stikhi. Parizh 1928.—Georgii Raevskii: Strofy. Parizh. 1928.—Anatolii Shteiger: Etot den'. Stikhi. Parizh, 1928.—Vladimir Pozner: Stikhi na sluchai. Parizh, 1928." *Sovremennye zapiski* 38 (1929): 521–25.

———. "Novye pisateli." *Poslednie novosti* 3256 (February 20, 1930): 3.

———. "Literaturnaia nedelia: 'Vecher u Kler' G. Gazdanova." *Illiustrirovannaia Rossiia* 11, no. 252 (March 8, 1930): 14.

——— "Literaturnaia nedelia." *Illiustrirovannaia Rossiia* 30, no. 271 (July 19, 1930): 22.

———. "Literaturnye zametki." *Poslednie novosti* 3515 (November 6, 1930): 2.

———. "André Gide." *Cahiers de la Quinzaine* 20, no. 6 (1930): 21–30.

———. "Kommentarii." *Chisla* 1 (1930): 136–43.

———. "Nachalo." *Sovremennye zapiski* 41 (1930): 500–511.

———. "Soiuz molodykh poetov v Parizhe: Sb. III, 1930. Perekrestok. Sb. stikhov, Parizh 1930." *Chisla* 2–3 (1930): 239–40.

———. "O literature v emigratsii." *Poslednie novosti* 3732 (June 11, 1931): 2.

——— "Andre Zhid i SSSR." *Poslednie novosti* 4201 (September 22, 1932): 2.

———. "'Sovremennye zapiski' kn. 50-ia." *Poslednie novosti* 4236 (October 27, 1932): 3.

————. "Literaturnye zametki." *Poslednie novosti* 4257 (November 17, 1932): 2.

————. "O literature v emigratsii." *Sovremennye zapiski* 50 (1932): 327–39.

————. "Chelovecheskii dokument." *Poslednie novosti* 4369 (March 9, 1933): 3.

————. "Puteshestvie vglub' nochi." *Poslednie novosti* 4418 (April 27, 1933): 3.

————. "Na raznye temy." *Poslednie novosti* 4649 (December 14, 1933): 3.

————. "V. Ianovskii: Mir." *Sovremennye zapiski* 52 (1933): 457–58.

————. "Sirin." *Poslednie novosti* 4670 (January 4, 1934): 3.

————. "Parizhskie vpechatleniia." *Poslednie novosti* 4767 (April 12, 1934): 2.

————. "Sovremennye zapiski, kn. 55-ia." *Poslednie novosti* 4809 (May 24, 1934): 2.

————. "Chisla: Kniga desiataia." *Poslednie novosti* 4844 (June 28, 1934): 2.

————. "Sovremennye zapiski, kniga 56." *Poslednie novosti* 4977 (November 8, 1934): 3.

————. "Zhizn' i 'zhizn'.'" *Poslednie novosti* 5124 (April 4, 1935): 2.

————. "Otsenki Pushkina." *Poslednie novosti* 5145 (April 25, 1935): 2.

————. "Eshche o 'zdes'' i 'tam.'" *Poslednie novosti* 5208 (June 27, 1935): 3.

————. "Pamiati Poplavskogo." *Poslednie novosti* 5320 (October 17, 1935): 2.

————. "Kommentarii." *Sovremennye zapiski* 58 (1935): 319–27.

————. "Nesostoiavshaiasia progulka." *Sovremennye zapiski* 59 (1935): 288–96.

————. "Pis'ma o Lermontove." *Poslednie novosti* 5411 (January 16, 1936): 2.

————. "Perechityvaia 'Otchaianie.'" *Poslednie novosti* 5460 (March 5, 1936): 3.

————. "Literaturnye zametki." *Poslednie novosti* 5516 (April 30, 1936): 3.

————. "'Smert' v razsrochku' (novyi roman Selina)." *Poslednie novosti* 5620 (August 13, 1936): 3.

————. "Liubov' vtoraia." *Krug* 1 (1936): 187–88.

————. "'Sovremennye zapiski,' kniga 63." *Poslednie novosti* 5885 (May 6, 1937): 3.

————. "'Sovremennye zapiski,' kniga 64." *Poslednie novosti* 6039 (October 7, 1937): 3.

————. "Literaturnye zametki." *Poslednie novosti* 6088 (November 25, 1937): 3.

————. "Russkie zapiski." *Poslednie novosti* 6109 (December 16, 1937): 3.

————. "'Sovremennye zapiski,' kniga 65." *Poslednie novosti* 6144 (January 20, 1938): 3.

————. "Druz'ia i vragi." *Poslednie novosti* 6214 (March 31, 1938): 3.

————. "Literatura v 'Russkikh zapiskakh.' Kniga 10-ia." *Poslednie novosti* 6416 (October 20, 1938): 3.

————. "'Sovremennye zapiski,' kniga 67." *Poslednie novosti* 6437 (November 10, 1938): 3.

————. "Otkliki." *Poslednie novosti* 6464 (December 8, 1938): 3.

————. "Literaturnye zametki." *Poslednie novosti* 6485 (December 29, 1938): 3.

————. "Kommentarii." *Krug* 3 (1938): 133–38.

————. "G. Gazdanov: Istoriia odnogo puteshestviia." *Poslednie novosti* 6513 (January 26, 1939): 3.

————. "Iz mira literatury." *Russkie zapiski* 13 (1939): 193–97.

————. *Odinochestvo i svoboda.* New York: Izdatel'stvo imeni Chekhova, 1955.

————. "Poeziia v emigratsii." *Opyty* 4 (1955): 45–61.

————. "Pis'ma Vasiliiu Ianovskomu." Edited by Vadim Kreid. *Novyi zhurnal* 218 (2000): 121–40.

Adamovich, Georgii [Sizif], et al. "Autour de Maïakovsky." *Nouvelles littéraires, artistiques et scientifiques* 404 (July 12, 1930): 6.

A. E. "Molodye zarubezhnye poety: Stikhotvorenie. Poeziia i poeticheskaia kritika." *Volia Rossii* 6 (1928): 117–20.

Aldanov, Mark. "Novye knigi: Sovremennye zapiski." *Poslednie novosti* 242 (February 3, 1921): 3.

———. "Marcel Proust: A la recherche du temps perdu." *Sovremennye zapiski* 22 (1924): 452–55.

———. "Nashi ankety." *Zveno* 112 (March 23, 1925): 2.

———. "O romane." *Sovremennye zapiski* 52 (1933): 433–37.

———. "'Vstrechi': Kniga 1 i 2." *Poslednie novosti* 4718 (February 22, 1934): 3.

———. "O polozhenii emigrantskoi literatury." *Sovremennye zapiski* 61 (1936): 400–409.

———. "Vechera 'Sovremennykh zapisok.'" *Poslednie novosti* 5788 (January 28, 1937): 3.

Alloi, Vladimir. "Iz arkhiva V. V. Nabokova." *Minuvshee* 8 (1992): 274–81.

Andersen, Hans Christian. *Andersen's Fairy Tales.* Translated by E. Lucas and H. Paull. New York: Grosset & Dunlap, 1945.

Andreev, Nikolai. "Sovremennye zapiski: Kniga XLIX, 1932." *Volia Rossii* 4–6 (1932): 183–86.

Andreev, Vadim. *Istoriia odnogo puteshestviia.* Moscow: Sovetskii pisatel', 1974.

"Anketa o Pruste." *Chisla* 1 (1930): 272–78.

Annenkov, Georges, et al. Letter to the editor. *Les Nouvelles littéraires, artistiques et scientifiques* 400 (June 14, 1930): 6.

Aragon, Louis. *Une vague de rêves.* 1924. Reprint, Paris: Seghers, 1990.

———. *Le Paysan de Paris.* 1926. Reprint, Paris: Gallimard, 1996.

———. *Traité du style.* 1928. Reprint, Paris: Gallimard, 1996.

Arland, Marcel, "Chroniques: Sur un nouveau mal du siècle." *Revue européenne* (April 1, 1924): 47–51.

———. "Examen de conscience." *Cahiers du mois* 21–22 (1926): 12.

———. "Chronique des romans." *Nouvelle revue française* 46, no. 273 (1936): 964–70.

———. "Essais Critiques." *Nouvelle revue française* 52, no. 309 (1939): 1039–43.

———. *Essais et nouveaux essais critiques.* Paris: Gallimard, 1952.

———. "Les Faux-Monnayeurs, par André Gide (N.R.F. édit.)." 1926. Reprinted in "Le Dossier de presse des 'Faux-Monnayeurs.'" *Bulletin des Amis d'André Gide* 22 (1974): 25–27.

———. *Terres étrangères.* 1923. Reprint, Paris: Gallimard, 1996.

Artaud, Antonin. "Enquête: Le suicide est-il une solution." *La Révolution surréaliste* 2 (1925): 12.

Averbakh, Leopol'd. "My stroim sotsialisticheskuiu literaturu." *Literaturnaia gazeta* 19 (188), (April 23, 1932): 2.

Avksent'ev, Nikolai, et al. "Ot redaktsii." *Russkie zapiski* 1 (1937): 7.

Aymé, Marcel et al. "Un appel des écrivains français." *Candide* 668 (December 31, 1936): 9.

Babel', Isaak. *Odesskie rasskazy. Konarmiia.* Moscow: Izvestiia, 1994.

Bakhrakh, Aleksandr. "Gazdanych." *Russkaia mysl'* 3292 (January 24, 1980): 8–9.

————. "Berlinskii 'Klub Pisatelei.'" *Novoe russkoe slovo* (September 6, 1981): 5.

————. "Po pamiati, po zapisiam . . . II." *Novyi zhurnal* 190–91 (1993): 330–417.

Bakunina, Ekaterina. "Bagrovoe solntse gliadelo kak glaz raz'iarennyi byka." *Chisla* 6 (1932): 5.

————. "Dlia kogo i dlia chego pisat'." *Chisla* 6 (1932): 254–56.

————. *Telo.* Berlin: Parabola, 1933.

Balakshin, Pavel. "Emigrantskaia literatura." In *Kaliforniiskii al'manakh*, 135–38. San Francisco: Izdanie literaturno-khudozhestvennogo kruzhka goroda San Frantsisko, 1934.

Bal'mont, Konstantin. "Romenu Rollanu." *Poslednie novosti* 2551 (March 17, 1928): 3.

Baudelaire, Charles. *Les Fleurs du mal.* Paris: Librairie Larousse, 1991.

Beauvoir, Simone de. *Mémoires d'une jeune fille rangée.* Paris: Gallimard, 1958.

Bem, Al'fred. *Pis'ma o literature.* Prague: Slovansky ustav-Euroslavica, 1996.

Berberova, Nina. "Zelenaia lampa. Beseda 3." *Novyi korabl'* 2 (1927): 42–43.

————. *Oblegchenie uchasti: Shest' povestei.* Paris: YMCA-Press, 1949.

————. *The Italics Are Mine.* Translated by Ph. Radley. New York: Alfred A. Knopf, 1992.

————. *Kursiv moi.* Moscow: Soglasie, 1996.

Berberova, Nina, et al. "Ot redaktsii." *Novyi dom* 1 (1926): 2.

Berdiaev, Nikolai. "Vérité et mensonge du communisme." *Esprit* 1 (1932): 104–28.

————. "Iskaniia sotsial'noi pravdy molodoi Frantsiei." *Novyi grad* 9 (1934): 56–64.

————. "O profeticheskoi missii slova i mysli (k ponimaniiu svobody)." *Novyi grad* 10 (1935): 56–65.

————. "Po povodu 'Dnevnikov' B. Poplavskogo." *Sovremennye zapiski* 68 (1939): 441–46.

Berge, André. "A propos du surréalisme." *Cahiers du mois* 8 (1925): 32.

————. *L'Esprit de la littérature moderne.* Paris: Perrin et Cie, 1930.

Berl, Emmanuel. "Marcel Proust en jugement." *Nouvelles littéraires, artistiques et scientifiques* 86 (June 7, 1924): 8.

Bethea, David M. "Pis'ma V. Khodasevicha k N. Berberovoi." *Minuvshee* 5 (1988): 228–327.

Betz, Marcel. "Sur une crise de la conscience artistique." *Cahiers du moi* 1 (1924): 57–71.

————. *L'Incertain.* Paris: Éditions Émile-Paul Frères, 1925.

Beucler, André. "Les Russes de France." *Revue de Paris* 2 (March-April 1937): 866–96.

Bibikov, Aleksandr. "V poiskakh literaturnogo napravleniia." *Vozrozhdenie* 2116 (March 19, 1931): 4.

Billy, André. *L'époque contemporaine (1905–1930).* Paris: Éditions Jules Talladier, 1956.

————. "Les Faux-Monnayeurs, par André Gide." 1926. In "Le Dossier de presse des 'Faux-Monnayeurs.'" *Bulletin des amis d'André Gide* 22 (1974): 24.

Bitsilli, Petr. "Paralleli." *Sovremennye zapiski* 48 (1932): 334–45.

————. "Venok na grob romana." *Chisla* 7–8 (1933): 166–73.

———. "Zhizn' i literatura." *Sovremennye zapiski* 51 (1933): 273–87.

———. "Iakor'. Antologiia zarubezhnoi poezii." *Sovremennye zapiski* 60 (1936): 463–65.

———. "Neskol'ko zamechanii o sovremennoi zarubezhnoi literature." *Novyi grad* 11 (1936): 131–35.

———. "Vozrozhdenie allegorii." *Sovremennye zapiski* 61 (1936): 191–204.

Blok, Aleksandr. *Sobranie sochinenii v vos'mi tomakh.* Moscow and Leningrad: Khudozhestvennaia literatura, 1960.

Boiffard, J.-A., et al. "Préface." *Révolution surréaliste* 1 (1924): 1–2.

"Boris Poplavsky." *Nouvelles Littéraires, Artistiques et Scientifiques* 631 (November 2, 1935): 3.

Breton, André. "Pour Dada." *Nouvelle revue française* 15, no. 83 (1920): 208–15.

———. *Les Pas perdus.* Paris: Gallimard, 1924.

———. "Liubovnaia lodka razbilas' o byt/La barque de l'amour s'est brisée contre la vie courante." *Le Surréalisme au service de la révolution* 1 (1930): 16–22.

———. *Clair de terre.* 1923. Reprint, Paris: Gallimard, 1996.

———. *Manifestes du surréalisme.* Paris: Gallimard, 1996.

———. *Nadja.* 1928. Reprint, Paris: Gallimard, 1996.

———. *Poisson soluble.* 1924. Reprint, Paris: Gallimard, 1996.

Breton, André, and Philippe Soupault. *Les Champs magnétiques.* 1921. Reprint, Paris: Gallimard, 1967.

Brousson, Jacques. "Témoignages russes et littéraires." *Nouvelles littéraires, artistiques et scientifiques* 333 (March 2, 1929): 3.

Buenzod, Emmanuel. "Les Faux-Monnayeurs." 1926. In "Le Dossier de presse des 'Faux-Monnayeurs.'" *Bulletin des Amis d'André Gide* 26 (1975): 13–14.

Céline, Louis-Ferdinand. *Cahiers Céline 1: Céline et l'actualité littéraire 1932–1957.* Paris: Gallimard, 1976.

———. *Romans.* 2 vols. Paris: Gallimard, Bibliothèque de la Pléiade, 1981.

———. *Lettres à Joseph Garcin.* Paris: Librairie Monnier, 1987.

"'C'était la première fois que mon fils prenait un stupéfiant,' nous dit la mère de Maurice Poplasky." *Paris Midi* 2768 (October 10, 1935): 5.

Chardonne, Jacques. *Oeuvres complètes.* 6 vols. Paris: Éditions Albin Michel, 1947–55.

Charpentier, John. "Les romans. Martin-Chauffier: Patrice ou l'indifférent." *Mercure de France* (November 1, 1924): 753–54.

———. "Les Faux-Monnayeurs, par André Gide." 1926. In "Le Dossier de presse des 'Faux-Monnayeurs.'" *Bulletin des amis d'André Gide* 22 (1974): 21–24.

Chauméix, André. "Les nouveaux enfants du siècle (1)." *Revue des deux mondes* 37 (1926): 693–704.

———. "Les Jeunes et les littératures étrangères (1)." *Revue des deux mondes* 28 (1927): 697–708.

Chuzeville, Jean. "Lettres russes." *Mercure de France* 662 (January 15, 1926): 518–22.

Cocteau, Jean. *Romans, poésies, oeuvres diverses.* Paris: La Pochothèque, 1995.

———. *Thomas l'imposteur.* Paris: Gallimard, 1997.

Cor, Robert. "Marcel Proust et la jeune littérature." *Mercure de France* (May 15, 1926): 46–55.

Crastre, Victor. "Sur le suicide de Jacques Rigaut." *Nouvelle revue française* 35, no. 203 (1930): 251–55.

———. "Trois héros surréalistes: Jacques Vaché, Jacques Rigaut, René Crevel." *Gazette des lettres* 39 (1947): 6–7.

Cravan, Arthur. *Oeuvres.* Paris: Ivréa, 1992.

Cravan, Arthur, Jacques Rigaut, and Jacques Vaché. *Trois suicidés de la société.* Paris: Eric Losfeld, 1974.

Crémieux, Benjamin. "Le Bilan d'une enquête." *Nouvelle revue française* 21, no. 120 (1923): 287–94.

———. "Sincérité et imagination." *Nouvelle revue française* 23, no. 146 (1924): 538–48.

———. *XX-e siècle.* Paris: Gallimard, 1924.

———. "L'Année littéraire 1924." *Nouvelles littéraires, artistiques et scientifiques* 116 (January 3, 1925): 1.

———. "Les Livres." *Les Annales politiques et littéraires* 89, no. 2 (October 1, 1927): 323–24.

———. *Du côté de Marcel Proust.* Paris: Lemarget, 1929.

———. "Le roman depuis 1918." *Cahiers de la Quinzaine* 20, no. 8 (1930): 3–13.

———. "Où en est Marcel Proust?" *Candide* (August 28, 1930): 3.

———. *Inquiétude et reconstruction.* Paris: Editions R.-A. Corrêa, 1931.

Crevel, René. "Après Dada." *Nouvelles littéraires, artistiques et scientifiques* 69 (February 9, 1924): 5.

———. "Enquête: Le suicide est-il une solution." *La Révolution surréaliste* 2 (1925): 13.

———. "Mais si la mort n'était qu'un mot." *Le Disque vert. Sur le suicide* 1 (1925): 29–31.

———. *Détours.* Paris: Société nouvelle des éditions Pauvert, 1985.

Damanskaia, Avgusta [Arsenii Merich]. "Privilegirovannyi klass." *Poslednie novosti* 1856 (April 22, 1926): 3.

———. "Na ekrane moei pamiati." *Novyi zhurnal* 201 (1996): 177–207; 202 (1996): 152–88.

Daniel-Rops, Henri. "Proust et ses quatre critiques." *Cahiers du mois* 13 (1925): 70–71.

———. "Notes sur le réalisme de Proust." *Rouge et le noir. Cahier spécial. Hommage à Marcel Proust* (April 1928): 16–26.

———. "Enquête sur l'inquiétude contemporaine." *Cahiers de l'Etoile* 18 (1930): 1073.

———. "Proust, par Pierre Abraham." *Revue nouvelle* 67 (1931): 97–98.

———. "Un bilan de dix ans: De l'inquiétude à l'ordre." *Revue de deux mondes* 11 (1932): 178–203.

———. *Notre inquiétude.* Paris: Librairie académique Perrin, 1953.

D'Artan'ian. "Iurii Fel'zen: Obman." *Nord-Ost* 2 (1931): 31–32.

Dashkov, N. [Vladimir Veidle]. "Ob odnoi popytke franko-russkogo sblizheniia." *Vozrozhdenie* 1563 (September 12, 1929): 3.

———. "Komsnobizm." *Vozrozhdenie* 1997 (November 20, 1930): 3.

———. "Iz evropeiskoi literatury: Bolezn' veka." *Vozrozhdenie* 2004 (November 27, 1930): 4.

Datz, Marcel. "Examen de conscience." *Cahiers du mois* 21–22 (1926): 68.

Delage, Jean. *La Russie en exil.* Paris: Librairie Delagrave, 1930.

Desnos, Robert. *Destinée arbitraire.* Paris: Gallimard, 1996.

"Deux réfugiés russes s'adonnaient aux stupéfiants." *Le Petit Parisien* (October 10, 1935): 8.

Dolinin, Aleksandr. "V. V. Nabokov: Vtoroe dobavlenie k 'Daru.'" *Zvezda* 1 (2001): 85–109.

Dommartin, Henri. "Benjamin Crémieux et la littérature moderne." *Disque vert* 2 (1925): 66–74.

Dostoevskii, Fedor. *Sobranie sochinenii v dvenadtsati tomakh.* 12 vols. Moscow: Pravda, 1982.

Drieu La Rochelle, Pierre. "La véritable erreur des surréalistes." *Nouvelle Revue Française* 25, no. 143 (1925): 166–71.

———. "Paris, ville d'exilés." *Nouvelles littéraires, artistiques et scientifiques* 537 (January 28, 1933): 1.

———. *État civil.* 1921. Reprint, Paris: Gallimard, 1977.

———. *Le jeune Européen.* 1927. Reprinted under the title *Le jeune Européen suivi de Genève ou Moscou.* Paris: Gallimard, 1978.

———. *Sur les écrivains.* Paris: Gallimard, 1982.

———. *Journal d'un homme trompé.* 1928. Reprint, Paris: Gallimard, 1986.

———. *Le Feu follet suivi de Adieu à Gonzague.* 1931. Reprint, Paris: Gallimard, 1997.

"Drug Maiakovskogo." *Poslednie novosti* 3361 (June 5, 1930): 4.

Duhamel, Georges. *Essai sur le roman.* Paris: Marcelle Lesage, 1925.

———. *Scènes de la vie future.* Paris: Mercure de France, 1930.

Ehrhard, Jean. *Le roman français depuis Marcel Proust.* Paris: Editions de la Nouvelle Revue Critique, 1932.

Eliot, T. S. *The Shock of Recognition.* 2 vols. New York: Grosset & Dunlap, 1955.

Éluard, Paul. *Oeuvres complètes.* 2 vols. Paris: Gallimard, Bibliothèque de la Pléiade, 1968.

———. *Capitale de la douleur.* 1926. Reprint, Paris: Gallimard, 1997.

"Enquête: Le suicide est-il une solution." *La Révolution surréaliste* 1 (1924): 2.

Fedotov, Georgii. "O smerti, kul'ture i 'Chislakh.'" *Chisla* 4 (1930–31): 143–48.

———. "Jean Maxence et Nadejda Gorodetzky. Charles Péguy: Textes suivis de débats au Studio franco-russe. 'Cahiers de la Quinzaine.'" *Novyi Grad* 1 (1931): 99–100.

———. "Rossiia, Evropa i my." *Novyi grad* 2 (1932): 3–14.

———. "Bor'ba za iskusstvo." *Novyi grad* 10 (1935): 29–43.

———. "Zachem my zdes'?" *Sovremennye zapiski* 58 (1935): 433–44.

———. "Chetverodnevnyi Lazar'." *Krug* 1 (1936): 139–43.

———. "O parizhskoi poezii." In *Kovcheg: Sbornik russkoi zarubezhnoi literatury,* 189–98. New York: Association of Russian Writers in New York, 1942.

Fel'zen, Iurii. "Literaturnaia molodezh' iz 'Kochev'ia.'" *Segodnia vecherom* 188 (August 22, 1930): 4.

———. "Eva ou le journal interrompu." *Chisla* 2–3 (1930): 255–56.

———. "Irène Némirovsky 'David Golder.' Grasset 1929." *Chisla* 1 (1930): 246–47.

————. "Na odnom strannom raute v Parizhe." *Segodnia* 274 (1930): 4.

————. "Neravenstvo." *Chisla* 1 (1930): 95–116.

————. *Obman*. Paris: J. Povolozky & Co., 1930.

————. "O literaturnoi molodezhi." *Mansarda* 1 (1930): 26–28.

————. "Parizhskie vstrechi russkikh i frantsuzskikh pisatelei." *Segodnia* 252 (September 12, 1930): 5.

————. "Marc Chadourne: Cécile de la Folie." *Chisla* 4 (1930–31): 278.

————. "O Pruste i Dzhoise." *Chisla* 6 (1932): 215–18.

————. *Schast'e*. Berlin: Parabola, 1932.

————. "Probuzhdenie." *Sovremennye zapiski* 53 (1933): 146–73.

————. "O sud'be emigrantskoi literatury." *Mech* 13–14 (August 5, 1934): 18–20.

————. "Avtobiografiia." In *Kaliforniiskii Al'manakh*, 121. San Francisco: Izdanie literaturno-khudozhestvennogo kruzhka goroda San Frantsisko, 1934.

————. "Mal'ro. (Frantsuzskie 'Tridtsatye gody')." *Vstrechi* 1 (1934): 30–32.

————. "Fransua Moriak—Akademik." *Vstrechi* 1 (1934): 32–33.

————. "Lichnost' i obshchestvo: Anketa." *Vstrechi* 3 (1934): 129–33.

————. "Sergei Sharshun: Put' pravyi. Roman. 1934." *Chisla* 10 (1934): 283–85.

————. "Vozvrashchenie." *Chisla* 10 (1934): 167–86.

————. *Pis'ma o Lermontove*. Berlin: Izdatel'skaia kollegiia parizhskogo ob'edineniia pisatelei, 1935.

————. "My v Evrope: Krug. Beseda 11, 3 maia 1936." *Novyi grad* 11 (1936): 154–60.

————. "Vecherinka." *Krug* 1 (1936): 21–31.

————. "Razroznennye mysli." *Krug* 2 (1937): 129–31.

————. "Umiranie iskusstva." *Krug* 2 (1937): 124–29.

————. "Vozvrashchenie iz Rossii." *Krug* 2 (1937): 120–24.

————. "Kompozitsiia." *Sovremennye zapiski* 68 (1939): 88–113.

————. "Figuratsiia." *Bodrost'* 257 (January 14, 1940): 3–4.

Fernandez, Ramon. "La Figure de la vie dans les Faux-Monnayeurs." *Nouvelle revue française* 27, no. 189 (1926): 98–103.

————. *Messages*. Paris: Gallimard, 1926.

"Feuillets de la Semaine: Ce qu'on lit. A la recherche du temps perdu." *L'Opinion* (May 27, 1922): 581.

Fokht, Vsevolod. "Soirées de Paris." *France et Monde* 135 (1929): 59–63.

————. "Quelques aspects du roman russe depuis 1918." *Cahiers de la Quinzaine* 20, no. 8 (1930): 15–26.

Frank, N. "A la recherche du temps perdu." *Vendredi* 71 (March 12, 1937): 7.

Gabory, Georges. *Essai sur Marcel Proust*. Paris: Le Livre, 1926.

Garf, Andrei. "Literaturnye pelenki." *Novoe slovo* 12, no. 184 (March 20, 1938): 6.

Gayraud, Régis. "Iz arkhiva Il'i Zdanevicha: Perepiska s bratom." *Minuvshee* 5 (1988): 123–64.

Gazdanov, Gaito. "Zametki ob Edgare Po, Gogole i Mopassane." *Volia Rossii* 5–6 (1929): 96–107.

————. "Literaturnye priznaniia." *Vstrechi* 6 (1934): 259–62.

————. "O molodoi emigrantskoi literature." *Sovremennye zapiski* 60 (1936): 404–8.

————. "Boris Poplavskii: Snezhnyi chas." *Sovremennye zapiski* 61 (1936): 465–66.

———. "Krug: Al'manakh, Kniga tret'ia, Parizh, 1938." *Sovremennye zapiski* 68 (1939): 480–81.

———. *An Evening with Claire.* Translated by Jodi Daynard. Ann Arbor, Mich.: Ardis, 1988.

———. *Sobranie sochinenii v trekh tomakh.* 3 vols. Moscow: Soglasie, 1996.

Germain, André. *De Proust à Dada.* Paris: Éditions du Sagittaire, 1924.

Gide, André. *Incidences.* Paris: Gallimard, 1924.

———. "Son o Marsele Pruste." *Zveno* 190 (September 19, 1926): 8.

———. *Retour de l'U.R.S.S. suivi de Retouches à mon Retour de l'U.R.S.S.* Paris: Gallimard, 1950.

———. *Journal, 1889–1939.* Paris: Gallimard, Bibliothèque de la Pléiade, 1955.

———. *Journal des Faux-Monnayeurs.* Paris: Gallimard, 1995.

———. *Romans. Récits et soties: Oeuvres lyriques.* Paris: Gallimard, Bibilothèque de la Pléiade, 1998.

Gippius, Zinaida [Anton Krainii]. "Polet v Evropu." *Sovremennye zapiski* 18 (1924): 123–38.

———. "Nashi ankety." *Zveno* 113 (March 30, 1925): 3.

———. "Cherty liubvi." *Krug* 3 (1938): 139–49.

Golenishchev-Kutuzov, Il'ia. "Franko-russkaia studiia." *Vozrozhdenie* 2550 (May 26, 1932): 4.

———. "Sovremennye Zapiski: Kniga 49." *Vozrozhdenie* 2557 (June 2, 1932): 3–4.

Gomolitskii, Lev. *Arion.* Paris: n.p., 1939.

Gorlin, Mikhail. "Pokhval'noe slovo Gaito Gazdanovu." *Rul'* 2841 (March 30, 1930): 8.

Gorodetskaia, Nadezhda. "Les Débats." *Cahiers de la Quinzaine* 20, no. 5 (1930): 55.

———. "Spor pokolenii." *Vozrozhdenie* 2417 (January 14, 1932): 5.

Gourmont, Jean de. "Revue de la quinzaine. Léon Pierre-Quinte: Marcel Proust, sa vie, son oeuvre." *Mercure de France* (October 1, 1925): 178–80.

Gul', Roman. *Odvukon': Sovetskaia i emigrantskaia literatura.* New York: Most, 1973.

———. *"Ia unes Rossiiu": Apologiia emigratsii.* 2 vols. New York: Most, 1984.

Honnert, Robert. "L'Apport humain de Marcel Proust." *Cahiers de la Quinzaine* 20, no. 5 (1930): 11–22.

———. "Les Faux-Monnayeurs." 1926. In "Le Dossier de presse des 'Faux-Monnayeurs.'" *Bulletin des amis d'André Gide* 36 (1977): 74–75.

Ianovskii, Vasilii. *Koleso.* Paris and Berlin: Novye pisateli, 1930.

———. "Trinadtsatye." *Chisla* 2–3 (1930): 129–43.

———. *Mir.* Berlin: Parabola, 1931.

———. *Sachka: L'Enfant qui a faim.* Translated by E. Gaebelé-Cekhanovski. Paris: Éditions des Portiques, 1932.

———. "Rasskaz medika." *Chisla* 7–8 (1933): 149–53.

———. *Liubov' vtoraia: Parizhskaia povest'.* Paris: Izdatel'skaia kollegiia Parizhskoe ob'edinenie pisatelei, 1935.

———. "Ee zvali Rossiia." *Krug* 2 (1937): 55–66.

———. "Iurii German: 'Nashi znakomye.' Moskva. 1936." *Krug* 2 (1937): 158–59.

———. "Vol'no-amerikanskaia." *Sovremennye zapiski* 63 (1937): 90–118.

———. *Portativnoe bessmertie.* New York: Izdatel'stvo imeni Chekhova, 1953.

———. "Mimo nezamechennogo pokoleniia." *Novoe russkoe slovo* (October 2, 1955): 5.

———. *Polia Eliseiskie.* New York: Serebrianyi vek, 1983.

Iegulov, S. "Georgii Ivanov: Raspad Atoma. Izd. 'Dom knigi.'" *Gran'* 2 (1939): 79–80.

"Iskusstvo i politika." *Poslednie novosti* 3557 (December 18, 1930): 3.

Iulius, Anatolii. "Russkii literaturnyi Parizh 20-kh godov." *Sovremennik* 13 (1966): 84–90.

Ivanov, Georgii. "Sovremennye zapiski: Kniga XXXV-ia." *Poslednie novosti* 2626 (May 31, 1928): 3.

———. "Anketa o Pruste." *Chisla* 1 (1930): 272–73.

———. "V. Sirin: 'Mashen'ka,' 'Korol', dama, valet', 'Zashchita Luzhina,' 'Vozvrashchenie Chorba.'" *Chisla* 1 (1930): 233–35.

———. "Boris Poplavskii. Flagi. Izd. 'Chisla' Parizh: 1931." *Chisla* 5 (1931): 231–33.

———. *Raspad atoma.* Paris: Dom knigi, 1938.

———. *Sobranie sochinenii v trekh tomakh.* 3 vols. Moscow: Soglasie, 1994.

Ivask, Iurii. "Chudaki." In *Tri iubileia Andreia Sedykh,* 183–87. New York: Litfund, 1982.

Izvol'skaia, Elena. "Commerce." *Zveno* 123 (June 8, 1925): 2–3.

———. "Sud i pravosudie: 'Bella' Zhana Zhirodu." *Poslednie novosti* 1800 (February 25, 1926): 3.

———. "Affirmations." *Esprit* 18 (1934): 1051–53.

———. "Frantsuzskaia molodezh' i problemy sovremennosti." *Novyi grad* 12 (1937): 122–31.

———. "Twenty-Five Years of Russian Émigré Literature." *The Russian Review* 1, no. 2 (1942): 61–73.

Jaham-Desrivaux, Louis. "L'Esthétique des Faux-Monnayeurs." 1928. In "Le Dossier de presse des 'Faux-Monnayeurs.'" *Bulletin des amis d'André Gide* 26 (1975): 3–13.

Jakobson, Roman. "O pokolenii, rastrativshem svoikh poetov." In *Smert' Vladimira Maiakovskogo,* 8–34. The Hague and Paris: Mouton, 1975.

Jaloux, Édmond. *L'Esprit des livres.* Paris: Plon, 1923.

———. "Souvenirs du jardin détruit, par René Boylesve (Ferenczi)." *Nouvelles littéraires, artistiques et scientifiques* 107 (November 1, 1924): 3.

———. "L'Évolution de M. Henry Bernstein." *Candide* (November 6, 1924): 3.

———. "Esprit des livres: Sur Jean Paul et sur Marcel Proust." *Nouvelles littéraires, artistiques et scientifiques* 202 (August 28, 1926): 3.

———. "Esprit des livres: L'Autre sommeil, par Julien Green. Le Feu follet, par Drieu La Rochelle." *Nouvelles littéraires, artistiques et scientifiques* 450 (May 30, 1931): 3.

———. "Voyage au bout de la nuit." *Nouvelles littéraires, artistiques et scientifiques* 530 (December 10, 1932): 3.

———. "Les Faux-Monnayeurs, par André Gide (Nouvelle Revue Française)." 1926. In "Le Dossier de presse des 'Faux-Monnayeurs.'" *Bulletin des amis d'André Gide* 27 (1975): 9–15.

Josephson, Matthew. *Life among the Surrealists.* New York: Holt, Rinehart & Winston, 1962.

Kantor, Mikhail. "Nado pomnit'." *Novoe russkoe slovo* (March 7, 1955): 2.

Kel'berin, Lazar'. "V. Ianovskii. Koleso." *Chisla* 2–3 (1930): 251.

———. "L. F. Céline. Voyage au bout de la nuit." *Chisla* 9 (1933): 223–24.

———. "Iurii Fel'zen. 'Pis'ma o Lermontove' Parizh. 1935." *Krug* 1 (1936): 183–85.

Kelli, D. "Andre Morua o russkoi literature." *Novaia gazeta* 2 (March 15, 1931): 1–2.

Khlebnikov, Velimir. *Tvoreniia.* Moscow: Sovetskii pisatel', 1987.

Khodasevich, Vladislav. "O formalizme i formalistakh." *Vozrozhdenie* 646 (March 10, 1927): 2–3.

———. "Poeticheskaia beseda." *Vozrozhdenie* 1640 (November 28, 1929): 3.

———. "'Chisla.'" *Vozrozhdenie* 1759 (March 27, 1930): 3.

———. "O Maiakovskom." *Vozrozhdenie* 1787 (April 24, 1930): 3–4.

———. "Letuchie listy." *Vozrozhdenie* 1864 (July 10, 1930): 3–4.

———. "Knigi i liudi." *Vozrozhdenie* 2431 (January 28, 1932): 3–4.

———. "Podvig." *Vozrozhdenie* 2529 (May 5, 1932): 3.

———. "Knigi i liudi." *Vozrozhdenie* 2781 (January 12, 1933): 3.

———. "Rossica." *Vozrozhdenie* 2956 (July 6, 1933): 3–4.

———. "Krizis poezii." *Vozrozhdenie* 3235 (April 12, 1934): 3–4.

———. "Novye stikhi." *Vozrozhdenie* 3585 (March 28, 1935): 3–4.

———. "Zhalost' i 'zhalost'.'" *Vozrozhdenie* 3599 (April 11, 1935): 3–4.

———. "Knigi i liudi." *Vozrozhdenie* 3732 (August 22, 1935): 3.

———. "O smerti Poplavskogo." *Vozrozhdenie* 3788 (October 17, 1935): 3–4.

———. "O zadachakh molodoi literatury." *Vozrozhdenie* 3851 (December 19, 1935): 3–4.

———. "Pis'ma o Lermontove." *Vozrozhdenie* 3858 (December 26, 1935): 3–4.

———. "'Sovremennye zapiski.'" *Vozrozhdenie* 3935 (March 12, 1936): 3–4.

———. "Dva poeta." *Vozrozhdenie* 3984 (April 30, 1936): 3.

———. "Avtor, geroi, poet." *Krug* 1 (1936): 167–71.

———. "'Sovremennye zapiski,' kn. 63-ia." *Vozrozhdenie* 4078 (May 15, 1937): 9.

———. "'Sovremennye zapiski,' kniga 64." *Vozrozhdenie* 4101 (October 15, 1937): 9.

———. "Raspad atoma." *Vozrozhdenie* 4116 (January 28, 1938): 9.

———. "'Sovremennye zapiski,' kn. 65." *Vozrozhdenie* 4120 (February 25, 1938): 9.

———. "'Sovremennye zapiski,' kniga 66." *Vozrozhdenie* 4137 (June 24, 1938): 9.

———. "Knigi i liudi." *Vozrozhdenie* 4157 (November 11, 1938): 9.

———. "Istoriia odnogo puteshestviia." *Vozrozhdenie* 4163 (December 23, 1938): 9.

———. *Literaturnye stat'i i vospominaniia.* New York: Izdatel'stvo imeni Chekhova, 1954.

———. *Koleblemyi trenozhnik.* Moscow: Sovetskii pisatel', 1991.

Khokhlov, German [G. Kh., Al. Novik]. "Gaito Gazdanov: 'Vecher u Kler.'" *Russkii magazin* 1 (1930): 25–27.

———. "Iurii Fel'zen: Obman. Izd. Ia. Povolotskii i K-o, Parizh, 1930." *Volia Rossii* 1–2 (1931): 198–99.

———. "Iurii Fel'zen: Obman. Izd. Ia. Povolotskii. Parizh, 1930." *Sovremennye zapiski* 46 (1931): 499–501.

———. "Da byl li mal'chik? . . ." *Literaturnaia gazeta* 30, no. 346 (March 12, 1934): 2.

Knut, Dovid. "Russkii Monparnass." *Poslednie novosti* 2444 (December 1, 1927): 3.

———. "Zelenaia lampa: Beseda 3." *Novyi korabl'* 2 (1927): 39–47.

———. "Materialy Soiuza Russkikh Pisatelei i Zhurnalistov v Pol'she." *Mech* 3–4 (May 27, 1934): 18–19.

———. *Sobranie sochinenii v dvukh tomakh.* 2 vols. Jerusalem: The Hebrew University of Jerusalem, 1997–98.

Kostrov, Mikhail. "Lui Aragon." *Vozrozhdenie* 905 (November 24, 1927): 3.

"Krug: Beseda piataia 16 dekabria 1935 goda." *Novyi grad* 11 (1936): 138–39.

Kul'man, Nikolai. "Novyi dom: 3-ia kniga." *Vozrozhdenie* 653 (March 17, 1927): 3.

Kuskova, Ekaterina. "O nezamechennom pokolenii." *Novoe russkoe slovo* (September 11, 1955): 2.

Lacretelle, Jacques de. *La Vie inquiète de Jean Hermelin.* Paris: Bernard Grasset, 1920.

———. "Une heure avec M. Jacques de Lacretelle." *Nouvelles littéraires, artistiques et scientifiques* 138 (June 6, 1925): 1–2.

Lalou, René. *Défence de l'homme. (Intelligence et sensualité).* Paris: Éditions du Sagittaire, 1926.

———. *Histoire de la littérature contemporaine (1870 à nos jours).* Paris: Les éditions G. Crès et Cie, 1928.

———. "Les Débats." *Cahiers de la Quinzaine* 20, no.5 (1930): 49–50.

Lanoë, J. "Le Corps, par Catherine Bakounine." *Nouvelle revue française* 43, no. 255 (1934): 919.

Larnac, Jean. "Le roman, d'après André Gide: À propos des 'Faux-Monnayeurs.'" 1927. In "Le Dossier de presse des 'Faux-Monnayeurs.'" *Bulletin des amis d'André Gide* 26 (1975): 15 –19.

Ledré, Charles. *Les émigrés russes en France.* Paris: Spes, 1930.

———.*Trois romanciers russes: Ivan Bunine, Alexandre Kouprine, Marc Aldanov.* Paris: Nouvelles Éditions Latines, 1935.

Leiris, Michel. *L'Âge d'homme.* Paris: Gallimard, 1995.

Leis, D. [Vladimir Veidle]. "Pontin'i." *Zveno* 191 (September 26, 1926): 2–3.

———. "Bolezn' veka." *Zveno* 220 (April 17, 1927): 5–6.

Lemonnier, Léon. *Manifeste du roman populiste.* Paris: Jacques Bernard, 1929.

Leonidov, A. "Boris Poplavskii. Flagi." *Novaia gazeta* 1 (March 1, 1931): 5–6.

Leving, Iurii. "Literaturnyi podtekst palestinskogo pis'ma Vladimira Nabokova." *Novyi zhurnal* 214 (1999): 116–33.

Levinson, Andrei. "Svoe i chuzhoe. 'Mir iskusstva.' Dva khudozhnika." *Sovremennye zapiski* 6 (1921): 247–52.

———. "Siuares." *Sovremennye zapiski* 7 (1921): 351–62.

———. "La poésie chez les Soviets: Le suicide de Mayakovsky." *Nouvelles littéraires, artistiques et scientifiques* 398 (May 31, 1930): 6.

———. Letter to the editor. *Les Nouvelles littéraires, artistiques et scientifiques* 400 (June 14, 1930): 6.

"Lichnost' i obshchestvo: Anketa." *Vstrechi* 3 (1934): 129–33.

"Literatura ne kormit." *Poslednie novosti* 3207 (January 2, 1930): 3.

Liubimov, Lev. "Skandal na sobranii 'Chisel.'" *Vozrozhdenie* 2858 (March 30, 1933): 3.

Livak, Leonid. "K istorii 'Parizhskoi shkoly'. Pis'ma Anatoliia Shteigera, 1937–1943." *Canadian-American Slavic Studies* 37, no. 1–2 (2003): 83–120.

Lukash, Ivan. "Zametki na poliakh: O literaturnom dvizheni." *Vozrozhdenie* 1906 (August 21, 1930): 3–4.

Lunts, Lev. *Rodina i drugie proizvedeniia.* Jerusalem: n.p., 1981.

L'vov, Lolii. "Belletristika 'Chisel.'" *Rossiia i slavianstvo* 97 (October 4, 1930): 3.

Malespine, Emile. "Côté doublure." *Manomètre* 5 (1924): 77.

Mandel'shtam, Iurii. "Poteriannoe bezrazlichie." *Vozrozhdenie* 3193 (March 1, 1934): 4.

———. "Dnevnik obmanutogo cheloveka." *Vozrozhdenie* 3557 (February 28, 1935): 4.

———. "Smert' v kredit." *Vozrozhdenie* 4035 (July 18, 1936): 5.

———. "Frantsuzskie pisateli o russkikh." *Vozrozhdenie* 4060 (January 9, 1937): 9.

———. "Evoliutsiia Selina." *Vozrozhdenie* 4063 (January 30, 1937): 9.

———. "Dnevnik pisatelia." *Vozrozhdenie* 4148 (September 9, 1938): 9.

Mandel'shtam, Osip. *Sobranie sochinenii.* 2 vols. Moscow: Terra, 1991.

Manziarly, Irma. "La soirée chez Claire, par Gaito Gazdanov." *Cahiers de l'Etoile* 14 (1930): 306.

Marcel, Gabriel. "Souvenirs de ma vie littéraire, de Maxime Gorki." *Nouvelle revue française* 22, no. 125 (1924): 253–54.

———. "Proust, alchimiste spirituel." *Europe nouvelle* 14 (January 31, 1931): 138–39.

Marin, Robert. "André Gide, Les Faux-Monnayeurs." 1925–26. In "Le Dossier de presse des 'Faux-Monnayeurs.'" *Bulletin des amis d'André Gide* 65 (1985): 122–24.

Martin-Chauffier, Louis. "Besedy v Pontigny." *Chisla* 1 (1930): 253–54.

Massis, Henri. *Réflexions sur l'art du roman.* Paris: Librairie Plon, 1927.

———. "Faillite d'André Gide." *La Revue universelle* (September 15, 1929): 737–43.

Martineau, Henri. "Les Faux-Monnayeurs." 1926. In "Le Dossier de presse des 'Faux-Monnayeurs.'" *Bulletin des amis d'André Gide* 31 (1976): 31.

Mauriac, François. "Sur la tombe de Marcel Proust." *Revue hébdomadaire* 12 (1922): 5–9.

———. "Une heure avec M. François Mauriac." *Nouvelles littéraires, artistiques et scientifiques* (May 26, 1923): 1–2.

———. "Le Bon apôtre, par Philippe Soupault." *Nouvelle revue française* 21, no. 122 (1923): 610–11.

———. *Proust.* Paris: Marcelle Lesage, 1926.

Maxence, Jean. "Les Débat." *Cahiers de la Quinzaine* 20, no. 6 (1930): 44.

———. "Les Débat." *Cahiers de la Quinzaine* 20, no. 8 (1930): 37.

Merezhkovskii, Dmitrii. "O svobode i Rossii." *Novyi korabl'* 1 (1927): 20–22.

Mirskii, Dmitrii. "Zametki ob emigrantskoi literature." *Evraziia* 7 (1929): 6.

Mochul'skii, Konstantin. "Nishchie dukhom." *Zveno* 199 (November 21, 1926): 3–4.

———. "Novoe vo frantsuzskoi literature." *Zveno* 221 (April 24, 1927): 2–4.

———. "Krizis voobrazheniia." *Zveno* 2 (1927): 75–81.

———. "Novyi chelovek." *Poslednie novosti* 2913 (March 14, 1929): 3.

———. "Molodye poety." *Poslednie novosti* 3004 (June 13, 1929): 2.

———. "Romantizm i my." *Poslednie novosti* 3354 (May 29, 1930): 3.

Mogilianskii, Nikolai. "Mir iskusstva." *Poslednie novosti* 368 (June 30, 1921): 2.

Montfort, Eugène. "Chronique des romans." *Marges* 30, no. 122 (August 15, 1924): 299–304.

Monthérlant, Henri de. "Partageons la liberté." *Candide* 668 (December 31, 1936): 9.

Morand, Paul. *Tendres Stocks*. Paris: Gallimard, 1921.

———. *Ouvert la nuit suivi de Fermé la nuit*. Paris: Gallimard, 1983.

———. *L'Art de mourir*. Paris: L'Esprit du temps, 1992.

Muratov, Pavel. "Iskusstvo prozy." *Sovremennye zapiski* 29 (1926): 240–58.

Nabokov, Vladimir. "Anketa o Pruste." *Chisla* 1 (1930): 274.

———. "Arest Chernyshevskogo (iz neizdannoi glavy romana 'Dar')." *Bodrost'* 256 (December 31, 1939): 3–4.

———. "Literaturnyi smotr. Svobodnyi sbornik. Parizh, 1939." *Sovremennye zapiski* 70 (1940): 283–85.

———. *Dar*. New York: Izdatel'stvo imeni Chekhova, 1952.

———. *Lolita*. New York: G. P. Putnam's Sons, 1955.

———. *Vesna v Fial'te i drugie rasskazy*. New York: Izd. im. Chekhova, 1956.

———. *Lectures on Russian Literature*. Edited by Fredson Bowers. New York: Harcourt Brace Jovanovich, 1981.

———. *Rasskazy. Priglashenie na kazn'. Roman. Esse, interv'iu, retsenzii*. Moscow: Kniga, 1989.

———. *Kamera obskura: Romany*. Moscow: Sovremennik, 1990.

———. *Strong Opinions*. New York: Vintage International, 1990.

———. *The Gift*. New York: Vintage International, 1991.

———. *Sobranie sochinenii russkogo perioda v piati tomakh*. 5 vols. St. Petersburg: Simpozium, 1999–2000.

———. *Nabokov's Butterflies: Unpublished and Uncollected Writings*. Translated by Dmitri Nabokov. Edited by Brian Boyd and Robert Michael Pyle. Boston: Beacon Press, 2000.

"O bditel'nosti i otvetstvennosti." *Pravda* 83, no. 8329 (March 25, 1935): 1.

Odoevtseva, Irina. *Na beregakh Seny*. Paris: La Presse Libre, 1983.

Osokin, Sergei. "Boris Poplavskii.—'V venke iz voska.'" *Russkie zapiski* 11 (1938): 197–98.

Osorgin, Mikhail. "'Sovremennye zapiski': Knizhka 30-ia." *Poslednie novosti* 2136 (January 27, 1927): 2.

———. "Vecher u Kler." *Poslednie novosti* 3242 (February 6, 1930): 3.

———. "Kniga Chisel." *Poslednie novosti* 3284 (March 20, 1930): 3.

———. "Bez kliukvy." *Poslednie novosti* 3326 (May 1, 1930): 3.

———. "Pozhelaniia." *Novaia gazeta* 1 (March 1, 1931): 3.

———. "Chisla.— Sborniki pod redaktsiei I. V. de Mantsiarli i N. A. Otsupa. Kn. 4-aia. Parizh, 1930–1931 g." *Sovremennye zapiski* 46 (1931): 505–8.
———. "Podvig." *Poslednie novosti* 4236 (October 27, 1932): 3.
———. "Sud'ba zarubezhnoi knigi." *Sovremennye zapiski* 54 (1934): 385–90.
———. "V. Sirin: 'Kamera obskura.'" *Sovremennye zapiski* 54 (1934): 458–60.
———. "Liubov' vtoraia." *Poslednie novosti* 5222 (July 11, 1935): 3.
———. "O 'molodykh pisateliakh.'" *Poslednie novosti* 5474 (March 19, 1936): 3.
———. "Literaturnye razmyshleniia." *Poslednie novosti* 6169 (February 14, 1938): 2.
———. "Anri Truaia." *Poslednie novosti* 6471 (December 15, 1938): 3.
"Ot redaktsii." *Chisla* 1 (1930): 5–7.
"Ot redaktsii." *Lloid-zhurnal* 1 (1931): 3–4.
Otsup, Nikolai. "Gaito Gazdanov: Vecher u Kler." *Chisla* 1 (1930): 232–33.
———. "Ne tol'ko v nash poslednii chas." *Chisla* 1 (1930): 23.
———. "Iz dnevnika." *Chisla* 2–3 (1930): 155–66.
———. "V. S. Ianovskii. Mir. Iz-vo Parabola. Berlin, 1932." *Chisla* 6 (1932): 262–64.
———. "Klim Samgin." *Chisla* 7–8 (1933): 178–83.
———. "Iz dnevnika." *Chisla* 9 (1933): 130–34.
———. *Literaturnye ocherki.* Paris: n.p., 1961.
Pachmuss, Temira. "Zinaida Gippius: Istoriia emigrantskoi intelligentsii." *Russian Language Journal* 26, no. 93 (1972): 3–13; no. 94–95 (1972): 3–19.
Péguy, Marcel. "Les Débats." *Cahiers de la Quinzaine* 20, no. 5 (1930): 54–55.
P.-H.-S. "Catherine Bakounine: Le Corps." *Esprit* 30 (1935): 969.
Picard, Gaston. "Faut-il revenir aux Écoles littéraires? Grande enquête dirigée par Gaston Picard." *Revue mondiale* 192 (1929): 233.
Pierre-Quint, Léon. *Marcel Proust: Sa vie, son oeuvre.* Paris: Éditions du Sagittaire, 1925.
Pikel'nyi, Roman. "Na temu 'iskusstvo i byt.'" *Versty* 1 (1926): 187–92.
Pil'skii, Petr. "Gaito Gazdanov: Vecher u Kler." *Segodnia* 62 (March 3, 1930): 6.
———. "Novyi zhurnal—'Chisla' 1." *Segodnia* 69 (March 10, 1930): 6.
———. "Kniga. V. S. Ianovskii. Koleso. Povest'." *Segodnia* 76 (March 17, 1930): 6.
———. "Tikhii gospodin s mikroskopom." *Segodnia* 326 (November 22, 1930): 8.
———. "Iurii Fel'zen. Obman." *Chisla* 4 (1930–31): 267–69.
———. "'Sovremennye zapiski,' kniga 63." *Segodnia* 117 (April 29, 1937): 3.
"Po literaturnym sobraniiam." *Chisla* 9 (1933): 197–200.
Poplavskii, Boris. "Zametki o poezii." *Stikhotvorenie* 2 (1928): 28–29.
———. "Molodaia russkaia zhivopis' v Parizhe." *Chisla* 1 (1930): 192–96.
———. "O misticheskoi atmosfere molodoi literatury v emigratsii." *Chisla* 2–3 (1930): 308–11.
———. "Po povodu . . ." *Chisla* 4 (1930–31): 161–75.
———. "O smerti i zhalosti v 'Chislakh.'" *Novaia gazeta* 3 (April 1, 1931): 3.
———. "Literaturnaia anketa: Chto vy dumaete o svoem tvorchestve." *Chisla* 5 (1931): 287.
———. "Sredi somnenii i ochevidnostei." *Utverzhdeniia* 3 (1932): 96–105.
———. "Chelovek i ego znakomye." *Chisla* 9 (1933): 135–38.
———. "Vokrug 'Chisel.'" *Chisla* 10 (1934): 204–9.
———. "Pis'ma Iu. P. Ivasku." *Gnozis* 5–6 (1979): 201–11.

————. *Sobranie sochinenii.* 3 vols. Berkeley, Cal.: Berkeley Slavic Specialties, 1980–81.

————. *Domoi s nebes: Romany.* St. Petersburg and Düsseldorf: Logos-Goluboi vsadnik, 1993.

————. "Dnevnik T." *Novyi zhurnal* 195 (1994): 175–211.

————. *Neizdannoe.* Moscow: Khristianskoe izdatel'stvo, 1996.

————. *Pokushenie s negodnymi sredstvami.* Moscow: Gileia-Goluboi vsadnik, 1997.

————. *Avtomaticheskie stikhi.* Moscow: Soglasie, 1999.

————. *Dadafoniia.* Moscow: Gileia, 1999.

Poplavskii, Iulian. "Boris Poplavskii." *Nov'* 8 (1935): 144–48.

Postnikov, Semen. "O molodoi emigrantskoi literature." *Volia Rossii* 5–6 (1927): 215–25.

Pourtalès, Guy de. *De Hamlet à Swann.* Paris: Crès, 1924.

Pozner, Vladimir. "L'âme slave et l'esprit gaulois." *Nouvelles littéraires, artistiques et scientifiques* 193 (June 26, 1926): 6.

————. "Les Débats." *Cahiers de la Quinzaine* 20, no. 8 (1930): 33.

"Proletarskaia poeziia na pod'eme." *Literaturnaia gazeta* 19, no. 188 (April 23, 1932): 1.

"Protiv burzhuaznykh tribunov pod maskoi sovetskogo pisatelia: Protiv pereklichki s beloi emigratsiei." *Literaturnaia gazeta* 20 (September 2, 1929): 1.

Proust, Marcel. *Le Temps retrouvé.* Paris: Gallimard, 1996.

————. *Albertine disparue.* Paris: Gallimard, 1997.

————. *A l'ombre des jeunes filles en fleurs.* Paris: Gallimard, 1997.

————. *Contre Sainte-Beuve.* Paris: Gallimard, 1997.

————. *Du Côté de chez Swann.* Paris: Gallimard, 1997.

————. *La Prisonnière.* Paris: Gallimard, 1997.

————. *Le Côté de Guermantes I & II.* Paris: Gallimard, 1997.

————. *Sodome et Gomorrhe.* Paris: Gallimard, 1997.

Pushkin, Aleksandr. *Polnoe sobranie sochinenii v desiati tomakh.* Moscow: Izdatel'stvo Akademii Nauk SSSR, 1956–58.

Quincey, Thomas de. *Collected Writings.* New York: Johnson Reprint Corporation, 1968.

Raevskii, Georgii. "O russkoi trevoge i nemetskoi Sensucht." *Vozrozhdenie* 1297 (December 20, 1928): 4.

————. "O 'kontse' iskusstva." *Vozrozhdenie* 1794 (May 1, 1930): 3–4.

Rambaud, Henri. "Sur la tombe de Marcel Proust." *Nouvelles littéraire, artistiques et scientifiques* 8 (December 9, 1922): 3.

Rappoport, Iurii. "Konets zarubezh'ia." *Sovremennye zapiski* 69 (1939): 373–81.

Raskol'nikov, Fedor. "Pis'mo v redaktsiiu." *Literaturnaia gazeta* 20 (September 2, 1929): 1.

Remizov, Aleksei. "Samoe znachitel'noe proizvedenie russkoi literatury poslednego piatiletiia." *Novaia gazeta* 3 (April 1, 1931): 1–2.

Reznikov, Daniil. "Chto budet s nashei literaturoi?" *Novaia gazeta* 1 (March 1, 1931): 4.

Ribemont-Dessaignes, Georges. *Déjà jadis.* Paris: René Julliard, 1958.

Rigaut, Jacques. Untitled article. *Littérature* 17 (1920): 5–8.

———. "Jacques Rigaut." *La Révolution surréaliste* 12 (1929): 55–57.

———. *Écrits posthumes.* Paris: Gallimard, 1970.

———. *Écrits.* Paris: Gallimard, 1997.

Rimbaud, Arthur. *Poésie. Une saison en enfer. Illuminations.* Paris: Gallimard, 1994.

Rivière, Jacques. "Reconnaissance à Dada." *Nouvelle revue française* 15, no. 83 (1920): 216–37.

———. "La Crise du concepte de littérature." *Nouvelle revue française* 22, no. 75 (1924): 159–70.

———. *Quelques progrès dans l'étude du coeur humain: Cahiers Marcel Proust* 13, nouvelle série. Paris: Gallimard, 1985.

Robertfrance, Jacques. "Freud ou l'opportunisme." *Nouvelles littéraires, artistiques et scientifiques* 104 (October 11, 1924): 5.

Romashov, Boris. "Unichtozhit' vragov, pokhoronit' manilovshchinu." *Literaturnaia gazeta* 48, no. 611 (August 27, 1936): 4.

Rozental', Mikhail, and Evgenii Usievich. "Zadachi literaturnoi kritiki (V poriadke obsuzhdeniia voprosa na plenume pravleniia Soiuza pisatelei)." *Pravda* 60, no. 8306 (March 2, 1935): 4.

Rudnev, Vadim. "W. Ch. Huntington: The Homesick Million." *Sovremennye zapiski* 55 (1934): 449–50.

Saurat, Denis. *Tendances.* Paris: Éditions du monde moderne, 1928.

———. "Lettres de Marcel Proust à la Comtesse de Noailles." *Nouvelle revue française* 35, no. 286 (1931): 340–44.

Sautel, Léon. "Découverte de Proust." *Rouge et le noir. Cahier spécial. Hommage à Marcel Proust.* (April 1928): 99–102.

Savel'ev, A. [Savel'ev, S., Savelii Sherman]. "Chisla, no. 1." *Rul'* 2837 (March 26, 1930): 2–3.

———. "G. Gazdanov, Vecher u Kler." *Rul'* 2843 (April 2, 1930): 5.

———. "Iurii Fel'zen: Obman." *Rul'* 3098 (February 4, 1931): 3.

———. "V. S. Ianovskii: Liubov' vtoraia. Izd. Koll. Par. Ob''ed. Pisatelei. Parizh. 1936." *Sovremennye zapiski* 62 (1936): 443–44.

———. "Iu. Fel'zen: Pis'ma o Lermontove. Izdatel'skaia Kollegiia Parizhsk. Ob''edin. Pisatelei. Parizh. 1936." *Sovremennye zapiski* 62 (1936): 444–45.

Sazonova, Iuliia. "V zashchitu . . . tsenzury." *Poslednie novosti* 3130 (October 17, 1929): 3.

———. "Vstrecha frantsuzskikh i russkikh pisatelei." *Poslednie novosti* 3324 (April 29, 1930): 5.

———. "K. Fedin: 'Brat'ia.' Petropolis, Berlin 1929." *Chisla* 1 (1930): 237–39.

———. "Slavianskaia dusha." *Poslednie novosti* 4460 (June 8, 1933): 3.

Sedykh, Andrei. "U V. V. Sirina." *Poslednie novosti* 4243 (November 3, 1932): 2.

———. "Tragicheskaia smert' Borisa Poplavskogo." *Poslednie novosti* 5313 (October 10, 1935): 4.

Ségur, Nicolas. "La Jeune littérature." *Revue mondiale* 166, no. 18 (1925): 181–85.

Shakespeare, William. *The Complete Works of William Shakespeare.* New York: Avenel Books, Crown Publishers Inc., 1975.

Shakhovskaia, Zinaida. *Otrazheniia.* Paris: YMCA-Press, 1975.

———. *V poiskakh Nabokova.* Paris: La Presse Libre, 1979.

Shapiro, Gabriel. "Desiat' pisem Dovida Knuta." *Cahiers du Monde russe et soviétique* 27, no.2 (1986): 191–208.

Sharshun, Sergei. "Magicheskii realizm." *Chisla* 6 (1932): 229–31.

———. "Moe uchastie vo frantsuzskom dadaisticheskom dvizhenii." *Vozdushnye puti* 5 (1967): 168–74.

Shenshin, K. "O Marsele Pruste." *Zveno* 1 (January 1, 1928): 24–29.

Shklovskii, Viktor. "Serapionovy brat'ia." *Knizhnyi ugol* (1921): 20–21.

———. "Pamiatnik nauchnoi oshibke." *Literaturnaia gazeta* 4, no. 41 (January 27, 1930): 1.

———. *Khod konia: Sbornik statei.* Moscow: Sol', 1999.

Shletser, Boris. "Zhizn' slova. (Pol' Klodel')." *Sovremennye zapiski* 4 (1921): 308–20.

———. "Zerkal'noe tvorchestvo (Marsel' Prust)." *Sovremennye zapiski* 6 (1921): 227–38.

———. "Marsel' Prust." *Zveno* 2 (February 12, 1923): 2.

———. "Novoe v zapadnoi literature." *Zveno* 45 (December 10, 1923): 2.

Shmelev, Ivan. "Anketa o Pruste." *Chisla* 1 (1930): 277–78.

Slonim, Mark. "Literaturnyi dnevnik." *Volia Rossii* 7 (1928): 58–75.

———. "Bunin molodym pisateliam." *Volia Rossii* 1 (1929): 119–20.

———. "Novyi korabl'." *Volia Rossii* 1 (1929): 121–22.

———. "Gibel' literatury: Ot estetizma k khudozhestvennoi znachitel'nosti." *Volia Rossii* 3 (1929): 53–63.

———. "Molodye pisateli za rubezhom." *Volia Rossii* 10–11 (1929): 100–118.

———. "Literaturnyi dnevnik: Dva Maiakovskikh—Roman Gazdanova." *Volia Rossii* 5–6 (1930): 446–57.

———. "Novye zarubezhnye zhurnaly." *Volia Rossii* 10 (1930): 892–93.

———. "Literatura v emigratsii." *Novaia gazeta* 1 (March 1, 1931): 1.

———. "O 'Chislakh.'" *Novaia gazeta* 2 (March 15, 1931): 3–4.

———. "Zametki ob emigrantskoi literature." *Volia Rossii* 7–9 (1931): 616–27.

———. "Nezamechennoe pokolenie." *Novoe russkoe slovo* 5500 (July 31, 1955): 8.

———. "Russkii Parizh dvadtsatykh godov." *Russkaia mysl'* 2948 (May 24, 1973): 6.

Slovtsov, R. [Nikolai Kalishevich]. "Russkie vo Frantsii." *Poslednie novosti* 1071 (October 19, 1923): 2.

Smirnov, Nikolai. "Solntse mertvykh: Zametki ob emigrantskoi literature." *Krasnaia nov'* 3, no. 20 (1924): 250–67.

———. "Na tom beregu." *Novyi mir* 6 (1926): 141–50.

Smolenskii, Vladimir. "Materialy Soiuza Russkikh Pisatelei i Zhurnalistov v Pol'she." *Mech* 3–4 (May 27, 1934): 18–19.

Sosinskii, Vladislav. "Konurka." *Voprosy literatury* 6 (1991): 167–207.

Souday, Paul. "Les Faux-Monnayeurs." 1926. In "Le Dossier de presee des 'Faux-Monnayeurs.'" *Bulletin des amis d'André Gide* 22 (1974): 33–41.

Soupault, Philippe. *A la dérive.* Paris: J. Ferenczi et fils, 1923.

———. "Déposition." *Cahiers du Mois* 21–22 (1926): 149–61.

———. *Mémoires de l'Oubli: 1914–1923.* Paris: Lachenal & Ritter, 1981.

———. *En Joue!* Paris: Lachenal & Ritter, 1984.

————. *Mémoires de l'Oubli: 1923–1926*. Paris: Lachenal & Ritter, 1986.

————. *Le bon apôtre*. Paris: Lachenal & Ritter, 1988.

Stepun, Fedor. "Porevoliutsionnoe soznanie i zadacha emigrantskoi literatury." *Novyi Grad* 10 (1935): 12–28.

"Stikhi Borisa Poplavskogo." *Poslednie novosti* 5425 (January 30, 1936): 3.

Struve, Gleb. "Zametki o stikhakh." *Rossiia i slavianstvo* 24 (May 11, 1929): 3.

————. "Dva romana o liubvi." *Rossiia i slavianstvo* 102 (November 8, 1930): 4.

————. "Na vechere 'Perekrestka.'" *Rossiia i slavianstvo* 158 (December 5, 1931): 4.

————. "O molodykh poetakh." *Rossiia i slavianstvo* 191 (July 23, 1932): 3.

————. "K istorii russkoi zarubezhnoi literatury: Kak sostavlialas' antologiia 'Iakor'.'" *Novyi zhurnal* 107 (1972): 222–54.

————. "K istorii zarubezhnoi literatury: O parizhskom zhurnale 'Vstrechi' s prilozheniem perepiski dvukh redaktorov." *Novyi zhurnal* 110 (1973): 216–46.

Suarès, Carlo. "Anketa o Pruste." *Chisla* 1 (1930): 275–76.

Sushchev, Iurii [Vladimir Veidle]. "Novoe vo frantsuzskoi belletristike." *Zveno* 154 (January 10, 1926): 7.

————. "Novoe vo frantsuzskoi literature." *Zveno* 173 (May 23, 1926): 4–6.

Tatishchev, Nikolai. "Poet v izgnanii." *Novyi zhurnal* 15 (1947): 199–207.

————. "Boris Poplavskii: Poet samopoznaniia." *Vozrozhdenie* 165 (1965): 26–37.

Terapiano, Iurii. "Zhurnal i chitatel'." *Novyi korabl'* 1 (1927): 23–26.

————. "O smerti i umiranii." *Rossiia i slavianstvo* 138 (July 18, 1931): 3.

————. "Chelovek 1930-kh godov." *Chisla* 7–8 (1933): 210–12.

————. "Iu. Fel'zen: 'Schast'e,' izd. 'Parabola.' Berlin, 1932." *Chisla* 7–8 (1933): 267–69.

————. "'Na Balkanakh.'" *Chisla* 9 (1933): 139–40.

————. "Rytsar' bednyi. (Eshche o krizise poezii)." *Mech* 8 (June 24, 1934): 9–10.

————. "Puteshestvie v glub' nochi." *Chisla* 10 (1934): 210–11.

————. "Pamiati Borisa Poplavskogo." *Nov'* 8 (1935): 148.

————. "Soprotivlenie smerti." *Krug* 1 (1936): 144–47.

————. "O novykh knigakh stikhov." *Krug* 3 (1938): 171–75.

————. *Vstrechi*. New York: Izdatel'stvo imeni Chekhova, 1953.

————. "Po povodu nezamechennogo pokoleniia." *Novoe russkoe slovo* (November 27, 1955): 5.

————. "O zarubezhnoi poezii 1920–1960 godov." *Grani* 44 (1959): 3–12.

————. "Boris Poplavskii." *Sovremennik* 16 (1967): 142–46.

————. "'V pamiati eta epokha zapechatlelas' navsegda': Pis'ma Iu. K. Terapiano k V. F. Markovu (1953–1966)." *Minuvshee* 24 (1998): 240–378.

Thérive, André. "Les Faux-Monnayeurs." 1926. In "Le Dossier de presse des 'Faux-Monnayeurs.'" *Bulletin des amis d'André Gide* 22 (1974): 41–49.

Thibaudet, Albert. *Le Liseur de romans*. Paris: Crès et Co., 1925.

————. "Les Faux-Monnayeurs." 1926. In "Le Dossier de presse des 'Faux-Monnayeurs.'" *Bulletin des amis d'André Gide* 26 (1975): 19–22.

"Tragicheskaia gibel' B. Poplavskogo." *Vozrozhdenie* 3782 (October 11, 1935): 4.

"Tragicheskaia smert' Borisa Poplavskogo." *Poslednie novosti* 5314 (October 11, 1935): 3.

Travérsey, Guy de. "Les Débats." *Cahiers de la Quinzaine* 21, no. 1 (1930): 63.

Troyat, Henri. *Un si long chemin*. Paris: Stock, 1993.

Tsetlin, Mikhail. "Anri Barbius." *Sovremennye zapiski* 1 (1920): 241–43.

———. "Ob Anatole Franse." *Sovremennye zapiski* 23 (1925): 431–40.

———. "Emigrantskoe." *Sovremennye zapiski* 32 (1927): 435–41.

———. "Anketa o Pruste." *Chisla* 1 (1930): 276–77.

———. "Iurii Fel'zen. Schast'e. Roman. Izd. 'Parabola,' Berlin." *Sovremennye zapiski* 51 (1933): 459–61.

———. "O sovremennoi emigrantskoi poezii." *Sovremennye zapiski* 58 (1935): 452–61.

Tsvetaeva, Marina. "Les Débats." *Cahiers de la Quinzaine* 20, no. 5 (1930): 50–51.

Turgenev, Ivan. *Polnoe sobranie sochinenii i pisem*. 28 vols. Moscow and Leningrad: Nauka, 1961–65.

Valéry, Paul. "Les Débats." *Cahiers de la Quinzaine* 21, no. 2 (1930): 65.

———. *Oeuvres*. 2 vols. Paris: Gallimard, Bibliothèque de la Pléiade, 1957.

Vandérém, François. "Les lettres et la vie." *Revue de France* 1 (1921): 603.

Varshavskii, Vladimir. "Iz zapisok besstydnogo molodogo cheloveka: Optimisticheskii rasskaz." *Chisla* 2–3 (1930): 55–70.

———. "Neskol'ko rassuzhdenii ob Andre Zhide i emigrantskom molodom cheloveke." *Chisla* 4 (1930–31): 216–22.

———. "Uedinenie i prazdnost'." *Chisla* 6 (1932): 51–76.

———. "O 'geroe' emigrantskoi molodoi literatury." *Chisla* 6 (1932): 164–72.

———. "V. Sirin: 'Podvig.' Izd. 'Sovrem. Zap.' 1932." *Chisla* 7–8 (1933): 266–67.

———. "O proze mladshikh emigrantskikh pisatelei." *Sovremennye zapiski* 61 (1936): 409–14.

———. *Nezamechennoe pokolenie*. New York: Izdatel'stvo imeni Chekhova, 1956.

Vasilevskii, Mikhail [Ne-Bukva]. "My." *Poslednie novosti* 245 (February 6, 1921): 2.

"Vechera 'Chisel.'" *Chisla* 1 (1930): 252–53.

Veidle, Vladimir. "Zhivopis' siurrealistov." *Zveno* 224 (May 15, 1927): 6–7.

———. "Andre Zhid." *Vozrozhdenie* 1178 (August 23, 1928): 3–4.

———. "Sovremennye zapiski XXXIX." *Vozrozhdenie* 1493 (July 4, 1929): 3.

———. "O frantsuzskoi literature." *Sovremennye zapiski* 39 (1929): 491–502.

———. "Russkaia literatura v emigratsii: Novaia proza." *Vozrozhdenie* 1848 (June 19, 1930): 3–4.

———. "Kriticheskie zametki." *Vozrozhdenie* 1920 (September 4, 1930): 3.

———. "Paul Valéry et la poésie pure." *Cahiers de la Quinzaine* 21, no. 2 (1930): 37–45.

———. "Pol' Moran." *Vozrozhdenie* 2165 (May 7, 1931): 3.

———. "Les Débats." *Cahiers de la Quinzaine* 21, no. 4 (1931): 42.

———. "Monparnasskie mechtaniia." *Sovremennye zapiski* 47 (1931): 457–67.

———. "Odinochestvo khudozhnika." *Novyi grad* 8 (1934): 52–62.

———. "Mekhanizatsiia bessoznatel'nogo." *Sovremennye zapiski* 58 (1935): 461–69.

———. "Angliiskaia kniga o sovetskoi literature." *Poslednie novosti* 5669 (October 1, 1936): 3.

———. "Chelovek protiv pisatelia." *Krug* 2 (1937): 139–45.

———. "G. Gazdanov: Istoriia odnogo puteshestviia." *Russkie zapiski* 14 (1939): 200–201.

———. "Franko-russkie vstrechi." In *Russkii al'manakh.* Edited by Z. Shakhovskaia, R. Guerra, and E. Ternovskii. Paris: n.p., 1981: 397–400.

———. "O tekh, kogo uzhe net." *Novyi zhurnal* 192–93 (1993): 313–424.

Vering, A. "O 'novom gumanizme' v zhivopisi." *Novaia gazeta* 2 (March 15, 1931): 14.

Vinaver, Evgenii. "Ugolovnyi roman." *Vstrechi* 6 (1934): 256–59.

Vishniak, Mark. *"Sovremennye zapiski": Vospominaniia redaktora.* Bloomington: Indiana University Press, 1957.

V. L. [Vera Lur'e]. "Novye knigi. V. S. Ianovskii. Koleso." *Vozrozhdenie* 1714 (February 10, 1930): 3.

Volin, Boris. "Emigrantskaia poeziia." *Na literaturnom postu* 3 (May, 1926): 20–23.

———. "Nedopustimye iavleniia." *Literaturnaia gazeta* 19 (August 26, 1929): 1.

Voloshin, Gleb. "V. S. Ianovskii: Liubov' vtoraia." *Sovremennye zapiski* 59 (1935): 476–77.

Vysheslavtsev, Boris. "Proust et la Tragédie objective." *Cahiers de la Quinzaine* 20, no. 5 (1930): 23–31.

Woolf, Virginia. *A Room of One's Own.* New York and London: Harcourt Brace Jovanovich, 1981.

Zaitsev, Boris. "Nashi ankety." *Zveno* 117 (April 27, 1925): 2.

———. "Dnevnik pisatelia." *Vozrozhdenie* 1981 (November 4, 1930): 3.

———. "Les Débats." *Cahiers de la Quinzaine* 20, no. 8 (1930): 36.

Zaitsev, Kirill. "Fal'shivomonetchiki." *Vozrozhdenie* 282 (March 11, 1926): 3.

———. "'Vecher u Kler' Gaito Gazdanova." *Rossiia i slavianstvo* 69 (March 22, 1930): 3.

———. "Chisla." *Rossiia i slavianstvo* 71 (April 5, 1930): 3.

———. "Les Débats." *Cahiers de la Quinzaine* 20, no. 6 (1930): 40–42.

Zakovich, Boris. "Vecher soiuza molodykh poetov." *Chisla* 4 (1930–31): 258–59.

Zdanevich, Il'ia [Iliazd]. "Boris Poplavskii." *Sintaksis* 16 (1986): 164–69.

———. "En approchant Éluard." *Carnets de l'Iliazd Club* 1 (1990): 35–76.

———. *Ledentu le Phare.* Paris: Allia, 1995.

Zeeler, Vladimir. "Neobkhodimye popravki." *Poslednie novosti* 5342 (November 8, 1935): 2.

Zelinskii, Kornelii. "Rubaki na sene." *Za rubezhom* 4, no. 6 (February 5, 1933): 10.

Zenzinov, Vladimir. "Ivan Boldyrev: Mal'chiki i devochki.—V. S. Ianovskii: Koleso. Izdatel'stvo 'Novye Pisateli.' Parizh-Berlin. 1929–1930." *Sovremennye zapiski* 42 (1930): 525–29.

Secondary sources

REFERENCE WORKS

Alekseev, Anatolii. *Literatura russkogo zarubezh'ia: Knigi 1917–1940. Materialy k bibliografii.* St. Petersburg: Nauka, 1993.

Belin de Ballu, Eugène, and Tatiana Ossorguine. *Catalogue des périodiques russes des origines à 1970, conservés à la Bibliothèque nationale.* Paris: La Bibliothèque, 1978.

Beyssac, Michel. *La Vie culturelle de l'émigration russe en France. Chronique (1920–1930).* Paris: Presses Universitaires de France, 1971.

Dienes, Laszlo. *Bibliographie des oeuvres de Gaito Gazdanov.* Paris: Institut d'études slaves, 1982.

Foster, Liudmila. *Bibliography of Russian Émigré Literature.* 2 vols. Boston: G. K. Hall & Co., 1970.

Gladkova, Tatiana, and Tatiana Ossorguine. *L'Émigration russe: Revues et recueils, 1920–1980: Index général des articles.* Paris: Institut d'études slaves, 1988.

Hagglund, Roger. *Georgy Adamovich: An Annotated Bibliography—Criticism, Poetry, and Prose, 1915–1980.* Ann Arbor, Mich.: Ardis, 1985.

Mikhailov, O. N., ed. *Literatura russkogo zarubezh'ia: 1920–1940,* vol. 2. Moscow: IMLI-Nasledie, 1999.

Mnukhin, Lev, et al. *L'Émigration russe: Chronique de la vie scientifique, culturelle et sociale. 1920–1940 France.* 4 vols. Paris: YMCA-Press, 1995–97.

Ossorguine-Bakounine, Tatiana. *L'Emigration russe en Europe: Catalogue collectif des périodiques en langue russe 1855–1940.* Paris: Institut d'études slaves, 1976–77.

Vil'danova, R., V. Kudriavtsev, and K. Lappo-Danilevskii. *Kratkii biograficheskii slovar' russkogo Zarubezh'ia.* In Gleb Struve, *Russkaia literatura v izgnanii.* Paris and Moscow: YMCA-Press and Russkii put', 1996.

COLLECTIONS OF SOURCES

Etkind, Efim, et al, eds. *Histoire de la littérature russe: Le XX-e siècle.* 2 vols. Paris: Fayard, 1988.

Genette, Gérard, and Tzvetan Todorov, eds. *Recherche de Proust.* Paris: Éditions du Seuil, 1980.

Paperno, Irina, and Joan Grossman, eds. *Creating Life: The Aesthetic Utopia of Russian Modernism.* Stanford: Stanford University Press, 1994.

Poltoratskii, Nikolai, ed. *Russkaia literatura v emigratsii: Sbornik statei.* Pittsburgh: University of Pittsburgh Press, 1972.

Rosenthal, Bernice, ed. *Nietzsche in Russia.* Princeton, N.J.: Princeton University Press, 1986.

INDIVIDUAL AUTHORS
(MULTIPLE ENTRIES ARE LISTED CHRONOLOGICALLY)

Alden, D. W. *Marcel Proust and His French Critics.* Los Angeles: Lymanhouse, 1940.

Aleksinskaia, Tat'iana. "Emigrantskaia pechat' i pisateli-emigranty." *Vozrozhdenie* 70 (1957): 33–58.

Alexandrian, Saran. *Le surréalisme et le Rêve.* Paris: Gallimard, 1974.

Alexandrov, Vladimir. "A Note on Nabokov's Anti-Darwinism; or, Why Apes Feed on Butterflies in *The Gift.*" In *Freedom and Responsibility in Russian Literature: Essays in Honor of Robert Louis Jackson.* Evanston, Ill.: Northwestern University Press, 1995, 239–44.

Bancquart, Michel, and Pierre Cahné. *Littérature française du XX siècle*. Paris: Presses universitaires de France, 1992.

Baranoff-Chestov, Nathalie. *Vie de Léon Chestov*. Vol. 1. Paris: Éditions de la Différence, 1991.

Barthes, Roland. *Mythologies*. Paris: Éditions du Seuil, 1970.

———. *Le Degré zéro de l'écriture suivi de Nouveaux Essais critiques*. Paris: Éditions du Seuil, 1972.

Beaujour, Elizabeth. *Alien Tongues: Bilingual Russian Writers of the "First" Emigration*. Ithaca, N.Y.: Cornell University Press, 1989.

Béhar, Henri, and Michel Carassou. *Le Surréalisme*. Paris: Le Livre de Poche, 1992.

Behr-Sigel, Elisabeth. *Un Moine de l'Église d'Orient: Le Père Lev Gillet*. Paris: Les Éditions du Cerf, 1993.

Bersani, Jacques. "Proust et Dada." *Revue d'histoire littéraire de la France* 65, no. 2 (1965): 260–68.

Bethea, David M. *Khodasevich: His Life and Art*. Princeton, N.J.: Princeton University Press, 1983.

———. *Joseph Brodsky and the Creation of Exile*. Princeton, N.J.: Princeton University Press, 1994.

Blackwell, Stephen H. "Boundaries of Art in Nabokov's *The Gift:* Reading as Transcendence." *Slavic Review* 58, no. 3 (1999): 600–625.

Blium, Arlen. "Pechat' russkogo zarubezh'ia glazami Glavlita i GPU." *Novyi zhurnal* 183 (1991): 264–82.

Boldt, F., Dmitrii Segal, and Lazar' Fleishman. "Problemy izucheniia literatury russkoi emigratsii pervoi treti XX veka." *Slavica Hierosolymitana* 3 (1978): 75–88.

Bowlt, John. *Russian Art of the Avant-Garde: Theory and Criticism. 1902–1934*. New York: Thames & Hudson, 1988.

Boyd, Brian. *Vladimir Nabokov: The Russian Years*. Princeton, N.J.: Princeton University Press, 1990.

Boym, Svetlana. *Death in Quotation Marks: Cultural Myths of the Modern Poet*. Cambridge, Mass. and London: Harvard University Press, 1991.

Brée, Germaine. *Du temps perdu au temps retrouvé*. Paris: Les Belles Lettres, 1969.

Brodsky, Anna. "Homosexuality and the Aesthetic of Nabokov's *Dar*." *Nabokov Studies* 4 (1997): 95–115.

Brosman, Catharine S. "The Novelist as Natural Historian in 'Les Faux-Monnayeurs.'" *Essays in French Literature* 14 (1977): 48–59.

———. "Le Journal des Faux-Monnayeurs: Oeuvre accessoire ou oeuvre autonome." *Bulletin des amis d'André Gide* 18 (1990): 535–44.

Buks, Nora. *Eshafot v khrustal'nom dvortse*. Moscow: Novoe Literaturnoe Obozrenie, 1998.

Calinescu, Mattei. *Five Faces of Modernity: Modernism, Avant-Garde, Decadence, Kitsch, Postmodernism*. Durham, N.C.: Duke University Press, 1987.

Carrouges, Michel. *André Breton et les données fondamentales du surréalisme*. Paris: Gallimard, 1967.

Chénieux, Jacqueline. *Le Surréalisme et le roman*. Lausanne: L'Age d'Homme, 1983.

————. *Surrealism*. Translated by V. Folkenflik. New York: Columbia University Press, 1990.

Chertkov, Leonid. "Debiut Borisa Poplavskogo." *Kontitent* 47 (1986): 375–77.

Chudakova, Marietta. *Masterstvo Iuriia Oleshi*. Moscow: Nauka, 1972.

Clark, Katerina. *The Soviet Novel: History as Ritual*. Chicago and London: University of Chicago Press, 1981.

Conover, Roger, Terry Hale, and Paul Lenti. *Four Dada Suicides: Selected Texts of Arthur Cravan, Jacques Rigaut, Julien Torma & Jacques Vaché*. London: Atlas Press, 1995.

Crespelle, Jean-Pierre. *La Vie quotidienne à Montparnasse à la Grande Époque 1905–1930*. Paris: Hachette, 1976.

Dällenbach, Lucien. *Le récit spéculaire: Essai sur la mise en abyme*. Paris: Éditions du Seuil, 1977.

Davydov, Sergei. *"Teksty-matreshki" Vladimira Nabokova*. Munich: Verlag Otto Sagner, 1982.

Décaudin, Michel. *Panorama du XX siècle français*. Paris: Seghers, 1987.

Dienes, Laszlo. *Russian Literature in Exile: The Life and Work of Gajto Gazdanov*. Munich: Verlag Otto Sagner, 1982.

Dolinin, Aleksandr. "'Dvoinoe vremia' u Nabokova (ot 'Dara' k 'Lolite')." In *Puti i mirazhi russkoi kul'tury*, edited by V. Bagno and M. Virolainen, 283–322. St. Petersburg: Severo-Zapad, 1994.

————. "The Gift." In *The Garland Companion to Vladimir Nabokov*, edited by V. Alexandrov, 135–69. New York: Garland Publishing, 1995.

————. "Dve zametki o romane 'Dar.'" *Zvezda* 11 (1996): 173–80.

————. "Tri zametki o romane Vladimira Nabokova 'Dar.'" In *V. V. Nabokov: Pro et Contra*, 697–740. St. Petersburg: Russkii khristianskii gumanitarnyi institut, 1997.

————. "Clio Laughs Last: Nabokov's Answer to Historicism." In *Nabokov and His Fiction. New Perspectives*, edited by Julian W. Connolly, 197–215. New York: Cambridge University Press, 1999.

————. "Doklady Vladimira Nabokova v berlinskom literaturnom kruzhke." *Zvezda* 4 (1999): 7–22.

————. "V. V. Nabokov: Vtoroe dobavlenie k 'Daru.'" *Zvezda* 1 (2001): 85–109.

Eiseley, Loren. "The Cosmic Orphan." *Saturday Review/World* (February 23, 1974): 16–19.

Eliade, Mircea. *Aspects du mythe*. Paris: Gallimard, 1997.

————. *Le Mythe de l'éternel retour*. Paris: Gallimard, 1997.

Fleishman, Lazar'. "O gibeli Maiakovskogo kak 'literaturnom fakte.'" *Slavica Hierosolymitana* 4 (1979): 126–30.

————. *Boris Pasternak v dvadtsatye gody*. Munich: Wilhelm Fink Verlag, 1980.

————. *Boris Pasternak v tridtsatye gody*. Jerusalem: Magness Press & Hebrew University, 1984.

————. *Boris Pasternak: The Poet and His Politics*. Cambridge, Mass.: Harvard University Press, 1990.

Fokkema, Douwe. "A Semiotic Definition of Aesthetic Experience and the Period Code of Modernism: With Reference to an Interpretation of the *Faux-Monnayeurs*." *Poetics Today* 3, no. 1 (1982): 61–79.

Fondane, Benjamin. *Faux Traité d'ésthétique.* Paris: Plasma, 1980.

Foster, John B. *Nabokov's Art of Memory and European Modernism.* Princeton, N.J.: Princeton University Press, 1993.

Foster, Liudmila. "K voprosu o siurrealizme v russkoi literature." In *American Contributions to the Seventh International Congress of Slavists,* vol. 2, 199–219. The Hague and Paris: Mouton, 1973.

Freidin, Gregory. *A Coat of Many Colors: Osip Mandelstam and His Mythologies of Self-Presentation.* Berkeley and Los Angeles: University of California Press, 1987.

Furet, François. *Le Passé d'une illusion.* Paris: Robert Laffont & Calmann-Lévy, 1995.

Geertz, Clifford. *The Interpretation of Cultures.* New York: Basic Books, 1973.

Genette, Gérard. *Figures II.* Paris: Éditions du Seuil, 1969.

———. *Figures III.* Paris: Éditions du Seuil, 1972.

Gerbod, François, and Pierre Gerbod. *Introduction à la vie littéraire du XX siècle.* Paris: Bordas, 1986.

Gibault, François. *Céline.* 2 vols. Paris: Mercure de France, 1977.

Gibson, Aleksey. *Russian Poetry and Criticism in Paris from 1920 to 1940.* The Hague: Leuxenhoff Publishing, 1990.

Ginzburg, Lidiia. *On Psychological Prose.* Princeton, N.J.: Princeton University Press, 1991.

Godard, Henri. *Voyage au bout de la nuit de Louis-Ferdinand Céline.* Paris: Gallimard, 1991.

Goux, Jean-Joseph. "La Métaphore monétaire dans les Faux-Monnayeurs." *Stanford French Review* 7, no. 1 (1983): 91–108.

Greenleaf, Monika. "Fathers, Sons and Impostors: Pushkin's Trace in *The Gift.*" *Slavic Review* 53, no. 1 (1994): 140–58.

Guillén, Claudio. *Literature as System: Essays toward the Theory of Literary History.* Princeton, N.J.: Princeton University Press, 1971.

———. "On the Literature of Exile and Counter-Exile." *Books Abroad* 50, no. 2 (1976): 271–80.

Habermas, Jurgen. "Modernity—An Incomplete Project." In *Interpretive Social Science: A Second Look,* edited by P. Rabinow and W. M. Sullivan, 141–56. Berkeley: University of California Press, 1987.

Hagglund, Roger. "The Adamovich-Xodasevich Polemics." *Slavic and East European Journal* 20, no. 3 (1976): 239–52.

Heurgon-Desjardins, Anne. *Paul Desjardins et les Décades de Pontigny: Études, témoignages et documents inédits.* Paris: Presses universitaires de France, 1964.

Hutcheon, Linda. *Narcissistic Narrative: The Metafictional Paradox.* Waterloo: Wilfred Laurier University Press, 1980.

Jakobson, Roman. *Language in Literature.* Cambridge, Mass.: Belknap Press, 1987.

Jelen, Christian. *L'Aveuglement.* Paris: Flammarion, 1984.

Johnson, D. Barton. "The Key to Nabokov's *Gift.*" *Canadian-American Slavic Studies* 16, no. 2 (1982): 190–206.

———. *Worlds in Regression: Some Novels of Vladimir Nabokov.* Ann Arbor, Mich.: Ardis, 1985.

Jünger, Ernst. *La Guerre comme expérience intérieure*. Paris: Christian Bourgois, 1997.

Karlinsky, Simon. "Surrealism in Twentieth-Century Russian Poetry: Churilin, Zabolotskii, Poplavskii." *Slavic Review* 26, no. 4 (1967): 605–17.

———. "In Search of Poplavsky: A Collage." In *The Bitter Air of Exile: Russian Writers in the West 1922–1972*, edited by S. Karlinsky and A. Appel Jr. Berkeley, 311–33. University of California Press, 1977.

Kondrat'eva, Tatiana. *Bolcheviks et Jacobins: Itinéraire des analogies*. Paris: Éditions Payot, 1989.

Kopper, John M. "Surrealism under Fire: The Prose of Boris Poplavsky." *Russian Review* 55, no. 2 (1996): 245–64.

Kovalevskii, Petr. *Zarubezhnaia Rossiia*. Paris: Librairie des cinq continents, 1971.

Kristeva, Julia. *Pouvoirs de l'horreur: Essai sur l'abjection*. Paris: Éditions du Seuil, 1980.

Krysinski, Wladimir. *"Les Faux-Monnayeurs* et le paradigme du roman européen autour de 1925." In *André Gide 6*, 233–65. Paris: La Revue des Lettres Modernes, 1979.

Latin, Danièle. *Le "Voyage au bout de la nuit" de Céline: Roman de la subversion et subversion du roman. Langue, fiction, écriture*. Bruxelles: Palais des Académies, 1988.

Léonard, Albert. *La Crise du concept de littérature en France au XXe siècle*. Paris: Librairie José Corti, 1974.

Levin, Iurii I. "Ob osobennostiakh povestvovatel'noi struktury i obraznogo stroia romana V. Nabokova *Dar*." *Russian Literature* 9 (1981): 191–230.

Levin, Harry. *Refractions*. New York: Oxford University Press, 1966.

Lieberman, Lisa. "Romanticism and the Culture of Suicide in Nineteenth-Century France." *Comparative Studies in Society and History* 33, no. 3 (1991): 611–29.

Lilienfeld, A. de. "Le problème international des réfugiés et apatrides." *Esprit* 82 (1939): 579–605.

Livak, Leonid. "Histoire de la littérature russe en exil: La 'période héroïque' de la jeune poésie russe à Paris." *Revue des études slaves* 73, no. 1 (2001): 1–15.

———. "The Place of Suicide in the French Avant-Garde of the Inter-War Period." *The Romanic Review* 91, no. 3 (2000): 245–62.

Lotman, Iurii. *The Semiotics of Russian Cultural History*. Edited by A. D. Nakhimovsky and A. S. Nakhimovsky. Ithaca, N.Y.: Cornell University Press, 1985.

———. *Izbrannye stat'i v trekh tomakh*. 3 vols. Tallin: Aleksandra, 1992–93.

———. *Iu. M. Lotman i tartussko-moskovskaia semioticheskaia shkola*. Edited by A. D. Koshelev. Moscow: Gnozis, 1994.

Louria, Yvette. "Nabokov and Proust: The Challenge of Time." *Books Abroad* 48, no. 3 (1947): 469–76.

Magny, Claude-Edmond. *Histoire du roman français depuis 1918*. 2 vols. Paris: Éditions du Seuil, 1950.

Maguire, Robert. *Red Virgin Soil: Soviet Literature in the 1920s*. Princeton, N.J.: Princeton University Press, 1968.

Man, Paul de. *Blindness and Insight*. New York: Oxford University Press, 1971.

Marty, Eric. "Les Faux-Monnayeurs: Roman, mise-en-abyme, répétition." In *André Gide 8*, 95–118. Paris: Lettres Modèrnes-Minard, 1987.

Matthews, J. H. *Surrealism and the Novel*. Ann Arbor: University of Michigan Press, 1966.

Mel'nikov, Nikolai. "'Do poslednei kapli chernil . . .' Vladimir Nabokov i 'Chisla.'" *Literaturnoe obozrenie* 2 (1996): 73–82.

Menegaldo, Hélène. "L'Univers imaginaire de Boris Poplavsky (1903–1935)." Ph.D. diss., Université de Paris X-Nanterre, 1981.

—— "La jeune génération des avant-gardistes russes à Paris, 1921–1930." *Slavica Occitania* 10 (2000): 249–60.

—— "Boris Poplavski. Rencontres à Montparnasse (1922–1935)." *Pleine Marge* 33 (June 2001): 121–43.

Michihiko, Susuki. "Le 'je' proustien." *Bulletin de la société des amis de Marcel Proust et des amis de Combray* 9 (1959): 69–82.

Milly, Jean. *La Phrase de Proust*. Paris: Editions Champion, 1983.

Mints, Zara. "Poniatie teksta i simvolistskaia estetika." *Materialy vsesoiuznogo simpoziuma po vtorichnym modeliruiushchim sistemam* 1, no. 5 (1974): 134–41.

Nadeau, Maurice. *Histoire du surréalisme*. Paris: Éditions du Seuil, 1964.

Nesbet, Ann. "Suicide as Literary Fact in the 1920s." *Slavic Review* 50, no. 4 (1991): 827–35.

Nikonenko, S. "Neskol'ko slov o Gaito Gazdanove." In *Novo-Basmannaia 19*, 727–31. Moscow: Khudozhestvennaia literatura, 1990.

Oualid, William. "Pour une politique de l'immigration en France." *Esprit* 82 (1939): 547–61.

Paperno, Irina. "How Nabokov's *Gift* Is Made." *Stanford Slavic Studies* 4, no. 2 (1992): 295–322.

——. *Suicide as a Cultural Institution in Dostoevsky's Russia*. Ithaca, N.Y. and London: Cornell University Press, 1997.

Passeron, René. *Histoire de la peinture surréaliste*. Paris: Le Livre de Poche, 1968.

Peterson, Ronald. "Time in *The Gift*." *The Vladimir Nabokov Research Newsletter* 9 (1982): 36–40.

Petrunkevich, Aleksei. "S. F. Platonov—Istorik 'Smutnogo vremeni.'" *Vozrozhdenie* 189 (1967): 72–95.

Poggioli, Renato. *The Theory of the Avant-Garde*. Cambridge, Mass.: Belknap Press, 1968.

Pomerand, George. "Trois suicides significatifs: Jacques Vaché, Jacques Rigaut, René Crevel." *Psyché: Revue internationale des sciences de l'homme et de psychanalyse* 20 (1948): 697–701.

Prior, Roy. "Auteur et narrateur dans *Les Faux-Monnayeurs*." *Bulletin des amis d'André Gide* 44 (1978): 33–44.

Racine, Paul. "La main-d'oeuvre étrangère en France." *Esprit* 82 (July 1939): 620–32.

Raeff, Mark. *Russia Abroad: A Cultural History of the Russian Emigration, 1919–1939*. New York: Oxford University Press, 1990.

——. "V pomoshch' issledovaniiu zarubezhnoi Rossii." *Novyi zhurnal* 196 (1995): 348–58.

Raimond, Michel. *La Crise du roman: Des lendemains du Naturalisme aux années vingt.* Paris: Corti, 1966.

Ricoeur, Paul. "The Model of the Text: Meaningful Action Considered as a Text." In *Interpretive Social Science,* edited by P. Rabinow and W. Sullivan, 73–101. Berkeley: University of California Press, 1979.

Rieder, Dolly. "*Les Faux-Monnayeurs:* Gide's Essay on Bad Faith." *The Romanic Review* 62, no. 2 (1971): 87–98.

Riffaterre, Michael. *La Production du texte.* Paris: Seuil, 1979.

Rigaud, Albert. "L'Argot littéraire (II): La langue verte du roman noir." *Information littéraire* 238 (1972): 50–55.

Ronen, Irena, and Omri Ronen. "'Diabolically Evocative': An Inquiry into the Meaning of a Metaphor." *Slavica Hierosolymitana* 5–6 (1981): 371–86.

Rouayrenc, Catherine. "Le Langage populaire et argotique dans le roman français de 1914 à 1939." Ph.D. diss., Université de Paris III, 1988.

Rovskaia, Natal'ia. "Sergei Sharshun." *Novyi zhurnal* 163 (1986): 119–27.

Russell, Charles. *Poets, Prophets, and Revolutionaries.* New York: Oxford University Press, 1985.

Said, Edward. "The Mind of Winter." *Harper's Magazine* (September 1984): 49–55.

Sanouillet, Michel. *Dada à Paris.* Paris: Jean-Jacques Pauvert, 1965.

Segal, Dmitrii. "Literatura kak okhrannaia gramota." *Slavica Hierosolymitana* 5–6 (1981): 151–244.

Shlapentok, Dmitrii. "The Images of the French Revolution in the February and Bolshevik Revolutions." *Russian History* 16, no. 1 (1989): 31–54.

Skonechnaia, Olga. "'People of the Moonlight': Silver Age Parodies in Nabokov's *The Eye* and *The Gift.*" *Nabokov Studies* 3 (1996): 33–52.

Spitzer, Leo. "Une habitude de style chez M. Céline." *Français moderne* (June 1935): 193–208.

———. *Études de style.* Paris: Gallimard, 1979.

Steel, David. "To be or not to be un personnage des Faux-Monnayeurs." *Bulletin des amis d'André Gide* 88 (1990): 477–90.

Steiner, George. *Extraterritorial: Papers on Literature and the Language Revolution.* New York: Atheneum, 1971.

Struve, Gleb. "The Double Life of Russian Literature." *Books Abroad* 28, no. 4 (1954): 389–406.

———. "Russian Writers in Exile: Problems of an Émigré Literature." In *Comparative Literature: Proceedings of the Second Congress of the International Comparative Literature Association,* vol. 2, edited by W. P. Friedrich, 592–606. Chapel Hill: University of North Carolina Press, 1959.

———. *Russkaia literatura v izgnanii.* Paris: YMCA-Press, 1984.

Tadié, Jean-Yves. "Proust et le 'nouvel écrivain.'" *Revue d'histoire littéraire de la France* 67, no. 1 (1967): 79–81.

———. *Proust et le roman.* Paris: Gallimard, 1971.

Tammi, Pekka. *Problems of Nabokov's Poetics: A Narratological Analysis.* Helsinki: Suomalainen Tiedeakatemia, 1985.

Toker, Leona. *Nabokov: The Mystery of Literary Structures.* Ithaca, N.Y.: Cornell University Press, 1989.

Uspenskii, Boris. *Izbrannye trudy*. 2 vols. Moscow: Gnozis, 1994.
Vishniak, Mark. *The Legal Status of Stateless Persons*. New York: American Jewish Committee, 1945.
Vitoux, Frédéric. *La Vie de Céline*. Paris: Bernard Grasset, 1988.
Waite, Sarah Tiffany. "On the Linear Structure of Nabokov's *Dar:* Three Keys, Six Chapters." *Slavic and East European Journal* 39, no. 1 (1995): 51–72.
Weiner, Andrew. *By Authors Possessed: The Demonic Novel in Russia*. Evanston, Ill.: Northwestern University Press, 1998.
Wellek, René, and Austin Warren. *Theory of Literature*. New York: Penguin Books, 1956.
Wichs, Ulrich. "Onlyman." *Mosaic* 8, no. 3 (1975): 21–31.
Winspur, Stephen. "Ethical Loops in Eluard." In *Conjunctions: Verbal-Visual Relations,* edited by L. Edson, 169–85. San Diego: San Diego State University Press.

Index

Adamovich, Georgii Viktorovich: as critic, 206; cyclical regeneration and, 101; disintegration, 156; Dostoevsky and, 140; on émigré Hamlets, 28; on European decline, 25; on France, 207; on French literary culture, 14, 21–22, 31; on Gazdanov's works, 104; on Gide, 22; on Mme Granier and self-sacrifice, 141; on his own critical work, 154; on Ianovskii, 148–50; on invention and imagination, 139; Ivanov and, 163; Nabokov and, 19, 181, 186, 193, 196; Poplavskii and, 71, 79; on Proust, 139; on "Russian soul," 17, 18–19; on Russian tradition, 15; on simplicity of style, 32; on sincerity, 154; and solitude of émigrés, 26–27; Soviet literature and, 33; on Troyat, 19; "Za vse, za vse spasibo," 27

Air, 59

Andersen, Hans Christian, 115, 207

Annenkov, Iurii (Temiriazev, B.), 30

Antipositivism, 39, 92, 189–90

Apollon Bezobrazov (Poplavskii), 37, 73–79, 152

Aragon, Louis, 75, 82, 205

Arland, Marcel, 23–24, 173

Asceticism: form / content dichotomy and, 142; Poplavskii

and, 81–82; in Russian literary tradition, 42–43

Author-narrators: in Celine's works, 137–38; Gazdanov, autobiographical readings of works, 103; in Gide's works, 170–71; merged with text / identified with protagonist, 137–38; in Nabokov's works, 170–71, 174, 182; in Poplavskii's works, 75–79; Proust and conflation of author and narrator, 94; sincerity and, 103; surrealism and, 75–76

Automatic writing and automatism, 46, 51, 53, 66; Poplavskii's use of, 57–58, 79

Avant-garde art: Poplavskii and, 47, 82; Proust and, 91; Soviet political context and, 63

Bakunina, Ekaterina, 40, 148

Bal'mont, Konstantin, 34

Berberova, Nina, 35

Bethea, David, 204

Betz, Marcel, 99

Beyssac, Michel, 11

Blok, Aleksandr, 28, 118–20; Poplavskii and, 66, 68, 72–73

Boldt, F., 12

Bolshevism: émigré literary culture and, 36–38; Khodasevich on literature and, 30

European Hamlets, 111–12; death
and, 135–36; history and, 92;
Ivanov as, 157; referential illusion and, 93–94
Exile: archetypes of, 3; counterexile,
207; cultural influences on, 49;
exiles *vs.* émigrés, 10; literature
in exile *vs.* émigré literature, 5–6
Existentialism, 206

Failure, cult of, 11, 42–43
Les Faux-Monnayeurs (Gide), 15, 17,
24, 165, 167, 168–70
Fedotov, Georgii, on Christian concepts and art, 148
Fellow travelers, suppression of
works by, 32–33
Fel'zen, Iurii (Nikolai Berngardovich
Freudenstein), 121; career of,
206; Christianity in works of,
131; criticism of works, 121; émigré Hamlets in works of, 129;
employment of, 42; on exile and
foreign influences, 41; Freud
and, 133; Gazdanov and, 125;
Ivanov on, 18; "Kompozitsiia,"
128; Lermontov's influence on
works of, 129–30; love in works
of, 126; Nabokov and, 121–23,
134, 166; *Obman*, 40, 121, 126,
127, 130; parodies of works, 121–
23; *Pis'ma o Lermontove*, 121, 125,
126, 130; politics in works of, 37;
on Proust, 22, 101; Proustian influences, 121, 125–30; publishing history, 12; regeneration in
works of, 130; religion in works
of, 131, 132–33; *Schast'e*, 121,
126–27; sincerity in works of,
126–28; style of, 123–25; unconscious in works of, 131; as "un-
Soviet," 129
Feuds, émigré literary culture and,
17–19, 49, 143. *See also specific authors*
Flagi (Poplavskii), 66, 68, 71, 73

Fleishman, Lazar', 12
Fokht, Vsevolod, 21
Formalism, 6–7; antiformalism, 31–
32, 36, 39; émigré rejection of
and opposition to, 7, 31, 36, 50;
as French quality, 14; Soviet literary tradition and, 7, 28–29, 36,
102; *vs.* spirituality, 14–15
Form / content issues: émigré poetics and, 16; esthetic asceticism
and, 142; in esthetic debates and
feuds, 18; RAPP and, 36; Russian
literary tradition and, 15–16, 39;
Soviet literature and, 7, 28–29,
36, 102. *See also* Formalism;
Structure and composition issues; *specific literary forms*
Foster, Liudmila, 11
Fragmentation of personality, 94, 99,
116
Freidin, Gregory, 9
French language, as "un-Russian"
option, 19
French literary culture: anti-émigré
sentiments, 35; as context for
émigré literary culture, 6, 206;
émigré-French-Soviet triangle,
204–5; *Enquête sur les maîtres de la
jeune littérature*, 91–92; Fel'zen on
positive influences of, 129; of
Gazdanov's works, 120–21; Russian tradition and, 14, 16–17; Soviet literature, equated with, 31.
See also specific authors
Freud, Sigmund, 92–93, 133, 183
Freudenstein, Nikolai Berngardovich. *See* Fel'zen, Iurii
Futurism, 51; Dada and, 49;
Poplavskii and, 47–49, 54, 71; Soviet literature and, 28–29, 30

Gatarapak, 49
Gazdanov, Gaito (Georgii Ivanovich
Gazdanov), 206; autobiographical readings of works, 103; Blok's
poetic imagery and works of,

Water, 78; in Poplavskii's works, 57–
    58
Wellek, René, 6
"The Wild Swans" (Andersen), 115,
    207
Woolf, Virginia, 41
Writing: about writing, 125–26; as
    love or erotic fulfillment, 185; as
    substitute for love, 133–34

Zaitsev, Boris, 22
Zaitsev, Kirill, 15, 22

Zamiatin, Evgenii, 32–33
Zashchita Luzhina (Nabokov), 19
"Za vse, za vse spasibo"
    (Adamovich), 27
Zdanevich, Il'ia, 50–51, 63–65;
    Poplavskii and, 73
"Zhizneopisanie pisaria"
    (Poplavskii), 58
Zhiznestroenie (life building), 49
Zhiznetvorchestvo (life creation), 47,
    49
Zlobin, Vladimir, 162